Aesthetics of Music

Volume 5

Books by David Whitwell

Philosophic Foundations of Education
Foundations of Music Education
Music Education of the Future
The Sousa Oral History Project
The Art of Musical Conducting
The Longy Club: 1900–1917
A Concise History of the Wind Band
Wagner on Bands
Berlioz on Bands
Chopin: A Self-Portrait
Liszt: A Self-Portrait
Schumann: A Self-Portrait In His Own Words
Mendelssohn: A Self-Portrait In His Own Words
La Téléphonie and the Universal Musical Language
Extraordinary Women

Aesthetics of Music Series

Aesthetics of Music in Ancient Civilizations
Aesthetics of Music in the Middle Ages
Aesthetics of Music in the Early Renaissance
Aesthetics of Music in Sixteenth-Century Italy, France and Spain
Aesthetics of Music in Sixteenth-Century Germany, The Low Countries and England

The History and Literature of the Wind Band and Wind Ensemble Series

Volume 1 The Wind Band and Wind Ensemble Before 1500
Volume 2 The Renaissance Wind Band and Wind Ensemble
Volume 3 The Baroque Wind Band and Wind Ensemble
Volume 4 The Classical Period Wind Band and Wind Ensemble
Volume 5 The Nineteenth-Century Wind Band and Wind Ensemble
Volume 6 A Catalog of Multi-Part Repertoire for Wind Instruments or for Undesignated Instrumentation before 1600
Volume 7 Baroque Wind Band and Wind Ensemble Repertoire
Volume 8 Classic Period Wind Band and Wind Ensemble Repertoire
Volume 9 Nineteenth-Century Wind Band and Wind Ensemble Repertoire
Volume 10 A Supplementary Catalog of Wind Band and Wind Ensemble Repertoire
Volume 11 A Catalog of Wind Repertoire before the Twentieth Century for One to Five Players
Volume 12 A Second Supplementary Catalog of Early Wind Band and Wind Ensemble Repertoire
Volume 13 Name Index, Volumes 1–12, The History and Literature of the Wind Band and Wind Ensemble

www.whitwellbooks.com

David Whitwell

Aesthetics of Music

VOLUME 5
AESTHETICS OF MUSIC IN
SIXTEENTH-CENTURY GERMANY,
THE LOW COUNTRIES AND ENGLAND

EDITED BY CRAIG DABELSTEIN

WHITWELL PUBLISHING • AUSTIN, TEXAS, USA

Whitwell Publishing, Austin 78701
www.whitwellbooks.com

© 1996, 2013 by David Whitwell
All rights reserved. First edition 1996.
Second edition 2013

Printed in the United States of America

Paperback
ISBN-13: 978-1-963512-58-4
ISBN-10: 1936512580

Composed in Minion Pro

CONTENTS

	Foreword	vii
	Acknowledgements	xi
1	*The Low Countries in the Sixteenth Century*	1
2	*Erasmus*	7
3	*The German-Speaking Countries in the Sixteenth Century*	57
4	*Martin Luther*	79
5	*Music Theorists in the German-Speaking Countries*	103
6	*Music Practice in the German-Speaking Countries*	133
7	*Praetorius*	153
8	*Sixteenth-Century England*	183
9	*Royal Music of Sixteenth-Century England*	223
10	*Civic Music of Sixteenth-Century England*	237
11	*Sixteenth-Century English Poetry*	249
12	*Sixteenth-Century English Fiction*	287
13	*Elizabethan Playwrights*	315
14	*Shakespeare*	341
	Bibliography	387
	Index	393
	About the Author	399

FOREWORD

We define Music to be that form of music performed live before listeners. We define Aesthetics in Music to be a study of the nature of the perception of music by the listener.

We believe the performance of music in actual practice falls naturally into four classes. These are Art Music, Educational Music, Functional Music and Entertainment Music.

I. Art Music

Art Music we believe is defined by four conditions, *all* of which *must always be present*. These are:

1. *Art music is inspired.* Art music is music in which it seems evident that the composer has made an honest attempt to communicate genuine feelings. Feelings, which may range from lofty and noble to superficial and vulgar, must be presumed to be generally recognizable in music, as they are in any other art form, including painting, sculpture, dance, and architecture. In Art Music, lofty and noble feelings are paramount.

    Due to the common genetically understood nature of emotions, it must also be understood that in music emotions or feelings cannot be 'faked.' They will always be recognized as such by any contemplative listener.

2. *Art Music has no purpose other than the communication of its own aesthetic content.* Art Music is free of any purpose or function, save the spiritual communication of pure beauty.

3. *Art Music is that which enjoys a performance faithful to the intent of the composer.*

4. *Art Music must have a listener capable of contemplation.*

If any of these conditions are missing, the performance must result in a lesser aesthetic experience. For example, the *Ninth Symphony* of Beethoven played in a stadium, during the half-time of a professional football game, would fail for the lack of the presence of Condition Number Four. The same Symphony heard in a concert hall, but in a poor performance, not faithful to the intent of the composer, would fail for the lack of the presence of Condition Number Three.

II. Educational Music

Educational Music may or may not have the same conditions as Art Music, excepting Condition Number Two; it may or may not occur within an educational institution. Educational Music is didactic music, music which has the specific and *additional* aim to educate. In the strictest sense, if the *primary purpose* of Music is to educate, it cannot be Art Music—for Art Music has no purpose.

III. Functional Music

Functional Music is music put at the service of something else. We include here, for example, all kinds of religious music, music for weddings, music for the military, and occupational music. Functional Music may share the same conditions as Art Music, excepting Condition Number Two.

One may ask, How can a Mozart Mass be called Functional Music, and not Art Music? If the observer were not contemplatively listening to the music, but were rather contemplating religious thoughts, then the Mozart Mass becomes merely a very high level of Functional Music. If, on the other hand, the observer is a contemplative listener of music, forgetting about religion, then the Mozart Mass is Art Music, but has failed in its purpose as church music.

Military and wedding music are examples of music in which the contemplative listener is missing entirely. How about airport, supermarket and elevator music where there is no listener at all? According to the definition we have given above, recorded music without listeners is not to be considered music at all.

IV. Entertainment Music

Entertainment Music is music with no object other than to please. It will always be missing Condition Four, the contemplative listener. For this reason, Entertainment Music may be inspired music, but the composer is unlikely to be inspired by lofty and noble emotions, knowing there will be no contemplative listener. Entertainment Music and Art Music can never be the same thing because of Condition Number Two: Art Music has no purpose other than the communication of its own aesthetic content. It is inconsistent with the nature of great art to have any extrinsic purpose, including the purpose to entertain.

The first philosopher to address the impact which Art has on an observer was Aristotle, in his *Poetics*, as part of a discussion of Tragedy, which like music has both a material, written form and a live performance form. In this treatise, Aristotle first considers the nature and contribution of each of the specific components of the written form of the Tragedy in his typically methodical style. His great contribution, however, comes when he has completed this discussion, for he then goes beyond the material form of the play itself to discuss the observer. He makes it clear that not only is the end purpose of the elements of the play to produce a specific experience in the observer, but that the nature of this experience is what distinguishes Tragedy from other dramatic forms, such as Spectacle. It was in this moment that he created a new branch of Philosophy which we call 'Aesthetics.'

Our purpose is to provide a source book of representative descriptions of actual performances, observations by philosophers, poets and other commentators which contribute insights to our understanding of what music meant to listeners during the early Renaissance. It is for this reason that when discussing contemporary treatises on music that we concentrate on those passages which offer insights relative to the aesthetics of music and musical performance rather than the usual technical subjects such as scales, modes and counterpoint which fill most books on Renaissance music.

Since traditional musicology has focused almost exclusively on sacred and secular vocal music of the Renaissance, we have also included numerous references which we hope will reveal a much wider world of music during this period.

We are also interested in contemporary views on the physiology of knowing, especially with regard to the relationship of the senses and Reason, and related psychological ideas, such as Pleasure and Pain and the Emotions, which might offer a frame of reference for their perspective on the perception of music.

This is the fifth volume in a series of eight, ranging from the music of the ancient civilizations through the Baroque Period.

David Whitwell
Austin, Texas

ACKNOWLEDGMENTS

This new edition would not have been possible without the encouragement and help of Craig Dabelstein of Brisbane, Australia. His experience as a musician and educator himself has contributed greatly to his expertise as editor of this volume.

David Whitwell
Austin, 2013

1 THE LOW COUNTRIES IN THE SIXTEENTH CENTURY

THE EVIDENCE OF THE STRONG MUSICAL HERITAGE of the Low Countries is most clearly seen in her many distinguished musicians who made careers in other countries. Even a city so relatively distant as Lisbon used only musicians from Flanders in their civic bands between 1495 and 1521.[1] And the same can be said for poets.

> We should not forget the role played by the Low Countries humanist-poets who settled in Paris, the most prolific perhaps being Petrus Caecus de Ponte.[2]

The Eighty Years' War, which began in 1568, restricted patronage of the arts somewhat and encouraged more artists to leave. We can sense the negative effects of the political atmosphere during the second half of the century in an observation by Corneille Verdonck (1563–1625), one who stayed behind working for wealthy burghers. In the preface of his chanson collection of 1599, he comments on this scene and worries,

> whether these sweet harmonies have been interrupted by the tempests of war [Mars], who has too long been master of these provinces, or whether [music] has ceased to be esteemed by those who, filled with [religious] confusion ... cannot value what is full of agreement and harmony.[3]

The same pessimism is found in another famous native son, Erasmus.

> Only in my own country are we still backward, and barbarism, defeated elsewhere, seems to have fled to us as its last refuge. The reason is partly that the court here has not yet learnt to treat good literature with respect; partly the personal pretensions of a few men, who are convinced that humane studies will interfere with the distinction they have hitherto enjoyed among the common herd.[4]

The university created by papal bull in Louvain in 1425 had become a vital humanistic center until the turmoil following Luther somewhat derailed it. In any case we can see by its

---

1   George Grove, *The New Grove Dictionary of Music and Musicians,* ed. Stanley Sadie (London: Macmillan, 1980), XI, 25.
2   I. D. McFarlane, 'Clément Marot and the World of Neo-Latin Poetry,' in *Literature and the Arts in the Reign of Francis I* (Lexington: French Forum, 1985), 108.
3   Quoted in Gustave Reese, *Music in the Renaissance* (New York: Norton, 1959), 398.
4   Letter of Erasmus to Louis Ruzé, Mechelen, 1519, in *The Collected Works of Erasmus* (Toronto: University of Toronto Press, 1992), VI, 273.

statutes that it closely followed the model of Paris, with music still firmly tied to mathematics. Further, Erasmus frequently complained that the Catholic conservatives were seeking to diminish the humanities taught in this university.

> But in Louvain the trouble has been that the leading men prevent anyone from giving instruction in any humane subject, even without a fee! I cannot tell you how they conspired against something which would be a great benefit and a great credit, not only to the university but to the whole region. An ancient regulation was produced that no one had ever heard of. The authority of the whole university was brought to bear; the protection of the king's court was invoked; lay magistrates were summoned to give aid; finally the police were called in. No stone was left unturned, no expedient untried.[5]

He returns to this topic again in a letter to Cardinal Wolsey in England, in which he mentions that two of the theologians at Louvain 'hate me for the sake of the humanities, of which they are more terrified than of dog or snake.'[6]

ON THE AESTHETICS OF MUSIC

One of the great men of the Low Countries was Tielman Susato (d. 1561), trombonist,[7] leader of the town wind band in Antwerp and an important publisher. Although he published the first music in the Dutch tongue, his publication of many French chansons point to the close relationships between these two countries. His publications of chansons always carry a phrase indicating that they are suitable to be sung or played any kind of musical instruments, which is a reflection on his days as a member of the Antwerp town band. In the 'Apology' to Susato's 1551 publication of the first music in the Flemish tongue, we find a touching statement on the purpose of music.

> Music is a remarkable gift, instituted by order of God and offered to man to be used not for dishonest or thoughtless ends but, above all, to render thanks and praise to the Lord, to shun idleness and make good use of his time, to drive out melancholy and dark thoughts, and in order to restore joy to hearts sorely tried. And wherefore then should this not be done henceforth in our own mother tongue with the same skill and the same harmony as, until now, have been lavished on Latin, French and Italian? Our art and our harmony being the equal of those others, for what reason should one language be scorned to the profit of another?

---

5   Letter to Juan Vives [1520], in Ibid., VII, 308.
6   Letter to Thomas Wolsey [1522], in Ibid., IX, 40.
7   Reese, *Music in the Renaissance*, 290, incorrectly identifies Susato as a trumpeter.

ART MUSIC

An occasional reference speaks of the performance of art music in the homes of the nobles residing in the Low Countries. For example, a letter of Paschasius Berselius to Erasmus, in 1518, speaks of 'feeding my ears on sweet music' and the guests singing 'grace to the powers above' after the tables had been cleared after dinner.[8]

By the sixteenth century virtually all the more prosperous towns in the Low Countries had regularly employed wind bands of at least six members. A document from Ghent, in 1540–1541, provides a standard instrumentation.

> Item, paid to Pieter de Coninc, Goldsmith ... for two silver sackbuts, two descant and two tenor shawms ... to be delivered to the six shawm players of the city.[9]

As one finds elsewhere, these players doubled on all the standard instruments. In Ghent, for example, Corneilis Van Winckle was hired in 1542 as a trombonist, but is mentioned in a document of 1552 as having the city's bombard.

The Antwerp civic wind band enjoyed a large collection of city owned instruments and received uniforms. One of the members of this band was the famous Hans Nagel. Soon after Susato joined this wind band he himself transcribed for it thirty-three volumes of six-part music, running to about four hundred folio pages![10] His famous instrumental dances, published in four part-books in 1551 are almost certainly taken from the repertoire of this band.[11]

Another town which had a fine wind band was Mechelen, which profited from the presence of the court of Margaret of Austria. An extant contract for these players, from 1505, says they were to play on cornetts and other instruments during solemn masses; they were to perform concerts at the town hall late mornings, every Saturday, Sunday, holiday and on days preceding public festivities and they were to play for civic banquets and could not refuse to participate in any service required by the town. In order to maintain a desirable standard of performance, they were ordered to rehearse together at least twice weekly and to obey a leader.[12] A later contract for Mechelen, in 1568, calls for concerts on Sundays, Holy Days, and feast days.[13]

---

8 Quoted in *The Collected Works of Erasmus*, V, 258.

9 Ghent, *Stads Rekeningen*, 1540–1541, vol. 246v. Similar documents ordering 'cases' (consorts) of instruments exist in great numbers for many of these towns. In general, string instruments are not mentioned until after mid-century.

10 John Murray, *Antwerp in the Age of Platin and Brueghel* (Norman: University of Oklahoma Press, 1970), 147.

11 As a publisher, Susato's principal competitor was Pierre Phalèse, who stole much of his music from other editions. It is only due to this plagiarism, that the original dances of d'Estrée (1564) have survived.

12 Robert Wangermeé, *Flemish Music and Society in the Fifteenth and Sixteenth Centuries* (New York: F. A. Praeger, 1968), 180.

13 Raymond Van Aerde, *Ménestrels Communaux ... à Malines, de 1312 a 1790* (Mechelen, 1911), 39ff.

A contract of the Mons civic band, of 1532, demands the performance of concerts for the citizens twice a day, at eleven o'clock in the morning and at six o'clock in the evening.[14] A similar contract for the Bruges civic wind band requires concerts each Sunday at eleven o'clock in the square in front of the city hall and in the St. Donaes Church after the evening prayer.[15] The repertoire for these concerts was specified as sacred and devotional.

A more informal performance can be seen in an engraving by Lucas Valckenborck called 'Spring Landscape,' of 1587.[16] Here one sees a consort of wind players in a large 'nest,' in a tree, performing in the town square.

While the civic statutes addressed the performances required by the town, much of the actual control of civic performance rested with the civic musician guilds. The by-laws of the Bruges guild for 1534 stipulates fines if a member steals a performance opportunity from a brother member or criticizes a brother's talent. If one accepts a wedding or feast performance, one cannot withdraw to take a job that might pay more without the written permission of the first client.[17]

The by-laws of the Antwerp guild, for 1541, says the members cannot refuse engagements if they are free, cannot make double bookings or cut short performances and must teach dancing.[18]

By 1588, in Mons, new members were now expected to play string instruments, in addition to shawm, cornett and recorder, in the performance of 'such songs as the masters see fit to choose.'[19]

FUNCTIONAL MUSIC

The most frequently documented public performances by the civic bands of the Low Countries were those associated with a civic-religious celebration called the *ommegang*. These often featured allegorical pageants, as for example those given in Antwerp, 'The Return of Peace and Abundance' (1561), 'The Vicissitudes of all Things Mortal in War and Peace and Richness and Poverty' (1562) and 'The Good and Evil Use of Wealth' (1564).

An earlier *Ommegang*, in 1520, in Antwerp was observed by Albrecht Dürer and is discussed in his diary. He describes hearing 'long old Frankish trumpets of silver,'[20] and in addition,

---

14 Leopold Devillers, *Essai sur l'historie de la musique à Mons* (Mons, 1868), 16.

15 Louis Gilliodts-Van Severen, 'Les ménestrels de Bruges,' in *Essais d'Archéologie Brugeoise* (Bruges: L. de Plancke, 1912), II, 134.

16 London, Victoria and Albert Museum.

17 Edmond Vander Straeten, *La Musique aux Pays-Bas* (Brussels, 1867), IV, 96.

18 Murray, *Antwerp in the Age of Platin and Brueghel*, 143ff.

19 Wangermeé, *Flemish Music*, 182.

20 Albrecht Dürer, *Albrecht Dürer, Diary of his Journey to the Netherlands* (Grennwish, CT: New York Graphic Society, 1971), 60ff.

> There were also in the German fashion many pipers and drummers. All the instruments were loudly and noisily blown and beaten.

He describes the procession of the various guilds, including Goldsmiths, Painters, Masons, Sculptors, Joiners, Carpenters, Sailors, Fishermen, Butchers, Leatherers, Clothmakers, Bakers, Tailors and Cordwainers. He was particularly moved to see a group of widows, clad in white, 'very sorrowful to see.' From where he stood, it took two hours for the procession to pass.

The civic musicians were always engaged in the ceremonies welcoming visiting nobles. When Prince Francis, Duke of Brabant visited Antwerp in 1581, an eyewitness records a procession that included twenty thousand knights. Given the size, this observer was surprised by the quiet and orderly nature of the procession.

> Why, they made so little noise that if it had not been for the thundering of the cannons, the sounding of the trumpets, clarions, halboies [shawms], and other instruments, there was no more noise than is among a councell of grave men.[21]

Along the procession route were a number of allegorical pageants. The first featured the 'Maiden of Antwerp,' and consisted of 'Concord, Wisedome, and Defense' (a pelican killing herself for her young birds) and 'Offense' (a hen brooding over her chicks). At St. Katharines bridge a triumphal arch was constructed,

> cunninglie painted, garnished with His Highnesses armes, and with torches and cressets, and with musick of holboies and clarions.

Here also were torches constructed of barrels of pitch on poles, 'five stories high,' and a great mechanical giant which turned its head to greet the visitors.

Another triumphal arch held the Antwerp civic band, together with the allegorical goddesses Flora, Ceres, and Pomona, together with the 'hellhounds, Discord, Violence and Tyrannie.'

Later in the week another pageant was given, representing the Nine Muses, 'playing on diverse kinds of instruments, and a sweet singer.' Near the musicians was a 'cave, verie hideous, darke, and drierie to behold,' in which lurked the three hell-hounds, Discord, Violence and Tyrannie. These three would come sneaking to the mouth of the cave only to hear the music, which would cause them to scamper back into the cave. This was to instruct all observers that as long as the realm was interested in the arts, it would not be disturbed by discord, violence and tyranny!

When the English Earl of Leicester visited Amsterdam in 1586, an eyewitness reports that not only were there one thousand ships in the harbor, but 'sundry great [mechanical] whales and other fishes of hugeness,' which carried the civic officials who read Latin orations of welcome.[22]

---

21 John Nichols, *The Progresses and Public Processions of Queen Elizabeth* (London, 1788).
22 John Motley, *History of the United Netherlands* (New York, 1860), I, 15ff.

2 ERASMUS

DESIDERIUS ERASMUS (1469–1536) was the greatest humanist, scholar and writer of prose of the sixteenth century. He was born near Rotterdam and left an orphan while still a teenager. The executor of his parents estate, in order obtain everything for himself, gave Erasmus over to a monastic career. Erasmus in time became an ordained priest and, although he studied at the University of Paris, his viewpoints always reflected to a surprising degree his background in Church dogma.

His fame was such that he was constantly being offered the protection of various kings, as well as high office in the Church, but he foresaw that he could not write freely unless he was independent. Thus he supported himself through his publications as well as through gifts which resulted from his frequent travels. He made a lasting impression on everyone he met in these travels and we will let one famous acquaintance, Sir Thomas More, speak for them all.

> I cannot get rid of a prurient feeling of vanity … when it occurs to my mind that I shall be commended to a distant posterity by the friendship of Erasmus.[1]

Erasmus once described himself, in the third person, as follows:

> His health was always delicate, and thus he was often attacked by fevers, especially in Lent on account of the eating of fish, the mere smell of which used to upset him. His character was straightforward, and his dislike of falsehood such that even as a child he hated other boys who told lies, and in old age even the sight of such people affected him physically. Among his friends he spoke freely—too freely sometimes, and though often deceived he never learned not to trust them. Having a touch of pedantry, he never wrote anything with which he was satisfied; he even disliked his own appearance … For high office and for wealth he had a permanent contempt, and thought nothing more precious than leisure and liberty. A charitable judge of other mens' learning, he would have been a supreme [teacher] of gifted minds had his resources run to it. In promoting the study of the humanities no one did more, and great was the unpopularity he had to suffer in return for this from barbarians and monks.[2]

But this description hardly does justice to a man whose intellectual brilliance was so astonishing and whose knowledge of ancient Greek and Latin literature seems almost incredible.

---

1   Desiderius Erasmus, *Epistles* (London, 1901), III, 94.

2   Letter to Conradus Goclenius [1524], quoted in *The Collected Works of Erasmus* (Toronto: University of Toronto Press, 1992), IV, 409.

His overpowering knowledge and the scope of his writings made him probably the most widely known person of his time and certainly the most influential scholar. We get a sense of his influence in a description by a contemporary.

> He enjoys a reputation such as no one, I believe, has enjoyed during his lifetime for many generations past. He holds a unique position of respect, admiration, and esteem among the great host of scholars who are to be found throughout Germany, Belgium, and Britain; they compete in singing his praises, and while they themselves are sometimes brought low by the wounds which they are prone to inflict on one another with their pens, Erasmus sits *en dehors de la mêlée*, watching the gladiators from a ringside seat, while he is acclaimed by both sides with compliments and shouts of approbation. Nowadays no one produces a book or a speech or a page without, at the first opportunity, working in a complimentary reference to Erasmus' name, which is set in capital letters and adorned with the most flattering eulogies, with the object, presumably, of gaining the favor of the public. Nothing is more likely to win customers for the booksellers than to have the name of Erasmus on the title-page of all their publications, whether as expert reader, redactor, or annotator; and there is no book so expensive or so cheap and insignificant that it does not receive some added dignity and authority from the mention of Erasmus' name.[3]

This international respect which Erasmus enjoyed made it impossible to enjoy the life of humanist scholar, for he lived at one of the pivotal moments of history. Against his desire, he was thrust into the greatest drama of the sixteenth century, the rise of the Protestant movement and its impact on the Church and states of Europe.

The earliest extant letter from Luther to Erasmus, two years after his famous posting of his ninety-five theses on the door of the Castle Church in Wittenberg, finds them on friendly terms.

> Who is there in whose heart Erasmus does not occupy a central place, to whom Erasmus is not the teacher who holds him in thrall? I speak of those who love learning as it should be loved.[4]

As the Lutheran movement gained support there was tremendous pressure on Erasmus by Catholic leaders for him to write and speak out against Luther. In 1522 even Pope Adrian VI pleaded in a letter to Erasmus to write against 'the heresies, as stupid and boorish as they are godless … Can you then refuse to sharpen the weapon of your pen against the madness of these men?'[5]

Erasmus went to great lengths to attempt to remove himself from the fight, often pleading that he did not know Luther and had not read his books. Putting him in the best light, one can say that he preferred to encourage the fight against Luther, but not participate in it.

---

3   Letter of Juan de Vergara to Diego López Zúñiga [1521], in Ibid., VIII, 339.
4   Letter of Martin Luther to Erasmus, Wittenberg, [1519], in Ibid., VI, 281.
5   Letter of Pope Adrian VI to Erasmus [1522], in Ibid., IX, 206ff.

Indeed, he once compared himself to 'those who sound the trumpet on the battlefield while remaining themselves outside the fray.'[6]

But a less genuine side of Erasmus is often seen in his correspondence, where he attempted to tailor his views to please the reader. For example, in a letter to Albert of Brandenburg, in 1519,[7] he could untruthfully say that he had attempted to prevent the publication of Luther's works. On the other hand, to the Luther supporter, Philippus Melanchthon, he could seem almost sympathetic.

> Luther's supporters—and they include almost all men of good will—would wish that some of what he has written were more courteously and moderately expressed. But it is too late to tell him so now. I can see that things are heading towards civil strife.[8]

In the correspondence of Erasmus we can follow the progress of the Lutheran movement, step by step. By 1520 he had become fully aware of the impact of Luther's views. A correspondent at this time writes of Luther's publications, 'You would hardly believe their universal popularity.'[9] Erasmus, who first thought the Church should simply ignore Luther, now saw the Church beginning to blame everything on the humanist movement. Erasmus, reflecting on the failure of the Church leaders to properly confront Luther, was becoming alarmed.

> I saw that the business took its rise in hatred of the classical languages and what they call liberal studies. I saw that it was carried on with bitter strife and seditious clamor in public, the only result of which was to make Luther's works famous and arouse the common run of men to read them eagerly. Had they first refuted Luther and taken him out of men's minds, and then burnt his books, they might have done away with the whole of Luther without setting the world by the ears.[10]

By 1524 he concludes it is already too late to stop the new movement—too late to simply burn Luther at the stake!

> This business of Luther is very widely spread, and pushes further every day. And so I fear that the common remedies of public recantation, prison, and faggot will not get us very far.[11]

At the same time his strong traditional faith made him wonder if this were not all the work of God.

---

6   Letter to Duke George of Saxony [1520], in Ibid., VIII, 5. Curiously, in another letter he referred to Luther as a trumpet, 'like a great trumpet for proclaiming the gospel truth.' [Ibid., 42]

7   Quoted in Ibid., VII, 110.

8   Letter to Philippus Melanchthon [1520], in Ibid., VII, 313.

9   Letter of Arkleb of Boskovice to Erasmus [1520], in Ibid., VIII, 76.

10 Letter to Leo X [1520], in Ibid., VIII, 52.

11 Letter to Archduke Ferdinand [1524], in Ibid., X, 423.

> Has it pleased God to use Luther, as once he used the Pharaohs, the Philistines, the Romans, and men like Nebuchadnezzar? For Luther's successes can hardly have come about without God's help, especially since many of the actors in the play are vile creatures of extraordinary depravity and stupidity.[12]

By the following year events had become so dramatic that even Erasmus' faith could not sustain his optimism.

> What began with theological argument and noisy protestations soon turned into a matter for papal bulls; then it came to the burning of books and finally to the burning of men. What, I should like to know, has been gained by all this? Here at this moment a bloody drama is being played out … How it will end I do not know.[13]

Already in 1523, Erasmus had found himself becoming the object of attacks by the followers of Luther. Otto Brunfels had written him,

> Meanwhile you publish a second edition of your misbegotten and miserable *Spongia*, designed now not so much to wipe off aspersions as to collect and soak up all the lowest filth you can find and disgorge it again when you squeeze it.[14]

By 1524 Erasmus was becoming worried about the impact of the religious strife on humanistic studies.

> Thanks to these new gospellers of ours the humanities are out in the cold more or less everywhere, and we must use every effort to assist them.[15]

The following year he observed,

> Throughout Germany, not just the humanities, but almost every form of learning has crumbled into ruin.[16]

And he could not fail to recognize the irony,

> In Germany and Switzerland all lovers of the humanities were enthusiastic supporters of Luther at the beginning.[17]

---

12   Letter to Duke George of Saxony [1524], in Ibid., X, 457ff.
13   Letter to Noël Béda [1525], in Ibid., XI, 150.
14   Quoted in Ibid., X, 138.
15   Letter to Caspar Velius [1524], in Ibid., X, 420.
16   Letter to Adrianus Barlandus [1525], in Ibid., XI, 177.
17   Letter to Alberto Pio [1525], in Ibid., XI, 330.

In 1525, as well, Erasmus was becoming alarmed at the general civil unrest.

> I had fair success in Germany in arousing interest in languages and polite letters, and the applause which greeted my efforts was not entirely grudging; but then there was this sudden and disastrous upheaval, which, with its controversies and senseless disputes, began to throw everything into confusion, and has now reached the point where human blood flows in torrents.[18]
>
> ......
>
> Here considerably more than 100,000 peasants have been killed, and every day priests are arrested, tortured, hanged, decapitated, or burnt at the stake.[19]

As if all these concerns did not weigh heavily enough on Erasmus, he was astonished at the actions of his own Catholic brothers. The thought among the Catholic conservatives was that the new heresies had sprung from the humanities.[20]

> Nothing is so brazen, so pig-headed, as ignorance. These are the men who conspire with such zeal against the humanities. Their aim is to count for something in the councils of the theologians, and they fear that if there is a renaissance of the humanities, and if the world sees the error of its ways, it may become clear that they know nothing, although in the old days they were commonly supposed to know everything ... It is they who run this conspiracy against the devotees of liberal subjects.[21]

By 1522 he mentions that the Pope, Adrian VI, 'is entirely a scholastic, and not wholly well disposed to the humanities.'[22]

As the Lutheran movement gained momentum, Erasmus was shocked to find inquisitors in the Low Countries 'astonishingly hostile to the humanities. They start by putting men in jail and only then look for something to accuse them of.'[23]

> You know what an epic struggle I had with certain theologians in support of the humanities, before Luther appeared on the scene. And now a sword has been put into the hand of two [Catholic inquisitors] who hate the humanities passionately, Hulst and Baechem.[24]

In 1525 a correspondent, Christoph Truchsess, writes to Erasmus of the extent of the hostility of the conservatives toward the humanities.

---

18 Letter to Benedetto Giovio [1525], in Ibid., XI, 341.
19 Letter to Erasmus Schets [1525], in Ibid., XI, 393
20 Erasmus mentions this specifically in a letter of 1519 to Petrus Mosellanus, in Ibid., VI, 313.
21 Letter to Maarten van Dorp [1515], in Ibid., III, 122.
22 Letter to John Fisher [1522], in Ibid., IX, 176.
23 Letter to Willibald Pirckheimer [1524], in Ibid., X, 173.
24 Letter to Jean de Carondelet [1524], in Ibid., X, 212.

> Recently a well-known lawyer stood up in a crowded [university] hall in Bologna and without a blush made an attack upon the Muses (I quote his actual words): 'Keep away, gentlemen, from the humane arts, as you would from a painted harlot.'[25]

One can see Erasmus becoming increasingly alarmed. He remarks that certain men ('if such creatures deserve the name of *men*') are conspiring in deadly earnest to destroy the humanities. To combat this, he says, what is needed is,

> a whole host of champions whose intelligence, virtue, and influence will match the folly, villainy, and insolence of our enemies, these being the qualities in which they indisputably excel. If studies of this sort are snuffed out, how, I wonder, will our life differ from that of cattle or fish or creatures of the wild?[26]

At this time he loses one of his few soul-mates with the death of Maarten van Dorp.

> He stood almost alone in his support of the humanities, which some are now desperately trying to destroy. I do not think they realize what effect this will have upon their own studies, whose success alone interests them; for, as events will prove, once the gentler forms of learning have been destroyed, the things which they are defending with more zeal than wisdom will perish also. Everything would turn out better if the doyens of the old learning graciously welcomed the humanities into a friendly partnership, like exiles returning home to resume their rightful place.[27]

By this time, 1525, he complains he is being attacked by both the Lutherans and the Catholics. Regarding the latter, he writes,

> I am the target of persistent and mindless attacks from monks and theologians whose implacable hostility I have brought upon myself through my support of the humanities, for these swine detest the humanities more than they detest Luther himself.[28]
>
> ......
>
> There are some [Catholic clergy], especially among the older generation, who can accept nothing that has the slightest odor of the humanities about it or departs at all from the preferences they acquired as children. They don't realize that times change and that we must change with them.[29]
>
> ......
>
> Even the theologians' dogs piss on me as they pass.[30]

---

25 Quoted in Ibid., XI, 379.
26 Letter to Alexius Thurzo [1525], in Ibid., XI, 103.
27 Letter to Adrianus Barlandus [1525], in Ibid., XI, 176ff.
28 Letter to Celio Calcagnini [1525], in Ibid., XI, 112.
29 Letter to Noël Béda [1525], in Ibid., XI, 148.
30 Letter to Claudius Cantiuncula [1525], in Ibid., XI, 288.

During this period of personal attacks by important figures of his own Church, we find Erasmus fighting back with stronger and stronger language. In a letter of 1519 to Pope Leo X, Erasmus characterizes the Catholic scholars who have criticized him for attempting a new translation of the New Testament.

> With astonishing unanimity it won the approbation of all save very few, some of whom were too stupid to be convinced by sound arguments, others too proud to be willing to learn, others too obstinate not to feel shame if they showed lack of firmness in pursuing the wrong course ... some too anxious for their own reputation to let it be thought that there was anything they had not known before.[31]

Another letter of the same year is more outspoken.

> There are gangs of conspirators who have consigned themselves on oath to the infernal powers if they do not utterly destroy the humanities and classical theology; and they have sworn to hold forth against Erasmus everywhere: at drinking-parties, in markets, in committees, in druggists' shops, in carriages, at the barber's, in the brothels, in public and private classrooms, in university lectures and in sermons, in confidential conversations, in the privacy of the confessional, in bookshops, in the taverns of the poor, in the courts of the rich ... There is no place they cannot penetrate, no lie they will not tell, to make me, a general benefactor, into an object of general hatred.[32]

The following year, after an attack by the English scholar, Edward Lee, the language of Erasmus becomes very personal.

> The English viper has burst out at last! Before us stands Edward Lee, an eternal blot on that isle so highly thought of. For eighteen months now he has been boasting of his 'pious annotations.' The whole world awaited a work of scholarship; and here before us is a book running over, raving mad I would say, with brawling and fishwives' abuse. Strip this from the book, and heavens! how worthless, how tedious is what remains! I would describe the monster for you, but I fear posterity will not believe that such a beast was ever born in human shape. No harlot was ever so brazen, no pimp a more abandoned liar.[33]

And in 1521, Erasmus actually writes an extraordinary personal letter to a critic.

> My own feeling for you is pity rather than resentment, and I pity you the more if you have still no pity for yourself. A large element of health lies in diagnosing one's disease. If nature has denied you the brains to become a great scholar, the eloquence to be an effective preacher, the skill to write so that you might publish books for the general good, you must at least try to become a good man. And he begins to become a good man who has ceased to be a bad one. He is a bad

---

31 Letter to Leo X [1519], in Ibid., VII, 57.
32 Letter to Thomas Lupset [1519], in Ibid., VII, 159.
33 Letter to Wolfgang Capito [1520], in Ibid., VII, 216.

man who speaks ill of his neighbor; doubly bad if he speaks ill of one who has done him some good. If you cannot do good to others for want of brains, eloquence, learning, common sense, and judgment, do what you can at least to do them no harm.[34]

One has to read these last letters with some sympathy, for with all his great gifts, Erasmus was also human and had his own share of human weaknesses. As mentioned above, he was capable of presenting quite different views to different correspondents. In 1501 he writes to the Princess of Veere, Anna van Borssele requesting her aid in obtaining an honorary doctorate for himself, 'that I should be able to style myself a doctor.'[35] But, he writes a friend in 1506,

> I have recently been awarded a doctorate in theology, against my own inclinations, which were overborne by my friends' insistence.[36]

And he was, sad to say, extremely anti-Semitic. We will let a single example of his remarks on this subject serve for many.

> I wish he were an entire Jew—better still if the removal of his foreskin had been followed by the loss of his tongue and both hands.[37]

ON THE PHYSIOLOGY OF AESTHETICS

Considering his Church background, together with a life spent in studying the ancient philosophers, is must be no surprise that Erasmus often makes the statement that he is 'ruled by reason and not by my feelings.'[38] He also observed, 'He who takes a man's life does him less harm than if he robbed him of his reason.'[39]

One of the most interesting statements by Erasmus, explaining why Reason must rule man, is found in his advice to the young prince. God, he tells us, has no emotions. Here we also see an example of the low regard Erasmus held for the common people.

> Although God is swayed by no emotions, he nevertheless orders the world with the greatest good judgment. Following his example in all his actions, the prince must disregard emotional reactions and use only reason and judgment.

---

34 Letter to Vincentius Theoderici [1521], in Ibid., VIII, 194.

35 Letter to Anna van Borssele [1501], in Ibid., II, 16.

36 Letter to Jan Obrecht [1506], in Ibid., II, 124.

37 Letter to Jacopo Bannisio [1517], in Ibid., V, 179.

38 Mentioned in an autobiographical essay, ca. 1525, quoted in Ibid., X, 218.

39 Letter to François I [1523], in Ibid., X, 116.

> Nothing is higher than God, and similarly the prince should be removed as far as possible from the low concerns and sordid emotions of the common people.[40]

Later, he adds,

> If there is any evil in the mind, it arises from being in contact with the body, which is at the mercy of the emotions; and whatever good the body has springs from the mind as from a fountain.[41]

In another place, however, he returns to the older Church dogma.

> Correct judgment has no use for any kind of emotion, least of all for excessive, uncontrollable, and overwhelming joy, which is wont not only to eradicate all judgment but often also to rob us of our senses entirely.[42]

This stern analysis is lightened only by the recognition that the mind must also have some rest.

> We relax lyre and bow in order to tighten them more effectively, and similarly the mind should be refreshed by repose to make its response to toil more lively.[43]

Erasmus viewed the senses again from the long-held Church position that all the senses distort the truth, thus only Reason can be depended upon.

> What we apprehend with our senses does not really exist, for it is not perpetual, nor does it always take the same form. Those things alone really exist which are apprehended by the contemplation of the mind ... Now although the philosopher, withdrawing from sensible things, practices the contemplation of things intelligible, yet he does not perfectly enjoy them except when the spirit, liberated from the material organs through which it operates now, exercises all its force.[44]

To support this view that the senses distort, Erasmus presents a long discussion of the Greek proverb, 'The Sileni of Alcibiades,' which meant something which appears other than it is. He gives as an example, by the way, a carved figure of wood which appears like a 'caricature of a hideous flute player,' but opens to reveal a deity.

> The real truth of things is always most profoundly concealed, and cannot be detected easily or by many people. The stupid multitude, judging things as they do upside down, and using of course

---

40 'The Education of a Christian Prince,' [1516] in Ibid., XXVII, 221. In his 'A Complaint of Peace Spurned and Rejected by the Whole World,' [Ibid., XXVII, 296], Erasmus again mentions 'the common people, who are swayed by their passions like a stormy sea.'
41 'The Education of a Christian Prince,' [1516] in Ibid., XXVII, 233.
42 'The Tyrannicide,' [1506] in Ibid., XXIX, 77.
43 'Parallels,' [1514] in Ibid., XXIII, 164.
44 Letter to Joris van Halewijn [1520], in Ibid., VII, 317.

as their criteria for every purpose what is most clearly obvious to the bodily senses, constantly make mistakes and go astray.[45]

While Erasmus writes little of the individual senses, one comment about hearing attracts our attention. In his 'The Tongue,' which deals mostly with talking, Erasmus observes,

> Men say fine tales are best told twice or three times, yet hearing, the most fastidious of the senses, can hardly bear even this.[46]

Erasmus also writes little of the value of individual experience as an aspect of the mind's development. In one place, however, we find something which has a clear 'we are what we eat' quality about it. In explaining the proverb, 'The cover is worthy of the cup,' Erasmus quotes his friend, John Colet, as saying, 'We are, what we are made by our daily conversation: we are shaped by what we hear around us every day.' Erasmus believed this was true of reading as well.

> And what he said about conversation is also to be understood of what we read. Those who spend their whole lives on gentile literature end up as pagans; those who read nothing but filthy books must needs develop in their own characters a streak of filth. For reading surely is a kind of conversation.[47]

In these books we have been calling attention to the reader of instances throughout early literature of preference for the right hand, which we understand today as an expression of the left hemisphere of the brain (the only side which can read, write or speak) and its curious denial of the the importance, and even existence, of the right hemisphere. We should like to mention a few such examples in Erasmus.

In a treatise, 'On Good Manners,' Erasmus discusses manners for young people. Among his rules, we find,

> If offering or pouring something see that you do not do it with your left hand.[48]

Similarly, in his discussion of the proverb, 'Admetus' dirge,' Erasmus mentions a curious Greek myth regarding Aesculapius, son to Apollo, who studied medicine with Cheiron. Acquiring blood from the veins of the Gorgon, 'he employed blood from the veins on the left side to destroy people, and blood from the right side to save their lives.'[49]

One of the important characteristics of the twin hemispheres is that they tend to operate one at a time, and not together on an equal basis. This, of course, is the essential problem for

---

45 'Adages,' in Ibid., 267.
46 'The Tongue,' [1525] in Ibid., XXIX, 283.
47 'Adages,' in Ibid., XXXII, 268.
48 'On Good Manners,' [1530] in Ibid., XXV, 286.
49 'Adages,' in Ibid., XXXIII, 302.

one composing music for words: does one want the listener to hear the words or the music? In opera, the invention of the alternating recitative and aria was one solution to this dilemma. Erasmus reveals he had observed this problem, in a treatise devoted to 'The Tongue,' where he noticed that when someone is chattering away, one cannot 'listen to the lute.'[50]

On Education

Erasmus, who would have been welcome at any sixteenth-century university, was clearly uncomfortable in that environment. While he shared many of the Church viewpoints with the professors, he was clearly bothered by their rigid approach to knowledge, a remnant of medieval Scholasticism. He mentions this in a letter of 1525, where he notes that he has tried to inspire a renewed interest in the liberal arts, both to bring them into religious discussion and to introduce languages and fine literature into the schools. But takes pains to disassociate himself from Scholasticism.

> With regard to the teaching of the scholastics, I have always kept away from it as much as possible, for I am very conscious that a person of my modest abilities should not enter this difficult field of dogmatic theology.[51]

In a letter to Henry VIII, Erasmus is less modest. He wonders who would have been willing to face martyrdom for the early Greek philosophies and 'Who gives a fig for those puzzling precepts of Pythagoras?' In a remarkable distortion of the truth, he claims that even Aristotle would be unknown were it not for the Christians.[52]

He takes the opportunity to again attack the world of the professor in discussing the proverb, 'The Sileni of Alcibiades,' which deals with appearances versus realities.

> Anyone who looked thoroughly into the driving force of things and their true nature would find none so far removed from real wisdom as those whose honorific titles, learned bonnets, resplendent belts, and bejeweled rings advertise wisdom in perfection. So true is this that you may not seldom find more real and native wisdom in one single ordinary man, who in the world's judgment is an ignoramus and a simple-minded fool, more or less, whose mind has been educated not by the subtle Scotus but by the heavenly spirit of Christ, than in many of our pompous theologians, Professors three and four times over, stuffed with their favorite Aristotle and swollen with a plethora of doctoral definitions, conclusions and propositions.[53]

---

50 'The Tongue,' [1525] in Ibid., XXIX, 279.
51 Letter to Noël Béda [1525], in Ibid., XI, 135.
52 Letter to Henry VIII [1523], in Ibid., X, 70.
53 'Adages,' in Ibid., XXXIV, 265ff.

Part of his attitude, of course, was due to the fact that these same university scholars were constantly attacking his writings. In his 'Complaint of Peace,' Erasmus has Peace bemoan this characteristic of the academic community.

> I shall seek refuge in the company of scholars, for good learning makes men, philosophy makes superior men, theology makes holy men. Surely I shall be allowed to settle down amongst them after all my wanderings. But woe is me! Here too there is warfare, another kind and not so bloody, but just as insane … The heat of the debate mounts from argument to insult, from insults to fisticuffs, and if they don't settle the matter by daggers or spears they take to stabbing with poisoned pens, tear one another with barbed wit, and attack each other's reputation with the deadly darts of their tongues.[54]

Preferring not to be part of this environment, Erasmus was resigned to the solitary life. In his 'Praise of Folly,' the narrator, Folly, proposes to compare the lot of a wise man to that of a fool. One cannot help but feel this passage is to some degree autobiographical, composed in some moment of self-pity.

> Imagine some paragon of wisdom to set up against him, a man who has frittered away all his boyhood and youth in acquiring learning, has lost the happiest part of his life in endless wakeful nights, toil, and care, and never tastes a drop of pleasure even in what's left to him. He's always thrifty, impoverished, miserable, grumpy, harsh and unjust to himself, disagreeable and unpopular with his fellows, pale and thin, sickly and bleary-eyed, prematurely white-haired and senile, worn-out and dying before his time. Though what difference does it make when a man like that does die? He's never been alive. There you have a splendid picture of a wise man.[55]

By way of introducing Erasmus' views on education, we might mention a letter of 1521 in which Erasmus makes the interesting observation that he has discovered a man who 'takes pains to give his whole household an education in good literature, setting thereby a new precedent which, if I mistake not, will soon be widely followed, so happy is the outcome.'[56] What he means by 'whole household' here is that the man is also educating his daughters! Until now, he admits that he was not entirely free of the opinion held by others that 'for the female sex, education had nothing to offer in the way of either virtue or reputation.' He attributes his change of opinion to the influence of Sir Thomas More and he adds that he doesn't think husbands should worry that educated wives would be less obedient!

Regarding the education of children, Erasmus often, and correctly, observed that the early years are the most fertile.

> Age is slow at any kind of learning, but especially at learning a language, a faculty which is given by nature to children. It is generally well known that children can learn to speak any tongue,

---

54 'A Complaint of Peace Spurned and Rejected by the Whole World,' [1516] in Ibid., XXVII, 297.
55 'Praise of Folly,' [1503] in Ibid., XXVII, 110.
56 Letter to Guillaume Budé [1521], in Ibid., VIII, 296.

while older people do not achieve it or imitate it very badly ... For this reason the character must be formed while the age is malleable; the mind accustomed to the best, while it is impressionable as wax.[57]

As with all ancients, however, he often makes the mistake of thinking of the education of the child as 'filling the blank page of your mind,'[58] whereas we know today that quite the reverse is the case.

Erasmus' ideas on the teacher begin with the question of the relative value of books and teachers, a topic we find in his discussion the proverb, 'Muti magistri' (Silent teachers).

> The question is often asked, and very sensibly, which is the more useful in the acquisition of knowledge, to use the living voice or silent masters. Each has its own particular advantages. What we learn from books is often more recondite, and there is more of it; for each reader learns as much as his quickness of mind will allow and the faithfulness of his memory retain ...
> On the other hand what we learn from listening to a teacher costs us less in mental effort, in eyesight, in health—particularly if the one who speaks is someone we admire and love.[59]

Eventually, he decides a combination of the two is best.

His ideal for the teacher of children he expresses in a letter to Johann von Vlatten,

> To this end it will be a great help to have in charge of the school a man of good character no less than good education ... Once he has laid the first foundations of both Greek and Latin, he should read all the best authors with the boys; and this means Cicero, and the others in proportion as they approach him. Among the poets he must choose those who are respectable; and in any case those who are worth reading for the amount they can tell us but are objectionable for their obscenity, of whom Martial is one, must in my view be presented in excerpts which can safely be read with the boys.[60]

In general, however, he seems to have found quite another kind of teacher. In his treatise, 'On the Writing of Letters,' he calls them 'this untaught race of experts, this illiterate horde of literates.'[61]

Erasmus was especially concerned with the treatment of children in school and he often lashes out at the cruel teacher.

---

57 'Adages,' in Ibid., XXXI, 200
58 'On the Pursuit of Virtue,' [1503] in Ibid., XXIX, 9.
59 'Adages,' in Ibid., XXXI, 163.
60 Letter to Johann von Vlatten [1523], in Ibid., X, 100.
61 'On the Writing of Letters,' [1522] in Ibid., XXV, 12. Erasmus, in 'The Right Way of Speaking Latin and Greek,' [1528] in Ibid., XXVI, 381, says that the word 'bachelor,' in the academic sense comes from *Baculus*, or 'rod,' referring to the beating of students.

> He flogs and tortures the poor creatures, and deafens them with shouting and abuse ...
> You may see this whip-cracking and untaught breed of elementary schoolmasters in power everywhere nowadays, and the caverns where they babble away reverberate on all sides with piteous howling like the realm of the Furies.[62]

And in another place,

> schoolmasters, always shouting and clouting and flogging the boys' skin off their backs, and can teach nothing for all that except bad grammar, which they will soon have to unlearn.[63]

This having been his experience, he is astonished at how casually teachers are hired.

> Nobody commissions a statue from a sculptor without having seen other statues from his workshop, yet we happily hand over our children to a stranger without having seen any example of what he has done.[64]

Erasmus also, however, places some importance on the attitude of the student.

> Outstanding ability can acquire a liberal education even under a bad and idle teacher; but if the pupil, on the other hand, is an ass listening to the lyre, even the best of teachers wastes both oil and toil.[65]

Erasmus found it curious that of all persons, the highest nobles were the least carefully educated.

> If anyone is to be a coachman, he learns the art, spends care and practice; but for anyone to be a king, we think it is enough for him to be born ...
> What actually happens is that no kind of man is more corruptly or carelessly brought up than those whose education is of such importance to so many people. The baby who is to rule the world is handed over to the stupidest of womenkind who are so far from instilling anything in his mind worthy of a prince, that they discourage whatever the tutor rightly advises, or whatever inclination to gentleness the child may have in himself—and they teach him to act like a prince, that is like a tyrant. Then no one fails to fawn and flatter. The courtiers applaud, the servants obey his every whim, even the tutor is obsequious; and he is not doing this to make the prince more beneficial to his country, but to ensure a splendid future for himself.[66]

---

62 'On the Writing of Letters,' [1522] in Ibid., XXV, 41.

63 Letter to Maarten Lips [1518], in Ibid., VI, 4.

64 'The Right Way of Speaking Latin and Greek,' [1528] in Ibid., XXVI, 374.

65 'Adages,' in Ibid., XXXIV, 16. The reference to the 'ass listening to the lyre,' is a comment often mentioned by ancient philosophers: an ass can hear music, but not listen to it.

66 'Adages,' in Ibid., XXXI, 232, 234.

The most famous discussion by Erasmus on the subject of the education of nobles is found in his 'The Education of a Christian Prince.' He begins by stressing that the proper teacher is one who has learned 'by long practical experience and not just by petty maxims.'[67] Oddly enough, Erasmus does not, in this treatise, outline a specific plan of studies for the prince, nor even mention the basic subjects by name. He does recommend the reading of books in general, however with some stipulations.

> Demetrius Phalereus [fourth century BC] shrewdly recommends the prince to read books, because very often he may learn from these what his friends have not dared to bring to his attention. But in this matter he must be equipped in advance with an antidote, as it were, along these lines: 'This writer whom you are reading is a pagan[68] and you are a Christian reader; although he has many excellent things to say, he nevertheless does not depict the ideal of a Christian prince quite accurately, and you must take care not to think that whatever you come across at any point is to be imitated straight away, but instead test everything against the standard of Christ.'
> ......
> But today we see a great many people enjoying the stories of Arthur and Lancelot and other legends of that sort, which are not only tyrannical but also utterly illiterate, foolish, and on the level of old wives' tales, so that it would be more advisable to put one's reading time into the comedies or the myths of the poets rather than into that sort of drivel.[69]

ON THE PSYCHOLOGY OF AESTHETICS

Emotions

In the 'Enchiridion' Erasmus states, as he often does, that 'in man Reason plays the role of king.' He then turns to the emotions and divides them into two general categories. Some are as nobles to the King Reason, such as love of parents, kindness towards friends and compassion for the afflicted. Those, however, which are sensuous in nature he places in quite a different category.

> As for those passions of the soul that are furthest removed from the dictates of Reason and are debased to the lowliness of beasts, consider these to be like the lowest dregs of the masses. Of this kind are lust, debauchery, envy, and similar disorders of the mind, which should all without exception be consigned to forced labor like vile and wicked slaves, so that, if they are able, they may produce the work and services required of them by their master, or, if not, at least not cause any harm.[70]

---

67 'The Education of a Christian Prince,' [1516] in Ibid., XXVII, 208.
68 No doubt Erasmus was thinking of Aristotle, whom he frequently attacks.
69 'The Education of a Christian Prince,' [1516] in Ibid., XXVII, 250.
70 'Enchiridion,' 'The Handbook of the Christian Soldier,' [1503] in Ibid., LXVI, 42.

While this passage would appear to admit the necessity of emotions only for reproduction, in another place Erasmus seems to recognize a more general contribution of emotions to the total man. He begins, nevertheless, with the old Church dogma.

> First of all, it's admitted that all the emotions belong to Folly, and this is what marks the wise man off from the fool; he is ruled by reason, the fool by his emotions. That is why the Stoics segregate all passions from the wise man, as if they were diseases. But in fact these emotions not only act as guides to those hastening towards the haven of wisdom, but also wherever virtue is put into practice they are always present to act like spurs and goads as incentives towards good deeds. Yet this is hotly denied by that double-dyed Stoic Seneca who strips his wise man of every emotion. In doing so he leaves nothing at all of the man, and has to fabricate in his place a new sort of god who never was and never will be in existence anywhere. Indeed, if I may be frank, what he created was a kind of marble statue of a man, devoid of sense and any sort of human feeling.[71]

Having said this, Erasmus emphasizes the importance of one not being carried away by one's feelings. In his famous book, 'The Education of a Christian Prince,' for example, he begins by describing the proper head of state as not being so old as to be senile, 'nor so immature as to be carried away by his feelings.'[72] As for himself, one remarkable comment seems to suggest this self-made man had little need of emotional support.

> Stage tragedies are different: in real disasters we do not need a character to grieve with us and join his tears with ours.[73]

Regarding specific emotions, an early poem, composed in 1487, speaks of the power of Love.

> Now I know what love is: love is a madness in
> the mind; love is a fire in the heart hotter than
> Aetna …
> Tender Love first enters
> the eyes; then with full force Love sticks in the
> marrow and pierces the bones. Love pierces
> the bones and eats away the innards with
> silent flames.[74]

As he became older the ideas in this poem took on a different tone. In his discussion of one of his proverbs, Erasmus comments that the unhappiness which accompanies Love is greater than the pleasure.[75]

---

71 'Praise of Folly,' [1503] in Ibid., XXVII, 104.
72 'The Education of a Christian Prince,' [1516] in Ibid., XXVII, 206.
73 'Parallels,' [1514] in Ibid., XXIII, 159.
74 'An Elegiac Poem on the Overmastering Power of Cupid,' in Ibid., LXXXV, 231ff.
75 'Adages,' in Ibid., XXXIII, 95.

As an adult, it was the dangers of physical love that most concerned him. In his 'On Disdaining the World,' Erasmus uses music as a context to explain the dangers of the young woman.

> Whose heart is calm enough, firm enough, hardened enough, to resist those wanton gestures, the rhythmical movement of arms, the song of the cither, and the voices of the young women? Whom could they fail to seduce, to shake, and to weaken in his resolve? Especially since they are always the kind of songs that could warm the cockles of any man ... And when the music-master touches the lute, as is the custom, and gives the sign to end the dancing, you will be considered a yokel if you do not heartily kiss the girl.[76]

In another place he describes physical love in much stronger terms.

> These are obscene, bestial pleasures, altogether unworthy of man, which make wild animals of us; they are impure as well, containing more bitterness than sweetness.[77]

Later in this work he returns to this subject, warning 'nothing does more to dull the mind's activity, to weaken bodily strength and to hasten old age.' He also takes advantage of this opportunity to reflect on,

> the hateful vices of the female sex, how few good, modest women there are to be found, how few men who do not regret that they entered upon wedlock. [The writer] will expose to view these all too common experiences, that wives are quarrelsome, impudent, shameless, and ... drive husbands to their death.[78]

Another emotion which Erasmus found to be thoroughly detrimental to man, was anger.

> Anger, which is intense among the young because of their hot blood and inexperience of life, takes on a new vigor among the old, doubtless because of the infirmities of age, unless experience and philosophy provide an effective cure.[79]

Thus in a letter to a young friend Erasmus advises him to overcome his hot temper.

> Take my word for it, unless you abstain from two things, disorder of the mind and unseasonable sexual relations, I would rather not confess what I fear for you.[80]

---

76 'On Disdaining the World,' [1521] in Ibid., LXVI, 152.
77 'On the Writing of Letters,' [1522] in Ibid., XXV, 36.
78 'On the Writing of Letters,' [1522] in Ibid., XXV, 147.
79 Letter to Alexius Thurzo [1525], in Ibid., XI, 105.
80 Letter to Pieter Gillis [1517], in Ibid., V, 156.

The following year, Erasmus writes this young man again.

> Above all, avoid all strong emotion, excessive joy, unrestrained laughter, too much walking, excessive study, and anger especially.[81]

One topic which all early philosophers comment on is the apparent conflict between emotions and Reason, most evident in the familiar observations that strong emotions inhibit speech and that speech cannot always express feelings. The latter was evident to Erasmus as well, for a poem of 1504 contains the line, 'My tongue is not adequate to my feelings.'[82]

Among early writers, Love is the emotion which usually prevents coherent speech. Erasmus, in an unusually obsequious paper praising Archduke Philip, pretends that it is the strong feelings of joy which prevent him from communicating his thoughts.

> Something strange has just happened: now I have reached the point where not even the most carefully chosen words could have been sufficient, even ordinary language suddenly fails me. It seems almost phenomenal, but the richness of my material is overwhelming my natural talent, the throng of events chokes and strangles the flow of my eloquence, and this strange and unwonted force of happiness, which does not permit silence, at the same time cuts off my power of speech. I have no idea what this can be, unless it must be what the tragic poet expressed so elegantly: light feelings can speak, strong feelings have no voice.[83]

The solution is, once again, for Reason to control the emotions. In the preface to the second edition of his *Spongia*, Erasmus cautions the young to acquire good sense, as well as good learning, and to 'rein in their mettlesome passions with the bridle of Reason.'[84] In another place, he writes,

> As the body cannot support pleasure unless it is in good health, so the mind is not capable of true happiness unless free from fear and the other emotions.[85]

One accomplishes this by engaging the mind in virtuous studies.

> Far more pleasant delights derive from honorable studies, as the mind is nobler than the body, and as man surpasses the beasts; as much more honorable as the glory of virtue outshines moral baseness; they are happily acquired and more happily retained; they do not remove us from ourselves, but restore us to ourselves, and do not change us from men into wild animals, but from men into gods.[86]

---

81 Quoted in Ibid., V, 390.

82 'A Congratulatory Poem [for] Prince Philip, Upon his Happy Return,' in Ibid., LXXXV, 139.

83 'Panegyric for Archduke Philip,' [1503] in Ibid., XXVII, 67. The 'tragic poet' is Seneca, Phaedra, 607.

84 Quoted in *The Collected Works of Erasmus*, X, 93.

85 'Parallels,' [1514] in Ibid., XXIII, 153.

86 'On the Writing of Letters,' [1522] in Ibid., XXV, 36.

But, of course, this is easier said than done and Erasmus admits that even he has not always been successful.

> Some people find me in places too outspoken, too passionate ... While I was proceeding with my actual work, the indignation that boiled within me at this monstrous affair was often restrained by reason, but I could not conceal it everywhere.[87]

Pleasure and Pain

In an early poem, composed in 1487, Erasmus deals with the importance of Joy driving away Sorrow. The poem concludes,

> Joy, without which nothing can be beautiful,
> nothing can be good. It makes our bodies
> strong and fends off gloomy old age, and it
> prolongs our days of joy. Joy increases our
> beauty and makes our faces more cheerful; joy
> tends to make our mental endowments more
> brilliant.[88]

Six years later he gives a Christian definition of Pleasure which reads like something by one of the medieval Church fathers.

> What is it that the pitiful masses call pleasure? Surely nothing less than what it is said to be. And what is that? It is pure insanity ... The sole true pleasure is the joy of a pure conscience. The study of the holy Scriptures is a sumptuous banquet; the psalms of the Holy Spirit are the pleasantest of songs; the communion of all the saints is a most joyous fellowship; the enjoyment of truth is the greatest delight.[89]

Erasmus joins nearly all early writers in recognizing that Pleasure and Pain seem always related one to the other. In an early poem, composed in 1490, he attributes to Fortune this mixing of Pleasure and Pain.

> For Fortune
> intermingles her gifts to her followers in such a
> way that a bit of honey masks a deal of
> wormwood. And just as the white lilies are
> surrounded by tangled briars and the sharp

---

87   Letter to Ludwig Baer [1517], in Ibid., IV, 177.
88   'An Elegiac Poem comparing Sorrow and Joy,' in Ibid., LXXXV, 220ff.
89   'Enchiridion,' 'The Handbook of the Christian Soldier,' [1503] in Ibid., LXVI, 89.

> thorn brings forth the crimson glory, so
> Fortune mixes sorrow with joy, the sweet with
> the bitter, and hope marches linked in an even
> pace with fear, delight keeps step with grief,
> and dancing is mingled with heavy-hearted
> mourning, freedom with cares, repose with
> hardship.[90]

From time to time he returns to the thought of life being a mixture of Pleasure and Pain. He writes to a correspondent,

> Such are the turns of human life, such the web of tragedy and comedy in which our brief days are spent.[91]

A similar thought is expressed in a poem of 1518.

> Here, where affairs are
> mixed and various, we bow down and sing
> hymns intermingled with wailing supplications.[92]

Another poem mentions 'tears of happiness.'[93]

From the perspective of his Christian faith, Erasmus was able to wonder if man were intended to obtain pleasure from this very mixture of Pleasure and Pain. He seems to be searching for an analogy for this idea in his discussion of the proverb, 'The most delightful sailing is by the land.'

> Everything is most delightful when tempered by some admixture of an opposite kind; as for instance if you mingle a little learning in your pastimes, and mix light relief with your studies ... In the same way we get more pleasure from philosophy when mingled with poetry, and poetry with an admixture of philosophy is more attractive.[94]

In the same vein, when discussing the proverb, 'The labors of Hercules,' Erasmus uses the opportunity to complain somewhat about the difficulty of his huge proverb project. The pleasure, he says, belongs only to the reader; 'Nothing comes the writer's way except ... unvarying toil.'[95] But then he remembers a comment by Aristotle that it is, nevertheless, some form of pleasure which makes possible extensive projects of this kind.

---

90 'An Elegiac Poem on Patience,' in Ibid., LXXXV, 253.
91 Letter to Gerardus Listrius [1517], in Ibid., V, 174.
92 'Ode in Praise of Michael,' in Ibid., LXXXV, 113.
93 Poem 'in Praise of St. Ann,' in Ibid., LXXXV, 11.
94 'Adages,' in Ibid., XXXI, 221.
95 'Adages,' in Ibid., XXXIV, 174.

ON THE PHILOSOPHY OF AESTHETICS

Erasmus appears to have had little appreciation for Art. Perhaps we must make allowances for one who probably read more and wrote more than anyone in the sixteenth century, as just not having time to study it. In a letter of 1525 he mentions the pyramids of Egypt, calling them 'a vain and foolish display of barbaric wealth.' Such monuments he admits delight by their marvelous skill and ingenuity, 'but are otherwise without value.' To him function was more important.

> Real distinction belongs to those who, by building bridges, harbors, baths, and aqueducts, have created works which combine grandeur with utility.[96]

Later in this same letter he mentions the writings of Pliny as deserving to be honored beyond anything which painters or sculptors have produced.

Whatever value Erasmus placed on Art, unlike earlier Christian writers who always defined Art as that being within the artist, he found Art to be in the Art object.

> The best picture is not that which displays by its material the wealth of the man who paid for it or the skill of the artist, but the most faithful likeness of the subject.[97]

In his 'Praise of Folly,' Erasmus has the narrator, Folly, condemn, one after the other, nearly every profession. When the artist is discussed, it seems clear that the purpose for Art for Erasmus was simply to please. We see here again Erasmus' frequent condemnation of the general public.

> As for those who teach and practice the arts—what shall I say about them? They all have their special form of Self-love, and you're more likely to find one who'll give up his family plot of land than one who'll yield an inch, where his ability is in question. This is especially true of actors, singers, orators, and poets; the more ignorant one of them is, the more immoderate his self-satisfaction, boastfulness, and conceit. They can always find like to meet their like, in fact anything wins more admiration the sillier it is. The worst always pleases the most people, since the majority of men, as I said before, are prone to folly. Besides, if an artist is all the more pleased with himself and the more generally admired the less skilled he is, why should he choose to undergo a proper course of instruction? It'll cost him a lot in the first place, then make him more nervous and self-conscious, and he'll end up pleasing far fewer people.[98]

---

96 Letter to Stanislaus Thurzo [1525], in Ibid., XI, 27.

97 'Parallels,' [1514] in Ibid., XXIII, 226.

98 'Praise of Folly,' [1503] in Ibid., XXVII, 116.

Later, Folly says of poets,

> Poets aren't so much in my debt, though they're admittedly members of my party, as they're a free race, as the saying goes, whose sole interest lies in delighting the ears of the foolish with pure nonsense and silly tales. Yet strange to say, they rely on these for the immortality and godlike life they assure themselves, and they make similar promises to others. Self-love and Flattery are their special friends, and no other race of men worships me with such wholehearted devotion.[99]

Similarly, in another place he says poets aren't so bad, as they can be excused on the basis of artistic inspiration.

> Less harm indeed is done by poets and orators, who are all by now well versed in the practice of taking the measure for a prince's praise not from his deserts but from their own inspiration.[100]

Finally, he seems to suggest in a more general sense that Art, whatever its value, is not worthy of being a profession.

> LION. People generally look down on the idea of anyone remaining a grammarian for life.
> BEAR. Why should they look down on it more than they look down on the idea of anyone remaining a painter?[101]

Regarding Beauty in Art, Erasmus seems to focus on only two definitions, but both of them are rarely mentioned by other early writers. The first is evident in the name of the proverb he discusses, 'Beauty bears repeating.'

> In general, there is such a power in excellent things that the more often and the more closely they are examined the more they please … On the other hand, things which are falsely colored or commonplace sometimes have a charm to begin with, through sheer novelty, but soon grow ugly on repetition.[102]

Erasmus mentions this definition again in a letter to William Warham, the Archbishop of Canterbury, when discussing painting.

> A picture of moderate quality is quite attractive on first inspection; if you study it more often, more closely, and more at leisure, it gradually loses its attraction. On the other hand, a painting by a distinguished artist becomes more and more admirable the more often and more attentively you look at it.[103]

---

99 'Praise of Folly,' [1503] in Ibid., XXVII, 123.
100 'The Education of a Christian Prince,' [1516] in Ibid., XXVII, 247.
101 'The Right Way of Speaking Latin and Greek,' [1528] in Ibid., XXVI, 384.
102 'Adages,' in Ibid., XXXI, 191.
103 Letter to William Warham, Archbishop of Canterbury [1524], in Ibid., X, 276.

Second, it would appear from a comment in his 'Apology Against Latomus,' that Erasmus regarded the environment in which Beauty is found to be inseparable from Beauty itself. This is a rather curious observation, as most people would probably regard the purposes of Art to be to improve the environment. It leads us to suspect, as we do with regard to Music, that Erasmus understood little beyond the superficial in Art. He was a left-brained man.

> I suppose truth has its own form of beauty wherever it is found. All the same I should prefer to see a beautiful shape naked, or simply and neatly dressed, than fouled by shabby rags. I would prefer to pick jewels from a golden vessel than from a muck-heap. I would prefer to eat fine food from a clean plate than a dirty dish.[104]

Regarding the most consistently discussed topic among early writers, whether Art should imitate Nature, there is little in the writing of Erasmus to imply much interest. In only one place does he address the central topic and here he clearly sides with Nature. In his discussion of the proverb 'Viva vox,' Erasmus notes, 'Natural things, in fact, have some quality of genuine grace which no artistic imitation can hope to copy.'[105] In discussing a proverb, 'As though in a mirror,' Erasmus touches around the edges, but avoids the obvious connection of Art and Nature.

> Nature, that most cunning designer of all things, has clearly constructed the eye in living creatures on the pattern of a mirror, for at the back of its translucent element she has fixed a dark layer, the removal of which immediately removes the faculty of vision. Hence the pointed saying that as the mirror is the eye of art, so the eye is the mirror of nature.[106]

ON POETRY

In his writings, Erasmus still speaks of poetry as a medium appropriate to either be read or sung.[107] His views regarding the essential value of poetry seem conflicting. On one hand he could say,

> As a young man I loved poetry, which I consider perhaps the most important element in a liberal education.[108]

---

104 'Apology Refuting Rumors and Suspicions … by Latomus,' in Ibid., LXXI, 78.
105 'Adages,' in Ibid., XXXI, 161.
106 'Adages,' in Ibid., XXXIII, 163.
107 See Ibid., LXXXV, 45, 47.
108 Letter to Noël Béda [1525], in Ibid., XI, 150.

And yet, he could curiously observe,

> One can find religious ceremonies with no flutes or dancing; one cannot find poetry without falsehood.[109]

In several places Erasmus apologizes for the poetry he wrote in his youth. A typical example is found in his explanation of a proverb, 'I'm sorry I gave what I did.' While not identifying himself, the implication seems clear.

> If someone wishes to convey his regret for the efforts he devoted in the past to a passion for poetry, and his intention to waste no more time on it, he might say, 'I'm sorry I gave what I did; what's left I will not give.'[110]

Nevertheless, his writings reflect that he continued to read and follow other poets during his life. In a letter to Conradus Rufus of 1518, for example, Erasmus recommends a young poet, Eobanus, whose poetry he says is so original 'you would think him a poet born, not made by practice.'[111] In a letter to Johannes Draconites he mentions this poet again, calling him a modern Ovid. Here he praises the poet for his ease and fluency, his natural style and with an absence of unnamed faults common to the Italians.[112] In another place he speaks of his own preferences.

> Some would have it that a poem is not a poem unless you summon up all the gods in turn from sky, sea, and land, and cram hundreds of legendary tales into it. I myself have always liked verse that was not far removed from prose, albeit prose of the first order … So do I take the greatest pleasure in rhetorical poems and in poetical rhetoric.[113]

It does seem clear that the purpose of poetry, for Erasmus, could be either as a virtue or a pleasure.

> As the bee gathers from flowers the nectar for her honey, where other creatures get only the pleasures of color and scent, so too the student of philosophy finds even in poetry things that can contribute to the good life, while others find only pleasure and relaxation.[114]

In another place he hints that poetry might have a greater purpose. In the 'Ciceronian,' a character wonders what appreciation a writer will get if he only imitates Cicero, or anyone else. The reply gives us some of Erasmus's ideals for poetry.

---

109 'Parallels,' [1514] in Ibid., XXIII, 182.
110 'Adages,' in Ibid., XXXIII, 222.
111 Letter to Conradus Rufus [1518], in Ibid., VI, 132.
112 Letter to Johannes Draconites [1518], in Ibid., VI, 133.
113 Letter to Andrea Ammonio [1513], in Ibid., II, 270ff.
114 'Parallels,' [1514] in Ibid., 186.

Only the sort acquired by those people who write patchwork poems—who possibly give pleasure, but only for a short while and only if one has nothing better to do; and they neither impart information, nor stir the emotions, nor rouse to action.[115]

In a world dominated by aristocrats there was still a need for epic poetry and in a letter to Duke Henry, in 1514, Erasmus reminds the duke of its importance with respect to posterity.

> Kings can indeed earn such fame by their glorious deeds, but poets alone can confer it through their learned [songs], for waxen effigies and portraits and genealogies and golden statues and inscriptions on bronze and pyramids laboriously reared, these things decay in the long course of the years; only the poets' memorials grow strong with the lapse of time, which weakens everything else.[116]

But the poet must be careful for, as Erasmus observes, regarding the proverb, 'Some have a tongue, others have teeth,'

> Poets have a tongue which they can use for attack; but princes have molar teeth with which they can make short work of poets.[117]

On Prose

Erasmus wrote little about his own craft, other than works on the proper use of Latin and Greek. We regard it as a genuine comment when he gives the highest purpose for prose that which combines pleasure and usefulness.

> Those who write nothing but agreeable things please only the readers who seek for pleasure, and those who produce useful writings only win approval of the readers in search of the useful. But the one who has combined pleasure with usefulness will win the approval of all.[118]

His few comments about this art deal with style and here, in general, he prefers that which is 'frank, simple and unspoilt.'[119] In one place he writes,

> Language above all is the mirror of the mind, and the mind should be without spot; if then we hold it a fault in a man if his clothes are filthy, I think it more incumbent on a good man to develop a pure clean style, and to this end I have always striven since my boyhood, so far as the

---

115 'The Ciceronian,' [1529] in Ibid., XXVIII, 368.
116 Quoted in Ibid., LXXXV, 27.
117 'Adages,' in Ibid., XXXIV, 252.
118 'Adages,' in Ibid., XXXI, 438.
119 Letter to Eobanus Hessus [1518], in Ibid., VI, 142.

land of my birth, my generation, my position in life, and above all as far as my scanty natural gifts permitted. And yet, though I saw that an artificial style wins such solemn approval from established men, I always aimed at pure and not elaborate language, and a solid masculine style, rather than something brilliant or theatrical, one designed to convey the subject-matter before displaying the writer's gifts … Besides which, a man has, I think, achieved something worth having who persuades his reader to devour his whole book eagerly and hurry on to the end without slacking speed.[120]

In his treatise, 'On the Writing of Letters,' Erasmus argues at length for the importance of achieving an elevated style. He reminds the reader that it takes 'no less ability to creep along the ground … than to soar through the air.'[121] He concludes this discussion with the observation,

Art is not absolutely necessary in a letter, but if it is lacking, the affectation of art will provoke ridicule.[122]

On Painting

Erasmus did not discuss painting at length, but he did seem to have an appreciation for contemporary achievement.

By now the art of painting, so rude in its beginnings, has reached such a pitch of subtlety that it can deceive not only men's eyes but even birds, and can make things be taken for real which are illusions in paint.[123]

However, in his 'Ciceronian,' Erasmus, through the character Bulephorus, comments on one inadequacy of painting. Painting, he says, gives us only the outer appearance of a man, but,

Where are the brain, the flesh, the veins, the sinews and bones, the bowels, blood, breath, humors? Where are life, movement, feeling, voice and speech? Where finally are man's special characteristics, mind, intelligence, memory, and understanding?[124]

---

120 Letter to Guillaume Budé [1517], in Ibid., IV, 233ff.

121 'On the Writing of Letters,' [1522] in Ibid., XXV, 21.

122 'On the Writing of Letters,' [1522] in Ibid., XXV, 22.

123 'Adages,' in Ibid., XXXIII, 163. The reference to birds refers to the Greek painter Zeuxis who painted grapes so natural looking that birds came to pick at them.

124 'The Ciceronian,' [1529] in Ibid., XXVIII, 375. Erasmus mentions this complaint again in a letter to Reginald Pole in 1525 [Ibid., XI, 314]

This is followed by a humorous story of a painter, whose subject was constantly changing his appearance, his hair style, shaving his beard, etc., so that the painter each day had to cover his previous work and could never finish.

A common debate was whether an artist should paint a man as he is, or make him look better than he is. Erasmus' conclusion is that 'the essence of art is to represent the object as it actually is.'[125] Another purpose of art which Erasmus mentions in this discussion is to delight.

> The art of the painter and the sculptor came into existence for the purpose of delighting the eyes, and once it has done that it has fulfilled its function.[126]

Finally, Erasmus offers two points of advice to painters. First, that the artist should not copy any one artist, but take the best from as many good artists as he can,[127] and second,

> Painters set their work aside for a time, in order to form a better judgment of it, for continuous attention is a reason why they find it very difficult to judge.[128]

On the Public

Throughout his writings Erasmus displays a pronounced contempt for the general public. His most frequent complaint has to do with the ability of the masses to judge, as he mentions in a letter to the Archbishop of Canterbury.

> 'I cannot but wonder at the absurd judgment of the multitude.'[129]

He mentions this again in a warning he gives a young prince.

> The true prince should avoid the degrading opinions and interests of the common folk to the same extent that the common run of princes are keen to avoid the dress and life-style of the lower classes. The one thing which he should consider degrading, low, and unbecoming to him is to think like the common people, who are never pleased by the best things.[130]

In one of the earliest poems of Erasmus, composed in 1489, he blames the judgment of the general public for the loss of ancient poetry.

---

125 'The Ciceronian,' [1529] in Ibid., XXVIII, 382.
126 'The Ciceronian,' [1529] in Ibid., XXVIII, 405.
127 'The Ciceronian,' [1529] in Ibid., XXVIII, 403.
128 'Parallels,' [1514] in Ibid., XXIII, 198.
129 Letter to William Warham [1516], in Ibid., III, 257.
130 'The Education of a Christian Prince,' [1516] in Ibid., XXVII, 214.

> I am forced (but what a shame!) by a
> host of bumpkins more numerous even than the stars.
> This arrogant herd, always goaded by their
> fierce passions, tramples under their worthless
> feet (Oh what a crime!) poems dear to bygone ages.[131]

Thus we can understand that it was not his goal to please the multitude, as he explains in a poem on the title-page of his *Enchiridion* (1503).

> I do not care about the praise or the insults of
> the superficial mob. The fine thing is to please
> either the learned or the pious. If I happen to
> do either of these, it is more than I hoped for.[132]

Erasmus condemns the public again when his thoughts turn to the critics which writers must face.

> The life of those who like myself write books is no better than that of the actors of antiquity who presented a play on the stage before the public. They had to learn their parts, to rehearse their production, to do all that was humanly possible to satisfy their audience—that motley throng, truly a beast of many heads, few of whose members have the same tastes, nor are they always consistent, and what is worse, the greater part of them are led by prejudice rather than judgment. On their thumbs the poor mountebank is wholly dependent; he must worship the lowest of the mob, and after superhuman exertions thinks himself happy if he has secured a hearing for his play. If he is hissed off the stage, he must find a tree and hang himself. Surely books have to face critics who are no less various, no less difficult to please, no less distorted by prejudice. In one way our fate is more unfair, in that we put on our show at our own expense, while the actors get their fee. And they, if the dance is a failure, merely look foolish; we, if we fail to please, are heretics.[133]

Having been a much criticized writer, Erasmus mentions the critic again in a letter to a friend.

> He who criticizes another man's writing gets, to begin with, as much of a name in one year as his author has acquired by the labors of many years. And then the critic is commonly thought cleverer than his victim. Last but not least, there are plenty of people to spur him on.[134]

---

131 'A Defense ... against Barbarous Persons ...,' in Ibid., LXXXV, 183ff.
132 Quoted in Ibid., LXXXV, 75.
133 Letter to Pedro Ruiz de la Mota [1522], in Ibid., IX, 60.
134 Letter to Thomas Lupset [1519], in Ibid., VII, 154.

ON THE AESTHETICS OF MUSIC

On the subject of music, Erasmus is a considerable disappointment. Although he studied music with Obrecht[135] and apparently could play the viol,[136] his references to music, and there are many, tend to be passive and dispassionate. His great mind is demonstrated in his wide knowledge of the literature on music, but it is not employed in original thinking on the nature of music. In this regard he will include important thoughts taken from the Greek philosophers, but offer the reader no explanation at all of their meaning. Some examples are:

> The composer who would set a serious subject to soft Lydian airs would be absurd.[137]
>
> ......
>
> There is more pleasure in hearing an old song than a new one, even if it is a better one.[138]
>
> ......
>
> A flute player produces sounds that are not his.[139]

He quotes the great testimonials of music found in ancient literature, but sometimes he seems to miss their true meaning and sometimes he distorts them. Take for example one of the most famous Greek myths, the story of Orpheus taming wild beasts with music. The purpose of the myth was to illustrate that music can affect and improve the nature of man. Erasmus, who surely knew better, offers two outrageously false explanations:

> Take those wild men sprung from hard rocks and oak trees—what power brought them together into a civilized society if not flattery? This is all that's meant by the lyre of Amphion and Orpheus.[140]
>
> ......
>
> The same poets record that Orpheus, poet and lute player, moved the hardest of stones with his singing. What did they mean? They meant to show that men as unfeeling as stone, who were living after the manner of wild beasts, were rescued from promiscuity by this wise and eloquent hero and initiated into the holy ways of marriage.[141]

It is clear that to some degree Erasmus was still thinking of music in the old medieval definition as a branch of mathematics, as was still taught in the major universities. For example, in a letter of recommendation for Henricus Glareanus, Erasmus says,

---

135 Clement Miller, ed., *The Dodecachordon of Heinrich Glarean* (Rome: American Institute of Musicology, 1965), II, 252. Glarean says he heard this from Erasmus himself.
136 P. E. Hallett, *The Life and Illustrious Martyrdom of Sir Thomas More* (London: Burns, Oates & Washbourne, 1928), 15.
137 'Parallels,' [1514] in *The Collected Works of Erasmus*, XXIII, 179.
138 'Parallels,' [1514] in Ibid., XXIII, 273.
139 'Parallels,' [1514] in Ibid., XXIII, 168. Early philosophers sometimes said the flute made the music, not the player.
140 'Praise of Folly,' [1503] in Ibid., XXVII, 101.
141 'On the Writing of Letters,' [1522] in Ibid., XXV, 135.

> He has a great knowledge of history, and in music, geography and all the other subjects that are commonly called mathematical he is most experienced, for this is the field in which he is a specialist.[142]

In a discussion of the Greek proverb, 'Double diapason,' Erasmus gets carried away, admitting, 'I have rashly—and as it were forgetting myself—gone further into musical matters than the nature of the work undertaken required.' While he rarely writes of music in detail, these pages clearly reflect his knowledge of the old Scholastic mathematics based theories of music, as well as the principal earlier treatises such as Boethius. Erasmus defines the common usage of this proverb to mean any two things very far apart. In the course of his musical discussion he seeks to make the principal point that the range of two octaves is a kind of natural furthermost limit, with respect to the ear hearing the mathematical proportions in music. Clearly concerned that he was sticking his neck out, he tells us that as he was writing, a famous philosopher, Ambrogio Leone of Nola, just happened to walk in and thus he attributes to this man the remainder of the discussion. Leone finds two reasons for calling the double octave the natural limit. First, he has observed that the [male] voice cannot reach beyond the fifteenth without becoming forced and artificial. The second argument is because Reason and the senses must work together. While Reason can comprehend numbers of any size, hence, for example, the possibility of a distance of a thousand octaves, the senses do not distinguish relationships beyond two octaves.

> But the physical senses have had their own limits prescribed for them by nature, and if they transgress these, they gradually become misty and wandering, and can no longer judge with certainty as they used to do, but through a cloud, as they say, or in a dream. It was not fitting that principles of art should be drawn from an uncertainty of judgment. But since the ancients understood that beyond the fifteenth note of the scale the judgment of the ears began to fail, they decided to fix the bounds of harmony there, so that no one could have any reason to bring up that adage of yours, 'unheard music is useless.'[143]

We suspect that it was this association with mathematics which caused Erasmus to think of music as being somewhat exclusive. In a series of objections to a treatise by Latomus, Erasmus adds, for example, that 'mathematics, metaphysics and music' are not needed by everyone, as for instance the baker and the tailor.[144] And it may have been the association with mathematics, with its world of order and exactness, that caused Erasmus on two occasions to connect music with the divine. In one case Erasmus writes that he found in the works of Augustine a reference (which cannot be identified today) which mentions the Greek philosopher, Zeno, saying that the soul itself is a 'self-moving harmony, and for this reason

---

142 Letter to Etienne Poncher [1517], in Ibid., IV, 220.

143 'Adages,' in Ibid., XXXI, 202ff. Erasmus discusses the last phrase in a discussion of the proverb, 'Hidden music has no listeners [and is thus worthless].' [Ibid., XXXII, 117ff.]

144 'Apology Refuting Rumors and Suspicions ... by Latomus,' in Ibid., LXXI, 47.

can be caught up and carried away by harmonious things.' Erasmus adds a comment which seems to suggest a divinely implanted understanding of music.

> [This is its nature] just as children too are affected by the modes of music through some natural affinity, even when they have no idea what music is.[145]

The other instance is a rather special case, for it is really one of the only documents which suggest that Erasmus was capable of being profoundly moved by music and the only place in all of his writings where he mentions any contemporary musician by name. This is a poem written in honor of Ockeghem a little more than a year after his death. Here Erasmus declares, 'Music is something divine.'

> Has it fallen silent then, that voice once so renowned, the golden voice of Ockeghem? Is the glory of music thus snuffed out? Sing, Apollo, come sing a sad dirge to your lyre. You also, Calliope, clad in mourning together with your sisters, pour forth loving tears. Mourn, all who are enraptured by the sweet pursuit of music, and extol this man with your praises. That sacred Phoenix of Apollo's art is dead.
>
> What are you doing, O envious Death? The golden voice has been silenced, the golden voice of Ockeghem, the voice that could move even stones, the voice that so often resounded in the vaulted nave with fluid and subtly modulated melodies, soothing the ears of the saints in heaven and likewise piercing the hearts of earthborn men.
>
> What are you doing, O envious Death? You are unjust precisely because you deal justly with everyone. It would be enough for you to take away indiscriminately the things that belong to mankind. Music is something divine. Why do you violate the divine?[146]

---

145 'Adages,' in Ibid., XXXI, 167.
146 'An Epitaph for the Superlative Musician Jan Ockeghem,' in Ibid., LXXXV, 77.

On the Purpose of Music

We suspect that for Erasmus the primary purpose of music was that of simple pleasure and leisure, something which he mentions many times. In a letter of 1519 for example, he seems to suggest by inference that music and reading are to be thought of as leisure, apart from the important things such as business.

> For it would be unwise in a man born for public affairs to gather dust by constant meditation in the company of what they call dumb teachers; on the contrary, just as Plato molds the spirit of his citizens by a judicious mixture of music and gymnastics, so the lives of great men should be kept in balance by interchanging leisure for study and the business of public affairs.[147]

In another letter of the same year, when he is discussing the attitude of the Catholic conservatives turning against the humanities, he again seems to join music with simple and temporary pleasures.

> I have never seen anything more determined than this conspiracy against humane studies. Food and drink, sleep, music and dancing—of all such pleasures one can have enough, as Homer says; but the love of mischief-making in these men is never satisfied.[148]

Similar purposes of music are mentioned in his discussion of proverbs. For example, Erasmus gives a Greek proverb, 'But the man who runs away won't stop to hear the fiddler [*lyrae*] play.' First he gives the obvious example of one running from battle not wanting to stop to 'listen to some musician.' His next comment is perhaps more revealing.

> This has many applications: for instance, if you were to say that one ought not to waste time on frivolous pleasures when our life here is exposed to so many dangers.[149]

Relative to another proverb, 'You keep hounds though you cannot keep yourself,' Erasmus writes,

> It will fit everyone who takes thought for the pleasures and grandeurs of life, and neglects the things that are more badly needed. The necessities of life should have our attention first, and after them our social position; otherwise we shall be like one who toils to become a good scholar, and gives no thought to his livelihood, which is at risk.[150]

---

[147] Letter to Guillaume de Croy [1519], in Ibid., VI, 339ff.

[148] Letter to Richard Pace [1519], in Ibid.,VI, 354. The editors suggest that the Homer reference is to the *Illiad*, xiii, 636.

[149] 'Adages,' in Ibid., XXXII, 251. He also mentions here a line from Ecclesiasticus, 'A tale out of season is as music in mourning.'

[150] 'Adages,' in Ibid., XXXIII, 281.

Another Greek proverb which Erasmus discusses is 'Singers tell many lies.' Of this, he says,

> It comes from the fact that singers, whose only object is to delight and give pleasure, produce for the most part what redounds to the credit of the audience [even though it is not true]; for nothing is more solemn than the truth, or more agreeable than flattery.[151]

His most interesting comment of this sort is regarding the Greek proverb, 'A wooer's life.' Erasmus says this represents a life of fastidious luxury, or 'A life of pure music.'[152]

The principal purpose of music found in most medieval literature is to soothe the listener. Erasmus first mentions this in an early poem of 1489.

> O brainless blockhead,
> you have need of the very Muse you reject.
> See how she confronts madness, soothes
> cruel-hearted savagery, subdues the demon.
> Since all these apply to you, hold poetry dear;
> take up once more the soothing lyre.[153]

Erasmus refers to this purpose twice in his book called 'Parallels,' and they are both quite interesting.

> They say that the tigress, if she hears the roll of drums all round her, is driven mad, and ends by tearing herself in pieces; even so, some people cannot stand what raises the spirits of others, as music, eloquence, and so forth.[154]

......

> As some magnets attract iron, but the themedes, which is found in Ethiopia, rejects and repels it, so there is one kind of music that calms the passions and another that rouses them.[155]

The purpose of music most emphasized by the ancient Greek philosophers was its capacity to affect the character of the listener. Erasmus discusses this idea, together with music therapy, in a lengthy letter to Pope Adrian VI in 1522. The subject of the letter was a new publication on the Psalms by the celebrated teacher of rhetoric, Arnobius. Erasmus begins with a lengthy metaphor in which he characterizes Arnobius as the harp of David. Of note here is a phrase which suggests, however indirectly, that Erasmus recognized that good music was not only sweet, but had emotions [fire].

---

151 'Adages,' in Ibid., XXXIII, 128. In another place [Ibid., XXXIII, 281] he writes of the proverb, 'The aulos player of Tenedos,' who lied in a law suit.
152 'Adages,' in Ibid., XXXIV, 116.
153 'A Defense ... against Barbarous Persons ...,' in Ibid., LXXXV, 185. In this poem he also speaks of the Greek myths of music, as well as the tributes by early Latin poets.
154 'Parallels,' [1514] in Ibid., XXIII, 175.
155 'Parallels,' [1514] in Ibid., XXIII, 225.

> This instrument produces not merely animating notes that are sweet in the ears of pious folk; it has its fire as well.[156]

Erasmus then proceeds to discuss the topics we have mentioned.

> To expel this vast contagion of moral corruption we need powerful spells, and some sort of enchanter, a master of his art, who can charm wisely. For this purpose I have provided almost a new weapon, not that the Psalms of David did not exist, but for most people they lay silent. It is a property, they say, of man-made music that it can either rouse the emotions or control them if a skilled performer makes an appropriate use of specific harmonies. It is said that Timotheus could kindle the heart of Alexander of Macedon with warlike fire by playing in certain particular modes. Pythagoras, by playing spondees in the Phrygian mode, transformed a young man mad with love and restored his sanity. A similar story is told of Empedocles, who is said by the use of some particular musical modes to have recalled to his proper wits a young man already beside himself with rage and hell-bent on murder. The tales told in antiquity of Mercury and Orpheus playing on the lyre look like fables; and yet these fictions were inspired by the wonders music can perform. Certainly Terpander and Arion in Lesbos and in Ionia are said by the historians to have cured many serious diseases as a regular thing by the use of musical harmonies. Ismenias of Thebes in Boeotia is recorded as relieving the torments of many sufferers from gout in the hip with appropriate melodies. When Virgil says that 'the clammy snake in the meadows is burst by the singing of spells,' this might be ignored as merely the utterance of a poet, had not our own Scriptures mentioned the charmer who charms so wisely and the adder that will not listen. David used his harp to come to the aid of Saul, whenever he was vexed by an evil spirit from the Lord.
>   If then man-made music has such power to change the affections of both body and soul, how much more effective we must suppose this heavenly and divine music to be in purging our hearts of spiritual diseases and the evil spirits of this present world! Ambition is an overmastering disease, ill will and jealousy are a most evil spirit; and the majority of Christians are victims of this kind of plague, even those being often not exempt whose duty it was to cure their fellow men. The pagans of old possessed 'both words and spells,' with which they could 'of their distemper lose the greater part, and soothe the gnawing canker of the heart.' And surely Christ's music has words and spells with which we can charm out of our hearts the love of things transient and charm into its place the love of heavenly things. Pythagoras commanded musical modes whereby he could recall to sanity a young man beside himself with infatuation; and does not the Christian psalmist command modes whereby he can recall to the love of peace the princes who are endlessly at loggerheads in these most crazy wars? But we must first use this music to cure ourselves before we attempt to cure other men's diseases. There is no part of the Holy Scripture that does not have these powerful modes at its command, provided that we do not stop up our ears like deaf adders for fear that the strong magic of the divine enchanter may penetrate into our hearts. But in my view no modes are more powerful than the music of the Psalms; for in this book it was the will of that divine spirit to lay up a store for us of his most secret and delightful mysteries; and in it he enshrined certain musical modes of greatest power, by which we might

---

[156] Letter to Adrian VI [1522], in Ibid., IX, 145ff.

be changed into a frame of mind worthy of Christ, provided only that there is someone at hand who can wake the strings of this psaltery with proper skill.

This is the special duty of bishops and priests; and yet every individual might learn to play for himself. The spirit will help him as he plucks the strings and will breathe secret power into his inmost parts, if only he provides a pure and fervent heart—the ears, that is, with which a mind that has been purified can listen. Oh that your Holiness might be our new David—that consummate master of this kind of music!—who not only played himself but taught many other singers to do the same. And David was a prototype of Jesus Christ, our psalmist, who, when his body was strung like a harp upon the cross, played nothing common, nothing earthly, but such a melodious music as the Father loves, the moving force of which we feel. What harmony of the divine love sounded in that chord: 'Father, forgive them, for they know not what they do!'

The world too has its instruments, but their infernal notes return an unlovely sound. How speak the strings of anger? 'Revenge and rapine, Cast them out, Cut them down!' What tune does ambition play? 'On, on! extend your realm, think not of oaths nor of religion, when dominion is the prize.' What twangling notes we hear from avarice! 'You see no man is happy save him who has great possessions; by fair means or by foul get, get and pile and keep!' How sound the chords of luxury and lust? 'Live now to please yourself, for you know not what your portion will be after this life.' No less discordant are the chords played by jealousy and spite. This is of course the music of the world, which by such dreadful strains calls up pestilential appetites within us, and like the Sirens lures us to destruction with notes as sweet as they are fatal. This is the music that intoxicates and maddens us, and so we fight wars, we raise rebellion, we are ambitious, greedy, wrathful, and vindictive; we bite each other and are bitten in turn.

The only other lengthy discussion by Erasmus on the subject of the effect of music on a person's character is found in a treatise on Christian marriage. Here, curiously, he seems to focus only on the negative implications.

It is customary now among some nations to compose every year new songs which young girls study assiduously. The subject matter of the songs is usually the following: a husband deceived by his wife, or a daughter guarded in vain by her parents, or a clandestine affair of lovers. These things are presented as if they were wholesome deeds, and a successful act of profligacy is applauded. Added to pernicious subject matter are such obscene innuendoes, expressed in metaphors and allegories, that no manner of depravity could be depicted more vilely.

Many earn a livelihood in this occupation, especially among the Flemish. If laws were enforced, composers of such common ditties would be flogged for singing these doleful songs to the licentious. Men who publicly corrupt youth are making a living from crime, yet parents are found who think it a mark of good breeding if their daughters know such songs.

Antiquity considered music to belong to the liberal disciplines. Since musical sounds have great power to affect the soul of man … the ancients carefully distinguished musical modes, preferring the Dorian to others. They believed this matter to be so important that laws were enacted so that music would not be permitted in the state if it corrupted the minds of citizens.

But in our music, apart from obscenity in texts and subjects, how much is frivolity, how much is folly? There existed in former times a kind of performance in which, without words and only by pantomime, anything that was desired could be represented. In the same way in modern songs, even if the text is not sung, the foulness of the subject can be understood from the nature of the music. Then add to this the sound of frenetic pipes and noisy drums combining with a frenzy of movements. To such music young girls dance, to this they are accustomed, and yet we think there is no danger to their morals.[157]

On Performance Practice

While Erasmus rarely goes into detail regarding performance practice he might have observed, some brief comments suggest a broader understanding than he reveals to the reader. In one place, for example, he calls practice, 'the best teacher of any subject.' He follows this with the specific example, that one learns music by playing.[158] He seems inclined toward sensitivity when he observes, 'The melodiousness of harmony depends on the *quality* of the lute'[159] and 'musicians win our hearts with a light touch on the strings, not heavy pounding.'[160]

One value which he appears to suggest was considered important in the sixteenth century was accuracy. He refers to this in a discussion of the proverb, 'To strike the same wrong note.'

> Adopted from musicians, for whom it is a terrible thing to play a wrong note more than once on the same string. It can well be said of those who frequently go wrong in the same matter, or commit the same fault over and over again. The first lapse may be ascribed to chance or rashness, but to do it again argues stupidity or inexperience.[161]

Another place where Erasmus seems to argue for expertise in music is in his explanation of the Greek proverb, 'When you're offered turtle-meat, either eat or do not eat,' which means do not do anything half-way. He then adds the thought,

> Remember how many activities there are which are admirable if you throw yourself into them, and do harm if you are lukewarm; or which do not admit of mediocrity, like music and poetry.[162]

---

157 Erasmus, *Opera omnia*, ed. J. Clericus (Leiden, 1703–1706), V, 717F, quoted in Clement A. Miller, 'Erasmus on Music,' *The Musical Quarterly* 52, no. 3 (July, 1966): 347ff, http://www.jstor.org/stable/3085961

158 'Adages,' in *The Collected Works of Erasmus*, XXXII, 25.

159 'Puerpera' [1526], in Desiderius Erasmus, *The Colloquies of Erasmus*, trans. Craig Thompson (Chicago: University of Chicago Press, 1965), 280.

160 'Parallels,' [1514] in *The Collected Works of Erasmus*, XXIII, 136.

161 'Adages,' in Ibid., XXXI, 393.

162 'Adages,' in Ibid., XXXII, 260.

A few comments suggest Erasmus had a particular sensitivity to inaccuracy in singers.

> Singers often take little trouble when singing in chorus in the theater, but put them into competition with one another and every note is studied.[163]
>
> ......
>
> When a singer has a flute accompaniment, he can make many mistakes which his audience does not detect.[164]

Erasmus seems to have held instrumentalists in some awe, if not resentment, for the amount of money they were paid. In a discussion of the hiring of teachers for children, Erasmus says in passing,

> Flute players and trumpeters by the dozen are maintained with huge salaries, yet no one more rightly deserves a large and attractive salary than a learned schoolmaster.[165]

One of the proverbs discussed by Erasmus, 'You live the life of an aulos player,' he says may be applied to anyone who lives in comfort at other people's expense.

> Aulos players were employed in the old days at sacrifices, and so they were habitually present at those grand dinners enjoyed by the priests, and what is more, they had nothing to pay.[166]

In several places Erasmus, like nearly all humanists, is critical of polyphonic music. His strongest statement in this regard is found in his treatise, 'The Tongue.'

> The other liberal arts have also degenerated from their original simplicity, just like the morals of society. They have grown more fluent and less authentic; the loquacity of the declamatory schools has ruined eloquence. Again, what is more elaborate than present-day music, mimicking the chatter of many birds with such a large number of vocal parts. What would the Spartan ephor Emerepes say now? He was the man who cut away two of the nine strings from the lyre of Phrynis the musician with his axe, telling him not to ruin the art of music. Supposing he heard one and the same instrument imitating trumpets, horns, bugles, recorders descant, tenor, and alto, thunder, and the voices of men and birds in our houses of God? The standard of our music reflects that of our fashion in clothing and furnishings and architecture. The original simplicity has vanished, and elaborate caprices grow daily more common.[167]

---

163 'Parallels,' [1514] in Ibid., XXIII, 189ff.

164 'Parallels,' [1514] in Ibid., XXIII, 177.

165 'On the Writing of Letters,' [1522] in Ibid., XXV, 23. He argues against any form of tenure for teachers, as well as against paying them too much.

> Otherwise there is danger that the same abuses will ensue that we observe in high priestly offices, where the more lucrative the position, the more unworthy the one who occupies it.

166 'Adages,' in Ibid., XXXIII, 147. The editors generally mistranslate *aulos* as 'flute.'

167 'The Tongue,' [1525] in Ibid., XXIX, 286ff.

He mentions a particularly curious example of polyphony he heard in Paris, a comment he arrives at in his discussion of the proverb, 'A band from Syrbene.' Erasmus says this proverb refers to any group of performers whose playing or singing is disorderly and chaotic. He quotes a passage from Athenaeus which mentions 'a band of Syrbenaens in which every individual plays or sings what he thinks fit, and pays no attention to the instructions of the conductor of the band, who tells them how they ought to play.' Then Erasmus adds,

> I once witnessed in Paris the performance of a ludicrous comic scene, in which a number of people were singing at the same time, but with the intervals between them so arranged that all was in perfect discord. This had been organized by an expert musician, for it would be beyond an unskilled person.[168]

But, on the other hand, in one place he seems to indicate a preference for multi-part music.

> Part-singing is more melodious than if everyone sang exactly the same note.[169]

In the general context of performance practice among singers, Erasmus makes some important associations between speech and music. His 'The Right Way of Speaking Latin and Greek' is interesting particularly in view of the belief of modern philologists that speech developed from music. We also find fascinating the natural examples he supplies for a phenomenon by which the brain alters our perception of sounds, resulting, in the case of music, for the aesthetic necessity of making lower tones more pronounced.

> BEAR. Some people are so insensitive that they cannot distinguish accent from quantity, even though they are altogether different things. Striking a high note is not the same as holding a note, nor is stressing a sound the same as prolonging it …
>
>   Yet anyone with a smattering of music can distinguish without any trouble the difference between long and short on the one hand and high and low on the other. And after all speaking is just an articulated sequence of voiced sound. Metrical principles exist in prose as well as in verse, even though the rules are less restrictive and definite. But if they are disregarded speech will no more be speech than singing would be singing if high and low, long and short, were indiscriminately muddled up. The accent can justifiably be called, as it was by some ancient grammarians, the soul of the word … I think you play the guitar?
>
> LION. After a fashion.
>
> BEAR. Do you not often find yourself making a low note long or a high note short as well as the other way round?
>
> LION. Yes. Though the contrast is still more marked with wind instruments.
>
> BEAR. So why should we be so crude and unmusical when we talk, making every syllable that is accented high long and all the others short? Even donkeys could have taught us better. When they bray they take longer over the low note than over the high one.
>
> LION. The cuckoo does much the same.[170]

---

168 'Adages,' in Ibid., XXXIV, 29.

169 'Parallels,' [1514] in Ibid., XXIII, 273.

170 'The Right Way of Speaking Latin and Greek,' [1528] in Ibid., XXVI, 422ff.

Erasmus continues this comparison of speech to music by mentioning that a speaker often begins slowly and then accelerates, as happens in music. When the question is raised regarding the relationship of short to long in syllables, the answer is given as one to two, although 'in ordinary speech there is no need to keep the ratio so exactly as there would be in choral singing or in dancing to a guitar.'[171]

In another treatise, Erasmus again compares speech and music and in one passage criticizes contemporary singers.

> For well-timed silence is a product of the same art as well-timed speech ... Singers who blunder during the rests that separate the vocal parts display their ignorance of music and suggest that they are not even singing their parts with artistic understanding.[172]

Erasmus was always observant of language itself and therefore was interested in the fact that each craft had its own unique expressions. Among these he gives the example of 'prelude' in music, which means preface in other disciplines. Some contemporary examples he cites are the use of 'top string, lowest string' to mean 'loud or deep tone' and 'to strike the same wrong note' to mean the repetition of a mistake.[173]

Comments on Ancient Music

Finally, from his extensive reading of ancient literature, Erasmus mentions a number of aspects of performance in early literature which we have not found elsewhere. First, he describes some of the performance practices of the ancient lyre players, information to which he credits a first-century writer named Asconius Pedianus, although no such writing by Asconius is extant today.

> Ordinary lyre-players while playing make use of both hands, holding the plectrum in the left hand, which they call 'outside playing,' and plucking the strings with the fingers of the left hand, which they call 'inside.' It was thought difficult to do as the player, Aspendus, did, who never used both hands, but played everything—the music in its entirety—'inside,' and encompassed it all with the left hand only. In this way the piece was entirely performed by the left hand, which touched the strings silently and with a light action, so that the sound was audible only to the player or to a person very close to him. Hence came the proverb: thieving fellows were often called in Greek 'Aspendus lyre-players,' because they kept their thefts to themselves, as the players did their music.[174]

---

171 'The Right Way of Speaking Latin and Greek,' [1528] in Ibid., XXVI, 424. Later [Ibid., 428], Erasmus suggests that in speaking a distinction be made between high, accented syllables, and lower sounds which might be as much as a fourth, fifth or even an octave—although he admits this might be 'ungraceful.'
172 'The Tongue,' [1525] in Ibid., XXIX, 288.
173 'Adages,' in Ibid., XXXI, 178.
174 'Adages,' in Ibid., XXXIII, 34.

In a brief discussion of a proverb, 'What need was there to play on the long pipes,' Erasmus refers to Plutarch saying that in Egyptian tomb paintings the long flutes were primarily associated with religious rites.[175] We believe, however, that the tomb paintings picture the long flute used in broader circumstances. In his discussion of the proverb, 'Carian music,' he gives a detailed history of another instrument he associates with dirges, the 'Carian flute.'[176]

In discussing a proverb, 'From Dorian to Phrygian,' which meant any extreme change of manner, Erasmus mentions that he has found a unique reference in Apuleius who calls Dorian 'warlike.' Since he understood it was usually considered more delicate, he wonders if this reference meant the use of this mode to calm soldiers when on the way to battle. Then, regarding the general discussion of modes by the ancients, he adds,

> I myself suppose that the Ancients have given us different accounts of the systems of harmony, because the system itself changed with changes in the behavior of society. In the early days the people of Asia were reputed for their discipline, before they were softened by luxury. The same happened to the Spartans, among whom were Dorians. Hence those names for mixtures of mode, hypodorian, mixolydian and hypermixolydian.[177]

In discussing the proverb, 'Babys plays the [aulos] even worse,' Erasmus mentions a Greek myth we have not read.

> Babys, they say, was a brother of Marsyas, the man who was not afraid to challenge Apollo himself to a musical contest. When he was defeated, he was suspended by Apollo from a pine-tree upside down, and flayed. Then, when Apollo was preparing to destroy Babys too, Pallas interceded for him, saying that his aulos playing was so unsuccessful and unskillful that clearly he was quite negligible; 'Babys' she said 'plays even worse.' Apollo was impressed by her words, and treated Babys with such disdain that he did not even think him worthy of punishment, but judged it better to abandon him to his incompetence.[178]

Regarding the proverb, 'Hipparchion loses his voice,' Erasmus observes,

> They say that in Greece in the old days there were two leading lyre players, Hipparchion and Rufinus. At the regular games celebrated every nine years at Juliopolis these two were to engage in a contest; and it so happened that Hipparchion was unnerved by the uproar in the theater and lost his voice; hence this became a popular joke.[179]

---

175 'Adages,' in Ibid., XXXI, 467.

176 'Adages,' in Ibid., XXXII, 167.

177 'Adages,' in Ibid., XXXIII, 283ff.

178 'Adages,' in Ibid., XXXIV, 18.

179 'Adages,' in Ibid., XXXIV, 43.

Of the proverb, 'Moschus singing a Boeotian strain,' Erasmus, without giving a source, says Moschus was 'an unskillful lyre player [and singer], who used to stretch out a note to great lengths without drawing breath.' 'Boeotian,' he says was a mode like Dorian or Phrygian.[180]

Finally, he mentions an ancient gladiator's song, 'Not you I seek, 'tis fish I seek,' which he says he found in Sextus Festus.[181]

ART MUSIC

Erasmus rarely describes the performances of music which he heard, yet we know that during his travels he was serenaded by church choirs and civic wind bands.[182] He does, however, mention the importance of the listener, one of the chief hallmarks of Art Music. In a discussion of a proverb, 'A jackdaw has no business with a lute,' Erasmus characterizes this bird as very noisy and then adds, 'But the lute requires silence and attentive ears.'[183] He cites another proverb, 'The pig heard the trumpet,' which he associates with people 'who are neither pleased nor moved by what they hear.'[184]

He touches on the listener in another Greek proverb, 'You sing in vain,' which he says had its origin in singers who were unpleasing to their audience and therefore no one listened. Implied here is the idea that to give delight is the primary purpose. He also notes that this proverb can apply to lute players and here he is thinking of *sung* poetry, for he says this refers to lute-players, 'who sing without being paid anything.'[185]

In one place, however, Erasmus observes that such is the nature of music that the performer receives some pleasure even if there is no contemplative listener.

> Singing has its own delight, even when the person to whom the song is sung with the tender tones of love does not move a limb in response.[186]

---

180 'Adages,' in Ibid., XXXIV, 307.

181 Quoted in a letter to François I [1523] in Ibid., X, 118.

182 P.S. Allen, *Erasmus* (Oxford, 1934), 15.

183 'Adages,' in *The Collected Works of Erasmus*, XXXI, 346.

184 Ibid.

185 'Adages,' in Ibid., XXXI, 377.

186 'Adages,' in Ibid., XXXI, 424. Earlier [Ibid., 84], Erasmus recalls a story by Aristotle of a flutist who was promised he would be paid more, the better he played. When he asked for his pay, he was told he had already been paid, as he had been repaid by his fine playing.

EDUCATIONAL MUSIC

In one interesting passage in his 'The Education of a Christian Prince,' Erasmus uses the analogy of music to demonstrate the importance of learning in early childhood. The additional point here is that *quality* music should be used with children.

> Pains will therefore have to be taken to accustom them from the outset to what is best, for any music sounds sweet to those who have become used to it. And nothing is harder than to withdraw someone from behavior which has already taken root in his character from habitual usage.[187]

FUNCTIONAL MUSIC

On Church Music

Because of Erasmus' background in the church, we are not surprised to find that it is here that he writes with the most passion about music. His greatest joy in music seems to have been in hearing the Psalms.

> But it was heavenly music that inspired the man who wrote, 'How amiable are thy tabernacles, O Lord of hosts! My soul longeth, yea even fainteth for the courts of the Lord.' And again, 'My heart is like wax; it is melted in the midst of my bowels.' Such were the harmonies whose power had breathed upon the apostles when they said, 'Lord, whither shall we go? Thou hast the words of life.' Sweet and tuneful indeed is the concerted sound when love, chastity, sobriety, modesty, and the other virtues sing together in harmonious variety. And this music has different styles to suit different themes. In some which, mournful though they are, are pleasing in the ear of God, we lament our sins. Some give us strength and courage boldly to resist the devil. Some are cheerful and full of joy, to use when we give thanks to God for his goodness to us. Some are used to console and comfort the afflicted. In a word, this life offers no kind of trouble that we cannot easily endure, if, as St. Paul puts it in his letter to the Colossians, we instruct and admonish each other, with psalms and hymns of praise and spiritual songs singing gratefully in our hearts to the Lord, and if, whatever we do in word or deed, we do all in the name of the Lord Jesus, giving thanks to God and the Father through the Son. And this music will be the more pleasing to God if performed by a numerous choir in harmony of hearts and voices.
>
> But to return to the Psalms of David, no man can appreciate how sweet this music making is unless he has perceived its mystic meaning. What is the reason, otherwise, why so many monks and priests find it so tedious to intone these famous psalms? Surely because they sing them with their mouths, not with their minds. And if any of them have no time to turn the pages of long commentaries by other authors, such men, though hard to please, will find Arnobius a help, for his note is often shorter than the psalm itself, and if they read his brief disquisition they will have sung the psalm and learned its meaning at one stroke. All priests should therefore take special

---

[187] 'The Education of a Christian Prince,' [1516] in Ibid., XXVII, 259.

care to master once and for all what they sing every day. As a result they will find more comfort in one psalm which they have learned to understand and have sung with the mind, than in forty sung merely with the mouth. Of one thing above all others our would-be psalm singer must be perfectly convinced, that it was the purpose of the Holy Spirit, and a very wise purpose too, to wrap up the mysteries of heavenly wisdom under these layers of metaphor.[188]

We have mentioned elsewhere that music history texts have failed to relate the full extent to which instruments were accompanying singers in the sixteenth-century churches. Erasmus evidently found little appreciation for this new style, preferring the old unaccompanied chant. He not only tells us that one customarily heard instruments accompany voices in village churches, but condemns this as a distraction to the Christian.

From every quarter of the world music of every style rises from every kind of instrument to assault the ears of the Blessed Virgin, who hears every day the song of the angelic choirs—unless I am mistaken, a far sweeter song than ours. It is only because men listen often to the din of voices and the noise of instruments and never or rarely to the message of the gospel that in our villages and even in some of our towns there is such naïveté and such ignorance of the Christian faith.[189]

Erasmus mentions the use of a surprising variety of instruments, together with objections to polyphony and another reference to improvisation in the service in the course of a discussion of I Corinthians 14.

In some countries the whole day is now spent in endless singing, yet one worthwhile sermon exciting true piety is hardly heard in six months … not to mention the kind of music that has been brought into divine worship, in which not a single word can be clearly understood. Nor is there a free moment for singers to contemplate what they are singing.

What else is heard in monasteries, colleges, and almost all churches, besides the clamor of voices? Yet in St. Paul's time there was no song, only speech. Later song was accepted by posterity, but it was nothing else than a distinct and modulated speech (such as we presently use in the Lord's Prayer), which the congregation understood and to which it responded. But what more does it hear now than meaningless sounds?

At present there is no end of psalms, songs, festal music, and dirges, from which we imagine we gain spiritual merit. And what is more serious, in the maintenance of these services, priests are bound by almost tighter chains than they are to Christ's teachings. The people are compelled to attend and thus are taken away from their labors. How are they to support their families, and what activity could be more meritorious? …

We have brought into sacred edifices a certain elaborate and theatrical music, a confused interplay of diverse sounds, such as I do not believe was ever heard in Greek or Roman theaters. Straight trumpets, curved trumpets, pipes and sambucas resound everywhere, and vie with human voices. Amorous and shameful songs are heard, the kind to which harlots and mimes dance. People flock to church as to a theater for aural delight.

---

188 Letter to Adrian VI [1522], Ibid., IX, 145ff.

189 Letter to Thiébaut Biétry [1525], in Ibid., XI, 106.

> To this end organists are maintained at large salaries, and crowds of children spend every summer in practicing such warblings, meanwhile studying nothing of value. The dregs of humanity, the vile and the unreliable (as a great many are drunken revelers), are kept on salary, and because of this pernicious custom the church is burdened with heavy expenses. I ask you to consider, how many paupers, dying in want, could be supported on the salaries of singers?
>
> These activities are so pleasing to monks, especially the English, that they perform nothing else. Their song should be mourned; they think God is pleased with ornamental neighings and agile throats. In this custom also in the Benedictine Colleges in Britain where young boys, adolescents, and professional singers are supported, who sing the morning service to the Virgin mother with a very melodious interweaving of voices and organs ...
>
> Those who are more doltish than really learned in music are not content on feast days unless they use a certain distorted kind of music called *Fauburdum*. This neither gives forth the pre-existing melody nor observes the harmonies of the art. In addition, when temperate music is used in church in this way, so that the meaning of the words may more easily come to the listener, it also seems a fine thing to some if one or other part, intermingled with the rest, produces a tremendous tonal clamor, so that not a single word is understood. Thus the whims of the foolish are indulged and their baser appetites are satisfied.[190]

A similar attack on Church music of his time, however, includes a guarded endorsement of polyphonic music.

> I was not speaking as much about any kind of ecclesiastical song as about unseemly music and alluring songs which the whims of naive women or simple men have added to religious services.
>
> Clamorers are so named because presently in many churches and monasteries, by thundering forth in a raucous bellowing, they so fill up the church that all sounds are obscured and nothing can be understood ...
>
> I call booming the nearly warlike sound of organs, straight trumpets, curved trumpets, horns, and also bombards, since these too are accepted in religious services ...
>
> But my judgment differs very much from those who condemn proper church song. I do not dispute about current polyphonic music if it is used with moderation and discretion.[191]

Finally, he complains of the use of instruments even during Vespers,

> which are done with the most ornate harmonies of singers and organs, and also trumpets, since they too are often heard in church in songs and prayers of psalmody.[192]

---

[190] Erasmus, *Opera omnia*, ed. J. Clericus (Leiden, 1703–1706), VI, 731C-732C, quoted in Miller, 'Erasmus on Music,' 338ff.

[191] Ibid., 340.

[192] Ibid., 341. In another place [*Opera omnia*, V, 718C], Erasmus complains that the instrumentalists sometimes 'converse together in the impudent manner of singers' during the service.

In spite of these attacks on the use of instruments in the Church, in three places Erasmus takes the opposite view in recommending these instruments in praise of the Lord. The first is an early (1499) poem written to celebrate Easter.

> Let that choir sing a heavenly melody;
> we on earth will applaud and mingle our
> earthly instruments with our weak voices. Let
> one strike his harp; let another pluck the
> resounding strings. Let one sing to the lyre; let
> another shake the jiggling tambourine. From
> one side let the blown horn sound; from
> another let the sweet flute blend its smooth
> notes, making music for the triumphant
> procession of the Lord.[193]

The second instance is found in a letter to William Roper, for whom Erasmus expresses the wish that he will have children. Erasmus recommends he sing of Jesus to the baby,

> to your lyre instead of nursery rhymes to please your little ones. For [Jesus] alone is worthy to be praised continually on the strings and pipe, with songs and every sort of music-making.[194]

A similar comment is made in a letter to a woman who had recently given birth. Erasmus, in a rare reference to the ancient Greek gods, recommends to her Jesus as the true Apollo,

> whose praises you will be able to sing to your lyre instead of nursery rhymes to please your little ones. For he alone is worthy to be praised continually on the strings and pipe, with songs and every sort of music making, but especially with the harmonious utterance of a true Christian heart.[195]

We have quoted some of Erasmus' views on the correspondence of speech and music. He returns to this subject in the context of contemporary Church choral singing.

> You know how they vary the pace of their singing, sometimes to double time, sometimes to triple, according to certain proportions or measures as they are now called. But there is no need in our case for this degree of discrimination. The point will be clear if you just conform with musical terminology to the extent of dividing breves into semi-breves …
>
> In my view though, the real difficulty in observing them is where one has many voices, particularly untrained voices, in unisons, and I imagine this must be why church choirs do not differentiate even between long and short when singing psalms and canticles, and indeed pay scant attention to differences of accent, but speak together in equal time units so that there is no

---

[193] 'A Heroic Poem on the Feast of Easter,' in *The Collected Works of Erasmus*, LXXXV, 309.
[194] 'Commentary on Prudentius' Hymn,' [1524] in Ibid., XXIX, Dedicatory Letter, 173.
[195] Letter to Margaret Roper [1523], in Ibid., X, 134.

getting out of step with each other or unseemly confusion introduced by varying vowel lengths. Even in hymns, where different lengths are put on different vowels, this is not done according to the natural lengths of the syllables, but by arbitrary arrangement. The stricter orders, though, do not admit this form of singing, and all their utterance is in spondees. But in my view Ambrose must have ordered his hymns to be sung with full regard for the differences between syllables, and I do not doubt that this was in fact how they were sung until the spread of illiteracy.[196]

Erasmus appears to have been opposed to congregational singing, especially after the model of the enthusiastic congregational singing of the earlier Christians. Better to leave the singing to the Church professionals.

> In early times the entire congregation sang and responded Amen to the priest. The consequent thunderous noise and ridiculous confusion of voices produced a spectacle unworthy of divine worship. In our day those who are appointed sing fittingly and the rest sing to the Lord [only] in their hearts.[197]

He was also opposed to the growing length of Church music,

> The Creed is shortened, the Lord's Prayer is not heard, and the singing of the prosa detains the congregation a full half hour. Added to this song are melismas [*caudae vocum*] which are just as long or even longer.[198]

and to any singing which is not strictly liturgical.

> Likewise ... the song now used in some churches for peace or against pestilence, or for a successful harvest, can be omitted without detriment to religious devotion.[199]

Erasmus was obviously bothered by the fact that many Church leaders were no longer simple, pious men, but lived in extravagance like secular princes. He satirizes this at some length in a witty little tract called 'Julius Excluded from Heaven.' Here we find the deceased pope, Julius II, finding the gates of heaven locked and being interrogated by the first pope, St. Peter. At one point Julius is telling Peter how much better the life of a pontiff is these days, and by way of example describes his own triumphal entry into Bologna.

> If you'd seen the ponies, the horses, the columns of armed soldiers, the panoply of the generals, the displays of hand-picked boys, the torches gleaming on all sides, the sumptuous litters, the procession of bishops, the stately cardinals, the trophies, the spoils; if you'd heard the cheers of people and soldiers resounding to the sky, the sound of applause echoing all round, the music

---

196 'The Right Way of Speaking Latin and Greek,' [1528] in Ibid., XXVI, 427.

197 Erasmus, *Opera omnia*, ed. J. Clericus (Leiden, 1703–1706), V, 959E, quoted in Miller, 'Erasmus on Music,' 334.

198 Ibid., 336.

199 Ibid., 336.

of trumpets, the thunder of cornets ... and myself, the leader and prime mover of the whole pageant, carried on high like some god ...[200]

He is critical of high Church leaders in another place where he complains that the Church princes will only offer their services for a fee, observing, 'without pay they sing no psalms.'[201]

On Trumpet Signals

Many early writers remark on the fear caused by the sound of the trumpet, for it was so identified with battle. According to Erasmus there was a Latin proverb, 'Ante tubam trepidas,' referring to those who were frightened even before they heard the trumpet play.[202]

Erasmus describes a police action against a criminal mob, known as the Black Band, in Germany when a trumpet signal was mistakenly sounded prematurely, resulting in confusion during which more than a thousand person were 'cut to pieces.'[203] In one of the poems of his 'Epigrammata,' Erasmus mentions the watchman's trumpet. In a kind of reverse reference to the 'Music of the Spheres,' he says the watchman 'sends his shrill trumpet notes up to the stars.'[204]

In one of many passages which reflect both the hostility Erasmus felt for the Jews and the dislike he had for the military trumpet, he makes the point that the birth of Jesus was announced not by trumpets, but by singing.

> When Christ was born, did the angels sound trumpets of war? The Jews heard the noise of the trumpet, for they were permitted to wage war, and this was the appropriate sign for men whose law told them to hate their enemies. But the angels of peace sing a very different song in the ears of a people seeking peace.[205]

---

200 'Julius Excluded from Heaven,' in *The Collected Works of Erasmus*, XXVII, 192ff.
201 'Adages,' in Ibid., XXXII, 186.
202 'Adages,' in Ibid., XXXIV, 77.
203 Details are found in letters to Thomas More and Cuthbert Tunstall [both of 1518], in Ibid.,V, 401, 409.
204 'The Castle Commonly called Hammes,' in Ibid., LXXXV, 51.
205 'A Complaint of Peace Spurned and Rejected by the Whole World,' [1516] in Ibid., XXVII, 300. Erasmus mentions the loud trumpets of war again in his colloquy, 'Militaria.' [1522]

ENTERTAINMENT MUSIC

It is difficult to imagine the somber Erasmus enjoying popular entertainment, something, indeed, which he rarely mentions. When he does mention it, it is usually a criticism of some sort and between the lines we always clearly see his own prejudices, as in this comment on hunting.

> In the same category belong those who care for nothing but hunting wild game, and declare they take unbelievable pleasure in the hideous blast of the hunting horn and baying of the hounds. Dogs' dung smells sweet as cinnamon to them, I suppose, and what delicious satisfaction when the beast is to be dismembered![206]

Among the upper classes, it appears that Erasmus particularly associated the courtiers with a meaningless life of seeking entertainment. This, to Erasmus, was life wasted.

> Now what shall I say about the courtiers? For the most part they're the most obsequious, servile, stupid, and worthless of creatures, and yet they're bent on appearing foremost in everything ... They sleep till midday, when a wretched little hired priest waiting at their bedside runs quickly through the mass before they're hardly out of bed. Then they go to breakfast, which is scarcely over before there's a summons to lunch. After that follows dice, draughts, fortune-telling, clowns, fools, whores, idle games, and dirty jokes, interspersed with one or two snacks. Then comes dinner, followed by a round of drinks, or more than one, you may be sure. In this way, hours, days, months, years, and centuries are frittered away without a moment's boredom.[207]

The lack of respect Erasmus had for professional entertainers is quite clear in his discussion of the Latin proverb, 'Once a buffoon, never an honest family man.'

> The meaning is that a man who has once lost all sense of shame, and with complete disregard for his reputation has taken to playing the buffoon in public, will scarcely ever return to respectability ... Fortune often showers wealth on the unworthy, but good character and good sense is not hers to give.[208]

In his discussion of the proverb, 'From horses to asses,' which refers to one's moving to a lower profession, the examples which Erasmus provides usually includes an entertainer as the lowest class. For example, a philosopher becoming a 'ballad-singer' and a blacksmith turned strolling player.[209]

We find in Erasmus only an occasional reference to the entertainment music heard at banquets. In discussing a proverb, 'You deserve no praise, even at a feast,' Erasmus recalls

---

206 'Praise of Folly,' [1503] in Ibid., XXVII, 112.
207 'Praise of Folly,' [1503] in Ibid., XXVII, 136ff.
208 'Adages,' in Ibid., XXXIII, 195.
209 'Adages,' in Ibid., XXXII, 83.

that in ancient Greece lyre players often sang of gods and famous men at almost every feast. He suggests, however, that often these performances were primarily for the entertainment of the audience.[210] Another reference makes it clear that most music heard on these occasions was intended for entertainment.

> Where pleasure's the object, the worst speaker deserves praise no less than the best, because he's no less entertaining; just as the only singer who gives pleasure is one who sings exceptionally well or exceptionally badly.[211]

The type of entertainment music heard seems to have varied greatly. An early poem, composed in 1490, describes rather elegant music.

> They do not care what aromas rise from the
> fully laden banquet tables or what vintage
> wines foam in full cups or what an abundance
> of song is plucked from melodious strings or
> what endless airs float about from lovely flutes.[212]

But a character in one of Erasmus' Colloquies speaks of a much different kind of music.

> I disagree emphatically with those who think a dinner party isn't fun unless it overflows with silly, bawdy stories and rings with dirty songs.[213]

Good music or bad, we can't imagine our somber Erasmus having much fun at any of these banquets.

> Ask a wise man to dinner and he'll upset everyone by his gloomy silence or tiresome questions ... Haul him off to a public entertainment and his face will be enough to spoil the people's enjoyment.[214]

---

210 'Adages,' in XXXIV, 8.

211 'Convivium fabulosum' [1524], in *The Colloquies of Erasmus*, 256.

212 'An Elegiac Poem on Patience,' in *The Collected Works of Erasmus*, LXXXV, 253.

213 'Convivium religiosum' [1522], in *The Colloquies of Erasmus*, 56.

214 'Praise of Folly,' [1503] in Ibid., XXVII, 101. This, perhaps Erasmus' most famous work, was an attempt to make serious points in a humorous context. However, his very strong and pointed comments about nearly every level of society, even the pope, caused the book to be repeatedly condemned and won numerous enemies.

3 THE GERMAN-SPEAKING COUNTRIES IN THE SIXTEENTH CENTURY

You know the times. No one really looks for a rebirth of the arts. They are so silent and neglected, it may well be feared that dolts will stamp them out. God alone can preserve them by inspiring the leaders of the city to water the seeds and nurture the plants.
    John Schöner, 1533[1]

No wonder that music is so utterly despised and rejected at this time, seeing that other arts, which after all we should and must possess, are so lamentably regarded by everyone as altogether worthless.
    Johann Walter, 1537[2]

These comments on life in early sixteenth-century Germany echo the concerns often expressed by Erasmus that the civil strife which accompanied the beginning of the Reformation had the consequence of greatly retarding the recognition of the studies of the humanists. The irony was that both the Catholic and Reformation leaders condemned the humanities, although for different reasons.

Humanism becomes prominent in Germany somewhat later than in France or Italy, although it apparently began under Italian influence. By the beginning of the sixteenth century it had begun to depart from Italian models, such as concentration on uniting humanism and the Church, to seek its own direction, which tended toward interest in poetry, philosophy and German history. One can see, from this alone, traces of those inevitable currents which were leading to the Reformation.

While humanism in Italy had strong support from the courts, in Germany the movement was centered on the universities where poets, in particular, were challenging traditional studies. These two forces, the humanist poets and the professors, were drawn together in the aftermath of a controversy which began in 1508 with the publication of books by Johannes Pfefferkorn, a converted Jew, which called for the destruction of all Hebrew books. The one person who spoke out strongly against this proposal was Johannes Reuchlin, a lawyer in Württemberg and a Hebrew scholar. After he himself came under attack by the faculty of the

---

[1] John Schöner, dedication in the 1533 publication of Johann Müller's *On Triangles* (1464), quoted in Johann Müller, *Regiomontanus on Triangles*, trans. Barnabas Hughes (Madison: The University of Wisconsin Press, 1967), 25.

[2] Johann Walter, *Wittenberg Gesangbuch* [1537], Foreword, quoted in Oliver Strunk, *Source Readings in Music History* (New York: Norton, 1950), 343.

University of Köln and the Dominican Order, humanists began to support him. It became a battle of the freedom of knowledge against the old Catholic Scholastic dogma, another obvious harbinger of the Reformation, and much of Europe was drawn into the debate.

While Pfefferkorn and Reuchlin were being debated on all sides, a book of satire called *Letters of Obscure Men* was published by Crotus Rubeanus, a teacher, and Ulrich von Hutten, a man of noble lineage who concerned himself with poetry and humanism. The debate was the focus of this book of fictitious letters, but much of the text ridicules the Catholic clergy, who are often characterized as being men of rather earthly interests. One letter, for example, describes a group of university students surprising a monk who was sleeping with a woman, causing him to flee naked into the night.[3] Another letter describes a Churchman visiting a woman and having to flee when the husband comes home.[4] One clergyman is described as being so much in love that he is blinded to the actual physical appearance of his lover. A writer informs him that in fact the lady has,

> a wart on her forehead, long red shanks, and clumsy brown hands, and her breath savoureth because of her foul teeth ... But you are so blinded by that devil-begotten passion that you perceive not her faults.[5]

Another letter claims that the monks of a monastery in Strasburg,

> brought women-folk to their cells by way of the river beneath their walls; and they trimmed their hair, so that for a long while they passed for monks.[6]

Finally, one letter suggests the Church did not worry much over such behavior.

> He hath been preaching too, of late, that priests should in no wise maintain concubines, and he declared that bishops are guilty of mortal sin when they take milktithes, and wink at priests consorting with their handmaidens, whereas they ought to drive them forth one and all.
>
> Be this as it may, we must sometimes be merry and have to do with a wench, when nobody is the wiser; after, we can make confession; and the Lord is merciful, wherefore we hope for forgiveness.[7]

Such openly satirical portraits of the clergy are found elsewhere and, again, their contribution toward preparing the climate for the coming Reformation can hardly be minimized. Already in 1503, Christopher, Bishop of Basel, had addressed the synod of his diocese on the subject of the immorality of the clergy as follows:

---

[3] Letter of 'Johann Kannegieszerr to Ortwin Gratius,' in Francis Stokes, *On the Eve of the Reformation* (New York: Harper & Row, 1909), 12.

[4] Letter of 'Magister Conrad of Zwickau to Ortwin Gratius,' in Ibid., 43.

[5] Letter of 'Magister Ortwin Gratius to Ortwin Gratius,' in Ibid., 69.

[6] Letter of 'Wendelin Tuchscherer, Choir member at Strasburg, to Ortwin Gratius,' in Ibid., 97.

[7] Letter of 'Magister Conrad of Zwickau to Ortwin Gratius,' in Ibid., 21.

Since we have learned with the greatest chagrin that the greater part of the priests of our city and diocese when they are called to conduct the funeral services of nobles and other persons, give themselves up to gaming and drunkenness, so that many of them at times sit the whole night at play; others exhaust themselves with swilling and drunkenness and sleep the whole night on the benches, and by other extraordinary excesses bring scandal, disgrace, and derision upon the clerical profession: Therefore, we command that all clergymen who are so invited, and all others, shall not give up themselves to dicing and card-playing, nor to other irregular and disgraceful actions at any time whatever, and especially in taverns …

The clergy shall see to it that during the worship in the church they do not walk up and down with laymen … nor shall they go out upon the market in choir dress during worship to buy eggs, cheese, or anything else.[8]

The *Letters of Obscure Men* also satirized professors, who were for the most part Churchmen. In the very first letter a dinner of 'Doctors, Licentiates and Magisters' is described, during which they eat and drink abundantly while arguing whether 'magister nostrandus' or 'noster magistrandus' is the more appropriate for a candidate of the Doctor in Divinity degree.[9] Especially attractive, regarding the majesty of the professors, is a letter which tells of a student who made the mistake of addressing the Rector of a university in the familiar form of German and who was consequently imprisoned![10]

The University of Paris is attacked in several letters, one calling it 'the mother of all foolishness' and accusing it of broadcasting 'superstition and folly' and calling its students numskulls.[11] One letter says of the university professors of the arts that they,

decoy youths and take their money, and make Bachelors and Doctors of them though they know nothing. And they have brought it about that students no longer desire to graduate even in Arts, but all wish to become Poets.[12]

We find the Catholic leaders of the university arguing against poetry, 'for it containeth falsehoods … [and] from an evil root springeth an evil plant.'[13] One Churchman accuses the professors of being not 'Masters of the Seven Liberal Arts, but of the Seven Deadly Sins.'[14] Another letter which attacks poetry is quite interesting in its detail.

---

8 Samuel Jackson, *Huldreich Zwingli* (New York: Putham, 1901), 26. Zwingli (1484–1531) was born, educated and served the Reformation in Switzerland.

9 Letter of 'Thomas Langschneider to Ortwin Gratius,' in Stokes, *On the Eve of the Reformation*, 5ff.

10 Letter of 'Magister Johann Krabacius to Ortwin Gratius,' in Ibid., 31. Not so many years ago I was giving a lecture at one of Europe's ancient universities and found, at a following social event, that the chief administrator of the university was addressed as 'Your Highness.'

11 Letter of 'Gerhard Schirrugel to Ortwin Gratius,' in Ibid., 46.

12 Letter of 'Anton Rübenstadt to Ortwin Gratius,' in Ibid., 53.

13 Letter of 'Petrus Hafenmusius to Ortwin Gratius,' in Ibid., 16ff.

14 Letter of 'Magister Johann Hipp to Ortwin Gratius,' in Ibid., 36.

> The old Magister furthermore told me that in his time there were full two thousand students at [the University of] Leipzig, and a like number at Erfurt; four thousand at Vienna and as many at Köln. Nowadays there are not as many students at all the universities put together as there were then in one or two. The Magisters at Leipzig bitterly lament the scarcity of scholars. It is the Poets that do them this hurt. Even when students are sent by their parents to hostels and colleges they will not stay there, but are off to the Poets to learn stuff and nonsense ... Among twenty students you will scarce find one with a mind to graduate. Yet all of them are eager to study the humanities.[15]

Another letter accuses such students of being 'uncivil in the streets, or having consorted with harlots' or, again, having addressed the Magister or a priest in the familiar form of German.'[16]

Unfortunately this satirical book rarely mentions music, which must be regretted for the lost insights on contemporary practice. One letter writer tells of writing a poem and then having it set to music in four parts, 'because songs sound best in four parts.'[17] Another 'correspondent' writes,

> I am a singer too, and am skilled in plainsong and [accompanied poetry], and I have a bass voice and can sing one note below contra-C.[18]

We see the increasingly hostile attitude toward the humanities again in a curious, and extremely negative, book by Henry Agrippa, called *Of the Vanities and Uncertaintie of Arts and Sciences*. This book, one of his later works, written in 1527 but not published until after his death, apparently stems from his disillusionment by his treatment by the French court, after which he began to doubt most humanistic studies. His premise can be seen early in his book.

> I see many were proud in Humane learning and knowledge, that therefore do despise and loath the Sacred and Canonical Scriptures of the Holy Ghost as rude and rustic, because they have no ornaments of words, force of syllogisms, and effective persuasions, nor the strange doctrine of the philosophers: but are simply grounded upon the operation of virtue.[19]

He returns to this theme at the end of the book when he observes that higher education ruins men as Christians.

> For they are so stiff and obstinate in their opinions that they leave no place for the Holy Ghost, and are so sure of themselves, and trust in their own strength and proper wit, that they allow

---

15 Letter of 'Magister Konrad Unckebunck to Ortwin Gratius,' in Ibid., 197ff.

16 Letter of 'Thomas Langschneider Magister Irus Perlirus to Ortwin Gratius,' in Ibid., 221.

17 Letter of 'Magister Peter Negelin to Ortwin Gratius,' in Ibid., 39.

18 Letter of 'Johannes Lucibularius to Ortwin Gratius,' in Ibid., 42.

19 Henry Cornelius Agrippa, *Of the Vanitie and Uncertaintie of Arts and Sciences*, ed. Catherine Dunn (Northridge: California State University, Northridge Press, 1974), 9. Agrippa [1486–1536] was born near Köln and graduated from the university there in 1499. The present work was first published in an English edition of 1569 [we have modernized the English].

no truth which they cannot prove with syllogistical reasons. They despise those things which they cannot search out or understand by their own strength and industry.[20]

Therefore, in his first chapter, 'Of Science in general' he observes that regarding 'the salvation of our souls, nothing is more hurtful and pestilent than the arts and sciences.'

> The sciences ought not to be extolled with such great praise, but rather for the most part, ought to be despised: and that there is none which is without just blame and reprehension, nor that of itself deserves praise.[21]

Agrippa then proceeds to discredit nearly all of man's disciplines (his comments on the arts will appear below). Historians, for example, because they rarely agree with each other, he decides are mostly liars.[22] The courts of the nobles, he complains, are filled with harpists, pipers and all kinds of musicians, together with actors, parasites, harlots, dancers, hunters and 'such like monsters of men.'[23]

ON THE PHYSIOLOGY OF AESTHETICS

One of the most curious philosophical books which is worthy of some attention is Henry Agrippa's three volume *De occulta philosophia*, written in 1509–1510 before the appearance of Luther on the German scene. In spite of the title, 'Occult Philosophy,' Agrippa was at this time a philosopher in the old mold of Catholic Scholasticism. In general, he uses the term 'occult' in reference to any phenomena which cannot be explained by Reason.[24]

Agrippa divides the universe into terrestrial, celestial, and intellectual, or spiritual regions, each with its own branch of magic.[25] By 'magic' he means the 'profound contemplation of most secret things, together with the nature, power, quality, substance and virtues thereof.' Agrippa adds that he who has not studied natural philosophy, mathematics, and theology, 'cannot be possibly able to understand the rationality of magic.'[26]

Agrippa assigns an order of importance to the external senses: sight, hearing, smell, taste, touch, in part a distinction made on the basis that the stronger ones are those effective at the greatest distance (sight and hearing). He also discusses four interior senses: common

---

20 Ibid., 380.
21 Ibid., 11ff.
22 Ibid., 35.
23 Ibid., 238.
24 Henry Cornelius Agrippa, *De occulta Philosophia*, I, x. The best modern edition, which is highly recommended, is Donald Tyson, *Three Books of Occult Philosophy* (St. Paul: Llewellyn Publications, 1993).
25 Ibid., I, i.
26 Ibid., I, ii. Much of this 'magic' is today explained by physics and natural science.

sense, imaginative power, inward sense and memory, as well as three appetites of the soul: natural, animal and intellective.²⁷

Those living in the south of Germany, which retained its ties to the old Church longer, also tended to reflect the older Church dogma. Lassus, for example, working in a Catholic environment of Munich, reflects the Church's view of Reason in the dedication of his *Cantiones sacrae* of 1593. He creates an analogy between his early and late works and young and old vines. In the course of this he makes the point that it is wrong to, 'rely solely on the judgment of our senses, disregarding the counsel of reason.'²⁸

Most philosophers of the Reformation, being unenthusiastic toward humanism and being absorbed with their struggle against the Catholic Church, found little time to write about the traditional philosophical topics of Reason and the senses. One of the more interesting who did was Philip Melanchthon. In a discussion of the 'greatest strengths' of man, after mentioning the ability to digest food, he calls the second great strength the five senses. Here he adds an additional three 'inner senses in his brain so that he can draw distinctions, find similarities, and remember.'²⁹ His next 'great strength' has the hallmark of medieval Church philosophy.

> Third, in his soul he has understanding and knowledge and can command some of his external members.

While earlier Church writers always used Reason as the distinction between man and beast, Melanchthon is somewhat more specific.

> The difference between human nature and the beasts is that the human reason understands order, and in all works should maintain suitable order and measure, but the beast knows nothing about order.³⁰

Later his comments reveal why he finds significance in such order for the Christian life.

> Although it is desirable that people live orderly lives because human nature is created so to live and because order contributes to good health, advancement in business, reasonable peace, contemplation, and prayer, nevertheless many people are so barbarous, especially in Germany, and indulge in so much eating, so many parties and various disorders, from which so many illnesses and obstacles follow, that we reasonably ought to complain.³¹

Like all Church philosophers, Melanchthon could not accept Reason alone as being sufficient to explain the needs of life, there must also be divine wisdom.

---

27 Ibid., I, lxi.

28 Strunk, *Source Readings*, 325.

29 Philip Melanchthon, *Loci Communes* [1555], in *Melanchthon on Christian Doctrine*, trans. Clyde Manschreck (New York: Oxford University Press, 1965), 51.

30 Ibid., 258. He makes the point again in Ibid, 312.

31 Ibid., 316.

The secret wisdom which God has revealed to his Church through his word is vastly different from the wisdom which comes from reason, such as one finds in philosophy, medicine, and government. And although such wisdom of reason is praiseworthy, we should not throw the two together as the papists, monks, and Anabaptists do.[32]

Perhaps it was with something like this in mind that the more puritanical Zwingli observed, 'Knowledge puffeth up and maketh conceited, but love edifieth.'[33]

It should be no surprise that traditional philosophers were somewhat suspect in this climate. In writing of the Liberal Arts, Melanchthon observed that only some are learned for the sake of the mind, while others are 'joined to the profit that will be gained.' Unlike his colleague in Wittenberg, Martin Luther, Melanchthon respected philosophy in general.

Philosophy should be sought—and by this term all antiquity especially has been included—in order that from that source one may seek a form of the better life.[34]

Later, however, he seems to suggest that the real virtue of philosophy is to recommend certain disciplines of life, but since philosophy is limited in what it can know of man it is necessary to combine it with the teachings of the church.[35]

Agrippa also, by 1527, had become somewhat disenchanted with traditional philosophy.

Philosophy disputes and judges all things, yet is certain of nothing. Wherefore I know not whether I should include philosophers among beasts, or among men: they seem to exceed brutish beasts because they have reason and understanding: but how shall they be considered men, when their reason can persuade no constant and certain thing, but always waivers in mutable opinions, whose understanding is doubtful of every matter.[36]

On Education

Regarding education, in the writings of Melanchthon we find the same kinds of criticism of the University of Paris that we find in his colleague Luther.

---

32 Ibid., 306.
33 Zwingli, 'Concerning Choice and Liberty Respecting Food' [1522], in Jackson, *Huldreich Zwingli*, 431.
34 Philip Melanchthon, 'Paul and the Scholastics' [1520], in *Melanchthon, Selected Writings*, trans. Charles Hill (Minneapolis: Augsburg Publishing House, 1962), 33ff.
35 Ibid., 38.
36 Agrippa, *Of the Vanitie and Vncertaintie of Arts and Sciences*, 143.

> Although the school of Paris indeed for so many years up to the present has pursued philosophy, in these times she has ceased to philosophize and only talks nonsense about their trifling *Logicalia*.[37]

In 1527 and 1528 he was engaged in a survey of the lower schools, which resulted in a *Book of Visitation School Plan*. The recommendations he makes here, however, are only a nearly word for word repetition of the recommendations of Luther's publication of 1525, which we give in the following chapter.[38]

A particularly interesting document is the *School Ordinance ... for the Town of Brunswick* of 1528 by Johann Bugenhagen.[39] He identifies the first purpose of school as being to teach,

> the ten commandments, the creed, the Lord's prayer, the Christian sacraments ... also to sing the psalms ... In addition they are to study the humanities from which one learns to understand such matters.

One purpose in the teaching of singing to children was to help provide music for the Sunday services. Therefore, Bugenhagen notes that 'the children shall attend the choir on the sacred evening and sacred days in that congregation to which their parents belong.'

Apparently in response to someone's objection to spending money on children who cannot learn, he argues,

> If our industry does not succeed with some children, it will with many others. A tree that bears many good apples, should not be hewn down because two or three are wormy. We must not neglect to do good, because it is thrown away on some individuals.

Of particular interest in this book is Bugenhagen's discussion of the payment of the teachers, for it offers insight on the value placed on the music teacher. He begins by arguing that teachers need enough to live on, adding 'we shall not keep them like beggars, but shall pay each one suitably according to his worth.' It is interesting that he insists that should the teacher become ill, 'we must not forsake them in need.' For the master of the St. Martin school he recommends a yearly salary of forty gulden. His assistant, as well as the music teacher (chorister) are to receive thirty and the fourth assistant twenty. The thirty gulden the music teacher receives here is the same that the master of a smaller school receives.

Interesting also is his insistence that the music teacher and his children are not to be used as a form of free music for extra services.

---

37 'Luther and the Paris Theologians' [1521], in *Melanchthon, Selected Writings*, 71.

38 One can find a translation of Melanchthon's plan, nevertheless, in Frederick Eby, *Early Protestant Educators* (New York: McGraw-Hill, 1931), 180ff.

39 See Frederick Eby, Ibid., 193ff. Bugenhagen (1485–1558) worked in the northern part of Germany and had considerable influence on the schools.

Moreover when some people during the funeral procession would have the pupils with one of the assistants sing before the coffin German psalms or other sacred songs not to help the dead but to admonish the living, also the Te Deum laudamus or any other song when the bride is led into the church, let the assistants divide the money among themselves. They are not to sing without pay.

Regarding the basic curriculum, he recommends the plan by Melanchthon (which was based on Luther's). In one place he describes the musical education in more detail, which seems to have been learning by experience.

The two choristers in the two schools shall perform their labors like the other assistants according to the command and will of their respective rectors. Furthermore it is the particular duty to teach all children, large and small, learned and ignorant, to sing … common songs in German and Latin.

......

Therefore he shall select three or four good boys who can hold the song for him with strong voices, but all the other boys in the parish shall accompany them. Some have poor voices which can be well controlled so that they shall sing low and listen to the others. In this way all children and youth shall learn to sing in the schools.

Bugenhagen says that after students have attended school until twelve years of age, 'the school master shall then announce to the parents in a straightforward way, if any are entirely unable to learn.' At age sixteen, those who have learned well, 'but are not so gifted that they can learn still further,' should be introduced to some vocation. Those who have demonstrated skill in helping to teach others should be given over to a career in Church or government.

Four schools (four so the children will be closer to their parents) shall be constructed for girls. They only require two hours of school per day, sufficient only to learn how to read and to learn the ten commandments, the creed, etc., so they can go home to help their parents and learn to keep house. The purpose of their education is to produce,

useful, skillful, happy, friendly, obedient, God-fearing, not superstitious, and self-willed housewives, who can control their servants, and train their children in obedience and to respect them and to reverence God.

A school ordinance for Hamburg of 1529 by Sternfeld[40] advocates the building of a library, which should contain books 'good and bad.' Emphasis is again given to the teaching of Christian singing. The ordinance specifies that the teachers are 'under obligation to have special Christian entertainment having to do with the studies' and that the teachers will not be paid until 'recitations from the Holy Scriptures, the catechism and Christian songs' have been learned.

---

40 Quoted in Ibid., 210ff.

This ordinance emphasizes the importance of the behavior of the students. For the higher schools, the entrance requirements require,

> each candidate to bring with him from his pastor and schoolmaster certificates regarding his scholastic attainments, talents, and correct conduct ... also [from] officials of the same locality certificates regarding his age, occupation, demeanor and the temporal means of his parents, and what sort of brothers and sisters he has ... [No young man is to be admitted] who is afflicted with a secret or repulsive disease.

Boys and girls are to be separated and the schoolmaster is 'by no means to allow them to run back and forth among each other.' The schoolmaster should not hurry the children in their studies. The students 'shall be taught not to mumble the last syllables.' When the children need correction it should 'be kindly spoken in a low tone and shown in a friendly way how each defect should be corrected.' There shall be no 'learning of any scandalous, shameful, sectarian books or any other kind of useless fictitious writings.'

A school ordinance from the Pomeranian church schools of 1563[41] now allow girls four hours of school per day before they return home to 'learn housekeeping with their parents.' Here again the teacher is admonished to allow his student to go to the church choir on Sundays.

Sternfeld provides extensive information on the music used in school dramatic performances, as well as singing for the community in the street, for banquets, weddings and funerals.[42] He finds the curriculum in German schools at all levels always included reading, music and Latin. Ability in singing was examined as part of the entrance requirements of many higher schools. Sternfeld mentions the Neckar School in Heidelberg which examined prospective students both by the rector in the arts and by the cantor in music.[43]

Documents from the reorganization of the Neckar School in 1587 are more specific in the use of music. Now there was two hours of instruction in singing each week by the cantor, which included singing in four-parts, in addition to the singing of a composition from part-books before and after meals.[44]

---

41 Quoted in Ibid., 228ff.

42 Frederick Sternfeld, 'Music in the Schools of the Reformation,' in *Musica Disciplina* (1948), 106ff. Gustave Reese, *Music in the Renaissance* (New York: Norton, 1959), 647, 691, identifies a work by Isaac apparently intended for school use, as well as motets by Lassus intended as exercises for the students of the Bavarian chapel. Nan Cooke Carpenter, in *Music in the Medieval and Renaissance Universities* (Norman: University of Oklahoma Press, 1954), 224ff, gives numerous references to music used in the universities of the German-speaking countries.

43 Sternfeld, Ibid., 112.

44 Carpenter, *Music in the Medieval and Renaissance Universities*, 235.

ON THE PSYCHOLOGY OF AESTHETICS

Agrippa, in his early *De occulta philosophia*, reflects the ancient Church view that Pleasure is the source of most evil. He ties the general subject of the emotions to this idea, maintaining that depraved appetites arise from four passions: oblectation, effusion, vaunting and loftiness, and envy, with,

> these four passions arising from a depraved appetite of pleasure, the grief or perplexity of produces many contrary passions, as horror, sadness, fear, and sorrow.[45]

The basic emotions, he says, are nothing else but certain motions or inclinations proceeding from the apprehension of anything, as of good or evil. In total he finds eleven basic emotions, existing in contrary pairs, except for the last. These are, love, hatred; desire, horror; joy, grief; hope, despair; boldness, fear; and anger.[46]

Although some of the early Reformation leaders were much more severe than Luther in all aspects of the Christian life, Zwingli, who was one of these, nevertheless recognized that some pleasures must be allowed.

> I am so far from condemning joy in moderation that I think he who takes it away from the pious will have to restore it with interest.[47]

ON THE PHILOSOPHY OF AESTHETICS

The financial hardships accompanying the civil strife associated with the beginning of the Reformation, together with the aesthetic views of some of its earlier leaders, resulted in an extremely bad climate for art in Germany. Commissions were not forthcoming either from Catholic or Lutheran churches. In the more rabid areas of the Reformation, such as in Switzerland, for example, where Zwingli believed that religious images were forbidden in the Bible,[48] one finds from about 1530 prohibitions against producing art works with Catholic content. Penalties included destruction of such art works, temporary imprisonment and even loss of citizenship.[49]

Such destruction was indeed carried out. Johannes Kessler, of St. Gall, reported that when his church was secularized, thirty-three altars were demolished, as well as sixty-three in the

---

45 Agrippa, *De occulta philosophia*, I, lxi.
46 Ibid., I, lxii.
47 Ulrich Zwingli, 'Refutation of the Tricks of the Baptists' [1523], in *Ulrich Zwingli, Selected Works*, ed. Samuel Jackson (Philadelphia: University of Pennsylvania Press, 1901), 71.
48 Charles Garside, *Zwingli and the Arts* (New Haven: Yale University Press, 1966), 120, 137, 163ff.
49 Carl Christensen, *Art and the Reformation in Germany* (Athens: Ohio University Press, 1979), 168.

cathedral in Constance.[50] In addition, fifty altars were taken from the great Münster in Ulm and twenty-five from the cathedral in Bern.[51] Not only were great art works thus lost, but also their function as models for younger artists. In this environment, one can imagine the concern of the artists. Thus Dürer wrote to a patron,

> If a thing, on which I have spent more than a year's work, were ruined it would be grief to me.[52]

A further detriment to the encouragement of art can be attributed to the fact that the emperor, Charles V, elected in 1519, did not make his residence in the German-speaking lands and gave his commissions to artists in Spain and Italy.

Finally the artists themselves were swept up in the movements which were so affecting Germany society. Jan Scorel, who went to Nürnberg to study with Dürer, was disappointed to find him preoccupied with the teachings of Luther.[53] In addition some artists were caught up in the peasants' uprisings of the 1520s. Among them were the painter, Jörg Ratgeb, who was quartered alive by horses for his participation, and the wood carver, Tilmann Riemenschneider who had his arms broken by the hangman.[54]

Taken together, it is not surprising that the artists were under considerable financial strain. In 1526 a group of painters requested aid from the town council in Basel, pleading that they,

> consider graciously that they, too, have wives and children, and to see to it that they can stay in Basel, because even so the painter's profession is in a bad way. Several painters have already abandoned their jobs, and if the situation is not improving in this and other respects, one will have to reckon with more of them giving up.[55]

Similarly, Heinrich Vogtherr, who was worried that a Christian Germany would turn to barbarism, wrote in 1538,

> By a special dispensation of his Holy Word, now in these our days brought about a noticeable decline and arrest in all the subtle and liberal arts, whereby numbers of people have been obliged to withdraw from these arts and to turn to other kinds of handicrafts. It might, therefore, be expected that in a few years there would scarcely be found any persons in German lands working as painters and carvers.[56]

---

50 Johannes Kessler, *Johannes Kesslers Sabbata mit kleineren Schriften und Briefen* (St. Gall: Fehr'sche Buchhandlung, 1902), 305, 311.

51 Christensen, *Art and the Reformation in Germany*, 171.

52 Albrecht Dürer, *The Writings of Albrecht Dürer*, trans. William Conway (New York: Philosophical Library, 1958), 70.

53 J. Saxl, 'Dürer and the Reformation,' in *Lectures* (London: Warburg Institute), I, 271.

54 Christensen, *Art and the Reformation in Germany*, 178.

55 Wolfgang Stechow, *Northern Renaissance Art 1400–1600* (Englewood Cliffs, N.J.: Prentice-Hall, 1966), 131.

56 Gerog Stuhlfauth, 'Künstlerstimmen und Künstlernot aus der Reformationsbewegung,' in *Zeithscrift für Kirchengeschichte* (1937), LVI, 3rd Ser. 7, 509ff.

At first some artists donated works to their towns, in hope of reward from the town council. One such case was Albrecht Dürer, who was given one hundred gulden for his panels, the *Four Apostles*.[57] Eventually the Lutherans began to help by commissioning some art works, in addition to the graphic arts needed for their new Bibles, but for many artists this came too late. One only has to think of the great artist, Holbein, who was forced to leave the country.

In the context of this turbulence, there was little philosophical discussion in the German-speaking countries regarding the aesthetics of art in general. We do find one interesting reference by Melanchthon, which, although addressing the subject of teaching, seems to suggest that he regarded art as being within the mind of the artist, rather than in the art object.

> Whoever wishes profitably to teach himself or intelligently to instruct others must first comprehend from beginning to end the principal pieces in a thing, and carefully note how each piece follows the one preceding—just as a builder, when he wishes to build a house, must first construct the entire building in his thoughts and himself project a picture.[58]

Poetry was still considered by many in the sixteenth century to be a form associated with music, although the humanists went to great lengths to emphasize that feelings were communicated by the words, not by the music. The implication of the humanists was that in poetry, the words were more important than the music.

Such thinking also influenced the practice of the Meistersinger. While today we think of these musicians as participating in singing contests, as indeed they did, the fact is that only one of the four judges judged music, and that was only the form of the melody, and not the singing in its technical aspects. The other three judges concerned themselves with the strophic structure of the text, the number of syllables in each line and the faithfulness to the Luther Bible with respect to the text where appropriate.[59] Thus, because of the emphasis on the text, rather than the music, the Meistersinger's art coincides more with the aesthetics of poetry than of music.

The negative Agrippa finds the distinguishing characteristic of poetry to be one of lies. He complains that he finds in ancient literature that the reasons for the construction of the great theaters and public buildings were based on the fables of the poets,

> an Art that was devised for no other end but to please the ears of foolish men, with wanton rhythms and meter, weightiness of syllables, and with a vain arrangement of words, and to deceive the minds of men with the delectation of fables and lies. Wherefore, she deserves to be called the principal author of lies.[60]

---

57 Carl Christensen, 'Dürer's "Four Apostles" and the Dedication as a Form of Renaissance Art Patronage,' in *Renaissance Quarterly* 20, no. 3 (Autumn, 1967): 333ff, http://www.jstor.org/stable/2859654.

58 Melanchthon, *Loci Communes*, xlvi.

59 Clair Bell, in 'A Glance into the Workshop of Meistergesang,' in *Publications of The Modern Language Association of America* (June, 1953), 630ff, discusses an extant 'score card' from one of these contests.

60 Agrippa, *Of the Vanitie and Vncertaintie of Arts and Sciences*, 30.

Among the Italian painters of the sixteenth century known as the 'Classicists,' there was a tendency to return to a more mathematical approach to drawing. Albert Dürer, on a visit to Venice, became acquainted with these views and began making detailed tabular measurements of various human models. He wrote at this time,

> I hold that the perfection of form and beauty is contained in the sum of all men ... Doubtless those arts and methods which approximate most to measurement are regarded as noblest and most honorable; and, excepting only the sacred arts, such as theology, metaphysics, and the love of natural wisdom, there is no art by which measurement is more and more variously, needed, than the art of painting, which not only requires geometry and arithmetic, the foundations of all measurement, but, much more than any other art, depends upon perspective, catoptics, geodesy, choreography ...[61]

While complaining of nearly all the professions, Agrippa almost seems to endorse painting. He begins with an incorrect understanding that painting was formerly a member of the Liberal Arts.

> Wherefore painting is a monstrous art, but very effective for the copying of natural things which consist of lines and colors. This, in times past, had so great a value that it held the first degree of the Liberal Arts ... It is said that painting is nothing else but a silent poetry, and poetry a speaking picture, so near are they allied together. For as poets express fables and histories, so do painters.[62]

He observes that painting far surpasses engraving and that it can even express emotions, thoughts and almost the very voice of its subjects.

With regard to the theater, Agrippa returns to a purely medieval perspective.

> To exercise this Art, is not only a dishonest and wicked occupation, but also to view it and to delight in it is a shameful thing, because the delight of a wanton mind is an offense. In times past no name was more infamous than stage players and all those who played interludes in the theater were by law deprived of all honor.[63]

ON THE AESTHETICS OF MUSIC

Without question, the most original commentary on aesthetics in music in sixteenth-century Germany is found in Agrippa's early work, his *De occulta philosophia*. Here, in a chapter entitled, 'Of Musical Harmony, of the Force and Power thereof,' he begins by observing that,

---

61 Quoted in Frank Chambers, *The History of Taste* (New York: Columbia University Press, 1932), 70.
62 Agrippa, *Of the Vanitie and Vncertaintie of Arts and Sciences*, 79.
63 Ibid., 73.

Musical harmony also is not destitute of the gifts of the stars; for it is a most powerful imaginer of all things, which whilst it follows opportunely the celestial bodies, doth wonderfully allure the celestial influence, and doth change the affections, intentions, gestures, motions, actions, and dispositions of all the hearers, and doth quietly allure them to its own properties, as to gladness, lamentation, to boldness, or rest, and the like; also it allures beasts, serpents, birds and dolphins to the hearing of its pleasant tunes.[64]

He then gives numerous anecdotes from ancient accounts of specific animals and their reaction to music, as well as ancient accounts of music therapy. One of his examples reads,

Saxo the Grammarian, in his *History of the Danes*, tells of a certain musician, who boasted that he could by his music make everyone that heard it mad; and when he was constrained by the King's command to perform the same, he endeavored to work several ways upon the affections; and first, but a tone of musical gravity filled the hearers with a kind of sadness and unsensibleness; then by a more lively sound he made them rejoice, and dance; and lastly, he by a more earnest music, reduced them to fury and madness.

Agrippa discusses the question of how Music achieves such power over men from two perspectives. The first, in a chapter he calls, 'Of Sound, and Harmony, and whence their Wonderfulness in Operation,' also offers an interesting explanation for the universal popularity of the consort principle in the sixteenth century.

Singing can do more than the sound of an instrument, in as much as it arising by an harmonical consent, from the conceit of the mind, and imperious affection of the imagination [*phantasy*] and heart, easily penetrates by motion, with the refracted and well tempered air, the aerious spirit of the hearer, which is the bond of soul and body; and transferring the affection and mind of the singer with it, it moves the affection of the hearer by his affection, and the hearer's imagination by his imagination, and mind by his mind, and strikes the mind, and strikes the heart, and pierces even to the inwards of the soul, and by little and little, infuses even dispositions: moreover it moves and stops the members and humors of the body.

From hence in moving the affections harmony confers so much, that not only natural, but also artificial and vocal harmony doth yield a certain power both to the souls and bodies: but it is necessary that all consorts proceed from fit foundations, both in stringed instruments, in pipes, and vocal singing, if you would have them agree well together: for no man can make the roaring of lions, the lowing of oxen, the neighing of horses, the braying of asses, the grunting of hogs to be harmonious: neither can the strings made of sheep's and wolf's guts, be brought to any agreement, because their foundations are dissonant.[65]

Agrippa's second contention for the power of music is found in its relationship with the familiar topic of ancient Greek philosophy, the 'Music of the Spheres.' In his chapter, 'Concerning the Agreement of them with the Celestial Bodies, and what Harmony and Sound is

---

64 Agrippa, *De occulta philosophia*, II, xxiv.
65 Ibid., II, xxv.

Correspondent of every Star,' he goes far beyond any earlier philosopher in his explanation of this topic.

> But understand now, that of the seven planets, Saturn, Mars, and the Moon have more of the voice than of the harmony. Saturn hath sad, hoarse, heavy and slow words, and sounds, as it were pressed to the center; but Mars, rough, sharp, threatening, great and wrathful words; the Moon observeth a mean between these two.
>
> But Jupiter, the Sun, Venus and Mercury, do possess harmonies; yet Jupiter hath grave, constant, fixed, sweet, merry, and pleasant consorts; the Sun venerable, settled, pure and sweet, with a certain grace; but Venus lascivious, luxurious, delicate, voluptuous, dissolute and fluent; Mercury hath harmonies more remiss, and various, merry and pleasant, with a certain boldness: but the tone of particulars, and proportionated consorts obeys the nine Muses. Jupiter has the grace of the octave, and also the quinte, viz. the diapason with the diapente: the Sun obtains the melody of the octave voice, viz. diapason: in like manner by fifteen tones, a disdiapason: Venus keeps the grace of the quinte or diapente: Mercury has diatessaron, viz. the grace of the quarte.

Then quoting some unnamed 'ancients,' he associates particular pitches with the planets, as well as the 'humors' and the modes.

> Moreover, they that followed the number of the elements, did affirm, that the four kinds of music do agree to them, and also to the four humors, and did think the Dorian music to be consonant to the Water and phlegm, the Phrygian to choler and Fire, the Lydian to blood and Air, the mixed-Lydian to melancholy and Earth: others respecting the number and virtue of the heavens, have attributed the Dorian to the Sun, the Phrygian to Mars, the Lydian to Jupiter, the mixed-Lydian to Saturn, the hypo-Phrygian to Mercury, the hypo-Lydian to Venus, the hypo-Dorian to the Moon, the hypo-mixed-Lydian to the fixed stars …
>
> Moreover there are some who find out the harmony of the heavens by their distance one from another. For that space which is between the Earth and the Moon, viz. an hundred and twenty-six thousand Italian miles,[66] makes the interval of a tone; but from the Moon to Mercury being half that distance, makes a half-tone; and from Mercury to Venus another half-tone; but from there to the Sun, as it were three tones and a half, and that makes a diapente; but from the Moon to the Sun, a twofold diatessaron with a half; again from the Sun to Mars is the same space as from the Earth to the Moon, making a tone; from there to Jupiter half of the same making a half tone; so much likewise from Jupiter to Saturn, consisting of an half tone; from whence to the starry firmaments is also the space of an half tone.

He concludes,

> Hence there are not any songs, sounds, or musical instruments more powerful in moving man's affections, or introducing magical impressions, than those which are composed of numbers, measures, and proportions, after the example of the heavens.[67]

---

66 Or about 116,000 English miles, whereas the correct distance is 240,000 miles.

67 *De occulta philosophia*, II, xxvi.

We must point out that Agrippa makes no attempt to explain why we cannot hear any of this 'Music of the Spheres.' Rather, he simply follows this discussion with an extensive one on astrology.

We have commented above on the general distrust of the humanities in early sixteenth-century Germany. Music was not immune, as we see in the later writings of Agrippa. While the universities of sixteenth-century Germany continued the medieval Scholastic misunderstanding of including music as a branch of mathematics, Agrippa does give it a separate chapter. However, this chapter follows one on 'Arithmetic,' which Agrippa concludes by ridiculing those mathematicians who count themselves among the divine, because they work with numbers. He quickly adds, 'Musicians hardly grant them his prerogative, as they are more willing to give this honor to their Harmonie.'[68] Agrippa does refer to ancient and medieval writings, which associate music with a variety topics, from the soul to mathematics, and admits, therefore, that one cannot treat the subject of music apart from all other disciplines. Nevertheless, he writes that his intent is to discuss music as an art unto itself.

> But I speak of that which consists of pleasant tunes, which is in agreement with strings or voices, according to their tune and meter, without offending the ears …[69]

In his earlier *De occulta philosophia* he had discussed the impressive references to the ethos of the various modes by the ancients, but fifteen years later he finds that in his experience music has been degraded in practice by the character of the men who perform it.

> Although men confess that this art has much sweetness, yet the common opinion is, and everyone may see it by experience, that it is the exercise of base men, and of unprofitable and intemperate wit … For this reason Music has ever been wandering here and there for price and pence and is the servant of bawdy which no grave, modest, honest or valiant man ever professed … But in very deed what is more unprofitable, more to be despised, and more to be eschewed, than these pipers, singers, and other sorts of musicians, which with so many and diverse voices of songs, surpassing the chirping of all birds, with a certain venomous sweetness, like the Mermaids, with voices, gestures, and lascivious sounds, do destroy and corrupt men's minds?
>
> ……
>
> And yet for this, these musicians do much boast, as though they were more able to move the emotions than Rhetoricians, that, so much misled by their madness, they affirm the Heavens themselves sing, yet with voices never heard by any man, except perhaps by means of their *Euouae*,[70] drunkenness or dreaming.

He makes an interesting observation, which we have not seen in earlier literature, that music, unlike other disciplines of the Liberal Arts, has no terminal point of completion, but must be a lifelong study.

---

68 Agrippa, *Of the Vanitie and Vncertaintie of Arts and Sciences*, 63.
69 Ibid., 64ff.
70 A joyous shout during the drinking festivals of Bacchus.

They say, moreover, that music is an endless art, and that it cannot be thoroughly learned with any wit: but that daily according to the capacity of every man, it gives fresh melody.[71]

Agrippa includes the dance as a branch of music, and again condemns the former with all the enthusiasm of a Puritan.

> To Music, moreover, belongs the Art of Dancing, very acceptable to maidens and lovers, which they learn with great care, and without tediousness do prolong it until midnight, and with great diligence do devise to dance with framed gestures, and with measurable passes to the sound of the cymbal, harp, or flute, and do, as they think very wisely, and subtly, the fondest thing of all and, little differing from madness, which except that it is tempered with the sound of instruments … There is no sight more ridiculous, taken out of context, than dancing: this is a liberty to wantonness, a friend to wickedness, a provocation to fleshly lust, enemy to chastity, and a pastime unworthy of all honest persons.[72]

In Switzerland we find another curious prohibition of dancing. A civic ordinance in Zurich in 1500 reads, 'In order that God the Lord may protect the harvests which are in the field, and may give us good weather, let no person dance.'[73] Another in 1519 reads,

> Let it be announced in the pulpits of the city and written notice sent into the country that since dancing has been forbidden, it is also forbidden to musicians or anyone else to provide dances in courts or other places, whether it be at public weddings or church festivals.

Agrippa, in his discussion of moral philosophy, provides amusing characterizations of the men of various nations. In addition to comparing them as lovers, in their speech and dress, he adds,

> We know moreover that the Italians do bleat in their singing, the Spaniards wail, the Germans howl and the French sing with pleasant tone and accent.[74]

Church singing, together with organs, bells, etc., he says exists for ignorant people, who have no respect for anything but what they see before them.[75]

Regarding the purposes of music, by mid-century we begin to find more modern understanding, especially that the chief purpose of music is to express feelings. Thus, the humanist Samuel Quickelberg, who was a physician in the court of Albert V in Munich wrote of Lassus' *Penitential Psalms* of 1560,

---

71   Agrippa, *Of the Vanitie and Vncertaintie of Arts and Sciences*, 68.

72   Ibid., 69. Interestingly enough, he associates the origin of dance to the movement of the planets and the 'music of the spheres.'

73   Quoted in Jackson, *Huldreich Zwingli* (New York: Putham, 1901), 24.

74   Agrippa, *Of the Vanitie and Vncertaintie of Arts and Sciences*, 161.

75   Ibid., 187.

He expressed so aptly with lamenting and plaintive melody, adapting where it was necessary [the music] to the subject and the words, expressing the power of the different emotions ... that one cannot know whether the sweetness of the emotions more adorns the plaintive melodies or the plaintive melodies the sweetness of the emotions.[76]

One still finds, however, the purpose given in all early literature, to soothe the feelings of the listener. A typical reference on this subject is that by Martin Agricola, in his *Melodiae Scholasticae* where he recommends music as an aid in restoring 'fagged minds and bodies.'[77]

Agrippa, in his *De occulta philosophia*, offered a unique explanation for the source of music's ability to soothe. He begins with a discussion of 'divine frenzy,' which is so often mentioned by the ancient poets. This comes from the Muses, he says, and the Muses, in turn, are the souls of the separate planets. Of these only the Sun is given a musical soul.

> The fourth degree belongs to the sphere of the Sun; this possesses voices, words, singing and harmonical sounds, by the sweet consonancy whereof it drives forth of the mind any troublesomeness therein, and cheers it up.[78]

Agrippa also contributes a very unique purpose of music, which is for calling upon the spirit world. After considerable discussion of good and evil spirits, Agrippa mentions that there are some rather friendly spirits, 'even affected with human passions, and many of these delight in man's society, and willingly dwell with them.' These include fairies and hobgoblins, who live in the fields; naiades, who live in fountains; nymphs, who live in marshes and ponds, etc.

> He therefore that will call upon them, may easily do it in the places where their abode is, by alluring them with sweet fumes, with pleasant sounds, and by such instruments as are made of the guts of certain animals and peculiar wood, adding songs, verses, enchantments suitable to it.[79]

On Church Music

Some Reformation leaders were much more puritanical than Luther and included in their reforms of Catholic tradition a drastic reduction in music. John Calvin is well-known for such actions in the French-speaking areas, but we find even more remarkable the example of Zwingli. Even though he loved music, sang well and played several different instruments, nev-

---

76 Quoted in Reese, *Music in the Renaissance*, 513. Reese also points to the music of Leonhard Lechner (b. 1553) as being 'marked by unusual intensity of feeling.' [Ibid., 686].
77 Sternfeld, 'Music in the Schools of the Reformation,' 101.
78 Agrippa, *De occulta philosophia*, III, xxxii.
79 Ibid.

ertheless in 1525 he suspended choir singing in his Zurich church and in 1527 had the organ of Great Munster broken up.[80] All that remained was unaccompanied congregational singing.

We mention in the following chapter, Luther's various objections to the practice of music in the old Catholic tradition. Agrippa was particularly critical of the current practice, including polyphony.

> But now days the unlawful liberty of music is so much used in churches, that together with the Canon of the Mass, very filthy songs have like tunes in the organs, and the Divine Service is sung by lascivious musicians hired for a great stipend, not for the understanding of the listeners, but for the stirring up of the mind. But for dishonest lasciviousness, not with manly voices, but with beastly [effects],[81] while the children bray the Discant, some bellow the Tenor, some bark the Counterpoint, some howl the Treble, some grunt the Bass, and cause many sounds to be heard, and no words or sentences to be understood.[82]

After the death of Frederick the Wise in 1525, his successor dissolved the choir of the Castle Church of Wittenberg in order to put the money to use for 'better purposes.' In response, Melanchthon wrote the new elector,

> We have need of such people, not only in order that the good music that has been used might not be buried, but also that new and better music be written. I consider retaining the services of such people a good work from which God derives pleasure. Thus far many people in many places maintained music groups for unnecessary pomp and other unbecoming purposes. Why should the noble art of music not remain active now for God's sake?[83]

The English educator, Roger Ascham, traveling in Germany in 1551 was impressed by the seriousness of purpose in the singing of the Lutheran faithful. In Augsburg, he found,

> the whole church sings psalms ... there is not one young nor old man, woman, nor child, but they sing ... Verily here, young and old commonly can sing perfectly without the book the whole psalter. The praecentor begins the psalm, all the church follows without any square, none behind, none before, but there doth appear one sound of voice and heart amongst them all.[84]

---

80 Jackson, *Huldreich Zwingli*, 290. In 1523 he had to defend himself against charges that he was too slow in eliminating choral music because he liked it. [Ibid., 201]

81 Agrippa gives 'skeekinge,' the meaning of which, in old English, is no longer understood.

82 Agrippa, *Of the Vanitie and Vncertaintie of Arts and Sciences*, 68.

83 Quoted in Walter Buszin, 'Luther on Music,' in *The Musical Quarterly* 32, no. 1 (January, 1946): 86, http://www.jstor.org/stable/739566.

84 Letter to Edward Raven, in Roger Ascham, *The Whole Works of Roger Ascham*, ed. Rev. Giles (London: John Russell Smith, 1864), I, Part II, 269ff.

And in Magdeburg he found,

> Every one in his own house, morning and evening, see their whole household kneel down, and sing psalms.[85]

Finally, when we arrive chronologically at those dates where we draw chalk lines for our students to indicate the separation of the major periods of music history, it is interesting to observe to what extent persons actually living at these moments were aware of the changes taking place. As we shall see below, Praetorius as late as 1619 could see no evidence of what we call the Baroque appearing on the horizon. He said, in effect, 'music has developed as far as it can.' Lassus, on the other hand, seemed to sense something was in the air. In 1593, in the dedication of his *Cantiones sacrae*, he wrote,

> In this age of annually renewed fertility, abounding in *cantiones* of every kind and in rival composers who daily come forward with the desire of pleasing, nay of winning for themselves the foremost place, it seems not easy to determine whether this divine art has attained its full growth, not to say the peak, the summit of its perfection, or whether it is decking itself with flowers after a new birth.[86]

---

[85] Ibid., 314.
[86] Strunk, *Source Readings*, 325.

4 MARTIN LUTHER

TEN YEARS BEFORE Luther posted his famous ninety-five theses on the door of the Castle Church in Wittenberg he was a model Catholic priest preparing, at age twenty-four, to conduct his first mass. In a letter inviting a friend to attend, Luther describes himself in these words.

> God, who is glorious and holy in all his works, has deigned to exalt me magnificently—a miserable and totally unworthy sinner—by calling me into his supreme ministry, solely on the basis of his bounteous mercy.[1]

By 1517, Luther was serving as a lecturer at the university in Wittenberg, in addition to his duties as a priest. Now thirty-four, nothing remarkable had happened in his life when one day a papal representative appeared selling indulgences to help raise money for the renovation of St. Peter's in Rome. When members of Luther's flock showed him the documents they had purchased which, among other things, obtained the entry into Heaven for their long dead ancestors who were never even believers, Luther refused to play the game. His 'Theses' were in effect statements in opposition which he offered to discuss or debate with whomsoever. This was the last chance the Church had either to deal with him rationally or, as Erasmus volunteered, to burn him at the stake. Instead, he was told to recant his views.

They picked the wrong man, for Luther, aside from being a strong and rather earthy German, happened to be a thorough scholar of the Scriptures. He could quote Scriptural support for everything he said and in his 'trials' he drove the authorities mad by simply saying, 'I will recant if you can prove I'm wrong.' The Reformation had begun, but by the following year Luther himself still had little enthusiasm for the great battle.

> While this thought was still agitating me, behold, suddenly around us the new war trumpets of indulgences and the bugles of pardon started to sound, even to blast, but they failed to evoke in us any prompt zeal for the battle.[2]

Even three years later, in an 'Open Letter' to Pope Leo X, in 1520, Luther seems to want to honor the pope, although he is quick to admit that he will fight back if attacked.

---

1 Letter to John Braun [1507], in *Luther's Works* (St. Louis: Concordia, 1961), XLVIII, 3.
2 Letter to John von Staupitz [1518], in Ibid., XLVIII, 68.

> I have never alienated myself from Your Blessedness to such an extent that I should not with all my heart wish you and your see every blessing, for which I have besought God with earnest prayers to the best of my ability. It is true that I have been so bold as to despise and look down upon those who have tried to frighten me with the majesty of your name and authority.[3]

But Luther was growing in confidence and in another three years he would call the pope 'a miserable bag of maggot-fodder'[4] and by 1541 a 'stupid ass.'[5]

In addition to his debates with the Church, Luther's publications after 1517 are also characterized by strong attacks against the universities, which with their long Scholastic tradition had been one of the pillars of support for the Church. When one reads these statements, one cannot help but wonder if a bright younger Luther had had some bad personal experience as a university student.

In his treatise, *To the Christian Nobility*, of 1520, Luther attacks the universities for using Aristotle, in particular. Sounding like a medieval Church Father, he makes an outrageously vain plea to the reader: just believe me, I know best!

> The universities, too, need a good, thorough reformation ... My advice would be that Aristotle's *Physics*, *Metaphysics*, *Concerning the Soul*, and *Ethics*, which hitherto have been thought to be his best books, should be completely discarded along with all the rest of his books that boast about nature, although nothing can be learned from them either about nature or the Spirit. Moreover, nobody has yet understood him, and many souls have been burdened with fruitless labor and study, at the cost of much precious time ...
>
> For the same reasons his book on ethics is the worst of all books. It flatly opposes divine grace and all Christian virtues, and yet it is considered one of his best works. Away with such books! Keep them away from Christians. No one can accuse me of overstating the case, or of condemning what I do not understand. Dear friend, I know what I am talking about. I know my Aristotle as well as you or the likes of you. I have lectured on him and been lectured on him, and I understand him better than St. Thomas or Duns Scotus did ...[6] It makes no difference to me that so many great minds have devoted their labor to him for so many centuries. Such objections do not disturb me as once they did, for it is plain as day that other errors have remained for even more centuries in the world and in the universities.[7]

Almost as an after thought, Luther recommends keeping Aristotle's *Logic*, *Rhetoric* and *Poetics* to train young men to speak and to preach properly, as he recommends in a proposal for a university curriculum.

---

3 Quoted in, 'The Freedom of a Christian' [1520], in Ibid., XXXI, 334.

4 'Exhortation to the Knights of the Teutonic Order' [1523], in Ibid., XLV, 144.

5 'Against Hanswurst' [1541], in Ibid., XLI, 221.

6 In a conversation of 1538 reported by Anthony Lauterbach, in Ibid., LIV, 264, Luther is quoted as remarking that in the time of St. Thomas and Scotus, since the Church gave the official answers for everything these philosophers 'had to embroider their thoughts with fantasies because they had no serious tasks to perform.'

7 'To the Christian Nobility' [1520], in Ibid., XLIV, 200ff.

> The universities only ought to turn out men who are experts in the Holy Scriptures, men who can become bishops and priests, and stand in the front line against heretics, the devil, and all the world.[8]

In another treatise he attacks the University of Paris, where he was once a student.

> In particular it is the Parisian school that is condemned in this connection, that impure and foul whore which has declared that Aristotle's teachings on morals are not in conflict with the teachings of Christ, since he teaches nothing other than that virtue is acquired by works, saying, 'By doing good we become good.' The Christian conscience curses this statement as bilge water of hell.[9]

By 1524, in the process of pleading for the foundation of public schools, Luther's language in attacking the universities is extraordinary.

> We have today the finest and most learned group of men, adorned with languages and all the arts, who could also render real service if only we would make use of them as instructors of the young people. Is it not evident that we are now able to prepare a boy in three years, so that at the age of fifteen or eighteen he will know more than all the universities and monasteries have known before? Indeed, what have men been learning till now in the universities and monasteries except to become asses, blockheads, and numskulls? For twenty, even forty, years they pored over their books, and still failed to master either Latin or German, to say nothing of the scandalous and immoral life there in which many a fine young fellow was shameful corrupted.
>
> ......
>
> We have taken upon ourselves the support of a host of doctors, preaching friars, masters, priests, and monks; that is to say, great, coarse, fat asses decked out in red and brown birettas, looking like a sow bedecked with a gold chain and jewels. They taught us nothing good, but only made us all the more blind and stupid. In return, they devoured all our goods and filled every monastery, indeed every nook and cranny, with the filth and dung of their foul and poisonous books, until it is appalling to think of it.[10]

---

8   Ibid., 207.
9   'The Judgment of Martin Luther on Monastic Vows' [1521], in Ibid., XLIV, 300.
10 'To the Councilmen of All Cities in Germany That They Establish and Maintain Christian Schools' [1524], in Ibid., XLV, 351, 375.

ON THE PHYSIOLOGY OF AESTHETICS

In the early years Luther's few observations on Reason are the perspectives of a genuine man of faith. His views on this subject are different from those of the medieval Church fathers, but in their own way they are just as narrow. In a treatise addressed to the German nobility, Luther sounds like the medieval Church Fathers who said, basically, don't think, depend on faith.

> The first and most important thing to do in this matter is to prepare ourselves in all seriousness. We must not start something by trusting in great power or human reason, even if all the power in the world were ours. For God cannot and will not suffer that a good work begin by relying upon one's own power and reason. He dashes such works to the ground, they do no good at all.[11]

Similarly, because Luther could cite Joshua 10:12, where Joshua commanded the sun to stand still, and not the earth, he rejected without further thought the findings of Nicholas Copernicus (1473–1543).[12]

It is in this period when he seems almost to ignore traditional concepts of Reason that he becomes so vigorous in his attack on Aristotle.

> I am working on short notes on the *First Book of Physics* with which I am determined to enact the story of Aristaeus against this, my Protheus. He is the most subtle seducer of gifted people, so that if Aristotle had not been flesh, I would not hesitate to claim that he was really a devil.[13]

Luther refers to Aristotle's *Physics* in another letter.

> This whole book is a debate about nothing ... It is just a rhetorical exercise, having no value, unless you want to see in it a model for oratorical practice, as if someone were exercising his talents and skills studying and playing with dung or other worthless stuff.[14]

And in another letter of this period, Luther predicts,

> Aristotle is gradually falling from his throne, and his final doom is only a matter of time.[15]

When Jerome Emser published an open letter to the Bohemian Catholics saying he did not believe Luther intended to follow the errors of the Hussites, Luther jumped to the con-

---

11 'To the Christian Nobility' [1520], in Ibid., XLIV, 125.

12 In a conversation of 1539 reported by Anthony Lauterbach, in Ibid., LIV, 359.

13 Letter to John Lang [1517], in Ibid., XLVIII, 38.

14 Letter to George Spalatin [1519], in Ibid., XLVIII, 112. Spalatin (1484–1545) was an official of the court of the elector Frederick and liaison between the court and the University of Wittenberg. Regarding the strong language in some of these passages, in a conversation of 1536 reported by Anthony Lauterbach, in Ibid., LIV, 213, Luther remarked of his early books, 'they are offensive not only to my adversaries but also to me.'

15 Letter to John Lang [1517], in Ibid., XLVIII, 42.

clusion that it was a plot against him and responded with a treatise against Emser. Included now were some strong attacks against philosophy.

> I think [Emser's] holy priesthood found this and everything else in the asses' stable with Aristotle.[16]

Later in the same work,

> What has become of your philosophy now which teaches 'not to beg the question?' I think it is idiotic and your Aristotle is an arch-fool. The same fate awaits a poet who wants to be a philosopher and theologian as awaited the ass with the bagpipes.[17]

And,

> If I did not know logic and philosophy, you crude asses might well dare to make a name for yourselves as logicians and philosophers, even though you know as much about these things as an ass knows about music.[18]

By the 1530s Luther was still at heart a man of faith, but he was beginning to have a broader view of Reason and philosophy. Conrad Cordatus reports a conversation with Luther in which he asked 'since it is necessary to exclude reason from articles of faith, does reason have any value at all for Christians?' He reports Luther's answer as follows.

> Prior to faith and a knowledge of God, Reason was darkness, but in believers it's an excellent instrument. Just as all gifts and instruments of nature are evil in godless men, so they are good in believers. Faith is now furthered by reason, speech and eloquence, whereas these were only impediments prior to faith.[19]

By 1536 Reason seems to have achieved a higher recognition in Luther's estimation. In a treatise of this year, in which Luther attempts to establish where philosophy fails and the Word of God supplies the correct answers, he nevertheless begins by agreeing with the ancient philosophers that,

> it is certainly true that Reason is the most important and the highest in rank among all things and, in comparison with other things of this life, the best and something divine.[20]

---

16 'Answer to the HyperChristian,' in Ibid., XXXIX, 146. Jerome Emser (1477–1527) was a secretary to cardinal von Gurk, papal legate, and a lecturer in the humanities at the Universities of Erfurt (where he claimed Luther was among his students) and Leipzig.
17 'Answer to the HyperChristian,' in Ibid., XXXIX, 197.
18 Ibid., 209. The reference means that an ass can hear music, but not listen to it.
19 Quoted in Ibid., LIV, 183.
20 'The Disputation Concerning Man' [1536], in Ibid., XXXIV, 137.

He continues by contending that Reason 'is the inventor and mentor of all the arts,' but here he is probably thinking of the the traditional 'Liberal Arts.'

As this last statement suggests, Luther did have some sympathy with the Liberal Arts, which did not traditionally include philosophy. Thus as early as 1523 he seems to support those humanistic studies which the Church had for so long questioned.

> I myself am convinced that without the knowledge of the humanistic studies, pure theology can by no means exist, as has been the case until now: when the humanistic studies were miserably ruined and prostrate [theology] declined and lay neglected ... I certainly wish there would be a tremendous number of poets and orators, since I realize that through these studies, as through nothing else, people are wonderfully equipped for grasping the sacred truths, as well as for handling them skillfully and successfully ... Therefore I beg also you to urge your young people at my request to study poetry and rhetoric diligently.[21]

This is not to suggest there were no limits to his interest in humanism.

> I am reading our Erasmus but daily I dislike him more and more ... Human things weigh more with him than the divine.[22]

On Education

While Luther's trial in 1518 was dragging on, he turned his attention to changes in the university curriculum for Wittenberg. Among other things, he wanted to eliminate some of the old Scholastic teachings and replace them with original sources such as Ovid.

> In this way the subtle hair-splitting finally may perish altogether, and genuine philosophy, theology, and all the arts may be drawn from their true sources.[23]

He appears to also have wanted to replace some of the professors.

> Unfortunately there are enough professors who drivel and really waste the time of the students who are here by God's grace.[24]

In 1524 Luther became very interested in promoting the idea of general public education. He publishes a treatise on this subject, pointing to the positive impact on society and cites

---

21 Letter to Eobanus Hessus [1523], in Ibid., XLIX, 32.
22 Letter to John Lang [1517], in Ibid., XLVIII, 39.
23 Letter to George Spalatin [1518], in Ibid., XLVIII, 96.
24 Letter to the Elector Frederick, in Ibid., XLIX, 76.

the ancient Roman example in which young men studied languages and the liberal arts, which of course included music.

> A city's best and greatest welfare, safety, and strength consist rather in its having many able, learned, wise, honorable, and well-educated citizens ...
>
> So it was done in ancient Rome. There boys were so taught that by the time they reached their fifteenth, eighteenth, or twentieth year they were well versed in Latin, Greek, and all the liberal arts, and then immediately entered upon a political or military career. Their system produced intelligent, wise, and competent men, so skilled in every art and rich in experience that if all the bishops, priests, and monks in the whole of Germany today were rolled into one, you would not have the equal of a single Roman soldier.[25]

Of more recent experience, he remarks that he is thankful that schools were not as they were, with 'flogging, trembling, anguish, and misery.' Then he presents the basic curriculum he would establish and we find music a central subject, although it is still in the context of the universities' dogma about its being a branch of mathematics.

> I would have them study not only languages and history, but also singing and music together with the whole of mathematics.[26]

Interestingly enough, he projects all of this would require only two hours of school per day! His closing remarks include a reference to the Dark Ages and the rediscovery of ancient literature during the Renaissance.

> This situation lasted until, as we have experienced and observed, the languages and the arts were laboriously recovered—although imperfectly—from bits and fragments of old books hidden among dust and worms. Men are still painfully searching for them every day, just as people poke through the ashes of a ruined city seeking the treasures and jewels.[27]

In a treatise of 1525, Luther again turns to education, saying 'The preachers are to exhort the people to send their children to school so that persons are educated for competent service both in church and state.'[28] He now presents more specific details on how this public education should be organized and again music is a core subject. First, instruction should be done in Latin, and only Latin, as including German, Greek or Hebrew for children is 'not only useless but even injurious.' Second, the students should not be burdened with too many books. And finally, he proposes dividing the children into three age groups.

---

25 'To the Councilmen of All Cities in Germany That They Establish and Maintain Christian Schools' [1524], in Ibid., XLV, 356.
26 Ibid., 369.
27 Ibid., 374.
28 'Instructions for the Visitors of Parish Pastors in Electoral Saxony' [1525], in Ibid., XL, 314ff.

The first group, or Division, are children just beginning to read. These children are to learn Latin a phrase or two at a time and are to be taught to write.

> These children shall also be taught music and shall sing with the others.

The second division includes those children able to read and now ready for grammar, which he says should only be taught in the hours before noon.

> Where the schoolmaster shuns [teaching grammar], as is often the case, he should be dismissed and another teacher found for the children, who will take on this work of holding the children to grammar. For no greater harm can be done to all the arts than where the children are not well trained in grammar.

While discussing this group Luther specifies,

> All the children, large and small, should practice music daily, in the first hour in the afternoon.

The Third Division, consisting of children well trained in grammar, are now given substantial literature, including Virgil, Ovid and Cicero. And once again,

> Along with the others these shall rehearse music the hour after noon.

We find perhaps one brief peek into Luther's conception of a music education classroom when, while discussing the ceremonies of the old Church, he says in passing,

> When the pupils kneel and fold their hands as the schoolmaster beats time with his baton during the singing of 'And was made man …'[29]

Finally, when the time came for Luther to send his own son to school, the boy's musical education was clearly on his mind.

> I am sending my son John to you so that you may add him to the boys who are to be drilled in grammar and music …
> Tell John Walter that I pray for his well-being, and that I commend my son to him for learning music. For I, of course, produce theologians, but I also would like to produce grammarians and musicians.[30]

---

[29] 'On the Councils and the Church' [1539], in Ibid., XLI, 137.
[30] Letter to Marcus Crodel [1542], in Ibid., L, 231ff.

ON THE PSYCHOLOGY OF AESTHETICS

Given Luther's attitude toward philosophy, not to mention the consuming demands on him by the revolution he had begun, it is no particular surprise that he writes little of matters relating to the psychology of aesthetics. Moreover, the entire question of Pleasure and Pain had, for him, moral implications rather than secular.

We do find it interesting that some references to Pleasure which are not related to religious concepts reflect some awareness on Luther's part that much of Pleasure is not related to Reason. We would say today, right brain pleasure rather than left brain pleasure, something he expresses when he speaks of the pleasure of music being different from those of the 'mind.'

> But in God in [music] more pleasure finds
> Than in all joys of earthly minds.[31]

We think he was experiencing the same distinction when he used to complain about his little son, Hans, singing while he was trying to write.[32] And he was perfectly correct when he observed that the intellect (left hemisphere) knows no emotions.

> [Types of] thoughts must be distinguished. Thoughts of the intellect do not make one sad, but considerations of the will do. They cause us to be vexed or pleased about something, and we have sad and melancholy thoughts when we sigh and complain.
> The intellect is not sad.[33]

All early writers speak of the curiosity they found in the fact that Pleasure and Pain seem always linked. Luther found hunting to be an ideal illustration of this association.

> Last Monday I went hunting for two days to see what this bittersweet pleasure of heroes is like. We caught two hares and a few poor partridges—a worthy occupation indeed for men with nothing to do. I theologized even among the snares and gods. However great the pleasure may be from these things, the mystery of pity and pain mixed into it is equally great.[34]

ON THE PHILOSOPHY OF AESTHETICS

Luther almost never mentioned any Art other than music. He was enthusiastic about painting, so long as it depicted scenes from the Bible. His purpose was, of course, an educational one and to this end he once exclaimed,

---

31 'A Preface for All Good Hymnals' [1538], in Ibid., LIII, 320.
32 In a conversation of 1532 reported by Veit Dietrich, in Ibid., LIV, 21.
33 In a conversation of 1533 reported by Veit Dietrich, in Ibid., 83.
34 Letter to George Spalatin [1521], in Ibid., XLVIII, 295.

> Yes, would to God that I could persuade the rich and the mighty that they would permit the whole bible to be painted on houses, on the inside and outside, so that all can see it. That would be a Christian work.[35]

We may suppose that what Art he knew contributed to an observation he made once about the public.

> Don't you know that the more wholesome something is, the less it is popular and the less it gains ground?[36]

ON THE AESTHETICS OF MUSIC

Luther, on several occasions, suggested that he found something of the divine in music. In part this reflects his awe of it and his inability to explain its effects. His longest discussion which reflects this feeling is found in his preface to Georg Rhau's *Symphoniae iucundae* of 1538.

> I would certainly like to praise music with all my heart as the excellent gift of God which it is and to commend it to everyone. But I am so overwhelmed by the diversity and magnitude of its virtue and benefits that I can find neither beginning nor end or method for my discourse. As much as I want to commend it, my praise is bound to be wanting and inadequate. For who can comprehend it all? And even if you wanted to encompass all of it, you would appear to have grasped nothing at all. First then, looking at music itself, you will find that from the beginning of the world it has been instilled and implanted in all creatures, individually and collectively. For nothing is without sound or harmony. Even the air, which of itself is invisible and imperceptible to all our senses, and which, since it lacks both voice and speech, is the least musical of all things, becomes sonorous, audible, and comprehensible when it is set in motion ...
>
> Philosophers have labored to explain the marvelous instrument of the human voice: how can the air projected by a light movement of the tongue and an even lighter movement of the throat produce such an infinite variety and articulation of the voice and of words? And how can the voice, at the direction of the will, sound forth so powerfully and vehemently that it cannot only be heard by everyone over a wide area, but also be understood? Philosophers for all their labor cannot find the explanation; and baffled they end in perplexity; for none of them has yet been able to define or demonstrate the original components of the human voice, its sibilation and (as it were) its alphabet, e.g., in the case of laughter—to say nothing of weeping. They marvel, but they do not understand.[37]

Some additional observations by Luther on the general nature of music are reported by Anthony Lauterbach. He reports Luther as saying,

---

35 'Against the Heavenly Prophets in the Matter of Images and Sacraments' [1525], in Ibid., XL, 99.
36 Letter to George Spalatin [1516], in Ibid., XLVIII, 35.
37 Ibid., LIII, 321ff.

> Oh, the art is a noble commodity. One shouldn't use it for pay, for purse or coffer. The art is easy to practice, is esteemed everywhere, benefits all people, and nevertheless preserves its own integrity. Yet nobody wants to learn or love it.[38]

In another conversation with Lauterbach, significant for a period in which music was still spoken of as being either theoretical or practical, Luther observed,

> It's so in all fields that activity and practice make men better informed than mere knowledge.[39]

Luther himself apparently had an ear for music sufficient to distinguish between the theory of music and that which was pleasing. When one, Lukas Edemberger, gave him some songs, Luther did not like them, responding,

> He has sufficient art and skill, but lacks sweetness.[40]

Having been educated in a choir school himself, he enjoyed participating in singing in his home, as one recollection by Johann Walter indicates.

> I spent many a pleasant hour singing music with him and often experienced that he seemingly could not weary of singing or even get enough of it; in addition, he was able to discuss music eloquently.[41]

Luther also mentions this in a letter of condolences to the parents of a young student who died, Luther mentions that the boy visited frequently and 'I made use of him many an evening for singing in my house.'[42]

And, as is generally known, Luther had sufficient skill to engage in some composition of his own, including at least one extant motet.[43] And there is no reason to believe he did not participate in writing some of the early hymn tunes.[44] At least two hymns exist in his

---

38 In a conversation of 1537 reported by Anthony Lauterbach, in Ibid., LIV, 246.

39 In a conversation of 1538 reported by Anthony Lauterbach, in Ibid., 274.

40 'Artis sat habet, sed caret suavitate,' quoted in Buszin, 'Luther on Music,' 90.

41 Mentioned in the *Syntagma Musicum* of Praetorius, quoted in Buszin, Ibid., 96. Johann Walter (1496–1570), close friend and musical adviser to Luther, was a musician and poet. Anthony Lauterbach reports, in 1537, in *Luther's Works*, LIV, 221, hearing Luther sing this song:

   > A red apple may look good and inviting.
   > And yet worminess hide;
   > A girl with the worst disposition
   > May be pretty outside.

42 Letter to Thomas Zink [1532], in *Luther's Works*, L, 51.

43 The music is reproduced in Ibid., LIII, 339ff.

44 Ibid., LIII, 191ff, documents his involvement in the early hymns at some length. His recognition as the composer of 'Ein feste burg' cannot be documented.

manuscript,[45] while in other cases he was careful to point out in print examples which had been attributed to him but were not his.[46] It seems clear, in the latter case, that publishers hoped to increase sales by using his name, prompting Luther to observe in his preface to the Weiss *Hymnal* of 1528,

> I realize that there is going to be no end to this haphazard and arbitrary revision which goes on from day to day, and that even our first hymns are more and more mutilated with each reprinting, I fear that this booklet will ultimately fare no better than good books everywhere, namely, to be corrupted and adulterated by blunderheads until the good in it will be lost and only the bad remain …
>
> In order to prevent this as far as possible, I have reviewed this booklet again and printed the hymns of our group separately with the names of the authors, something that I had heretofore avoided for fear of vainglory, but that I am now forced to do, lest worthless hymns by others be sold under our name.[47]

Regarding the purpose of music, Luther first recognized its traditional aesthetic virtue to soothe the listener. He mentions this in a lecture based on 2 Samuel 23, where he explains the first verse, 'the sweet psalmist of Israel.' Indirectly he reveals his definition of a good song, as well as giving the purpose of the psalms to soothe. He also follows the medieval Church fathers in implying that the real message is in the words, so it is not necessary to actually sing them. But then, he seems impelled to add a line on the importance of the music itself.

> When David uses the word *sweet* he is not thinking only of the sweetness and the charm of the Psalms from a grammatical and musical point of view, of artistic and euphonious words, of melodious song and notes, of beautiful text and beautiful tune; but he is referring much more to the theology they contain, to the spiritual meaning. That renders the Psalms lovely and sweet, for they are a solace to all saddened and wretched consciences, ensnared in the fear of sin, in the torture and terror of death, and in all sorts of adversity and misery. To such hearts the Book of Psalms is a sweet and delightful song because it sings of and proclaims the Messiah even when a person does not sing the notes but merely recites and pronounces the words. And yet the music, or the notes, which are a wonderful creation and gift of God, help materially in this, especially when the people sing along and reverently participate.[48]

Luther mentions this purpose again in a letter of advice to Melanchthon.

> Therefore, all of you, do not be downcast but sing the Lord's hymn which is appointed for the night. I will sing too; and so let us be anxious only for the Word.[49]

---

45   Ibid., 295.

46   Ibid., 333ff.

47   Ibid., LIII, 317ff.

48   'Lectures on the Last Words of David,' in Ibid., XV, 273ff.

49   Letter to Philip Melanchthon [1521], in Ibid., XLVIII, 233. His reference is to Psalms 42:8.

In a remarkable letter to the great composer of the court in Munich, Ludwig Senfl, Luther speaks not only of the power of music to soothe but also the virtues of music in general and of his own love for music.

> Even though my name is detested, so much that I am forced to fear that this letter I am sending may not be safely received and read by you, excellent Ludwig, yet the love for music, with which I see you adorned and gifted by God, has conquered this fear. This love also has given me hope that my letter will not bring danger to you. For who, even among the Turks, would censure him who loves art and praises the artist? Because they encourage and honor music so much, I, at least, nevertheless very much praise and respect above all others your dukes of Bavaria, much as they are unfavorably inclined toward me.
>
> There is no doubt that there are many seeds of good qualities in the minds of those who are moved by music. Those, however, who are not moved by music I believe are definitely like stumps and blocks of stone. For we know that music, too, is odious and unbearable to the demons. Indeed I plainly judge, and do not hesitate to affirm, that except for theology there is no art that could be put on the same level with music, since except for theology, music alone produces what otherwise only theology can do, namely, a calm and joyful disposition … This is the reason why the prophets did not make use of any art except music; when setting forth their theology they did it not as geometry, not as arithmetic, not as astronomy, but as music, so that they held theology and music most tightly connected, and proclaimed truth through Psalms and songs. But why do I now praise music and attempt to portray … such an important subject on such a little piece of paper? Yet my love for music, which often has quickened me and liberated me from great vexations, is abundant and overflowing.[50]

In a conversation held with Luther during dinner in his home, one present recalled a similar praise of music's ability to soothe.

> One of the most beautiful and most precious gifts of God is music. Satan is very hostile to it, since it casts out many scruples and evil thoughts. The devil does not remain near it, for music is one of the finest of all arts. Its notes instill life into its texts. Music drives away the spirit of sadness, as may be seen from the life of King Saul …
>
> For a person beset by grief music is the most effective balm, for through it the heart is made content, is inspired and refreshed.[51]

In another such conversation, Anthony Lauterbach reports Luther misinterpreting the ancient Greek's use of music in the schools as being for the purpose of soothing the students.

> Excellent was the arrangement of the ancients that required men to exercise, lest they fall into debauchery, drunkenness, and gambling. I especially admire these two noble exercises, music

---

50 Letter to Ludwig Senfl [1530], in Ibid., XLIX, 427ff.
51 Quoted in Buszin, 'Luther on Music,' 91ff.

and gymnastics. The first of these pertains to the spirit and serves to drive away care, while the second pertains to the body.[52]

An extraordinary testimonial to the ability of music to soothe and comfort the listener is found in a poem by Luther, found in his publication of 1538 called *A Preface for All Good Hymnals*, in which Music speaks as follows:

> Of all the joys upon this earth
> None has for men a greater worth
> Than what I give with my ringing
> And with voices sweetly singing.
> There cannot be an evil mood
> Where there are singing fellows good,
> There is no envy, hate, nor ire,
> Gone are through me all sorrows dire;
> Greed, care, and lonely heaviness
> No more do they the heart oppress.
> Each man can in his mirth be free
> Since such a joy no sin can be.
> But God in me more pleasure finds
> Than in all joys of earthly minds.
> Through my bright power the devil shirks
> His sinful, murderous, evil works …
> The best time of the year is mine
> When all the birds are singing fine.
> Heaven and earth their voices fill
> With right good song and tuneful trill.
> And, queen of all, the nightingale
> Men's ears will merrily regale
> With music so charmingly gay;
> For which be thanks to her for aye.
> But thanks be first to God, our Lord,
> Who created her by his Word
> To be his own beloved songstress
> And of *musica* a mistress.
> For our dear Lord she sings her song
> In praise of him the whole day long;
> To him I give my melody
> And thanks in all eternity.[53]

---

52 In a conversation of 1536 reported by Anthony Lauterbach, in *Luther's Works*, LIV, 206.

53 Ibid., LIII, 319ff.

Finally, in an unfinished treatise, 'Concerning Music,' Luther observed,

> Music drives away the devil and makes people happy; it induces one to forget all wrath, unchastity, arrogance, and other vices.[54]

In 1538 Luther wrote the preface for a collection of part-songs based on the suffering and death of Jesus. In addition to mentioning the emphasis on music in the Old Testament, together with his own awe of the art, Luther touches on the most fundamental purpose of music, to express feelings.

> I most heartily desire that music, that divine and most precious gift, be praised and extolled before all people. However, I am so completely overwhelmed by the quantity and greatness of its excellence and virtues, that I can find neither beginning nor end, nor adequate words and expressions to say what I ought; as a result, though I am full of the highest praise, I remain nothing more than a jejune and miserable eulogist.
>
> Here ought one to speak of the use one might make of so great a thing, but even this use is so infinitely manifold that it is beyond the reach of the greatest eloquence of the greatest orators. We are able to adduce only this one point at present, namely, that experience proves that, next to the Word of God, only music deserves being extolled as the mistress and governess of the feelings of the human heart.[55]

Luther makes an extended testimonial to music's ability to express feeling in his preface to Rhau's *Symphoniae iucundae*, published in the same year. He could not be more correct when he says 'music is a language [of feelings] without words.'

> Here it must suffice to discuss the benefit of this great art. But even that transcends the greatest eloquence of the most eloquent, because of the infinite variety of its forms and benefits. We can mention only one point (which experience confirms), namely, that next to the Word of God, music deserves the highest praise. She is a mistress and governess of those human emotions which as masters govern men or more often overwhelm them. No greater commendation than this can be found—at least not by us. For whether you wish to comfort the sad, to terrify the happy, to encourage the despairing, to humble the proud, to calm the passionate, or to appease those full of hate—and who could number all these masters of the human heart, namely, the emotions, inclinations, and affections that impel men to evil or good?—what more effective means than music could you find? ...
>
> Thus it was not without reason that the fathers and prophets wanted nothing else to be associated as closely with the Word of God as music. Therefore, we have so many hymns and Psalms where message and music join to move the listener's soul, while in other living beings and [sounding] bodies music remains a language without words.[56]

---

54 Quoted in Buszin, 'Luther on Music,' 88.
55 Ibid., 81.
56 *Luther's Works*, LIII, 323.

In several places, Luther also comments on the purpose of music so often mentioned by the ancient Greeks, the power of music to affect the character of the listener and to make them more well-rounded, 'fit for any task.' He seems to have noticed this first in the quality of people he knew who were also musicians. We may presume that it was his recognition of this purpose of music which fostered his frequent recommendation that music be part of the school curriculum.

> I have always loved music. Those who have mastered this art are made of good stuff, they are fit for any task. It is necessary indeed that music be taught in the schools. A teacher must be able to sing; otherwise I will not as much as look at him. Also, we should not ordain young men into the ministry unless they have become well acquainted with music in the schools.
>
> Music is a beautiful and glorious gift of God and close to theology. I would not give up what little I know about music for something else which I might have in greater abundance. We should always make it a point to habituate youth to enjoy the art of music, for it produces fine and skillful people.[57]

In 1524 Luther returned to this idea when he wrote the preface to his and Walter's *Geistliches Gesangbüchlein*.

> That it is good and God pleasing to sing hymns is, I think, known to every Christian; for everyone is aware not only of the example of the prophets and kings in the Old Testament who praised God with song and sound, with poetry and psaltery, but also of the common and ancient custom of the Christian church to sing Psalms …
>
> And these songs were arranged in four parts to give the young—who should at any rate be trained in music and other fine arts—something to wean them away from love ballads and carnal songs and to teach them something of value in their place, thus combining the good with the pleasing, as is proper for youth. Nor am I of the opinion that the gospel should destroy and blight all the arts, as some of the pseudo-religious claim. But I would like to see all the arts, especially music, used in the service of Him who gave and made them … As it is, the world is too lax and indifferent about teaching and training the young for us to abet this trend.[58]

Luther is reported to have mentioned this purpose in another dinner conversation.

> Music is a semi-discipline and taskmistress, which makes people milder and more gentle, more civil and more sensible. The wicked gut-scrapers and fiddlers serve the purpose of enabling us to see and hear what a fine and wholesome art music really is; for white is more clearly recognized when it is contrasted with black.[59]

---

57 Quoted in Buszin, 'Luther on Music,' 85.
58 *Luther's Works*, LIII, 315ff.
59 Quoted in Buszin, 'Luther on Music,' 92.

Given Luther's appreciation of the positive purposes of music, it follows that he was concerned that it might be misused. He mentions some specific examples of the misuse of music in the preface he wrote for a collection of part-songs published in 1538.

> Take special care to shun perverted minds who prostitute this lovely gift of nature and of art with their erotic rantings; and be quite assured that none but the devil goads them on to defy their very nature which would and should praise God its Maker with this gift, so that these bastards purloin the gift of God and use it to worship the foe of God, the enemy of nature and of this lovely art.[60]

In another place he seems to have had this same thought in mind, although he does not quite complete the analogy.

> Wine inflames to many evils, but especially to thirst and more drinking. What would the prophet have said to the Germans for whom natural capacity is insufficient to drain so much drink? Theirs are not feasts of joy but feasts of pigs. It is all right to eat and to drink, but to cultivate drunkenness is evil. So also music is a gift of God. Elisha says (2 Kings 3:15) 'Bring me a minstrel, etc.' Amos 6:5 says: 'Like David they invent for themselves instruments of music.' Certainly if you make use of music as David did, you will not sin.[61]

Since Luther's primary interest in music was centered on singing, his few remarks on performance practice are concerned with the proper spirit of the singer. In his preface to the Babst *Hymnal* of 1545, Luther writes of the proper manner of religious singing.

> As the prophet Malachi asks in the first chapter, 'Who is there even among you that would shut the doors for nought or kindle a light on my altar for nothing?' Now with a heart as lazy and unwilling as this, nothing or nothing good can be sung. Heart and mind must be cheerful and willing if one is to sing …
>
> Thus there is now in the New Testament a better service of God, of which the Psalm [96] here says: 'Sing to the Lord a new song …' For God has cheered our hearts and minds through his dear Son, whom he gave for us to redeem us from sin, death, and the devil. He who believes this earnestly cannot be quiet about it. But he must gladly and willingly sing and speak about it so that others also may come and hear it. And whoever does not want to sing and speak of it shows that he does not believe and that he does not belong under the new and joyful testament, but under the old, lazy, and tedious testament.[62]

Heydenreich reports hearing Luther make the observation during a dinner conversation, that music must be performed with a certain seriousness of purpose.

---

60 *Luther's Works*, LIII, 324.
61 'Lectures on Isaiah,' in Ibid., XVI, 62.
62 Ibid., LIII, 332ff.

> Music doesn't sound right when there is laughter in connection with it, for music is intended to cheer the spirit. The mouth gets no pleasure from it. If one sings diligently, the soul, which is located in the body, plays and derives special pleasure from it.[63]

Luther also makes one reference to the listener, drawing on an analogy often mentioned by ancient philosophers regarding the ass and the lyre, by which is meant the ass can hear music but not listen to it.

> No matter how much is said about this, the others neither understand nor heed it any more than a sow appreciates music played on the harp.[64]

On Church Music

Luther seemed to have had two central objections to the practice of music in the Catholic Church as he knew it in the sixteenth century. First, he was bothered by the use of money purely for the 'extras' of ceremony, although he suggests in one place that 'singing, churches, decorations, organs' are needed to coax the most childish of men to know the teachings of faith.[65] In any case, he complained in a publication of 1524 that instead of people giving money to the poor they give it to the Church for designated purposes, such as 'chapels, altars, towers, bells, organs, paintings, images, [and] singing.'[66] In this regard he also objected to a tradition of endowed masses, the paying for masses for particular private purposes.

> That is to say, they have been reduced to anthem singers, organ wheezers, and reciting decadent, indifferent masses to get and consume the income from the endowments.[67]

In an early treatise dealing with prayer, Luther suggests that the proper role for church music is not ceremonial, but to move the listener to devotional thought. In making the point that although one can pray silently, hearing the words stimulates thought, he uses the analogy of music.

> The spoken words have no other purpose than that of a trumpet, a drum, or an organ, or any other sound which will move the heart and lift it upward to God.[68]

---

63 In a conversation of 1542 reported by Caspar Heydenreich, in Ibid., LIV, 420.
64 'Sermon on the Fourteenth Chapter of St. John,' in Ibid., XXIV, 89.
65 'Treatise on Good Works' [1520], in Ibid., XLIV, 35.
66 'Trade and Usury' [1524], in Ibid., XLV, 284.
67 'To the Christian Nobility' [1520], in Ibid., XLIV, 192.
68 'An Exposition of the Lord's Prayer for Simple Laymen' [1519], in Ibid., XLII, 25.

One of his strongest objections to the old Church tradition was that as it had evolved there was no emphasis on God's Word, 'only reading and singing remain in the churches. This is the worst abuse.'[69] In particular, Luther complains that the foremost activity in monasteries and nunneries should be studying the Holy Scripture.

> But today these monasteries and nunneries have come to nothing but praying and singing.[70]

In a treatise dealing with monastic vows, Luther returns to this subject and strongly objects to the time spent in teaching monks to sing.

> If now some unbeliever were to enter into the midst of these men and heard them braying, mumbling, and bellowing, and saw that they were neither preaching nor praying, but rather, as their custom is, were sounding forth like those pipe organs (with which they have so brilliantly associated themselves, each one set in a row just like his neighbor), would this unbeliever not be perfectly justified in asking, 'Have you gone mad?' What else are these monks but the tubes and pipes Paul referred to as giving no distinct note but rather blasting out into the air? Is it any different from a man who seeking to lecture mounts the platform and talks for a whole hour in a language which is foreign to the people and which nobody understands? ... Would we not think this man mad? I grant that divine worship of this kind suits sacrilegious and blasphemous enemies of Christ, since they are not one whit better than those dumb, wooden pipes, sounding forth with much effort, teaching nothing, learning nothing, and praying nothing. And yet they boast that this senseless work is the highest worship, and draw to themselves the world's wealth on the merits of this work ...
>
> In this way audacious and blasphemous men adapt the divine oracles of Christ to fit in with this childish, ridiculous, and foolish performance, in which they actually stand in rows to worship God like rows of tubes, pipes, and trumpets, mute and insensate ... Do you think God wants a lot of dumb pipes to assemble themselves and delight him by blowing off into thin air?[71]

This passage and others seem to suggest that Luther had a certain hostility to the organ. Perhaps he was too sensitive a musician, or had sensitive ears, to appreciate the rough and loud instrument of the sixteenth century. In a list of things of the Catholic traditions which he found unnecessary he again includes the organ and, which is also perhaps a clue to his sensitivity as a listener, 'Not ringing, but *clattering* of bells.'[72] The possibility of his sensitivity to the loud sound of the organ is implied in another place, where he complains of people who say one thing in prayer and then contradict it in their hearts.

---

69 'Concerning the Order of Public Worship' [1523], in Ibid., LIII, 11.
70 'To the Christian Nobility' [1520], in Ibid., XLIV, 206.
71 'The Judgment of Martin Luther on Monastic Vows' [1521], in Ibid., XLIV, 324ff. In 'Concerning the Order of Public Worship' [1523], Ibid., LIII, 20, Luther mentions that the early Christians 'softly prayed one or two Psalms,' in a passage where he is discussing simplifying the service. He seems to be inferring that actual *music* is not necessary, perhaps unaware that the early Christians avoided music in the service as a matter of security, not theology.
72 'Exhortation to All Clergy Assembled at Augsburg' [1530], in Ibid., XXXIV, 55ff.

> They are like lead organ pipes which fairly drawl or shout out their sounds in church, yet lack both words and meaning.[73]

On the other hand, Luther liked much of the old Church music and had a personal preference for the music of Josquin, whose compositions he found,

> flow freely, gently, and cheerfully, are not forced or cramped by rules, and are like the song of the finch.[74]

It is clear in his writings that he wanted to preserve some of the older musical traditions. A case in point was the burial hymns. While he pointed out that the new church should not sing 'dirges or doleful songs,' but rather 'comforting hymns of the forgiveness of sins,' he nevertheless retained some of the older melodies in a collection of *Burial Hymns* of 1542, although he changed the text.

> This is why we have collected the fine music and songs which under the papacy were used at vigils, masses for the dead, and burials ... But we have adapted other texts to the music so that it may adorn our article of the resurrection, instead of purgatory with its torment and satisfaction which lets their dead neither sleep nor rest. The melodies and notes are precious. It would be a pity to let them perish. But the texts and words are non-Christian and absurd. They deserve to perish ...
>
> And indeed, they also possess a lot of splendid, beautiful songs and music, especially in the cathedral and parish churches. But these are used to adorn all sorts of impure and idolatrous texts. Therefore, we have unclothed these idolatrous, lifeless, and foolish texts, and divest them of their beautiful music ...
>
> But we do not hold that the notes need to be sung the same in all the churches. Let every church follow the music according to their own book and custom. For I myself do not like to hear the notes in a responsory or other song changed from what I was accustomed to in my youth. We are concerned with changing the text, not the music.[75]

Earlier, in 1525, he had recommended the German hymn, *Mitten in dem Leben*, for use in burial services.[76]

It appears that at one point, at least, Luther was thinking of retaining some of the old Catholic music for the purpose of promoting the Latin language.

> At vespers it would be excellent to sing three evening hymns in Latin, not German, on account of the school youth, to accustom them to the Latin. Then follow the simple antiphons, hymns, and responses, and a lesson in German ... Then one might sing the Magnificat or a Te Deum

---

73 'An Exposition of the Lord's Prayer for Simple Laymen' [1519], in Ibid., XLII, 39.

74 In a conversation of 1531 reported by John Schlaginhaufen, in Ibid., LIV, 129ff.

75 Ibid., LIII, 326ff.

76 'Instructions for the Visitors of Parish Pastors in Electoral Saxony' [1525], in Ibid., XL, 310.

Laudamus or Benedictus ... so that the youth remain close to the Scriptures. Thereupon the whole congregation may sing a German hymn ...

Since it is not fitting that singing should be uniform at all festivals, it would be well on high festivals to sing the Latin Introits, the Gloria in Excelsis, the Hallelujah, the simple sequences, the Sanctus, and Agnus Dei.[77]

The following year, in a publication dealing with the new order of the service, Luther mentions this again.

For in no wise would I want to discontinue the service in the Latin language, because the young are my chief concern. And if I could bring it to pass, and Greek and Hebrew were as familiar to us as the Latin and had as many fine melodies and songs, we would hold mass, sing, and read on successive Sundays in all four languages, German, Latin, Greek, and Hebrew. I do not at all agree with those who cling to one language and despise all others.[78]

On beginning to think about a new kind of church service, Luther recognizes the importance of keeping some traditions.

Let the chants in the Sunday masses and Vespers be retained; they are quite good and are taken from Scripture.[79]

But in general he seemed in favor of cutting back the amount of choral participation.

The Quadragesima graduals and others like them that exceed two verses may be sung at home by whoever wants them. In church we do not want to quench the spirit of the faithful with tedium.

By 1523, in a letter to George Spalatin, Luther was beginning to think of creating new music with German words.

Our plan is to follow the example of the prophets and the ancient fathers of the church, and to compose psalms for the people in the vernacular, that is, spiritual songs, so that the Word of God may be among the people also in the form of music. Therefore we are searching everywhere for poets ... But I would like you to avoid any new words or the language used at court. In order to be understood by the people, only the simplest and most common words should be used for singing; at the same time, however, they should be pure and apt; and further, the sense should be clear and as close as possible to the psalm. You need a free hand here: maintain the sense, but don't cling to the words ... I myself do not have so great a gift that I can do what I would like to see done here.[80]

---

77 Ibid., 307ff.
78 'The German Mass and Order of Service' [1526], in Ibid., LIII, 63.
79 'Concerning the Order of Public Worship' [1523], in Ibid., LIII, 13ff.
80 Letter to George Spalatin [1523], in Ibid., XLIX, 68.

One reason for favoring German was his preference for having the congregation participate in singing. In the same year, he wrote,

> I also wish that we had as many songs as possible in the vernacular which the people could sing during mass, immediately after the gradual and also after the Sanctus and Agnus Dei. For who doubts that originally all the people sang these which now only the choir sings or responds to while the bishop is consecrating?[81]

He mentions this again in 1525, in his *Against the Heavenly Prophets*.

> Although I am willing to permit the translating of Latin texts of choral and vocal music into the vernacular with the retention of the original notes and musical settings, I am nevertheless of the opinion that the result sounds neither proper nor correct; the text, the notes, the accents, the tune, and likewise the entire outward expression must be genuine outgrowths of the original text and its spirit.[82]

By 1524 he was beginning to think of a complete German Mass.

> I desire a German mass more than I can promise. I am not qualified for this task, which requires both a talent in music and the gift of the Spirit.[83]

The earliest church music which Luther published looked very much like chant, expect for German words. By 1538 he had apparently heard some new examples of polyphony, which he endorses in his preface to a collection of part-songs.

> But when learning is added to all this and artistic music which corrects, develops, and refines the natural music, then at last it is possible to taste with wonder (yet not to comprehend) God's absolute and perfect wisdom in his wondrous work of music. Here it is most remarkable that one single voice continues to sing the tenor, while at the same time many other voices play around it, exulting and adorning it in exuberant strains and, as it were, leading it forth in a divine roundelay, so that those who are the least bit moved know nothing more amazing in this world. But any who remain unaffected are unmusical indeed and deserve to hear a certain dunghill poet or the music of the pigs.[84]

His general enthusiasm for his new church music can be seen in a letter he wrote in 1525. After the death of Frederick the Wise, his successor dissolved the choir of the Castle Church of Wittenberg in order to put the money to use for 'better purposes.' In response, Luther wrote

---

81 'An Order of Mass and Communion' [1523], in Ibid., LIII, 36.

82 Quoted in Buszin, 'Luther on Music,' 95.

83 Letter to Nicholas Hausmann [1524], in *Luther's Works*, XLIX, 90.

84 Ibid., LIII, 324.

the new elector recommending that he fund the choir by selling the goods and possessions of the monasteries. 'God,' he said, 'would derive pleasure from such a transfer.'[85]

Finally, there are two instances in which Luther, based on the translations available to him, is in error in his reading of references to music in the Scriptures. The Psalms which carry a title 'Song of Ascent,' are psalms assumed today as having been intended to be sung on the steps. Luther rejects this, there being no other such biblical reference, and presumes it meant two-part music, with higher children or women's voices above those of the men.[86]

In his lectures on Isaiah, Luther finds in Isaiah 22:24 'musical instruments,' words which no longer appear in modern translations. He proceeds to say that musical instruments 'pertain to adornment and elegance, not to necessity.'[87]

---

85 Quoted in Buszin, 'Luther on Music,' 86.
86 'Exposition on Psalm 127' [1524], in *Luther's Works*, XLV, 320ff.
87 'Lectures on Isaiah,' in Ibid., XVI, 181.

5 MUSIC THEORISTS IN THE GERMAN-SPEAKING COUNTRIES

As with France and Italy, it was not to the universities of the German-speaking countries that one could look for new ideas in music. Here also they remained locked in the old medieval Scholastic notion that music belonged to mathematics. Thus, in 1505, the University of Leipzig appointed Sebastianus Müchelon as '*lector musicae et aritmetice*,'[1] a document of the University of Köln in 1515 specifies the teaching of 'the books on mathematics, that is geometry, arithmetic, music and astronomy' and in 1558 the University of Heidelberg employed a lecturer in mathematics who was expected to include music in his teaching.

Of course, at the beginning of the sixteenth century the universities had close ties with the Church and so even the exciting discussions of the humanists appear to have had little influence. A rare exception was the University of Vienna, where Maximilian I, in 1501, added to the arts faculty a '*Collegium poëtarum et mathematicorum*,' bringing poetry and oratory into the curriculum.[2]

In the present volume, as with the earlier ones in this series, we must remind the reader that our interest in these treatises is focused only on those portions which offer insight to aesthetics and performance practice. We leave out the mathematics.[3] It is where the author wanders away momentarily from mathematics that we find his personal aesthetic views.

We see in these sixteenth-century German music treatises documentation for a striking change in aesthetics. For several centuries, theorists wrote of speculative versus practical music, or as we might say today, theory versus performance. For centuries the speculative was always given the highest aesthetic value, as indeed it is in the early books of the sixteenth century. By mid-century, however, everything has changed and authors such as Coclico speak of a higher aesthetic value in performance. Music theorists have rarely been harbingers; they are followers. Thus, this change in view reflects what had already taken place towards the beginning of the sixteenth century. The growing sophistication of music patronage outside the Church, the influence of the humanists and the dramatic leaps forward in the art of instrument manufacture had resulted in an entirely new level of sophistication in performance.

---

[1] Nan Cooke Carpenter, *Music in the Medieval and Renaissance Universities* (Norman: University of Oklahoma Press, 1958), 251. Carpenter documents the association with mathematics extensively.

[2] Ibid., 228.

[3] Should we point out that universities still tie mathematics to music to some degree? We teach rhythm as mathematics and wonder why our students can't *feel* it.

Finally, it is also because of our specific focus that we omit discussion of two of the most familiar sixteenth-century music treatises, Virdung's *Musica getutscht* (1511) and Agricola's *Musica Instrumentalis Deutsch* (1528), both of which are important primarily for their discussion of contemporary instruments. The most important German treatise dealing with sixteenth-century practice, the *Syntagma Musicus* of Praetorius, we treat as a separate chapter.

JOHANNES COCHLAEUS, *TETRACHORDUM MUSICES* (1511)

Johannes Cochlaeus, would be only a footnote but for the fact that he was the teacher of Glarean and was *Magister Artium* at the University of Köln. Later he studied theology at Ferrara and eventually became rector at St. Lorenz school, in Nürnberg. It was for the students of this school that he wrote this treatise and to them that he dedicates a Latin poem.

> Everyone who delights in the arts of the muses, and who has concern for harmonious song, is supported by nature, guided by discernment, and rewarded by honor. Just as in former times poets and wise men were musicians, so also today they rejoice in churches with sweet sounding melody. Therefore, dear youth, accept these books with cheerful countenance, books written with labor and published with loving care.[4]

In a letter of dedication to the prior of the school, Cochlaeus reveals that he was hired with three areas of responsibility. The first was 'the education of our youth in literature and morals' (which also included grammar) and the second was 'ecclesiastical song.'[5] The third is quite interesting, for he was to see that 'polyphonic music (which is very pleasing to our people) should not be neglected entirely.' 'Our people,' meant the Church community, for this was a school which trained boys destined for the clergy. The phrase mentioning that polyphony should not be 'neglected entirely' reflects, quite contrary to the impression given by modern music history texts, that polyphony had long been considered by many people actually living in the Renaissance as archaic, Scholastic and irrelevant. The humanists, believing that the emotions in ancient Greek music were found primarily in the text, attacked polyphonic music for the obvious reasons. Cochlaeus adds a comment on the importance of this instruction in music for these boys,

> so that they do not continue on to the priesthood without knowledge of music, always singing like laboring oxen, and, being ignorant of the rules of music, deriving no profit or enjoyment from such poor singing.

Cochlaeus follows the medieval categorization of music into three divisions: Mundane, Human and Instrumental, although he greatly expands these fields. Mundane music now

---

4   Johannes Cochlaeus, *Tetrachordum Musices*, trans. Clement Miller (Rome: American Institute of Musicology, 1970), 90.

5   Ibid., 17.

includes not only the 'music of the spheres,' but the calendar, the seasons and the phases of the moon as well. Human music concerns the soul and its relationship with Reason and the body. Instrumental music includes both instruments and the voice. He follows this with another general division, the Natural and Artificial. In the latter, dealing essentially with notation, we see the relationship with mathematics.

> Indeed, all four mathematical sciences are concerned with quantity, for arithmetic is concerned with absolute numerals, music with numerals related to each other, geometry with magnitudes individually and without motion, and astronomy with mobile magnitudes.[6]

His final division is Theoretical Music and Practical Music ('the practical application of sounds and consonances').

We find his most interesting chapter, called 'Four Kinds of Musicians,' one which does reflect the influence of humanism, for it recalls that the ancient Greeks considered both poetry and dance as types of music. Cochlaeus defines his four categories of musicians as follows:

1. Those who are concerned with prose, and who express their thoughts in words rather than in melody. They are orators, lecturers and those who sing antiphons and psalms.
2. Those who not only express their thoughts, but who also declaim them in long and short syllables according to a metric plan, as in the case of poets.
3. Those devoted to the histrionic and mimic art, and who move with bodily gestures in imitation of musical sound.
4. Those who create sweet melody with mutually sonorous intervals. These are truly called musicians and singers.

Since the fourth of these seems to make performance stand as self-sufficient, he quickly adds the old medieval qualification that a performer must also be a musician, meaning he must understand the speculative definitions of music.

> But some wish to distinguish between a singer and a musician in the same way as between an orator and a rhetorician. For a singer brings to performance the musical concepts of a musician, just as an orator declaims in speech the rhetorical concepts of a rhetorician. Yet, just as one is not worthy to be called an orator unless he is also a rhetorician, so one should certainly not be considered a singer unless he is also a musician. Therefore, mimes and other performers of unskillful music are not really musicians.[7]

Finally, in his discussion of instrumental music we find some curious and interesting trivia.[8] The organ in ancient times, he says, was powered by 'a bag made of two elephant skins

---

6   Ibid., 21.
7   Ibid., 23.
8   Ibid., 28ff.

attached,' and could be heard from Jerusalem to the Mount of Olives.[9] It is interesting that he includes under *tuba* not only the traditional trumpet but also the trombone, reminding the reader that during most of the Renaissance the slide trumpet and early trombone differed in design but not in principle. It is under *tympanum* that he mentions female musicians for the first time in his book, as performers on this instrument he calls them *tympanistria*.

ANDREAS ORNITHOPARCHUS
MUSICE ACTIVE MICROLOGUS (1517)

Andreas Ornithoparchus was associated with several universities, in particular Leipzig and Tübingen. This treatise was widely used as an educational text in sixteenth-century Germany, republished in several editions and even translated and published in English in 1609.[10] The earliest extant publication is dated Leipzig, 1517, but the author says it first appeared in Rostock so it may be older. One immediately notices that its organization of topics is identical with the 1511 treatise of Cochlaeus, but perhaps they both reflect a basic syllabus followed by many universities at the beginning of the sixteenth century.

The treatise by Ornithoparchus is, however, unique among early sixteenth-century German treatises in two regards. First, it is almost a source book of quotations from ancient and medieval treatises, indeed he admits 'whatever flowers the volumes of other men had in them, like a bee I sucked them out.'[11]

Ornithoparchus typically cites earlier authors before making his own observations and, if nothing else, it marks him as being well read and very industrious. He recalls that this effort,

> made me travel to many countries, not without financial loss, to search out the Art; these made me often become wearied, when I might have [remained home] at rest; filled with grief, when I might have solaced myself; disgraced, when I might have lived in good reputation; impoverished, when I might have lived in plenty.[12]

Second, this treatise, more than any other of its time, concentrates on the ethical values of music. The very purpose of his book, he announces, is to provide the youth of all of Germany with a book which would introduce them to good fashions, the honest delights of music and 'little by little stir them to virtuous actions.'[13] He continues,

---

9   Ibid., 28. From old Jerusalem to the Mount of Olives is not a great distance and before our noisy century probably any instrument could be heard over that distance.

10 By John Dowland, whose work we quote here, in modernized English.

11 Andreas Ornithoparchus, *Musicae active mirologus* and Dowland, *Introduction: Containing the Art of Singing* (New York: Dover, 1973), 157.

12 Ibid., 117.

13 Ibid.

> Among those things by which the mind of man is wont to be delighted, I can find nothing that is more great, that appeals to any age or sex … There is no breast so savage and cruel, which is not moved with the touch of this delight. For it drives away cares, persuades men to gentleness, represses anger, nourishes arts, promotes concord, inflames heroic minds to gallant deeds, cures vice, breeds virtues and nourishes them when they are born and introduces men to good fashion … Therefore this Art is of a holy, sweet, heavenly, divine, fair and blessed nature.

Ornithoparchus returns to this subject again at the end of Book I when he discusses the character of the various modes.[14] Dorian, he says, bestows wisdom to and causes chastity in the listener, while Phrygian causes wars and inflames fury. Aeolian calms the tempest of the mind and, after having done so, lulls it to sleep. Lydian sharpens the wit of the dull and moves the mind from earthly to heavenly desires. No wonder Ornithoparchus warns that the musician must diligently observe which mode he plays for specific listeners! The men of our time, he says, know how to do this according to the nature of the occasion.

> But our men of a more refined time do use sometimes the Dorian, sometimes the Phrygian, sometimes the Lydian and sometimes other modes, because they judge that according to differing occasions they are to choose differing modes. And that is not without cause, for every habit of the mind is governed by songs. For songs make men sleepy and wakeful, careful and merry, angry and merciful. Songs heal diseases and produce diverse wonderful effects, moving some to vain mirth, some to a devout and holy joy, yes often to godly tears.

At the beginning of Book II, Ornithoparchus produces Nero as a considerably exaggerated illustration of how a man is affected by music.

> Even Nero, while he gave himself to music, was most gentle. But when he abandoned music in favor of the diabolical Art of Necromancy, then first appeared that fierce cruelty of his. Then he was changed from a lamb into a wolf and from a most mild prince into a most savage beast.[15]

Ornithoparchus, like many theorists before him, begins by dividing music into Mundane, Human and Instrumental Music. Mundane music, he finds in the 'harmony caused by the motion of the stars and the violence of the spheres,' which he also relates to elements and climate. Here he quotes a nice phrase, from a lost work by the philosopher, Dorilaus, 'The world is God's organ.' Even, as he admits, if we cannot hear the music of the spheres, one has to admit that God (whom Dowland calls, 'the Work-master of this Mundane Fabricke') has created in all things number, weight, and measure. Since these are also the principal properties of music, therefore it is reasonable to believe that the music of the spheres exists.

Again following earlier writers, especially the ancient Greeks, Human Music is associated primarily with the soul of man. In his conclusion he explains the importance of this idea.

---

14 Ibid., 156.

15 Ibid., 159. We have difficulty finding a period when Nero was not cruel, for he was scarcely twenty when he succeeded in murdering his mother—after a number of failed attempts!

> What other power so orders and glues the spiritual strength, which is invested with an intellect, to the mortal and earthly body, than Music, which every man that looks inside himself finds in himself? For everyone prefers what he likes and is disturbed by his dislikes. Hence it is, that we loath and abhor discords, and are delighted when we hear concords of harmony, because we know there is in ourselves the same concord.[16]

Ornithoparchus next turns to the virtues of speculative versus practical music, or theory versus performance. He admits that speculative understanding of music judges not by the ears, but by 'wit and reason.' In defense of the importance of speculative, or theoretical, knowledge of music, Ornithoparchus concludes,

> It is therefore no small praise, no little profit and labor which should not be lightly esteemed, which makes the Artist both a judge of those songs which have been composed, a corrector of those which are false and an inventor of new [ones].[17]

This leads him to establish three categories of musician: performers, poets and critics (those who judge music only by 'speculation and reason'). It is the first category which he discusses at length, following the old Church prejudices against musicians who are 'merely' performers. The basic logic here is that the performer is merely a kind of craftsman who engages in performance while understanding nothing he does. One would like to think that this is the last time we shall confront this relic of the worst of medieval Scholastic values, but alas this attitude is still found in some universities today. Here is Ornithoparchus on the performing musician:

> The first category deals with instruments, such as harpists, organists and all others who prove their skill by instruments. They are removed from the intellectual part of music, being as servants, and using no Reason, void of all speculation and following their sense only. Now though they may seem to do things with learning and skill, yet it is plain that they have no knowledge, because they do not comprehend what they profess. Therefore we deny that they have Music, which is the Science of making melody. One can have knowledge without practicing and this is a greater end than being an excellent practitioner. We do not associate nimbleness of fingers with Science, which resides in the soul, but rather to practice. If it were otherwise the more one knew about the Art, the more he would automatically become swift in his fingerings.[18]

Ornithoparchus includes singers among instrumentalists, which is to say performers, and again he says their performance means nothing if it is without 'the rules of Reason.' Thus, as regards the speculative versus the practical musician (theoretical versus performer), Ornithoparchus accepts the old Church dogma that it is more honorable to know than to do. Sup-

---

16　Ibid., 121.

17　Ibid., 123.

18　Ibid., 123.

posing the reader may wonder about the performers in the Old Testament, Ornithoparchus quickly adds that, well, they were also prophets and wise men!

Given this very limited definition of what a true musician is, one can understand Ornithoparchus' concern that the art was dying out.

> Hence it is, that excepting those which are, or have been in the chapels of princes, there are none, or very few true musicians. Whereupon the Art itself doth grow into contempt, being hidden like a candle under a bushel, the praising of the almighty Creator of all things decreases and the number of those which seek the overthrow of this Art increases daily throughout Germany.

We have no doubt that he was aware of the attacks of the humanists on the old contrapuntal Church style and that he saw the harbingers of the Reformation.

Ornithoparchus returns to the subject of the importance of musicianship based on theoretical learning in his discussion of mensural music. Now it is the composer who is the object of his attention and he lashes out at those who compose without 'following the rules.' In mid-stream he suddenly recalls having heard some effective music by composers not trained in theoretical knowledge, which is something he cannot quite explain. We know today that theory is left hemisphere of the brain but that the experiential form of music is in the right. It was the lack of this knowledge, together with the fact that the left hemisphere tends to deny the very existence of the right, which explains much of the early attacks on 'practical' musicians by 'speculative' musicians.

> I cannot but scorn certain composers (for so they will be called, though indeed they are Monsters of Music), who, though they know not so much as the first elements of the art, yet proclaim themselves 'the musicians' musician,' being ignorant in all things, yet bragging of all things and do … disgrace, corrupt and debase this art, which was in many ages before honored and used by many most learned, most wise men. They use any signs at their pleasure, neither reckoning of value, nor measure, seeking rather to please the ears of the foolish with the sweetness of the melody … I know such a man, who has been hired to be the organist at the castle in Prague, who though he know not (and I conceal his greater faults) how to distinguish a perfect time from an imperfect, yet maintains publicly that he is writing from the very depth of music … Many more have violently inundated the art of music, as those which are not compounders of harmonies, but rather corruptors, children of the furies rather than the Muses, not worthy of the least grace I may do them. For their songs are ridiculous, not grounded on the principles of the art, though perhaps true enough. For the artist does not grace the art, but the art graces the artist. Therefore a composer does not grace music, but the contrary. There are some who make true songs not by art, but by custom, as having happily lived among singers all their life, yet do not understand what they have made, knowing that such a thing is, but not what it is.[19]

Among his comments focusing on education, Ornithoparchus mentions some 'forbidden intervals,' such as the tritone, 'very rare and forbidden to young beginners.' His implication

---

19 Ibid., 169.

is that only the most experienced composers can use these. He also praises the use of the monochord, 'a rude master which makes learned scholars.' The value of this instrument, apart from ear training is to 'show hair-brained false musicians their errors.'

Ornithoparchus makes some additional interesting observations on performance practice which touch on aesthetics. He wonders why it is that sounds are more pleasing when they are closer to each other, rather than separated by large intervals. And he has noticed that 'high sounds are heard sooner than bass sounds.'

> As a sharp sword pierces quickly, whereas a blunt one enters slowly, so when we hear an high forced voice, it strikes into us, but a bass voice is dull, as if it were thrust at one.[20]

Soon he returns to the subject of singing and first contrasts the vocal qualities of various nationalities.

> Various nations have diverse fashions and differ in clothes, diet, studies, speech and song. Hence it is that the English carol, the French sing, the Spaniards weep, the Italians caper with their voices and others bark. But the Germans, I am ashamed to say, howl like wolves ... Germany nourishes many cantors, but few musicians. For very few, excepting those which are or have been in the chapel of princes, truly know the art of singing. For those magistrates to whom this charge is given, appoint ... young cantors, whom they choose by the shrillness of their voices, not for the cunning of their art, thinking that God is pleased with bellowing and braying.[21]

This, he says, we know is not pleasing to God, for in the Song of Solomon (2:14) one finds 'let me hear your voice, for your voice is sweet.'

Now Ornithoparchus offers some precepts necessary for every singer, for he has noticed many abuses 'some by moving their body indecently, some by gaping unseemly and some by changing the vowels.' Later he returns to this, saying 'the uncomely gaping of the mouth and the ungraceful motion of the body is a sign of a mad singer.'

Most of his precepts stress the importance of the singer knowing the theoretical rules of music. One of these is the necessity of keeping the beat, 'for to sing without law and measure is an offense to God himself.'

> Whole Vigils are performed with such confusion, haste and mockery ... that neither one voice can be distinguished from another, nor one syllable from another, nor one verse sometimes throughout a whole Psalm from another. An impious fashion to be punished with the severest correction. Think you that God is pleased with such howling, such noise, such mumbling, in which there is no devotion, no expressing of words, no articulating of syllables?

---

20 Ibid., 198.
21 Ibid., 208ff.

Ornithoparchus stresses the importance of making the voice coincide in emotion with the words of the text, 'sad when the words are sad and merry when they are merry.' Here he pauses to recognize a curious exception.

> I cannot but wonder at the Saxons (the most gallant people of all Germany …) in that they use in their funerals a high, merry and *joconde* emotion, for no other reason, I think, than that either they hold death to be the greatest good that can befall a man or that they believe the souls return to the original sweetness of music that is in heaven.

In this regard, Ornithoparchus even cautions the singer to be careful to make his singing correspond to the specific nature of holidays, 'least on a slight holiday he make the service too solemn, or too slight on a great one.'

He mentions the abuse of the Saxons again when he comments on the quality of the voice.

> Let a singer take heed, least he begin too loud, braying like an ass, or when he has begun at an unusual height, disgracing the song. For God is not pleased with loud cries, but with lovely sounds. As Erasmus says, it is not the noise of the lips, but the ardent desire of the art, which most impresses God's ears … But why the Saxons, and those that dwell on the Baltic coast, should so delight in such clamoring I know of no reason, unless they have a deaf God or they think he has gone to the South side of heaven and therefore cannot so easily hear the singers from the East.

Ornithoparchus' last warning to singers in the Church is to remember their purpose.

> Above all things, let the singer study to please God and not men. There are foolish singers who condemn the devotion they should seek and affect the wantonness which they should shun, because they intend their singing for men, not God; seeking for a little worldly fame, so that they may lose eternal glory; pleasing men while they may displease God … and seeking the favor of the creature, condemning the love of the Creator.

As for himself, as the author of a book, Ornithoparchus knows from experience that he will have critics.

> I doubt not that there will be some who will snarl at it and backbite it, condemning it before they read it and disgracing it before the understand it. Some would rather seem, than be, musicians, not obeying authors, or precepts or reasons, but whatsoever comes into their hair-brain Cockscomb … To whom I beg you (gentle Readers) to lend no ear … Neither listen to those that hate the art, they who dissuade others from that which their dullness will not allow them to attain, for it is in vain to harp before an ass.[22]

Finally, we must report Ornithoparchus' assertion that the inventor of music, Tubal (according to the Old Testament), engraved the rules of music on two tablets, one of slate

---

22 Ibid., 211.

and one of marble. He records having heard that the marble one survived the flood and can be found in Syria.²³

NICHOLAUS LISTENIUS, *MUSICA* (1537)

Nicolaus Listenius (ca. 1500–1550) matriculated at Wittenberg in 1529, when both Luther and Melancthon were teaching there. As a theorist, his most important work was his *Musica*, which was largely a revision of a *Rudimenta musicae* of 1533. This work was one of the two most popular instruction books in Germany during the sixteenth century, and was reissued in numerous editions.

The work is dedicated to Johann Georg, son of Joachim II, the Elector of Brandenburg, and it seems rather daring to us when Listenius tells the prince that by cultivating music he will be worthy of his ancestors. In this same Foreword, Listenius provides a moving review of the purpose and virtue of music. Of particular importance is his observation that music is a 'serious art.'

> Many great and serious reasons are established by learned and intelligent men, for all men of genius particularly free princes, must be versed in music and habituated to it. It influences souls to humanity, suavity, even-temper; it restrains all immoderate affections, grief, wrath; it represses violence and obscene desires, for it calms them; as in sounds and songs, so in all the actions of life we may conserve harmony. Hence we see the highest kings in old monuments singing and playing on strings, not only as a pastime for the enjoyment of the arts, but even more, however, making it a serious art, tying music to the harmony of the soul. David used music in deeply exciting the serious and spiritual affections. For this same reason, with all peoples at all periods of music, it has been used in sacred observances, not as a useless voluptuousness, to play some kind of game, but in song, as souls are made more tranquil and are aroused to understand the harmony of divine guidance and are attuned to the correct movement of heavenly teaching; hence its doctrines will more efficiently move souls when song arises. Homer describes Achilles playing the cythara and adds more to the argument, for he says that this most outstanding prince sang the praises of strong men, in which, since by both words and song the soul was moved, it was much more deeply inflamed by the admiration and love of virtue ...
>
> This art invites the soul to virtue.²⁴

Listenius begins his book with one of the old medieval definitions, 'Music is the science of singing correctly and well.' However, in his next sentence he clearly dates himself in the Renaissance by stating that the knowledge of music consists of three kinds: theoretical, practical and *poetic*. The theoretical is concerned only with understanding the subject. Hence, he says, the 'theoretical musician' is content in this knowledge and 'presents no example of his work in performance.'

---
23 Ibid., 125.
24 Nicolaus Listenius, *Musica*, trans. Albert Seay (Colorado Springs: Colorado College Music Press, 1975), 1.

His definition of practical music, which he divides into Choral and Figured, or Mensural, goes considerably beyond the usual definitions given in the university circles in France, England, and Italy, where the term is given to mean little more than simply performance itself. Listenius speaks of something beyond skill and says the performer teaches the listener something more than mere appreciation.

> Practical, whose goal is doing, is that which delights not only in the intricacies of skill, but extends into performance itself, leaving out no part of the act of performance. Hence the practical musician, who teaches others something more than the recognition of art, trains himself in it for the goal of any performance.[25]

His third kind of knowledge is an aesthetic definition quite new to the Renaissance. Here he is thinking of the meaning left with the listener when the performance is concluded. This he calls 'total performance.' It is most important and enlightening that he observed that the practical and the poetic always include the theoretical, 'but the reverse is not true.'

> Poetic is that which is not content with just the understanding of the thing nor with only its practice, but which leaves something more after the labor of performance, as when music or a song of musicians is composed by someone whose goal is total performance and accomplishment. It consists of making or putting together more in this work which afterwards leaves the work perfect and absolute, which otherwise is artificially like the dead.[26]

Although his book deals with many aspects of polyphonic music, it is clear by some of his comments that he does not embrace all that he hears in this style. In speaking of 'hard' and 'soft' scales, for example, he mentions that some compositions mix these two, adding,

> This is not completely proven to me nor do I think that it can be done satisfactorily.[27]

Listenius finds mensural music to be the most sophisticated as it 'is far superior in smoothness, number of notes, diversity of signs, inequality of beats and proportions.' Like other sixteenth-century writers, he finds the three smallest note durations, semiminima, fusa and semifusa are used in instrumental music more than in vocal music, due to their excessive speed. We believe this carries the implication that instrumental improvisation based on vocal models probably was more complex than the surviving music would suggest.

His book concludes with a poem by Johann Spanberg, which again praises the virtues of music and suggests that in Germany musicians were well paid.

> Faithful music, acting as the hope of the poor, an anchor, a harbor,
> A solace, rest, lifting the miserable from the dust,

---

25 Ibid., 3.
26 Ibid.
27 Ibid., 12.

It adds to Caesarian strength and to royal courts.
Riches, gardens, temples and estates, garments,
It gives both illustrious titles and names of fame.
What more may I say? Singers touch the heavens,
They hover around all the world of men; they are paid each year
A hundred golden coins for their specified wages.[28]

HEINRICH GLAREAN, *DODECACHORDON* (1547)

Glarean (1488–1563) of Switzerland completed his higher education at the University of Köln where one of his teachers was Cochlaeus. Glarean was a man of many talents as is testified to in numerous letters by Erasmus, who gives the impression that he was unusually proficient in all the Liberal Arts. In letters of recommendation, Erasmus calls Glarean a mathematician, meaning four branches of the Liberal Arts. It was from this perspective that Glarean was interested in music[29] and our guess is that he probably did not think of himself as a performing musician, although on one occasion he so impressed Maximilian I in his singing of a poem that he was made poet laureate. Such a widely talented man is never universally popular and in the fictitious, satirical *Letters of Obscure Men*, of 1515, by Crotus Rubeanus and Ulrich von Hutten, Glarean is described as,

> a very headstrong man ... A terrible man, a choleric, for ever threatening fights—and he must be possessed of a devil.[30]

In any case, Glarean was the author of one of the most extensive music treatises of the sixteenth century, a work he had apparently finished writing by 1539. While our interest is in Glarean's open and honest observations on a wide variety of topics related to performance and aesthetics, the treatise was originally widely known for Glarean's extension of the eight church modes to twelve, by adding Aeolian and Ionian, together with their plagals.[31] Beyond this, it is a treatise which treats all elements of music theory in very great detail. Glarean, fully aware of this, and perhaps reflecting on his experience in the university, observes at one point,

---

28 Ibid., 45.

29 Glarean does say, in his prefatory letter to Cardinal von Waldburg, that he had spent twenty years thinking about the musical problems presented in his book. See Glarean, *Dodecachordon*, trans. Clement Miller (American Institute of Musicology, 1965), I, 39.

30 Letter of 'Demetrius Phalerius to Ortwin Gratius,' in Francis Stokes, *On the Eve of the Reformation* (New York: Harper & Row, 1909), 183.

31 Clement Miller, in 'The Dodecachordon: Its Origins and Influence on Renaissance Musical Thought,' in *Musica Disciplina* (1961), 155ff., traces the influence of this treatise.

Perhaps we have treated this in more detail than is necessary but it had to be done for the state of mind of the masses, to whom nothing is explained sufficiently.[32]

In another place, however, he seems to suggest the difficulty lay with the professors as much as the minds of the masses.

If by chance this has seemed insufficiently clear to anyone, I beg him to remember how uneducated and unpolished our present age is, that among the highly learned, even among those teaching mathematics, not one in twenty has a clear conception of this matter.[33]

In any case, it is clear that Glarean's purpose was one of education and early in the treatise he cautions the student regarding the broad knowledge necessary to master music.

I appeal to every earnest youth, I exhort and admonish you, if you desire to be initiated into the secrets of this science and want to become a priest truly worthy of this discipline, you will make use of three principal points without which this study cannot be fully mastered, however much you may speculate, and even may surpass Prometheus himself in observation. The first is that you have the precepts of arithmetic clearly in mind and also those of theory and practice. Then it follows that you cannot be entirely ignorant of the Greek language. For a great many of the terms of this study are Greek. The third is that you have some instrument at hand on which you can measure all sounds by ear.[34]

This last sentence is very important and represents one of the distinguishing hallmarks of this treatise. Many earlier treatises were written from the perspective that music was something to be understood intellectually. For Glarean, no matter how extensively he explains the cerebral definitions, in the end it was a matter of the ear. For this reason he also treats the practicing musician with more respect than earlier treatises. In a typical passage, Glarean writes,

Modes are also changed from one into another but not with equal success. For in some cases the change is scarcely clear even to a perceptive ear, indeed, often with great pleasure to the listener, a fact which we have frequently declared is very common today in changing from the Lydian to the Ionian. Those who play instruments and who know how to sing readily the verses of poets according to a musical play, understand this. Indeed, in this way they are frequently worthy of praise if they do it skillfully, especially if they change the Ionian into Dorian. But in other cases the changing seems rough, and scarcely ever without a grave offense to the ears, as changing from the Dorian to the Phrygian. And so whenever present day organists encounter this difficulty in changing church songs in such a way, if they are not well trained and quick, they often incur the derision of experienced listeners.[35]

---

32 Glarean, *Dodecachordon*, I, 79.
33 Ibid., I, 133. Glarean here was reviewing the history of the development of the cithara.
34 Ibid., I, 82ff.
35 Ibid., I, 129.

It is also from this perspective that Glarean begins his treatise by reminding the reader that music, as something heard by the ear, came before theory. After stating that music consists of theory and practice, the separation of the speculative and the practical so long favored by early theorists, he observes,

> Since truly all learning consists in demonstration and neither facts themselves can be computed nor tones be written musicians have invented symbols of the tones partly through figures which they now call notes partly through the naming of syllables.[36]

Glarean does not discuss the subject so dear to the ancient philosophers, the ability of music to affect the character of the listener. He does, however, comment on the subjective character of the various modes. He seemed to believe that the modes contained specific and unique characters, although he admits there is not universal agreement. As an example of this inconsistency, he points to the *de Harmonia musicorum instrumentorum*, by Franchinus, where he finds that in one place the author suggests the Phrygian is suitable for 'more agreeable and the lighter subjects,' while later he contends the same mode 'is suitable for incitement to war and therefore is to be portrayed by a fiery color.' Glarean himself finds Phrygian 'more suitable to severe, religious music, as elegies, laments, and funeral music.'[37]

The Ionian mode Glarean associates with dancing and because 'some men attribute a frivolous wantonness to this mode,' he finds it rarely used in older Church music. He obviously liked it, for he speculates,

> On the other hand, I believe that for the last four hundred years it has also been so deeply admired by church singers, that, enticed by its sweetness and alluring charm, they have changed many songs of the Lydian mode into this mode.[38]

Some other descriptions of the character of various modes which we find interesting are the Lydian, which Glarean calls 'harsh,' and the Hypoionian mode, which he finds 'has great charm in morning songs and love songs, especially in the Celtic tongue which the Swiss use.'[39] Later he says that the Dorian has a 'certain sublime and indescribable majesty'[40] and Mixolydian he identifies with 'a certain tranquil dignity which both moves and dominates the people.'[41]

---

36 Ibid., I, 41.
37 Ibid., I, 130.
38 Ibid., I, 153.
39 Ibid., I, 163, 173.
40 Ibid., II, 257.
41 Ibid., II, 262.

In summarizing, Glarean adds a few comments on the qualities of the various modes.

> If I am allowed to make a rough judgment concerning this and the preceding modes, I shall say it in a few words: Each mode seems to me to reflect beautifully the customs of the people from which the names are taken. The Athenians were truly Ionians, the Spartans were Dorians; the former, although lovers of pleasant things and students of eloquence, were still always considered capricious. Yet the Spartans, renowned in war and bound by military discipline and the severe laws of Lycurgus, have preserved longer the harsh customs handed down from their ancestors. These modes have the same characteristics. The Ionian, devoted entirely to dancing, contains much sweetness and pleasantness, almost no severity. On the contrary, the Dorian presents a certain majesty and dignity which it is easier to admire than to explain. It is very suitable for [epic] poetry, as I have myself experienced at one time as a youth in Köln in the presence of the celebrated Kaiser Maximilian and many princes, not without the reward of the merited laurel branch (which is said without boasting).[42]

In another place, however, Glarean seems to weaken any argument that the modes have specific identifiable characters, by suggesting they can be changed in character by the composer.

> Yet, it cannot be denied that antiquity has changed these modes, but undoubtedly the nature of modes can be turned in another direction, so that a mode which seems light in character can be used with not much difficulty for serious subjects (provided that a propitious talent is at hand), and on the contrary, a serious mode can be used for light subjects.[43]

It is clear from some of Glarean's comments which touch on acoustics, that he had a very perceptive ear, especially with regard to the aesthetic quality of sound. He mentions the theory of the 'music of the spheres' as argued by Servius, that the planets existed in an order of decreasing volume, ranging from Saturn, Jupiter, Mars, the Sun, Venus, Mercury to the moon which was the softest. Glarean expresses some doubts about this,[44] but has observed that a similar arrangement is true for the strings of the cithara, meaning that the highest string sounds to the ear the loudest. He understands that for music to be pleasing, aesthetically, it must be performed in reverse proportion, with the lower tones louder than the upper ones.

> There is no song more pleasing than one in which the lowest voice resounds strongly, even if the highest voice caresses the ear more sweetly; for all the upper voices turn completely into chattering if they are deprived of the strength of the lowest voice.[45]

---

42 Ibid., I, 155ff.

43 Ibid., I, 164ff.

44 Later Glarean says his mention of the 'music of the spheres' is necessary only because so many great early writers had discussed it. As for himself, he agrees with Aristotle that there is no basis in fact for this theory. 'But this indulgence is allowed to antiquity, which has thought that the human mind must be raised in every possible way to the contemplation of heavenly objects.' [Ibid., I, 136ff.]

45 Ibid., I, 122.

Poor Glarean was at heart an old fashioned Churchman, born too late. He probably did not realize that his great book on modes had come near the end of the period of their functional use for general composition. But he must have been aware that Church music was rapidly changing. He preferred simple, sincere plain chant in the Church, in part for reasons which he gives following an interesting discussion of his theory that the music of the original Christians was in the Aeolian mode.

> But now it is worthwhile to observe ... with how much simplicity, also with how much seriousness the songs of the first church musicians were undertaken, with all ostentation completely removed, with all shallowness excluded, in a word, with such grace that everyone must approve them unless he does not possess any hearing. How justly we ought to be ashamed to have degenerated in such a degree from this![46]

Later, before quoting an example of chant which he thought beautiful, he makes one of several appeals on behalf of earlier, more simple Church music.

> Now let us listen to this Prosa after we have digressed too far in an unfamiliar subject, although I would like to see much explained in this way, but by someone who could present it more learnedly; the greatness of the church fathers certainly deserves this and also the remarkable vigilance by which they have endeavored to enlighten the church and have occasioned such beautiful songs, while our time invents nothing new that is worth hearing, and not only does not understand old tradition but even laughs at it. So very pious an undertaking is deserving, I say, of some Cicero who could both praise and explain everything according to merit. It would certainly not be a heavy burden to me, if I were as able as I should like. They undoubtedly have their reward with our Savior. I fear very much that we shall undergo deserved punishment for our sloth and ingratitude.[47]

Contrary to modern music history texts, polyphonic music did not dominate the sixteenth-century scene. Outside the Church it was now regarded as archaic and the humanists were attacking it for reasons of their own. Glarean was probably not too concerned about this as he sometimes reveals his own skepticism toward polyphonic music. Speaking of the Hyperaeolian mode, he gets off track and suggests that the ancients could have written polyphonic music but elected not to. He knew that was not true, but he is carried away by his passion against modern music.

> And yet our present time, affected as it were by tedium of all kinds and seeking novelties in every possible way, has arranged songs of this mode polyphonically, and at times shows us something ingenious it thinks it has invented that had been unknown to the ancients; but in fact, antiquity had not neglected this as unknown, but as unworthy for the ears of learned men.[48]

---

46 Ibid., I, 143.

47 Ibid., I, 171.

48 Ibid., I, 150ff.

As he continues, he seems to say, if we are going to have polyphonic music, why can't it at least be in the style of those fifteenth-century masters.

> Nonetheless, one still finds songs of this sort among composers who sink to such absurdities in their immoderate thirst for fame. I believe the reason for this error is that they, while despising the ancients, are pleased only with new things; thus we seek glory at present in a way in which we absolutely should not. In poetry, it is a fine thing to follow distinguished masters, as Virgil did not hesitate to follow Theocritus, Hesiod, and Homer. Yet in music, good god, how shameful this seems to some, if anyone should attempt to follow either Josquin des Prez, nearly comparable to Virgil in this matter, or Johannes Ockeghem, a very erudite man, or Pierre de la Rue, a most pleasing musician, although these men have expressed the nature of song with ingenuity and artistry, and have justly merited surpassing praise. In fact, in our time there are those who, just as they disdain the ancients, will not examine a song unless it has just recently come from a writer, still glowing hot from the anvil, as it were. Further, since they think it unseemly to imitate anyone, however much he is learned, and since all the old modes had been used, they turn of necessity to inventing novelties which, however, are foolish and bungling.

Glarean returns to his doubts about polyphony in a lengthy discussion of the differences between what he calls *phonasci* and *symphonetae*. His meaning for these terms he gives in a letter of 1538.

> I call a *phonacus* the inventor of a simple melody in some mode, a *symphoneta* the one who adds the remaing voices.[49]

In his discussion it is touching to read of Glarean's affinity for the old chants. We also observe here his belief that talent in composition is obtained by birth, and not learned.

> As we were hastening to the end of this very toilsome book, this not entirely inconsequential thought came to our mind about a matter which I say has been considered in doubt a long time now among men of our times, that is, which is more deserving of praise, the invention of a theme or the addition of several voices; namely, so that the uninitiated may also understand, whether it is of more value if one can invent a natural tenor, which affects all minds, which takes hold of a man's heart, in short, which so clings to our memory that it often steals upon us without our even thinking, and into which we break as if awakened from sleep, as we commonly see concerning many tenors; or if one adds three or more voices to the tenor invented in the aforementioned way, which voices, so to speak, embellish it with imitations, canons, changes of modus, tempus, and prolatio …
>
> Here is an example of this matter, so that one may comprehend so much the better what we say. Whoever first invented the tenor *Te Deum laudamus* or any other as *Pange lingua*, may he not be preferred in talent to one who afterwards composed a complete Mass according to it? First, indeed, to say as a preface, we cannot deny that this happens to each through the power of his talent, and through a certain natural and native capacity rather than through art. The reason

---

49 Letter to Johannes Aal, quoted in Miller, 'The Dodecachordon,' 160.

for this seems to be that very frequently those who are untrained in music are also surprisingly proficient in inventing tenors in our vernacular, whether Celtic or German, and further, that many who are proficient in adding voices likewise have learned music badly, to say nothing of other disciplines. Therefore, it is clear that neither talent is really possible for a man unless he is born to it, and, as it is commonly said, unless he received it from his mother. This is likewise true of painters, also of sculptors, and preachers ..., in short, of all works dedicated to Minerva ...

But indeed, if as Aristotle asserts, a man is truly deserving of praise who discovers the principles of any discipline, for it is very easy to add the rest (he says), I do not see why the first artist, the simple creator of a simple melody (now called a tenor) ought to be inferior to one who does not invent as easily as he adds to what has already been invented. Indeed, we see in the various disciplines that the first inventors always have merited the most praise. Thus Hippocrates is considered superior to Galen, even though Galen surpassed him with a thousand books ... Let everyone direct his attention to the following points as the most worthy of our consideration, namely, which of the two is older, which is more useful, and, finally, which yields to the other.[50]

In continuing his plea for the older chant, Glarean now reveals two basic aesthetic principles important to him: the art which appeals to the greater number of people is the higher, and art should be judged by the intellect and not by feelings.

Moreover, since music is the mother of pleasure, I consider much more useful that which pertains to the pleasure of many than what pertains to the pleasure of a few. And when a monophonic tenor, noble, distinguished, and having suitable words, has been brought forth among men, it is pleasing to many, educated as well as uneducated. For how many are there, even among the very highly educated, who truly understand a composition of four or more voices? Indeed, all praise it when they hear it, lest one may be considered less educated if he would disparage it ...

But those who do not understand the nature of modes, as singers in general in our time, and who do not judge the import of a song except through the consonances, since they have disregarded its moods and neglected its true beauty, disparage what they do not understand. I will spare the names here. For I could name some, more uncouth than any ass, who have rejected what has been successful, and in its place have instituted so much that is absurd, so much that is stupid, that they have shown themselves to be completely insensate. But such are the customs of this age. If one wished to remove some things it would be proper to substitute others, but they should be better. But I (for I must proclaim freely what I feel), am so far from wishing church songs to die, that I declare firmly that nothing more complete has ever been created, since in it those composers have demonstrated, with the clearest evidence, learning joined together with piety; I am speaking about the collection of Masses (called the Gradual), in which they have treated all modes successfully, not only treated but also have applied them as materials for the contents, and have so expressed the innate quality of the modes, that it is apparent to those who estimate the intrinsic value of these matters not by their feelings, as now happens, but by knowledge and considered judgment, that nothing more perfect could have been created by man.

---

50 Glarean, *Dodecachordon*, I, 205ff.

Now Glarean adds a general philosophical observation, frequently found in early literature, that in life the good always seems to be inseparable from the bad.

> Abuses may be tolerated, a sore may be cut off the unharmed leg, what has crept into the turbid fountain may be pumped out. And what has ever been so happily established in this world that its downfall may not follow immediately after? So grain has cockle, a purple garment has moths, and iron is subject to rust. Observe the elements, examine what has been mingled from them, consider the individual parts of nature, what then is there, I would like to know, which does not have weakness and evil immediately following on the heels of firmness and goodness?

Now Glarean returns to his original point, that we should praise these simple chants and if necessary modernize them, rather than neglect them.

> We ought to praise the best inventions of the most blameless and saintly men, not condemn or ridicule, and then, what the ravages of time or the malignity of Satan has corrupted, amend willingly with conscientious honesty. Since there are so many in other disciplines who correct successfully what has been made false for a long time, and improve it as to worth, is not the same clearly permissible in sacred songs? For which is of greater consequence, to have lost what pertains to the pomp of the world, or what pertains to the praise of Almighty God? Not to speak of this, that nothing is equally as useful in forming the speech of children as that pure music. For the other music exists in great measure for the comprehension of the few ... So here also in our times we see it happen that some who rejected church song have despaired of being able to invent anything like it themselves, and have given up entirely, while others have substituted such unsuitable harmonies for the psalms we sing that frequently their folly and stupidity completely amazes me.

Glarean concludes this long defense of chant by pointing to two specific objections he finds in those cases where chant has been turned into polyphony. First, he suggests that this is done sometimes just because the singers are ashamed to sing something so routine as a tenor and want to be heard in the higher voices. This he condemns as arrogance and vanity, 'as the perversity of singers is usually called.' Second, he complains of the unsuccessful attempts he has apparently heard in the improvisation of polyphony over a chant.

> For how often do you find, I should like to know, three or even two who will sing polyphony with you? I speak from experience, for something is always intervening at these times, some weariness or trouble is always at hand. Those who are skilled in this matter want to be asked, but one who does not understand it stands by, somewhat downcast, while the others are singing, either because he wished he were also able to sing or because he was ashamed that he had not learned this skill, or because he disdains what he neither understands nor attains; those who have progressed in this skill to some extent but are not sure of themselves, and their number is great, repeatedly make errors in singing, which produces great disgust among the skilled. Thus it is rare that even three can harmonize together in this manner.[51]

---
51 Ibid., I, 209.

We should mention that in another place Glarean objects to a different kind of improvisation, where singers improvise at the end of a chant, cadencing on the wrong tone. Which, he says, 'certain singers plainly do for pleasure ... and to turn up their noses at the listener.' Then he adds, somewhat sarcastically,

> But someone will say that nobody is so stupid not to understand that a song is corrupted in this way. Well, why then does the corruption generally occur in the Nicene Creed, also in the Lord's Prayer, and has no one at all observed this? Is the ear really more discerning in our time than formerly?[52]

If Glarean is thus discouraged at the lack of popularity of the old chants, in the following chapter he also is discouraged with contemporary efforts to compose. He seems to be aware, by ear at least, that the old modal system was turning into the major–minor system we know today. Hence he wants chant which sounds more like a popular song. Therefore, he issues a challenge. Based on the information he has given, Glarean asks one,

> to see if he can invent a harmony, or as it is usually said, a tenor, according to some form of a song in these odes, which tenor will sound sweetly in the ears, with words added suitably, and which will take hold of the heart and leave keen stimuli in the soul of the listener, in which the strength of its nature seems to have been expressed, and lastly, into which the mind of man may sometimes break, as if aroused from sleep, just as we mentioned in the preceding chapter. Although I cannot do this, as I have not been endowed with any such gift of talent, yet I shall not desist from encouraging others to attempt this ... Nevertheless, I see this attempted by many in our times, but very unsuccessfully, since they were entirely ignorant of the nature of the modes, and, relying only upon the freedom of their own practice, brought forth without any discernment whatever came into their mind. I am speaking about those who in this time have set four-voice songs to the Horatian odes, in which one finds absolutely no trace of distinguished talent, aside from the harmony. I am looking for a tenor which one may sing either by himself or to others, or which many may sing together, but as one, just as is customary with hymns and psalms in the choir.[53]

Having devoted his first two books to chant, Glarean now turns to polyphonic music. However, as we have indicated above, his heart was not really in this style and thus his explanations are relatively brief and taken mostly from the theorist Franchinus. He excuses his brevity by noting that there is no precedence for this style in antiquity and neither does he recognize anyone distinguished after Josquin.

As a mathematician, he was undoubtedly disturbed by the lack of universal practice in polyphonic music. He finds some symbols, such as the maxima, no longer in use and seems uncomfortable that the entire system of mensuration has no example in antiquity and is

---

52   Ibid., I, 196.
53   Ibid., I, 209ff.

a matter 'almost dependent on the decision of ordinary singers.'[54] He also finds the whole question of the beat and tempo a practice which varies from country to country.[55] In this regard the reason he gives for the alle-breve symbol is interesting.

> Whenever musicians wish to accelerate the *tactus*, which they consider should be done when they believe the hearing is fatigued, namely, in order to remove weariness, they draw a line downwards through the circle or semicircle.[56]

It is also interesting that he finds the idea of proportions largely ignored in practice. He admits there have been learned and complex treatises explaining this metrical system, but he says,

> Art ought to be transmitted as the art exists. But even the subject now proclaims that the observance of so many proportions is superfluous; no one, however much he is trained in song, can bear these in mind, and none of the most learned musicians of our time has deigned to adopt them, excepting a very few, in a composition, since there is greater trouble in learning them than there is sweetness or grace in singing them.[57]

Glarean now presents what must have been the most valued portion of his treatise at the time, a lengthy collection of actual music demonstrating the modes he had discussed at length earlier. But before he presents this music, once again he expresses his own doubts about polyphony, especially music in more than four-parts, which he believes was composed,

> not so much for aural pleasure as for the ostentation of the talented. For it could scarcely be possible that the human intellect, distracted by so many and varied sounds, could follow carefully all voices simultaneously ... Indeed, in my opinion, a distinguished [composer] can show the vigor of his talent no less in writing two or three voices than in the accumulation and chattering of many voices. I know it appears otherwise to others, nor do I reprove anyone's judgment; moreover, one may follow what one wishes, and I have stated my opinion.[58]

It is interesting that he was under the impression that polyphony began only about seventy years earlier (he seems unaware of Palestrina).

> But unfortunately, this art has now reached such unrestraint that learned men are almost wearied of it, and this has many causes, but especially, since it is ashamed to follow in the footsteps of

---

54 Ibid., II, 230.
55 Ibid., II, 232.
56 Ibid., II, 234.
57 Ibid., II, 242.
58 Ibid., II, 248. Interestingly, he says he omits from his collection a five-part 'Stabat mater' by Josquin, because everyone owns a copy of it.

predecessors who observed the relations of modes exactly, because we have fallen into a certain other distorted song which is in no way pleasing, unless because it is new.[59]

Having just written a book on the nature of the modes, this was, of course, of utmost importance to Glarean.

I am accustomed to consider as monstrous conceptions the songs which exceed the nature of a mode, and one finds many of such a kind everywhere.[60]

The one composer of polyphony whom Glarean praises above all others was Josquin, especially because he 'has never brought forth anything which was not pleasant to the ears.' But even Josquin was not above criticism.

But in many instances he lacked a proper measure and a judgment based on knowledge and thus in some places in his songs he did not fully restrain as he ought to have, the impetuosity of a lively talent, although this ordinary fault may be condoned because of the otherwise incomparable gifts of the man.[61]

As Glarean looks over the entire field of polyphonic composers, he finds, apart from the question of following his modal rules, a diversity of purpose.

Of these then there have been some (for such a kind must be mentioned briefly) who have composed solely for the ostentation of their own ability, and these are by far the largest crowd; others have composed in order to please the many and some to train the youth. Some have composed in order to support the majesty of ecclesiastical song. One also finds some who compose in this art in order to relieve their own compulsion and there are very many of these.[62]

For all of the questions which Glarean has raised about polyphonic music, in several of the descriptions he provides for the music he presents in his collection he reveals that he could in fact be deeply moved by such music. It is more significant that, having said several times that one must judge music by the intellect and not by feelings, we cannot help but observe that the works which move him most do so only by the emotions! For example, an elegy of Magdalene by Michael de Verona, Glarean hears as,

possessing great emotion and innate sweetness and tremendous power, so that one really believes he hears the weeping of a woman and her following ... At the end, through a certain confident hope, it rises so magnificently and is lifted to the heights with such tremendous exultation, and

---

59 Ibid., II, 248.
60 Ibid., II, 251.
61 Ibid., II, 264.
62 Ibid., II, 271.

then again, as if wearied and self-reproachful for immoderate joy, it falls back into deep and customary weeping.[63]

And similarly, he mentions a *Planxit autem David* by Josquin, intended for the mourner, whom Glarean finds,

at first is wont to cry out frequently, and then, turning gradually to melancholy complaints, to murmur subduedly and presently to subside, and sometimes, when emotion breaks forth anew to raise his voice again and to emit a cry ...[64]

In conclusion, Glarean presents a summary of his aesthetic values in Church music. Interestingly enough, he makes here a very rare Renaissance reference to humor in music.

I should like here to confess this about myself, namely, that we have always been displeased when all trivial songs have been composed, which offer nothing but a certain chattering and which allure the ears of the foolish, songs of a sort as are those pieces of patchwork poorly served together; then chiefly displeasing are wanton and shameful songs which now unfortunately sound through all Christian nations, which are everywhere filled with them. I desire [Church] song to be dignified, and directed to the greater honor of God, not to ostentation. I desire it to assist honorable pleasure. Finally, I desire it to be turned to the cultivation of talent, and especially to forming the stammering mouths of children.

Song has been sought and invented for the sake of pleasure, but it can be useful for many things besides; from this I do not exclude jesting, provided that it may be mature and honorable. Moreover, jesting is more praiseworthy and has true merit if it occurs with dignity and is selected for a favorable moment.[65]

ADRIAN COCLICO, *COMPENDIUM MUSICES* (1552)

The Flemish theorist Coclico was engaged as a music teacher at the university in Wittenberg in 1545. Although he remained only a brief time, due to lack of funds, he was popular not only with students but with Melanchthon. Coclico has left a very important treatise from this period, in so far as it documents the shift away from the old Scholastic complexities of speculative music to the more modern emphasis on expressive, practical musicianship.[66] In this work, written for the training of boys, he constantly warns against merely following the

---

63 Ibid., II, 258ff.
64 Ibid., II, 269.
65 Ibid., II, 284.
66 In Adrian Coclico, *Compendium Musices*, trans. Albert Seay (Colorado Springs: Colorado College Music Press, 1973), 30, Seay writes, 'Music by 1550 was less and less of a liberal art and more and more a fine art, while theory had begun to lose most of its speculative character in favor of the purely practical.'

rules. Indeed, in his 'Preface to Nordic Youth' he suggests that traditional books on music do not even treat what he calls the 'art' of music, 'which is seen more in practice than in rules.'[67]

In this Preface, Coclico also makes a statement for which this book is best known among modern musicologists. He has written this book,

> to bring back into the light that music which they praise as *reservata* from the masses ...

No one today knows for certain what this term means, other than some style not appreciated by the general public. We believe it probably refers to some form of sophistication probably based largely on improvisation.[68]

Coclico begins by stating his purpose as teaching 'correct, smooth and elegant singing.'

> I see today German youth not only ignorant of the traditions of music, of which many praises will be expounded elsewhere, but also ruined and kept back from the true force and reason of singing. As long as they pass over the memorizing of precepts, for them to learn to sing rapidly and correctly cannot be done.[69]

He quickly adds a significant qualification to the last sentence, noting,

> I would say that whoever keeps his students too long on precepts and theory lacks judgment and evidently is ignorant of the goal of music.

Coclico, no doubt from experience, is quite specific regarding the qualities which the student must bring to his study. He again stresses that it is performance not speculative music which produces a musician.

> First, adolescents or better, boys, ... should bring to their teacher a great zeal and desire for learning music, together with their natural enthusiasm, so that they may listen as eagerly and attentively as possible to whoever teaches and guides. For, if anyone by his nature is perhaps more estranged from the love of music or he may not have wanted to learn what he should, I cannot sensibly promise great things for him. He, however, who is possessed by a certain single-minded zeal for learning and does not have forces of nature repelling him from music, if they have molded him skillfully and carefully, this person I hold myself committed that he will be an excellent musician. In a Greek proverb it is beautifully stated: Love teaches music. Then, if the boy has this proposed goal for himself, so that he will become a better performer than theorist, I would not want to load him down with many precepts and almost overwhelm him. He who

---

67 Ibid., 1.

68 Gustave Reese, in *Music in the Renaissance* (New York: Norton, 1959), 511ff, reviews the few other sixteenth-century references to this term, as well as some modern deduction, but comes to no firm conclusion as to what this term meant in the sixteenth century.

69 Coclico, *Compendium Musices*, 5.

wishes first to explore all the reasonings of speculative music and turns himself to this rather than to singing; he will, in my opinion, only arrive at the hoped for and preset goal much later on.[70]

Later he adds an observation which might be found in any era,

> But I do not know how it happens that our youth not only despises work and does not submit well to good recommendations, but even grows angry.[71]

Coclico promises his book will give the necessary rules and knowledge which the student needs, but he seems eager to get beyond this to the purpose of the study. It is particularly important that he defines this purpose here as being to give pleasure and to exhilarate the listener, as well as stressing that it is the *ear* which must judge.

> When he has learned these things clearly and rapidly, he will then begin to sing, not only as [the music] is written but also with embellishments, and to pronounce skillfully, smoothly and meaningfully, to intone correctly and to place any syllable in its proper place under the right notes.
>
> As a singer, he will study especially how to please the ears of men and how to inspire pleasure in them, as well as admiration and favor for himself. He will also be continually guided by the judgment of his ears. The ears easily understand what is done correctly or badly and are truly the masters of the art of singing. What difference is there, I ask, between a dog's barking and he who does not hear or does not notice what and how he sings?
>
> To be avoided are the vices of certain nations, which, if they stay in us, must be corrected by zeal and industry. Insane clamor and huge roaring and that noise like the voice of certain ignorant men, lacks grace. While they weep, scream or bark, they please no one, they take away all pleasure from their hearers and deprive themselves of praise. A smooth song truly seeks this end, which the musician looks and hunts for, namely, to delight and to exhilarate.[72]

Almost as an afterthought, Coclico provides his credentials. His own study was with that 'most noble musician, Josquin,' from whom he learned 'incidentally, from no book.'

Now Coclico sets the framework for the 'rules' portion of his book by explaining that he divides musicians into four categories. We read his discussion as a virtual history of music, with a clear emphasis on the values of the sixteenth century. The first were the original musicians who discovered music, including Greek mythical figures, figures from the Old Testament and medieval theorists. These, he says, 'were only theorists.'[73]

The second type he calls mathematicians, and seems to have in mind the polyphonic Church composers of the fifteenth century. Everyone knows their compositions, he admits,

---

70 Ibid., 5ff.
71 Ibid., 7.
72 Ibid., 6.
73 Ibid., 8.

> But these men did not pursue the goal of music. Even if they understand the force of this art and also compose, they do not honor the smoothness and sweetness of song. What is worse, when they hope to spread their invented art widely and make it more outstanding, they rather defile and obscene it. In teaching precepts and speculation they have specialized excessively and, in accumulating a multitude of symbols and other things, they have introduced many difficulties. Disputing much a long time, they never arrived at the true rationality of singing.

The third type are the most outstanding musicians, who 'join theory and practice in the best and learned way.' These men, among whom he lists numerous sixteenth-century composers, understand 'how to embellish melodies, to express in them all the emotions of all kinds.'

The fourth type he calls poets, but he means those artistic singers who compose, improvise and sing 'smoothly, ornately and artfully for the delight of men.' He adds that he finds such singers particularly in France and Belgium and, once more, stresses that such ability rests more upon the practical than the theoretical.

Coclico now begins the theoretical portion of his book, but he repeatedly renews his criticism of rules-based learning. No sooner has he begun writing of scales, than he stops and observes that this can only be understood in performance.

> I have wished to train this boyish industry in music through but few words and precepts on that account, so that no youth running to the books of musician–mathematicians will waste his life in reading them and never arrive at the goal of singing well.[74]

Similarly, he barely introduces his discussion of mensural rules, when he promises to leave out 'a mass of definitions, lest boys staying for a longer time on precepts arrive too late at the purpose of singing well.'

> For this reason I do not cease to dissuade [students] from remaining tied to the prolix writings of musician–mathematicians who have drawn up so many types of signs of augmentation and diminution, from which no fruit, but rather controversy and discord arises.[75]

Having made this digression, he continues with some fascinating first-hand observations. Of great importance here is his emphasis on learning through performance itself, rather than through the conceptualization of music.

> In Belgian cities, where prizes are given to singers and, because of the prizes to be gained, no procedure or labor is undertaken unless it pertains to the goal of singing well, no music is written down or prescribed by precept.
> My teacher, Josquin des Près, never rehearsed or wrote out any musical procedures, yet in a short time made perfect musicians, since he did not hold his students back in long and frivolous

---

74 Ibid., 10.
75 Ibid., 16.

precepts, but taught precepts in a few words at the same time as singing through exercise and practice …

Josquin did not judge everyone capable of the demands of composition. He felt that it should be taught only to those who were driven by an unusual force of their nature to this most beautiful art.[76]

Once again, after giving his subject as the rules of prolations, he is able to produce only two sentences before returning to his chief concern.

I have wanted something here planned for adolescents so that they will not stick to the books of musician–mathematicians, who have contrived an infinite number of other signs and have turned away the souls of adolescents from the true use of music, making something clear in itself obscure, as when they write so many things about proportions of minor inequality, or sesquitertia.[77]

Coclico again interrupts his presentation of the rules of composition, this time to comment on the qualities of the fine singer. He first recommends that the student choose a teacher who sings beautifully and smoothly, who sings by,

special natural instinct and makes Music joyful by the ornaments of [improvisation], at the same time omitting throat clearings, shouting and other absurdities, leading most noble Music into the hatred of men.[78]

He again points to Belgium and France as the most likely source for fine singing and observes that in Germany the knowledge of such singing is rarely found. He cautions that the singing must come from the throat and that the student will not be able to do this unless he 'sweats and works a great deal.'

When discussing counterpoint, Coclico implies that in Germany polyphonic music had become unpopular among many musicians.

If anyone makes mention of counterpoint and demands it in a perfect musician, they destroy it with a more than snarling distaste, impudently asserting it as truth that many improper and corrupt types [of intervals] occur in counterpoint, ones that offend the ears and have no place in compositions.

Coclico admits the basic contention, but finds the reason for their views in their improper appreciation of the style.

I agree that counterpoint offends their ears, for theirs are like those of asses, to whom nothing is agreeable except that which they produce as braying or makes a sound like braying. If it has

---

76 Ibid., 16.

77 Ibid., 18.

78 Ibid., 20.

> offended the ears of men, why not more those of Josquin, Pierre de la Rue and their successors, whose ears were most delicate? …
>
> But knowledge has no enemy except the ignorant and, since the despisers of this art are ignorant of the practice of music, their foolishness easily adds many allies.
>
> A boy should curse the perverse judgment of these men as utter nonsense, and, as with the prince-singers, should hold as true that he will never become a perfect musician without the knowledge and use of counterpoint.[79]

Later he mentions that Josquin compared those inferior in counterpoint to trying to fly without wings.

After a brief discussion of intervals, Coclico briefly mentions improvisation, which he recommends should first be studied in note to note practice of the intervals, followed by more 'florid counterpoint.'[80] This art, he advises, requires constant practice. Later, he gives ability in improvisation even more weight.

> The first requirement of a good singer is that he should know how to sing counterpoint by improvisation. Without this he will be nothing.[81]

Perhaps because of the rules he has been presenting, Coclico now pauses to make the point that the urge to compose must be an inspired compulsion, not simply the next step after learning the necessary rules.

> [The Student] should be led to composing by a great desire, and by a certain natural impulse he will be driven to composition, so that he will not taste food nor drink until his piece is finished, for, since this natural impulse so drives him, he accomplishes more in one hour than others in a whole month. Composers to whom these unusual motivations are absent are useless.[82]

Returning to the art of singing, Coclico mentions the difficulties in singing multi-part polyphony. One must learn how to do this by study with a practical musician, otherwise 'he will leave in shame and be laughed at.' And, he adds, 'even if [the student] reads books for ten years, he will not advance at all without use and practice.'

Finally, we should point out that this book was published with two poems on music, which are important for their contemporary observations on the purpose and values of music. The first poem, by 'Griselius, a scholar of Wittenberg,' begins by praising the value of music for worship, for which the poet says it was first invented. More interesting are his views of how music affects the listener.

---

79 Ibid., 21.
80 Ibid., 23.
81 Ibid., 24.
82 Ibid.

She moves the emotions and not only softens breasts,
But also she influences the fibers of a living heart.
She frees hearts burdened by sad sorrow,
Often she takes away useless fears.

She will give to an afflicted mind sweet solace,
She also produces terror, when she wants it to be.
She takes away swollen pride from the breasts of men,
She does not permit us to have had cruel hands.

She calls forth overrunning sighs from an affected heart.
Often she causes eyes to grow wet with tears.
She controls illicit fevers of a passionate body
And, like a bridle, rules our breasts …

Let Music be the most esteemed in your studies,
For without it you cannot have the name of learned …

The second poem, by 'Noe Bucholczer' begins by praising the god, Jupiter, to whom he attributes the gift of music, and then offers more practical values.

She takes away our cares and brings back happy joys,
She amuses the young and the infirm aged,
She arouses the sweaty bodies of laborers,
Sleep overcomes the limbs of children by her song …

6 MUSIC PRACTICE IN THE GERMAN-SPEAKING COUNTRIES

GENERAL MUSIC HISTORY TEXTS usually give the impression that Renaissance music consisted primarily of unaccompanied Church polyphony. Only a moment's thought should tell one that this could not be a full accounting. What follows will perhaps give the reader some hint of the extensive music making which is not discussed in traditional music texts. In Germany much of this music was wind music, for, as Reese accurately points out,[1] winds were predominant until after the middle of the sixteenth century. This can be documented as well by Köchel reports that strings do not appear in the musical establishment of the emperor in Vienna until 1566.[2] Strings were introduced for the first time in the North German court of the Elector Johann Georg in 1571–1598.[3] When one considers that nobles sought out the best wind players available, even internationally, and contemporary accounts indicate they played the 'best pieces,' one has to ask, Why is virtually none of the following found in the famous Reese book? Why has this material been omitted from Grout?

On the other hand, one cannot pretend that culture in sixteenth-century Germany was by any means comparable to that found in Italy. We have mentioned above the worry expressed by John Schöner in 1533,

> You know the times. No one really looks for a rebirth of the arts. They are so silent and neglected, it may well be feared that dolts will stamp them out.[4]

His concern was focused more on the civic strife following the beginning of the Reformation, but by 'dolt' he was clearly thinking of the German nobles. And, again, it is certainly true that the general run of aristocracy in Germany consisted of a much rougher and unsophisticated man that his counterpart in Italy or France. We think the reader might best be introduced to the German noble by a few descriptions of his favorite pastime, hunting.

Albert V of Munich, between 1555 and 1579, personally slew 4,483 deer, 525 boar, 150 foxes and 2 bears. In the year 1564, he devoted no fewer than 103 days to hunting.[5] Philipps von

---

1 Gustave Reese, *Music in the Renaissance* (New York: Norton, 1959), 690.
2 Ludwig Ritter von Köchel, *Kaiserliche Hof-Musikkapelle in Wien von 1543–1867* (Hildesheim, 1976), 20.
3 Grove, *Dictionary* (1980), II, 566.
4 John Schöner, dedication in the 1533 publication of Johann Müller's *On Triangles* (1464), quoted in *Regiomontanus on Triangles*, trans Barnabas Hughes (Madison: The University of Wisconsin Press, 1967), 25.
5 Johannes Janssen, *History of the German People After the Close of the Middle Ages*, trans. A. Christie (New York, 1966), XV, 207.

Hessen was another who referred to slaughter as hunting. In a letter of 1559 to Duke Christopher of Württemburg, he writes complaining,

> At this boar hunt we had fine sport ... and caught over 1,120 boars. We had intended to have 60 more field days, but as we found that the boars had become thin, we did not go on hunting.[6]

Any starving peasant caught hunting on Philipps' land, however, was given severe punishment, the least of which was having the arms tied behind and being drawn upwards by a rope, pulling the arms backwards over the head, and left hanging.[7]

Moritz, Landgraf of Hesse-Cassel, was another great hunter. We can see how serious this activity was for the sixteenth-century German noble in the authority given Moritz's court official in charge. This Master Huntsman once shot a peasant who had lingered behind in the chase, struck off an ear of another who came up late with his hounds and slashed in two the head of a third. He was only brought to justice when he made the unfortunate mistake of addressing Moritz in an impolite manner.[8]

Similarly, to the North, Joachim II of Brandenburg issued an order that anyone taking a deer or pig from his forest would have both eyes put out. Taking a rabbit would result in having a hare branded on the cheek of the poacher! Christian I of Saxony on a single hunt, on October 4, 1562, according to his own statement, personally killed '539 wild swine.' In the year 1565 he personally killed 330 deer. To put the starving poacher at a disadvantage, he ordered that all dogs belonging to the peasants who entered his fields must first have a forefoot cut off![9] Christian was also a notorious drinker, and once wrote Prince Hans George of Anhalt,

> The reason why this letter is so stupid and badly written is that I have not yet altogether got over the last splendid orgy, and my hands tremble so that I can scarcely hold my pen.[10]

A few of these noble gentlemen were unusually interested in music, and when that was the case they devoted large amounts of money to assembling consorts of instruments. One of the prominent German princes of the sixteenth century was Moritz, Landgraf of Hesse-Cassel, whose interest in music is documented by his personal instrument collection of 44 strings, 10 keyboards and 142 wind instruments.[11] According to Henry Peacham, a contemporary, Moritz was also a composer.

---

6   Ibid., 202.

7   Ibid., 219.

8   Ibid., 212.

9   Ibid., 217.

10 Ibid., 233.

11 Anthony Baines, 'Two Cassel Inventories,' *The Galpin Society Journal* 4(June 1951): 32ff, http://www.jstor.org/stable/841260.

But above others who carrieth away the palm for excellency, not only in music, but in whatsoever is to be wished in a brave prince, is the yet-living Maurice, Landgrave of Hesse, of whose own composition I have seen eight or ten several sets of motets and solemn music set purposely for his own chapel, where, for the great honor of some festival, and many times for his recreation only, he is his own organist. Besides, he readily speaketh ten or twelve several languages. He is so universal a scholar that, coming, as he doth often, to his University of Marburg, what questions soever he meeteth with set up, as the manner is in the German and our universities, he will extempore dispute an hour or two, even in boots and spurs, upon them with their best professors. I pass over his rare skill in chirurgery, he being generally accounted the best bone-setter in the country.[12]

Another visiting Englishman describes him as follows:

His education prince-like, generally known in all things, and excellent in many, seasoning his grave and more important studies for ability in judgment, with studies of pastime for retiring, as in poetrie, musike, and the mathemitikes; and for ornament in discourse in the languages, French, Italian and English.[13]

We must assume this was written under a diplomatic necessity for exaggeration, for Moritz was also a drunk, spendthrift and egotist. Once on a visit to Berlin, he left for Spandau so drunk 'he could scarcely find the gate of the town.' On another visit to Berlin he traveled with a personal escort of 3,000 horses.[14]

Moritz was not so liberal when it came to his subjects, as we can see in one of his letters of 1600 when he speaks with disparagement of the middle class tradesmen who populated his domain.

On work days the masters and the journey men flock in shoals to christenings, weddings and wine bouts, and when they cannot go to these they drink brandy punch in the morning and go to beer parties in the taverns in the afternoon; all this time the buyers must wait for the sellers ... until the guild gentlemen have drunk themselves out, and then they must pay for the bespoken goods at whatever rate it pleases the besotted vendors to ask ... The handicraftsman does not provide for his house and his children, but for his own stomach, he invests his coins in liquid wares, and when he cannot wash his mouth with wine, or foreign beer, he must have roast capon ... when Monday comes they haven't a farthing left in their purses; then the lounge about idly in the market places, stare at the windows, fall to gossiping and chattering, or indulge in idlers' pastimes, which are profitable neither to civic life nor to the art of war, such as target shooting, nine-pins, football and other trumpery, whereby they often commit thefts, murders, and all kinds of misdeeds.[15]

---

12 Henry Peacham, *The Complete Gentleman*, ed. Virgil Heltzel (Ithaca: Cornell University Press, 1962), 111ff.

13 Edward Monings, quoted in Nichols, *The Progresses and Public Processions of Queen Elizabeth* (London, 1805), III.

14 Janssen, *History of the German People*, XV, 249 and 300.

15 Ibid., 122ff.

Perhaps the German duke who was most interested and knowledgable about music was Duke Albert of Prussia, who reigned in the second half of the century. From about 1540 he began to enlarge his musical establishment and there are numerous extant letters of his, to a number of instrument makers, dealing with these purchases.[16] For example, in December 1541, he purchased from Sebald von Thyll in Nürnberg twelve German trumpets, twelve 'Welch' (Italian) trumpets, a tenor and bass pomhart, two Welch cornetts, six cornetts 'voiced together, as well as mouthpieces for his trombones. A letter, written to the duke by the famous Nürnberg instrument maker, Georg Neuschel, in 1542, is very interesting.

> In addition I have a fine case of crumhorns, ten in all; the tenors also have keys and are made like the large one which is blown with a brass tube.

Correspondence between Albert and Neuschel reveals that the duke knew his instruments and was a tough bargainer when it came to prices. In an attempt to settle a dispute over prices in 1541, Neuschel writes that he has some less expensive instruments which he has acquired in Lyons and Venice, including a silver trombone, four ivory Zwergpfeiffen, five ivory cornetts, and some '*schreyendt peiffen*, which are much louder than the pumhart.'

Albert's interest in music must have been well known, for the composer Thomas Stoltzer, a court composer in Hungary, sent the duke one of his compositions especially arranged in order that it could be performed by the duke's crumhorns. In a letter attached to the manuscript, Stoltzer writes,

> It occurred to me in this work to specially serve your Lordship, to whom I owe all I have, and so I have thought of crumhorns and thus have set the psalm so that it completely suits them, which is not the case with every composition and especially those with many voices. However I have written the extra discant in the last section with some notes which do not suit them. This part can be omitted or played with another instrument or the human voice ... Since, your Lordship, I have thought to arrange the first part so that it suits crumhorns and lest I appear wanting, I am also sending your Lordship a Latin psalm, 'Exultabo te.'[17]

An important part of Duke Albert's wind band library is extant in a set of seven part-books containing 149 compositions.[18] Other extant works which should perhaps be associated with this court are the *Etliche Teutsche Liedlein*, by Paul Kugelmann and the *Concentus novi* by Johann Kugelmann, who calls himself 'concert trumpeter' [*tubicinae symphoniarum*].

Another noble who seems to have had an active musical establishment was the Elector August of Saxony. Duke Albert of Bavaria had written to August inquiring about the crumhorns he had heard in the elector's wind band when it performed at a meeting of the

---

16 Many of these details are recorded in Maria Federman, *Musik und Musikpflege zur Zeit herzog Albrechts* (Kassel, 1932).

17 Otto Johannes Gombosi, ed., *Das Chorwerk*, Nr. 6 (Wolfenbüttel, 1930).

18 Copenhagen (DK:Kk), MS. Gamle kongelige Samling, 1872/4, missing one part-book.

electors in Frankfurt in 1562. The elector answered this with a letter dated 13 May 1563, in which we find,

> When Your Lordship kindly asked us in an enclosed note to inform you where the crumhorns can be obtained, such as you heard in our band in Frankfurt, our instrumentalists and other servants have reported that some time ago our dear late brother elector Moritz ... bought these crumhorns from a merchant in Nürnberg and that they are said to have been made in Memmingen ... Our instrumentalists have no other information except that the cardinal of Trent also has a case full of crumhorns of this type which are supposed to be better than ours.[19]

During this century which we associate with the consort, an ensemble of like instruments, variety in tonal color was achieved through merely exchanging one consort for another. Hence, although most nobles employed only a small number of players, they sometimes have extensive inventories of actual instruments. A case in point was Duke Ludwig III of Württemburg, who reigned in Stuttgart from 1568 to 1593. In the year 1589 he employed 11 instrumentalists, 11 singers and 2 trumpet players, yet his instrument inventory lists 39 viols and vast numbers of wind instruments, as for example 220 flutes, 48 recorders, 113 cornetts and 14 crumhorns.[20] Similarly, an inventory of the instrument collection of the Hessian court at Kassel in 1573 lists 16 strings, 3 keyboards and 67 winds[21] and one of Christian I of Saxony included 120 wind instruments alone.[22] The inventory of Moritz, Landgraf of Hesse-Cassel, included separate consorts of *Bombartten*, bassoons, *Schriari*, *Bassanelli*, flutes, shawms, pommern, *Zwerchflöten*, *Zwerchpfeiffen*, white cornetts (separate consorts in three different pitches), black cornetts, *Krumbhörner*, *Racqueten* and trombones, to mention the winds alone.

Another collection which reflects this extraordinary variety was that of archduke Ferdinand II of Innsbruck. An inventory made after his death in 1595,[23] lists 37 violas de Gamba, 4 old 'Zitern,' and the following wind instruments:

27 trumpets
20 trombones, including 1 quart, 6 tenor and 2 bass
23 cornetts, 8 white and 15 black, including a discant, 6 tenor and 2 bass
5 unidentified bass wind instruments
8 sordune, including discant, tenor and bass
17 French fifes, including 4 discant, 5 tenor, 4 bass, 2 great bass, and 2 Zwerchpfeifen 'for concerts'
7 old German fifes, including 1 small discant, 12 discant, 3 tenor and 2 bass

---

19 R. Kade, 'Antonius Scandellus (1517–1580). Ein Beitrag zur Geschichte der Dresdener Hofkapelle,' in *Sammelbande der Internationalen Musikgesellschaft* (1913/1914), XV, 554.

20 Bossert, *Württemburgisches Vierteljahrheft für Landegeschichte* (1912) and Detlef Altenburg, *Untersuchungen zur Geschichte der Trumpete im Zeitalter der Clarinblaskunst* (Regensburg, 1973), I, 19.

21 Baines, 'Two Cassel Inventories,' 31ff.

22 Peter Panoff, *Militärmusik in Geschichte und Gegenwart* (Berlin, 1944), 74.

23 Walter Senn, *Musik und Theater am Hof zu Innsbruck* (Innsbruck, 1954), 166ff.

11 Zwerchpfeifen, including 2 tenor and 2 bass
6 bagpipes, including 1 discant, 3 tenor, 1 bass and 1 undesignated
6 flutes, including 2 discant, 3 tenor and one bass 'to be used with the trumpets'
1 great flute, 'to be used in concerts'
6 *Instrument per Concerta*, including 2 large flutes, 2 curtals, and 2 Zwerchpfeifen
12 shawms, including 3 discant, 4 tenor, 2 bass and 3 great bass
8 *Tolzanae*, including 2 discant, 4 tenors and 2 bass
1 dulzian
5 *Cabassi*, including 3 tenor and 2 bass
2 small drums
3 pair of timpani

ART MUSIC

The court in Munich appears to have employed primarily functional music until the sixteenth century. Even as late as 1514, a listing of the entire musical establishment shows ten trumpets and a drummer, together with three 'instrumentalists' and six singers.[24] With the employment of Ludwig Senfl, however, true art music begins to occur. Sandberger says of this period,

> It was the prevailing condition that zinks and trombones took over the performance of the works of Josquin, Isaac, Brumel, Mouton, and Willaert.[25]

The wind players in Munich, like the Renaissance itself, seem to have come primarily from Italy. One document speaks of a Hieronymus of Udine and his two brothers, described as Italian cornetto players [*Welch zink* players], visiting the court in Innsbruck.[26] Another document, in the hand of Hans Jakob Fugger, artistic advisor to the court, mentions the 'Bassani brothers,' in reference to a case of twelve crumhorns.[27]

The 1568 wedding banquet of Duke Albert of Bavaria to Renate von Lothringen began with trumpet fanfares, followed by a performance of the eight-part 'Battle music' by Annibale Padovano played as a 'concert' for the guests to listen to before the first course.[28]

The wedding of his son William, to Renée of Lorraine, also in 1568, shocked the government with its cost of 190,000 gulden.[29] After the banquet, which featured two hundred

---

24 M. Ruhnke, *Beiträge zu einer Geschichte der deutschen Hofmusikkollegien im 16. Jahrhundert* (Berlin, 1963), 251.

25 Adolf Sandberger, *Beiträge zur Geschichte der bayr. Hofkapelle unter Orlando di Lasso* [1894–1895], (Leipzig: 1894).

26 Walter Senn, *Musik und Theater am Hof zu Innsbruck* (Innsbruck, 1954), 148. See also Grove, *Dictionary*, XII, 615.

27 B. Wallner, 'Ein Instrumentenverzeichnis aus dem 16. Jahrhundert,' in *Festschrift zum 50. Geburtstag Adolf Sandberger* (Müchen, 1918), 277.

28 Quoted in Otto Kindeldey, *Orgel und Klavier in der Musik des 16. Jahrhundert* (1910).

29 Janssen, *History of the German People*, XV, 326. William, one of the few nobles known to always be sober, complained in 1587 of disorderly peasant weddings which resulted in 'hallooing, shouting and yelling, and rioting' in the church. [Ibid., 404]

different dishes, a concert was given which included the 'Providebam dominum' of Lassus, performed by cornetts and trombones, and a composition in twenty-four parts played by eight viols, eight violas, curtal, cornemusa, mute cornett, alto cornett, tenor cornett, flute, dolzaina and trombone.[30]

Sometimes special music, such as the *sonadas* mentioned by Praetorius, was performed by the aristocratic trumpet ensembles before the food was served at banquets. An interesting example of this is mentioned in a letter of 1584 by the Duke of Graz. His sister had heard such a performance and wrote to the duke asking for a copy of the music. The duke answered that this was impossible, as the music was not notated.[31] We might mention that beginning with the reign of the Emperor Maximilian II (1564–1576), the court records begin to distinguish between 'musical' trumpet players and 'not musical' ones. This is generally taken to mean a distinction between those who read music and those who only play memorized repertoire.[32]

All the German nobles had these trumpet corps, which must have followed them everywhere. One interesting eyewitness recalls hearing such an ensemble at the 1500 marriage of Duke Johann von Sachsen and Sofie von Mecklenburg in Torgau.

> With great joy the participating guests noticeably listened when the trumpets, in an old custom and tradition, blew the Passamezzo and Saltarella.[33]

Finally, all of the aristocratic musical establishments were considered to be a kind of aural symbol of the noble, much as his coat-of-arms was a visual symbol. Therefore we must assume they sometimes made out-of-court appearances on his behalf. To cite only one such example, there is an account from 14 March 1521, of the trombone consort of the Emperor Ferdinand I appearing in the palace of Margaret of Austria, regent for the Low Countries.[34]

The German civic wind bands, which were already giving concerts at the end of the fifteenth century, become increasingly active and proficient during the sixteenth century. Membership required ability on all the basic instruments, in order to handle the various consorts. One document from Rothenburg an der Tauber mentions three musicians who had applied to the city for employment and were found wanting, even though they were proficient on,

> trombones, cornetts, flutes, schreyerpfeifen, pipe and tabor, crumhorns, shawms, recorders, string instruments, organ and lutes.[35]

---

30 Massimo Trojano, *Discorsi Delli Triomfi, Giostre, Apparati, é delle cose piu notabile* (Munich, 1586), 150, fol. 111v, 112r. See also Andrew Kazdin, 'The Glorious Sound of Brass' (Columbia Recording, MS 6941). William also helped his brother, Duke Ernst of Bavaria, establish his own wind band by purchasing trombones, flutes and crumhorns for him in Rome in 1574. [B. A. Wallner, *Musikalische Denkmaler der Steinätzkunst* (Munich, Lentnersche Hofbuchhandlung, 1912)]

31 Helmutt Federhofer, *Musikpflege und Musiker am Grazer Habsburgerhof* (Mainz: Schott, 1967), 29.

32 Köchel, *Kaiserliche Hof-Musikkapelle in Wien*, 48ff.

33 Wilhelm Ehmann, *Tibilustrium* (Kassel: Bärenreiter, 1950), 12.

34 Edmond Vander Straeten, *La Musique aux Pays-Bas avant le XIXe Siècle* (1867–1888), VII, 501.

35 Georg Reichert, *Erasmus Widmann (1572–1634)* (Stuttgart: W. Kolhammer, 1951), 44.

Even the smallest German towns had some civic musicians by the sixteenth century and in some cases they must have also been exceptional. For example, in 1502 the Emperor, Maximilian I, wrote to the town council of Memmingen requesting that they send him 'two of your town musicians, Jörg Eyselin and Ulrich Plaser ... who are reputed to be good at playing high and low parts on shawms and trombones.'[36]

The towns were assembling large collections of instruments, again to make possible alternating consorts. Nürnberg, for example, which employed only four or five players for most of the sixteenth century,[37] had ninety instruments in its Ratsmusik Musikkammer in 1575.[38] One document of 1598 gives interesting details of a case of crumhorns in the town's collection.

> Item. 1 case with crumhorns, 1 bass with 2 keys, 1 bass with 1 key, 1 tenor with 1 key, 2 tenors without keys, 2 altos and 2 sopranos. Total 9. Note. All are there including a small box containing the reeds.[39]

It appears the Nürnberg civic players themselves were even proficient in making instruments. Civic records for 1538–1539 include the following note.

> It has been decided in the council to negotiate with the town musicians to make for the council a large bombard together with the Rauschpfeifen which go with it, such as they have made for Friedrich the Count Palatine, so that they can be used to the general honor of the town.[40]

Individual players, perhaps not trusting the state of repair of civic instruments, often acquired their own consorts as well. One Wolf Hueber, civic musician of Freistadt, Austria, owned three trombones, four trumpets, five cornetts, a shawm, nine Querpfeifen, eight viols and a zither![41]

During the sixteenth century we also see the first appearance of wealthy private citizens supporting their own establishments of musicians. A Krakow merchant, Jacobus Ellendus Augustanus (d. 1577)[42] maintained consorts of cornetts and crumhorns and a member of the

---

36 Memmingen, Stadtarchiv, MS. 1/1.

37 A miniature from ca. 1500 shows the Nürnberg civic band of two shawms and a slide trumpet playing for the butchers guild dance (Stadtbibliothek, MS. Nor. K. 444, fol. 1). A pencil drawing from 1519 still shows a three-man band, but with the trombone replacing the slide trumpet (Anonymous, in the *Nürnberger Schembarthandschrift* (D2, fol. 66) in Nürnberg, Germanisches Nationalmuseum (Hs. 5664). From 1520 there is a famous drawing by Albrecht Dürer, 'Nürnberger Stadtpfeifer,' which pictures a four-man band of two shams and two trombones, with two percussionists who are not playing. A mid-century engraving, 'Ball in the Town Hall,' shows a five-member civic wind band of cornett, three shawms and a sackbut (Anonymous, Nürnberg Stadtbibliothek).

38 Walter Salmen, *Musikleben im 16. Jahrhundert* (Leipzig: Deutscher Verlag für Musik, 1976), 16.

39 E. Nickel, *Der Holzblasinstrumentenbau in der Freien Reichsstadt Nürnberg* (München, 1971), 339.

40 Ibid., 58ff.

41 Salmen, *Musikleben im 16. Jahrhundert*, 15.

42 A. Chybinsky, 'Polnische Musik und Musikkultur der 16. Jahrhunderts in ihren Beziehungen zu Deutschland,' in *Sammelbände der Internationalen Musikgesellschaft* (1911–1912), XIII, 465.

wealthy Fugger family, Raimund Fugger of Augsburg, in 1566 owned 140 lutes, 82 cornetts, 59 recorders, 47 flutes, 13 bassoons, 2 doltzanas, 9 shawms and 8 crumhorns![43]

Regarding the music sponsored by private citizens, there were apparently also singing societies formed by educated citizens.[44] We might mention the *Krenzleinsgesellschaft* of Nürnberg, founded in the home of one, Niclas Nützel in 1568. This was a group of some twenty citizens which met every other week to rehearse instrumental and vocal music, accompanied by food and wine. A list of the members for 1568 shows that the participants came from a cross section of professions.[45]

Educators	5
Preachers	5
Lawyers	3
Doctors	3
Council officials	2
Musician	1
Businessman	1
Goldsmith	1

The wandering minstrel[46] was becoming increasingly rare by the sixteenth century and we begin to see considerable effort on the part of the civic musicians' guilds devoted to preventing him from playing for money in their towns.[47]

One form of public concert which is particularly associated with Germany is the regular performances by the civic wind bands, often from a tower, known as *Abblasen*. The city we most associate this practice with in the seventeenth century, Leipzig, is traditionally said to have begun this practice in 1599, for which an extant document orders them to play every morning at ten o'clock 'in honor of God.' We suspect the tradition began even earlier, for already in 1572 a similar civic order in Dresden calls for the civic musicians to play four-part music from a tower.[48]

In Lübeck the civic wind band first performed a chorale at four o'clock in the morning to awaken the farm hands and then another chorale to mark the mid-day pause (at ten

---

43 R. Schaal, 'Die Musikinstrumenten-Sammlung von Raimund Fugger,' in *Archiv für Musikwissenschaft* (1964), XXI, 212ff.

44 Reese, *Music in the Renaissance*, 636 and 677, mentions these only in passing.

45 Susan Gattuso, '16th-Century Nuremberg,' in *The Renaissance*, ed. Iain Fenlon (Englewood Cliffs: Prentice Hall, 1989), 289.

46 A woodcut in Olaus Magnus' *Historia de gentibus septentrionalibus* (Rome, 1555) shows three minstrels playing for a dancing bear. A copy is in the Kiel, Universitätsbibliothek.

47 More specific guilds also begin to appear in the sixteenth century. In Prague a 'Juden Spielleutezunft' was established [Salmen, *Musikleben im 16. Jahrhundert*, 14] and Kastner, in *Manuel Général de Musique Militaire* (Paris, 1848), 126, points out that in Lisbon there was separate shawm guild (20 members), a singers guild (150 members), a keyboard guild (20 members) and a trumpet and timpani guild (12 members).

48 Grove, *Dictionary*, V, 615.

o'clock). They performed again to signal the resumption of work at noon and at nine o'clock to indicate the time to sleep.[49]

Regular, non-tower, concerts are required in a Zürich contract 'at noon on Fridays, Sundays, holidays, and on *unserer Herren Tag*.'[50]

FUNCTIONAL MUSIC

During the sixteenth century in the German-speaking lands there is abundant evidence of the use of instrumental music with singers in the church service, both in Catholic and Lutheran polyphony. First, this can be viewed as only a logical extension of the music of the private chapels maintained by the aristocrats. The Emperor Maximilian I had trumpets, shawms and organists in his private church music, '*des kunigs cantarei*,' and during his visit to the Reichstag meeting in Trier, in 1512, he permitted only trombones, cornetts and trumpets with the church music.[51] His son, Philip, followed his example and one eyewitness describes hearing a Mass in Philip's chapel, during which the trombones joined in playing the 'Deo gratias' and the 'Ite messa est.'[52]

The Elector Moritz of Saxony hired six cornett and sackbut players in 1549 for his church music. One of those hired was the composer Antonio Scandello (1517–1580), who was also a cornettist of such fame that cornett students came from great distances to study with him.[53] The Elector Otto Heinrich of Heidelberg, in his will, espressed the hope that his chapel musicians would be maintained, especially his famous '*Organisten, pusauner, … zincKhenbleser vnd Trumpetter*.'[54]

Even the trumpet corps of the aristocrats performed in church, as we can see in a description of the ordination service of Bishop Amsdorf in Naumberg in 1542. The principal musical performance, *Nun bitten wir den heiligen Geist*, was heard in the first verse by the organ, the second verse by a five-part choir and the third verse was performed by a five-part trumpet choir.[55]

Another document, dated 1 May 1572, by Archduke Ferdinand II of Innsbruck, refers to the regular use of trumpets in church. This regulation seems to suggest he had been having some discipline problems with his trumpet corps for which he threatens to transfer them to another court. In addition, he orders,

---

49 Wilhelm Stahl, *Musikgeschichte Lübecks* (Kassel: Bärenreiter, 1952), II, 45ff.

50 Johann Steiner Cherbuliez, *Neujahrsblatter der Allgemeinen Musikgesellschaft Zürich* (Zürich, 1964), Bd. 148, 18.

51 Wolfgang Suppan, *Lexikon des Blasmusikwesens* (Freiburg: Blasmusikverlag Schulz, 1976), 23.

52 M. Brenet, 'Notes sur l'introduction des instruments dans les églises de France,' in *Riemann-Festschrift* (Leipzig, 1909), 281.

53 Grove, *Dictionary*, XVI, 547.

54 Quoted in Suppan, *Lexicon des Blasmusikwesens*, 24.

55 Ehmann, *Tibilustrium*, 149.

[The trumpet corps] must have diligent attention and must also appear for services on Sundays and holidays. Unless one has a better reason not to appear, he or they will receive serious punishment.[56]

In the following chapter we shall see fascinating discussion of this practice by Praetorius.

Naturally, any time the noble visited the church for a personal service, in particular for his wedding, his personal instrumentalists participated. That instruments performed with singers in the Mass during weddings is proved by an eyewitness account of the wedding of Duke Johann of Saxony to Sofia of Mecklenburg, in Torgau, speaks of a Te Deum, sung by a court singer with organ and 'my lord's trumpets, trombones, shawms, and other instruments of which the German princes have so many.' On the following Tuesday a Mass was sung in the castle chapel, under the direction of Adam von Fulda.

> On the Tuesday after Quinquagesima [1 March 1500] the bride and bridegroom together with the other princes and princesses heard Mass in the castle chapel; the singers belonging to my Most Gracious and Noble Lord sang two masses with the help of the organ, three sackbuts and a cornett, and also four crumhorns with the positive organ which were almost joyful to hear.[57]

For the wedding of Duke Ludwig of Württemberg in 1575, an eyewitness describes an eight-part work for singers and trombones which was 'so lovely and noble that the heart was refreshed.' Later, this same person, in a descriptive poem, makes reference to the duke's wind band.

> Zinks and five shawms,
> Held with flying fingers,
> Faster than an eye-blink,
> They played the best pieces.[58]

An eyewitness speaks of the combination of singers and wind players during a performance for Ludwig III of Württemburg's wedding to Ursula, Duchess of Bavaria, in 1585.[59] Similarly, an eyewitness of the wedding of Margrave Casimir of Brandenburg (d. 1527) and Dorothea Pfalzgrafin bei Rhein in 1518 reports of the music performed in the church, that it

---

56 Walter Senn, *Musik und Theater am Hof zu Innsbruck*, 135.

57 Adolf Aber, *Die Pflege der Musik unter den Wettinern und Wettinischen Ernestinern Von den Anfängen bis zur Auflösung der Weimarer Hofkapelle 1662* (Bückeburg, 1921), 82.

58 Nicodemus Frischlin, quoted in Josef Sittard, *Geschichte der Musik und des Theaters am Württembergischen hofe* (Stuttgart: Kohlhammer, 1890), I, 18ff. Another connection between the Württemberg court and the Church can be seen in the fact that the rector of Bempflingen served as the purchasing agent for instruments used by the court musicians. [G. Bossert, 'Die Hofhantorei unter Herzog Christof,' in *Württembergische Vierteljahresheftes für Landesgeschichte* (1898), Neue Folge, VII, 153]

59 G. Pietzsch, 'Beschreibungen deutscher Fürstenhochzeiten von der Mitte des 15. bis zum Beginn des 17. Jahrhunderts als musikgeschichtliche quellen,' in *Anuario Musical* (1960), XV, 53.

was solemn and elegant, 'especially through the triumphant performance of the Margrave's singers, organists and trombone and cornett players.'[60]

Of course the most important church service on behalf of the noble was his coronation. One can imagine the months of work by craftsman of all kinds which preceded the coronation of an emperor. If we can believe an English eyewitness, the coronation of Ferdinand I in 1562 required, among other things, 40,000 hunting horns!

> … suche pompe and triumph as ys thought not to have ben done the lyke at any tyme synce the great Charles … forty thousand … everi man … a lyttel bugl horn about his neck hunterlyk …[61]

As mentioned above, there is considerable evidence to suggest that it was not unusual for instrumentalists to join the singers in regular church services, an important fact which is hardly recognized in most music history texts. In fact, Polk finds the first definite evidence of wind players performing regularly with singers in liturgical music early in the sixteenth century.[62]

In the Catholic areas, as in the Lutheran, civic contracts specify that the civic wind bands will perform in church with the singers in polyphonic music. Such a contract is found for Munich in 1580[63] and a civic ordinance of 1571 in Ulm calls for the cornetts and trombones to play in Münster Cathedral.[64] A civic contract of 1572 in Dresden demands the civic musicians 'strengthen and enhance' the Kreuzchor,

> on feast days, Sundays and at weddings and other occasions when polyphony is performed.[65]

We find an account from St. Anne's Church in Dresden, for 1578, which gives the actual repertoire in which the Dresden civic wind band joined the choir. On this occasion they performed a six-part motet, *Jubilato Deo*, by Clemens non Papa and a six-Part motet, *Te Deum Patrem*, by Lassus.[66] Similarly, the Zwichau civic wind band was paid in 1559–1560 to perform the Mass in church ('*in der Kirchen in die Messe geblasen*').[67]

There is one interesting, and lengthy, account of the appearance of minstrels in the Catholic church festivities in Germany, written in 1553 by the Lutheran advocate, Thomas Kirchmai-

---

60 Tomaso Garzoni, *Allgemeiner Schauplatz aller Kunst, Professionen und Handwerker* (1659).

61 Dorothy McGuigan, *The Habsburgs* (Garden City, New York, 1966), 139.

62 Keith Polk, 'Instrumental music in the Urban Centres of Renaissance Germany,' *Early Music History* 7 (1987): 181, http://www.jstor.org/stable/853891.

63 Salmen, *Musikleben im 16. Jahrhundert*, 18; also Grove, *Dictionary*, XII, 781.

64 Salmen, Ibid., 18.

65 Grove, *Dictionary*, V, 615.

66 Ehmann, *Tibilustrium*, 149.

67 Arno Werner, *Vier Jahrhunderte im Dienste der Kirchenmusik* (Leipzig: Merseburger, 1933), 204.

er.[68] In his account of the celebration of the various feast days, he mentions the youth of the Church running through the streets on January 6, accompanied by minstrels, seeking donations. On Ash Wednesday, he says one found in the Church 'foolish plays, and doltish doggerel rhymes.' Again the youth go out into the streets and,

> the minstrel here doth fit amid the same, and drunken songs, with gaping mouth he sings …

During Easter, they 'lustily do sing … A bawling noise, while every man seeks highest for to sing … The Priests and schoolmen loud do roar, some use the instrument.'[69] And, finally, there would be a feast of celebration on the annual anniversary of the Church's dedication and for this 'Both jesters, rogues and minstrels with their instruments are here.' And dancing followed the banquet.

> The table taken up, they rise, and all the youth apace,
> The minstrel with them called go to some convenient place:
> Where when with Bagpipe hoarse, he hath begun his music fine,
> And unto such as are prepared to dance hath given sign,
> Comes thither straight both boys and girls, and men that aged be,
> And married folk of middle age, there also comes to see,
> Old wrinkled hags, and youthful dames, that mind to dance aloft,
> Then sundry pastimes do begin, and filthy dances oft …[70]

There are also a few sixteenth-century accounts of wind music in the Catholic convents and monasteries. Kellner writes that one often heard the local civic wind band perform during the important festivals at Kremsmünster in Austria.[71] Melk had a salaried cornettist at the end of the century,[72] while the convent at Hall (now Solbad Hall, near Innsbruck) had a full wind band of cornett and trombone players for which it was famous at the time.[73]

In the Lutheran areas one can also find many civic contracts which specify that the civic instrumentalist were to help out with the polyphony. A Stadtpfeifer contract in 1569 in Zwickau assigns the player to help out in the church with his instrument when polyphonic music is performed and an almost identical contract is found for Delitzsch in 1580.[74] Jakob Gallus wrote in his *Opus Musicum* (1587) that where there were small numbers of singers

---

68 Thomas Kirchmaier, 'The Popish Kingdome,' quoted in Philip Stubbs, *The Anatomy of the Abuses in England* (1583), ed. Frederick Furnivall (London: The New Shakespeare Society, n.d.), 323ff. Kirchmaier was born in 1511 in Straubingen, Bavaria.
69 Ibid., 336ff.
70 Ibid., 341.
71 Altmann Kellner, *Musikgeschichte des Stiftes Kremsmünster* (Kassel: Bärenreiter, 1956), 149ff.
72 Grove, *Dictionary*, XII, 107.
73 Ibid., X, 157.
74 Ehmann, *Tibilustrium*, 149.

the winds *must* help out.⁷⁵ A report by a trumpeter in the service of the Lutheran bishop of Halle a. d. Saale says that winds were used all the time for this kind of church music.⁷⁶

Regarding other accounts of the use of instruments in Lutheran churches, we find a rather complete account of the use of a civic wind band in a Lutheran church relative to the Easter celebration in Halle. On Palm Sunday there was a procession with trumpets and fifes and on Easter morning, during the service, a band of shawms performed, twice, a 'beautiful motet.' On Ascension Day trumpeters played for a procession which carried a picture of the Savior and the shawm band played an artistic piece from the roof of the church.⁷⁷

The Linz, Austria, civic wind band played in the Lutheran Landhauskirche after 1550.⁷⁸ In Berne, in 1572, the civic band was used to help accompany the congregational singing⁷⁹ and in Zwickau, in 1558, the band was ordered to play with the organ.⁸⁰ Towns which had no civic wind bands would import them, so the Würzen band appeared in Finsterwalde in 1581 and the Altenburg band in Oschatz in 1598.⁸¹

Finally, the extant music itself is a witness to the practice of the use of instruments in the church. One need only mention the *26 Fugen* (1542) by Johann Walter, Luther's musical advisor, composed 'especially for cornetts.'⁸²

When an important aristocratic wedding occurred at this time it was not unusual for the visiting nobles to bring their own musicians to join in the celebration. The result is sometimes rather large gatherings of musicians, especially trumpets One such case was the marriage of Joachim II of Brandenburg, who was married to Hedwig, daughter to Sigismund, in 1533. An eyewitness records that there were assembled no fewer than 156 trumpets, 28 timpani and 15 shawms.⁸³

For the marriage of Christian I of Saxony in 1582, a great allegorical pageant was held during which some of the musicians were required to perform while swimming in a reservoir, disguised as 'nymph-musicians.'⁸⁴

The marriage of Princess Anna of Saxony and the Prince of Orange in 1561, being celebrated in the Lutheran tradition, was held in the palace instead of the church. A contem-

---

75 In Part Three, 'Instructio ad musicos.'

76 Ehmann, *Tibilustrium*, 149.

77 Curt Sachs, *Musik und Oper am kurbrandenburgischen Hof* (Berlin: J. Bard, 1910), 25ff.

78 Grove, *Dictionary*, XI, 12.

79 Ibid., II, 621.

80 Ehmann, *Tibilustrium*, 156.

81 Werner, *Vier Jahrhunderte im Dienste der Kirchenmusik*, 219.

82 The manuscript is in DDR:LEu (MS. Cod. Mus. 50, 'Thomaskirche').

83 Aber, *Die Pflege der Musik unter den Wettinern und Wettinischen Ernestinern*, 109 and Ehmann, *Tibilustrium*, 13. No doubt Joachim rewarded these musicians well, for as a typical spendthrift, by 1540 he was so broke that in a desperate attempt to balance his books, he hired ten different alchemists in hopes that they could make gold! [Janssen, *History of the German People*, XV.]

84 Janssen, Ibid., 265.

porary account mentions that the banquet music in particular was 'the merriest and most ingenious.'[85]

In Duke Albert V's court in Munich even ordinary meals were accompanied by five musicians, according to the court singer Massimo Troiano.

> ... sometimes with corna-musa, sometimes with recorders or with flutes, or cornetts and trombones in French chansons or other light compositions.[86]

For Albert's wedding banquet in 1568, we have a detailed report by Troiano of the sixteenth-century custom of achieving instrumental variety through changing the instruments in the consort. During the first course the guests heard a seven-part motet by Lassus played by cornetts and trombones. The second course featured a six-part madrigal by Striggio performed by six *grosse* trombones, the bass of which was reported to have sounded an octave lower than the rest. Another course was served to an ensemble of dolzaina, cornamuse, shawm and mute cornett.[87]

The trumpet corps of the emperor Ferdinand I enjoyed the prestige of being entitled to horses, but they still were required to appear at every meal to perform.[88]

Another ancient pleasure for many nobles was dancing. Philipps von Hessen enjoyed dancing so much that his cornett and trumpet players who provided the music had apparently begun to complain. This noble immediately gave out an order in 1541 that henceforth they must perform for his dances with an attitude that is 'willing, unquestioning, and untiring!'[89]

An engraving by the anonymous 'F.A.,' called *Ballfest in der Wiener Hofburg, 1560*, pictures four trumpets leading the dancers to the dance floor, with an eight-member wind band playing from a special box in the foreground.

Aristocratic musicians must have also been ever present for the more somber occasion of a funeral. An often reproduced engraving by Georg Peham pictures the funeral procession of Archduke Karl II, of Graz, in 1590.[90] An eyewitness to this procession[91] mentions the timpani covered with black cloth and the trumpets, marching three by three, he says, all were using their 'small mouthpieces,' which we may assume to be a reference to a smaller sound, hence mutes.

In army music the trumpet performed the most important role of providing signals for the maneuvers of the troops. One source indicates that at this time there was found at least

---

85 'Acta des Printzen tzu Uranieun und Frawlein Annen tzu Saxen Beylager, 1561' (Dresden, Royal Archives).
86 Anthony Baines, *Woodwind Instruments and Their History* (New York: Norton, 1962), 256ff.
87 Frank Harrison and Joan Rimmer, *European Musical Instruments* (London: Studio Vista, 1964), 25.
88 Don Smithers, *The Music and History of the Baroque Trumpet* (London: Dent, 1973), 167ff.
89 Detlef Altenburg, *Untersuchungen zur Geschichte der Trumpete im Zeitalter der Clarinblaskunst* (Regensburg: G. Bosse, 1973), I, 100ff.
90 Graz Stadtmuseum (Inv.-Nr. M. 48/1–13).
91 Wallner, *Musikalische Denkmaler der Steinätzkunst*, 85.

one trumpet for each two hundred soldiers.[92] An interesting insight into the art of the field trumpeter is found in a publication of 1555 by Lienhart Fronsperger. Of the duties of the field trumpeter, he writes,

> Each squadron should have at least one trumpeter serving under his captain and he should be found day and night by his captain's tent ... He should know and be able to variously blow: when one mounts, when one eats, when one dismounts or sets out; also when the enemy is present ... a trumpeter should be bold, manly, intelligent, and honorable, as he may have to serve as an ambassador to the enemy.[93]

Among the very few extant examples of the trumpet corps repertoire which was actually notated are found in two North German manuscripts, by court trumpeters Hendrich Lübeck and Magnus Thomsen, which are thought to have been written out to help new members memorize their parts. Included are not only various signals for military use, but some 'concert' works including *Sonaten*, *Sersseneden* and *Tokkaten*, as well as an interesting early version of *In dulci jubilo*, here called *In dultzi gubilo*.[94]

A great deal more musical activity was associated specifically with civic life. The medieval tradition of having civic musicians serving watch duty, now primarily watching for fires during the night, continued to be maintained during the sixteenth century in Germany. A typical contract for a Stadtpfeifer, Abraham Hut, in Zwickau in 1569, demands that he keep careful watch day and night in the tower and announce each hour by blowing on his *hörnlein*, but in welcoming official guests he is to play the trumpet. In case of fire, he signals with a bell and hanging out a lantern at night and with a red flag during the day.[95] In one case we have an extant oath which a new watch musician in Wismar had to swear to in 1586.

> I swear that I shall be true, obedient and loyal to the honorable council of the town of Wismar, to bear in mind their and the town's best interest, and to avert harm to the best of my ability while on the tower of St. Nicholas where I have been appointed tower watch. I swear to watch carefully day and night, to look after light and fire with all diligence so no harm may come to the town and church from them; in other respects I also swear to behave modestly and peacefully with everyone and to lead an honorable and respectable life, so help me God.[96]

As mentioned above, in the Zwickau civic contract of 1569, these watch musicians also served as a surrogate clock at night when, as there were no lights, the citizens could not

---

92 Panoff, *Militärmusik in Geschichte und Gegenwart*, 54.

93 Lienhart Fronsperger, *Fünff Bücher von Kriegsregiment* (Frankfurt, 1555).

94 These manuscripts are discussed extensively in Georg Schünemann, 'Sonaten und Feldstücke der Hoftrompeter,' *Zeitschrift für Musikwissenschaft* (1935), XVII, 4ff. We have examined these manuscripts and it is our opinion that the solution for how this music was to be performed, as ensemble music, has not been satisfactorily solved, particularly in this article.

95 Werner, *Vier Jahrhunderte im Dienste der Kirchenmusik*, 275ff.

96 Smithers, *Music and History of the Baroque Trumpet*, 120ff.

see the town clock. In Köln the poor sleeping citizens were thus awakened by the sound of crashing cymbals!

> They are to give the time hourly with cymbals, and also every day in the morning around daybreak, at about three or four o'clock, they are to play on flutes, crumhorns, cornetts, or shawms; similarly around midday at eleven o'clock and then again in the evening at about nine or ten o'clock.[97]

In addition to this duty, the civic wind band in Delitzsch was required to wind the town clock regularly.[98]

An interesting Memmingen town council order in 1518 permits a civic musician to absent himself to participate in a contest so long as he obtains a watch replacement.

> Jack the town player is to be allowed to go with the other players for ten days to Augsburg, if they wish to win an award with the crumhorns, but in the meantime he must arrange for the watch to be maintained.[99]

The German town musicians also participated in the celebrations of universities in the sixteenth century, as for example providing trumpets for a procession of lawyers in Köln.[100] For a procession honoring the new Doctors of Theology of the university in Köln in 1591, the civic musicians were not only engaged but provided with wine and three persons to carry their instruments.[101] For the ceremonies surrounding the granting of degrees of Doctor of Medicine in Basel, in 1557, the civic wind band played in the cathedral before the ceremony and in the procession afterward.[102]

An account of the awarding of degrees ceremony at the University of Leipzig in 1541–1542 permits us to see how elaborate these festivities could be. On the evening before, the civic trumpeters announced the event to the entire city. At the first official ceremony, the *Promotionsakt*, the civic wind band played a musical interlude and were joined by the trumpets for a following procession. Later the same players, together with singers from St. Thomas Church, performed at a banquet in honor of the graduates.[103]

Of course civic wind bands were much in evidence when distinguished visitors visited. An eyewitness to the arrival of princes attending the wedding of Duke Ludwig of Württemberg to Dorothea Ursula, of Baden-Durlach, in Stuttgart in 1575, complains of,

---

97 H. Moser, 'Zur Mittelalterlichen Musikgeschichte der Stadt Köln,' in *Archiv für Musikwissenschaft* (1918), I, 136ff.
98 Smithers, *Music and History of the Baroque Trumpet*, 123.
99 Memmingen, Stadtarchiv, Ratsprotokollbuch, 1517–1519.
100 Hermann Keussen, 'Die alte Universität Köln,' in *Universität Köln* (Köln, 1929), 43.
101 Franz Joseph von Bianco, *Die alte Universität Köln und die spätern Gelehrten-Schulen dieser Stadt* (Köln, 1856), 89ff., 100.
102 Heinrich Boos, *Thomas und Felix Platter* (Leipzig, 1878), 309ff.
103 Georg Erler, *Leipziger Magisterschmäuse* (Leipzig, 1905), 150ff.

> Such a noise of cornetts and crumhorns, of bombards, racketts and shawms that one could not even hear oneself speak.[104]

An ink drawing by Johann Twenger pictures the Breslau civic wind band, consisting of a cornett, trombone, trumpet and dulzian, on a triumphal arch welcoming Rudolf II on 24 May 1577.[105]

Civic wind bands were also required to perform for all important civic banquets. A typical contract, from Zwickau in 1569, calls for the four-man band [*zwen Zincken, Posaun vnd Bohardt*] to play fanfares and dance music at all *Festtage*.[106]

The Stadtpfeifer were permitted to augment their incomes by performing for private weddings of citizens, although the city maintained careful watch over this activity as we can see in a civic regulation in Wissenfels. Here we read that when the civic wind band was requested to perform by the bridegroom, at the church, banquet, or dance, the band received four Groschen from each guest. If any bridegroom preferred not to have 'music,' but only fife and drums, there was a standard charge of twelve Groschen. The wind band, moreover, was permitted to 'pass the hat,' twice for a morning wedding and once for an evening wedding, but then they could make no further demands on the guests. For purposes of security, they could not be asked to remain later than ten o'clock in the evening, or nine o'clock in the winter. The band had the right to a 'Brautsuppe,' eating and drinking in the home of the bridegroom, but excesses by some band members led to a loss of this privilege in 1598![107]

A contract for the civic wind band in Reval (Tallinn) to perform for weddings in 1532 is also quite interesting.

> Item. After the evening meal they should play four popular double dances and then they can play a double dance with recorders or crumhorns, as well as a girl's dance and the bride's dance, which adds up to ten dances ... Whoever wishes to hold board for an evening in the hall or houses and wishes to be entertained on recorders and crumhorns with four double dances, one girl's dance and one bride's dance, for this the payment is six farthing.[108]

In addition, the resourceful civic musicians must have found numerous local opportunities for additional services to the town. In Delitzach the band, together with its apprentices, began a tradition on the first of the year called *Neujahrsblasen*, during which they performed in front of the citizens' houses for donations. We can judge the reaction of the townspeople

---

104 G. Pietzsch, 'Beschreibungen deutscher Fürstenhochzeiten von der Mitte des 15. bis zum Beginn des 17. Jahrhunderts als musikgeschichtliche Quellen,' in *Anuario Musical* (1960), XV, 46.

105 Nürnberg, Germanisches Nationalmuseum (Sign. HB 235).

106 Salmen, *Musikleben im 16. Jahrhundert*, 74.

107 Arno Werner, *Städtische und fürstliche Musikpflege in Weissenfels* (Leipzig: Breitkopf & Härtel, 1911), 36.

108 Moser, 'Zur Mittelalterlichen Musikgeschichte der Stadt Köln,' in *Archiv für Musikwissenschaft* (1918), I, 139.

by a civic order in 1599 in which the town council passed a special bonus of one Taler for the civic wind band, if they would *not* carry out this New Year's performance![109]

Finally, one special category of functional music must be mentioned with respect to the Bishop of Münster, who like many nobles in Germany suffered from common drunkenness.[110] In his case, he used to keep an ensemble of trumpets and drums at hand to wake him when he passed out from drink.[111]

---

109 Werner, *Vier Jahrhunderte im Dienste der Kirchenmusik*, 231.

110 Janssen, *History of the German People*, XV, 249. One duke quoted his pastor as saying, 'after the holy days you are free to drink well and to let the heavenly sackbuts ring on.' [Ibid., 239] This, we take it, is not what Brahms had in mind in his *Begräbnisgesang*, Op. 13, when he speaks of 'God's trombones.'

111 Ibid., 243.

7 PRAETORIUS

THE SINGLE MOST IMPORTANT BOOK which provides the most valuable insights into what sixteenth-century music was *really* like, that is to say its breadth in media, styles and practice, has never to this date, so far as we know, been published[1] in any modern language, much less English. Music historians have long been interested in, and have translated and published in modern editions, the first two volumes of Michael Praetorius' *Syntagma Musicum*, which deal basically with theory and physical descriptions of instruments, but not the third volume, which deals with how music functioned in society.[2]

Although he published his book in 1619, it is a description of late Renaissance style and not Baroque, for it is clear that Praetorius, in 1619, could see no evidence of what we call the Baroque on the horizon. In the preface to Volume III, he writes,

> I have included the most important facts a music director and practical musicians will need to know, especially at this time when music has reached such a high level that any further advance would seem inconceivable.[3]

And, of course, he was correct. Except for the beginnings of modern opera, for which we draw the chalk line on the blackboard for our students, we doubt that anyone alive in 1600 would have perceived that they had just entered a new period of music history.

Praetorius, in his preface, identifies several purposes for his having written this book. First, he says he has written this book for the benefit of present day musicians, as well as for those of the future 'who may be sincerely devoted to the noble art of music.' In terms of the scope of information available to us today in standard music history texts, it is most important that he promises to treat not only ecclesiastical music, but 'secular music, in free and honorable

---

[1] We hasten to add that this volume has been translated into English by Hans Lampl, as part of a doctoral program at the University of Southern California some twenty years ago, and a copy may be found in their music library. However, at the time we first wanted to examine this translation, this institution would neither provide xerox copies, microfilm, permit the work to circulate through interlibrary loan, nor did they participate in the Ann Arbor Dissertation collection. We are grateful to Dr. Lampl for the donation of a copy of an early draft for our use.

[2] Praetorius speaks of a fourth volume, which apparently he never actually wrote. Praetorius (1571–1621), whose real name was Schultheiss, studied in the Latin school at Torgau and worked in the court of the Duke of Brunswick and later as Kapellmeister in Wolfenbüttel.

[3] A facsimile of the original German publication has been printed by Bärenreiter Kassel, 1958. The page numbers we cite, therefore, are from the original print, in this case from the preface pages, which are unnumbered.

use for entertainment and pleasure outside the church.' He expresses the breadth of this in the actual title of Part One.

> Information concerning the definition and characteristics of forms currently used in the music of Italy, France, England and Germany in Church as well as for ethical, political and economic purposes.

If one will recall that music printing began at the beginning of this, the sixteenth century, in Italy, and that by the end of the century enormous quantities of Italian prints had been circulated over Europe, one will understand that one of the chief purposes of the third volume was to explain the 'great variety of unknown Italian terms which are so puzzling to many musicians.' Because the terms he is speaking of are very familiar to us today, words such as Motet, Sonata, Concerto and Thorough-bass ('a wonderful and useful new Italian invention'), this book has the great value of allowing us to see the initial meanings of these forms and styles. To this end, he promises the reader that he has made a thorough study.

> I have gathered together material from the prefaces of Italian composers, and from the oral accounts of various Italians and from those who have visited Italy, and also from my own thoughts and modest discoveries.

By the latter, he means, as he says later in the preface, his own experience as a music director in various courts. His purpose is therefore an educational one,

> so that the art of music, following the example of the Italians, may not only be taught in our German Fatherland like the other arts and disciplines, but for the glory and praise of God and for the recreation of God fearing citizens.

Praetorius says he had hoped someone better qualified would take on this work, but it appeared no one else would. In addition, he has observed that the real authorities, the best performing musicians, rarely talk about their art, preferring to teach by demonstration.

> Usually the most famous and excellent instrumentalists, organists and lutenists can hardly be persuaded to perform unless some fool has first violated all the rules of art, such as unrhythmical and clumsy groping and scratching, unpleasant fifths, and boorish, disagreeable melodies. Having their ears thus tormented, and filled with irritation, they will only then reach for a lute or some other instrument and, after preliminary toccatas or preludes, perform for their audience a most agreeable fantasy and fugue, with artful improvisation, *passaggi*, *tremoletti* and *tirate*.

This third volume is dedicated to the mayor and city council of Nürnberg, 'distinguished protectors and patrons of the art of music,' but in his preface he gives us valuable views of the larger society. After praising how these leaders have always recognized and rewarded the very best musicians, he recognizes the rapidly growing middle class.

To this must be added that many merchants of no mean significance have not only shown great love for music, but have also diligently practiced the art themselves so successfully that they have been able to publish their own musical works and thus make themselves famous.

And even private citizens and families in Nürnberg 'cherish, practice and foster vocal and instrumental music.'

As with our discussions of earlier treatises in these volumes, we must remind the reader that our purpose is to present only that information which offers insight to aesthetics and current performance practice. We omit material which is of a purely theoretical nature.

ON THE DEFINITION OF FORMS

Praetorius divides his study of forms into two general categories: works with text and works without text. After that, however, it is important and revealing, that he organizes his discussion of musical forms on the basis of aesthetics. Consequently, his first chapter (actually, Chapter 2) concerns those forms which he says are 'serious in nature.' These forms he finds used both in sacred and secular performances.

Starting with the category of works with text, he begins with the Concerto, which he seems to have understood both as a style and a form. Here he presents the meaning of the term as a style and below we shall see his extensive remarks on the practical application of this style. Before presenting Praetorius' comments on the concerto style, we should remind the reader that between the late Renaissance and the late Baroque, this term went through three distinct transformations in meaning. The term first meant the name of a group, as we might use the term 'ensemble' today, such as 'Concerto di Milano.' Then it became a style word and only later a form.

To Praetorius, 'Concerto' as a style was 'a dialog in which different voices or instruments are combined.'[4] In an apparent reference to Church polyphony, he adds that the pleasure comes not from the craft involved, but from the variety.

He associates the style of a concerto with a multi-voice composition in which separate choirs alternate. This follows from the term itself, which he says derives from *concertare*, 'to compete with one another.'

> Let us imagine several of the best and most competent musicians singing or playing on various instruments—such as cornetts, trombones, recorders or transverse flutes, cromornes, bassoons or dulcians, rackets, viols, large and small violins, lutes, harpsichords, regals, positives, or organs—alternating in the manner of choirs and striving, as it were, to outdo one another.[5]

---

[4] Ibid., 4. For 'Concerto' he gives *concertatio* in Latin and *ein Concert* in German. He also adds that *Cantio, concentus* and *symphonia* all mean at this time, 'a composition for several voices.'

[5] Ibid., 5.

When he adds, 'more properly a composition is called a concerto if a high and a low choir are heard in alternation and together,' we can see the roots of what we understand today as *concertato* style.

Curiously, when Praetorius speaks of the English practice, he reverts to an older use of this term, meaning simply a group of players.

> The English call this a Consort, from *consortium*, as when several people with various instruments such as harpsichord, large lyra, double harp, lute, theorbo, pandora, *penorcon*, cither, viol, small violin, transverse flute or recorder, sometimes also a soft trombone or rackett, play together quietly and softly, forming a pleasant and harmonious relationship with one another.[6]

In the case of the Motet, Praetorius seems at a loss to fulfill his earlier promise of explaining 'Italian terms which are so puzzling to many musicians.' It strikes the reader odd that he, not to mentions several Italian treatises he cites, did not recognize this as a French word. 'Opinions vary regarding the origin of the word *motet*,'[7] he says as he proceeds to give some possibilities which are incorrect. Philip de Monte, he maintains, thought it derived from *mutare*, 'to alter,' as in changing verses. Others believed it came from *modo tecta*, 'obscure as to mode' or even from *moda* in Italian for 'fashion.' We never arrive at the correct answer, but in the process Praetorius does provide more accurate descriptions of the style of the motet, in particular 'elegance' and a work which 'moves one most profoundly by its seriousness and artfulness.'

Praetorius also points out that this form is sometimes confused with Concerto, but he recognizes a distinction in style.

> The concerti should be set for several choirs and composed quite plainly, without particular elaboration and imitative passages; the motet, however, should be written with greater artfulness and care and for not more than eight voices.[8]

The next broad category of forms which Praetorius presents is the largest of his book: forms with a text, but of a lighter or humorous nature. Within this general designation, he begins with secular works based on recognized verse patterns, which he identifies as madrigals, stanzas, sestinas and sonnets. Accordingly, he reminds the reader that these names are derived from the text and therefore a 'madrigal' is a poem, not a musical composition.[9] Thus he does not discuss musical styles, but he does offer some interesting etymological possibilities for the word itself. He suspects it might have come from *Madre della gala*, 'mother of the verse,' *Madre della gaia*, 'mother of joy,' or even *madre galanate*, 'elegant mother.' It is

---

6   Ibid.

7   Ibid., 6ff. 'Motet,' of course, comes from *Mot*, French for 'word.'

8   Ibid., 8ff. He adds that Gabrieli has composed works for up to sixteen voices which are 'motets' in style, but organized into choirs as concerti.

9   Ibid., 12.

not to be confused with *Mandrigale* (from *mandra*, Italian for 'herd'), which is a pastoral song sung by shepherds.[10]

A Stanza he identifies as something like a paragraph, but in poetry. A Sestina is then six stanzas, each with six lines. The Sonnet he understands to have fourteen lines.

The following category is secular works without recognized, or specific, arrangements of verse and these include Dialogues, Canzoni, Canzonette and Arias. The Dialogue he does not define, because 'everyone knows what dialogues are.' It is interesting that he includes echo songs in this category.[11]

The Canzoni he understands first as 'rather worldly' songs with varying orders of verses. He is also familiar with the Italian instrumental form and he recognizes that many beautiful canzoni are being composed there, particularly by Gabrieli.[12] Shorter songs carry the diminutive, Canzonette, and usually have secular texts. It is interesting that he identifies this form with the German *Mestergesänge*.

By Aria, Praetorius seems to have understood a simple popular song, or as he states it, 'a pretty tune which a singer makes up by himself.' In Germany, he says the term is used for songs with 'fine, elegant texts,' which, on the other hand, the Italians call *scherzi*.

A special category of secular vocal music is the Quodlibet, a form by the way which remained popular until the beginning of the nineteenth century. A Quodlibet, for Praetorius, was a multi-part work in which the humor lay in the mixing up, or in the nature of the quotation, of the texts. It must have been more popular than we might think, for he distinguishes three main types: where there is a separate and complete text in each voice part, 'which I like very much'; with different text in each voice, but fragmentary and mutilated; and with the same text in all voices but with words suddenly broken off.[13]

The next group of secular vocal forms which Praetorius discusses are quite interesting as they are rarely mentioned in modern literature. These are songs which he associates with specific functional purposes, such as for social purposes, for entertainment or to be sung while at work.

The first of these is the Giustiniani, three-part love songs ('which someone called rude and wanton'). We are reminded here that Italian has not yet become a national language, for Praetorius specifies these songs are sung in the Bergamasca language.[14]

Another love song is the Serenata, called *Gassaten geht* by university students. He thinks of this as an evening song, sung 'while one goes through the streets in the evening courting the young ladies.' The form he gives as three or more parts, with a *ritornello* between each

---

10 Ibid.
11 Ibid., 16.
12 Ibid., 17.
13 Ibid., 18.
14 Ibid.

verse.[15] Later he mentions this again and says the ritornello, which alternates with the singing, was often played on a 'quintern, lute, chitarrone, theorbo, or other instruments.'[16]

The final social song he gives is the Balletti, a name which of course comes from *ballare*, 'to dance.' He mentions that in Italy these are sometimes sung, but the greater number are instrumental works. His description of these is of sufficient stylistic interest to quote in full.

> When these are played for dancing on shawms they are named *stampita*. In French this is called *un bal*, which means various dances in general such as branles, courantes, voltas, galliards, etc. But balletto signifies dances especially arranged for mummeries and pageants, or for the masquerade. Every balletto has three sections: First, the *intrada*, when persons taking part in the masquerade make their entrance; second, the figures which the maskers execute while standing, striding, changing places or letters—such as a circle, wreath, triangle, square, hexagon, or other patterns—and winding about among one another (these figures represent the entire inventions and substance of the balletto); and finally the *retrajecte*, or exit.[17]

He adds, that these balletti also can be played separately as instrumental works and make 'lovely pieces of music.'

The final songs in this group are the occupational songs, 'songs of laborers and peasants.' First among these is the Vinette, the song of the wine growers. Here Praetorius mentions a German variant, the *Vinate*, or 'drinking song.'

> If I should call them by their right name, they are booze songs, which here in Germany are not uncommon. I think there is nothing in the world base enough not to have been set to music.[18]

The Giardiniero is, of course, the song of the gardener. The Villanelle (from villa, 'village'), or *villotta* among the Bavarians, is the music of the peasants and common craftsmen. Some artistic composers write these using parallel fifths 'contrary to the rules of composition, just as the peasants do not sing according to the art but simply as it occurs to them.' He mentions a French version of this kind of music, the *villages*, 'made up by the peasants themselves, performed on shawms and viols, often with two, three and more people on a part.'[19]

Praetorius begins his second large division of forms, those without text (or instrumental music), with a broad category of preludes, which, in turn he separates into independent works and those which precede other compositions. The forms in this category which stand independently are the Fantasia, Fugue, Sinfonia and Sonata. The Fantasia he associates with the Capriccio, both being styles which begin like a fugue, but then proceed 'according to

---

15 Ibid.

16 Ibid., 128 (108). While printed as page 128, this is actually page 108. This printing error continues through the [first] printed 148 and then is corrected. We will refer to the printed page number with the correct page number in [ ].

17 Ibid., 18ff.

18 Ibid., 20.

19 Ibid., 21.

one's fancy.'[20] It is enlightening that, from the perspective of Praetorius, it is the very absence of text which grants freedom to the composer.

> One is free to make much or little of it, to digress or diminish, and treat it in any way. In such fantasies or capriccios one can display one's ability and craft equally well, since one may use without hesitation anything permissible in music, including suspensions, proportions, etc., yet one should not go too far beyond the limits of mode and melody [*Ariam*].

Praetorius was under the impression that Ricercar was merely the Italian name for Fugue. He devotes little space to these forms, although he notes that the composer who can write them suited to particular modes and construct them correctly will be held in the highest esteem.[21]

Sinfonia means, to the Italians, an instrumental work in four or more voices in the manner of a toccata, pavan, galliard or similar 'Harmony.' His most interesting observation is that while the sinfonia may be used at the beginning, it is often used inserted in the middle of a polychoral Concerto![22] This apparently corresponds to the practice of having instrumental canzoni or other works performed between movements of the Mass.

Praetorius' brief discussion of the Sonata is quite interesting. He finds the word itself is derived from *sonare* [Latin, 'to sound'], which he says simply refers to the fact that it is an instrumental work. He seems, moreover, to have associated the word with *style*, for he adds that beautiful examples of sonatas can be found *in* the canzoni and sinfonias of Gabrieli and other composers. He elaborates on the style association as follows,

> In my opinion there is this difference: the sonatas are composed in a stately and splendid manner like motets, but the canzoni have many black notes and move along crisply, gaily and fast.[23]

As an after thought, Praetorius adds that the word 'sonata' is often used in reference to the music performed by trumpet corps for banquets and dances.

Continuing with instrumental forms used as preludes, Praetorius mentions the Intrada, 'usually performed for the entry of great dignitaries or in processions.' More interesting is his reference to the keyboard prelude, the Toccata, which he says is performed before beginning a motet, madrigal or fugue. Praetorius knew the Toccata as a work of pure improvisation.

> It consists of plain chords and runs. Each player, however, has his own manner of executing Toccatas and I find it unnecessary to discuss them here at great length and consider myself too unworthy to dictate to anyone on this matter.[24]

---

20 Ibid.

21 Ibid., 21ff. In the original publication, page numbers 22 and 23 were mistakenly omitted.

22 Ibid., 24.

23 Ibid.

24 Ibid., 25.

Praetorius' final category of forms is dance forms, which he separates into those danced to specific dance steps, the paduana, passamezzo and galliard, and those danced without specific steps, the branle, courante, volta, allemande and mascherada. Of most interest to us, with respect to aesthetics, is the character he associates with various dance forms.[25] Limiting our discussion to this, we find, the Pavane is played by a consort of 'lovely instruments which furnish unique, delightful and splendid harmony. He associates this form with 'grave dancing.'

The Passaamezzo 'strides along quite gently.'

The Galliard he associates with Latin expressions of agility, strength, vigor and power, thus 'the galliard has to be executed with straightforwardness and a good disposition, more than other dances.' He notes that in Italy this dance is sometimes sung by the dancers, without instruments, in which cases it goes under the name *saltarello*.

The French Branle is derived from *branler* [to 'quiver, turn, stir' or 'move'].

> In these dances, however, the movements are not as violent as in the galliards and courantes, but quite gentle, from the knees only and without skips.

The Courante, from *currere* [Latin for 'to run'] is executed 'as if one were running while dancing.'

The Volta, from *vertere* [Latin for 'to turn'] is a dance in which the dancers swing and turn about with each other.

The Allemande is a term he associates with 'a little German song or dance.'

> This dance, however, is not as quick and nimble as the galliard, but somewhat heavier and slower, and makes no use of extraordinary motions.

The Mascharato he only mentions is a masked dance, known in Germany as *Mummerei*.

ON PERFORMANCE PRACTICE

Book Two, of his third volume, is devoted to 'Necessary Precepts' of music. Much of this is theoretical in nature, dealing with the modes, harmony and notation and we shall mention only a few passages which offer insight to performance.

We find it quite striking that he begins by suggesting that complex ligatures should be replaced with the [modern] slur indication, an example of which he actually draws.[26] Ligatures are usually presented in literature today as a kind of shorthand and we know of no place where there is a suggestion that there was a phrase association, such as would be indicated by a slur. The slur mark itself, of course, was new to notation at this time.

---

25 Ibid., 25ff.
26 Ibid., 29.

In discussing the necessity of *musica ficta*, the necessary alterations when changing modes, or to avoid the tritone, Praetorius advises the composer that this should *not* be left to the performers.

> Composers would do well, as an excellent precaution, to indicate clearly the two chromatic signs, the *cancellatum* [sharp sign] and *rotundum* [flat sign] whenever they are to be employed, in order to prevent hesitation or doubt. This is useful, convenient, and also most necessary to keep singers from becoming confused, as well as for the benefit of ignorant town musicians and organists who cannot read music, let alone sing correctly.[27]

Some of Praetorius' recommendations are of a very practical nature, such as advising that everyone should start expressing in numbers the number of rests in the various parts. He observes that he has learned from experience, 'not without some embarrassment,' that this is necessary as musicians are inclined not to pay strict attention or are sometimes caught up in listening to the music.[28]

He also offers a system he devised for numbering the separate parts of large concerti, to avoid confusion, since in polychoral works there will be several parts named 'tenor,' etc. He also mentions that he made it a habit to count the number of breves in a composition and notate it at the end of his score. Then, when planning the music for a service, by glancing at a chart he had worked out, he could immediately determine how long it would take to perform the composition.[29] This, he observes, is important so as not to delay the remaining church ceremonies. Similarly, he describes a system of marking cuts,[30] in case the latter does not work, which enables the musicians to stop in a hurry,

> in case the conductor finds the composition before or after the sermon threatens to last too long—since a musician is likely to overdo things.

Another instance of practical advice, which Praetorius has learned from his own experience, has to do with his recommended seating plan for singers.

> I have always put the sopranos together with the tenors and the altos with the bass … The reason is that I have not only seen most other composers do the same, but that it is because of the harmony and the intervals. If the singers stand close to each other and have to read and sing from one part, sopranos and tenors will produce pleasant sixths and the alto and basses fifths and octaves. Otherwise a singer would fill the other's ears with unpleasant fourths, the usual progressions between soprano and alto, or tenor and alto, spoiling the music and making singing distasteful, particularly if the performers carrying the other two parts are not placed near enough to complete and round out the harmony.

---

27 Ibid., 31.
28 Ibid., 33ff.
29 Ibid., 88. He had found, for example, that a composition of 640 breves required one hour to perform.
30 Ibid., 35.

Nevertheless I do not want to dictate to anyone in this or other matters, but merely to give my own modest ideas and to tell what I have found to be good from my own experience; for everyone will have his own ideas and will act accordingly.[31]

When discussing various time signatures at the beginning of compositions, Praetorius finds a general lack of agreement. He suggests that the slower common time signature is used in madrigals and the faster alle-breve sign is used in motets.[32] However, he has noticed that in *all* the compositions of Gabrieli, he uses only the alle-breve sign. In the works of Viadana, he finds the alle-breve sign in compositions with text and the common time sign in instrumental works. His own opinion, agreeing with what he has found in the works of Lassus and Marenzio, was that,

> the common time sign should be used 'for those motets and other sacred compositions which have many black notes, in order to show that the beat is to be taken more slowly … Anyone, however, may reflect upon such matters himself and decide, on the basis of text and music, where the beat has to be slow and where fast.

In concerti, where madrigal and motet *styles* are found, it is necessary to change tempo. Here, instead of using the common time and alle-breve signs, Praetorius suggests it might be better to employ the new practice of using Italian words, such as *adagio*, *presto*, etc.[33]

Praetorius also treats proportional signs and their meaning here, as a topic which he obviously related to the speed of a given beat. Here he feared the conductor might end up beating so fast that,

> we make the spectators laugh and offend the listeners with incessant hand and arm movements and give the crowd an opportunity for raillery and mockery.[34]

That tempo in the sixteenth century was a decision made by the performer, and not the composer, may surprise some readers. Praetorius clearly recommends[35] a level of rubato never mentioned in other treatises. First he makes two general rules, that a performance must not be hurried and that all note values must be observed. Then he adds,

> But to use, by turns, now a slower, now a faster beat, in accordance with the text, lends dignity and grace to a performance and makes it admirable … Some do not want such mixture of [tempi] in any one composition. But I cannot accept their opinion, especially since it makes motets and concerti particularly delightful, when after some slow and expressive measures at

---

31 Ibid., 90.
32 Ibid., 48ff.
33 Ibid., 51.
34 Ibid., 74.
35 Ibid., 79ff.

the beginning several quick phrases follow, succeeded in turn by slow and stately ones, which again change off with faster ones.

The purpose of this he says is to avoid monotony and he adds the same advice relative to dynamics.

> Besides, it adds much charm to harmony and melody, if the dynamic level in the vocal and instrumental parts is varied now and then.[36]

Later Praetorius returns to dynamics, mentioning that the Italians are beginning to use *forte*, *piano*, etc., to mark changes within a concerto. It is interesting that, in this case at least, he seems to suggest the two, dynamics and tempo, go together.

> I rather like this practice. There are some who believe that this is not very appropriate, especially in churches. I feel, however, that such variety [in dynamics] and change [in tempo] are not only agreeable and proper, if applied with moderation and designed to express the feelings of the music, and affect the ear and the spirit of the listener much more and give the concerto a unique quality and grace. Often the composition itself, as well as the text and the meaning of the words, requires that one [change] at times—but not too frequently or excessively—beating now fast, now slowly, also that one lets the choir by turns sing quietly and softly, and loudly and briskly. To be sure, in churches there will be more need of restraint in such changes than at banquets.[37]

It is particularly interesting here, that Praetorius gives one Latin term, *lento gradu*, which he says was understood to mean that the voice was both softer and slower.

Now Praetorius makes two quite extraordinary suggestions regarding performance, both having to do with the performance of cadences.[38] Moreover, he switches his text from German into Latin for this discussion, making us wonder if this were exclusive information allowed only to those conductors who were formally educated. In any case, the importance of these two observations cannot be stressed enough, in our view.

It is our general understanding today that a modern *ritard* is usually inappropriate for Renaissance music, especially as the composer so often accomplishes this effect through a gradual lengthening of note values at the final cadence. But we have never read elsewhere of making a fermata on the next-to-last harmony, which he suggests was common practice by fine musicians!

> It is not very commendable and pleasant when singers, organists, and other instrumentalists from habit hasten directly from the penultimate note of a composition into the last note without any hesitation. Therefore I believe I should here admonish those who have hitherto not observed

---

36 Later he mentions, with regard to concerti, that a softer dynamic level can also be achieved by simply not having as many instruments doubling in a particular choir. [Ibid., 128 (108)].

37 Ibid., 132 (112).

38 Ibid., 80.

this as it is done at princely courts and by other well-constituted musical organizations, to linger somewhat on the penultimate note, whatever its time value—whether they have [already] held it for four, five, or six *tactus*—and only then proceed to the last note.

His second 'secret' regarding the performance of cadences is based on a principle which can be found in earlier literature, having to do with acoustics. Most conductors today know that music sounds better if balanced in such a way that the lower tones are performed louder than higher tones. What is surprising here is the extent to which Praetorius carries this.

> As a piece is brought to a close, all the remaining voices should stop simultaneously at the sign of the conductor or choir master. The tenors should not prolong their tone, a fifth above the bass or lowest voice … after the bass has stopped. But if the bass continues to sound a little longer, for another two or four *tactus*, it lends charm and beauty to the music [*Cantilenae*], which no one can deny.

On the Requirements of Good Singing

One of the chapters in this volume Praetorius calls, 'The Method of Teaching Choir Boys who Love and Enjoy Singing, According to the new Italian Style.'[39] Praetorius begins this discussion by presenting his primary aesthetic purpose in music. As the orator must, through his style of speaking, arouse the emotions of the listeners, so,

> Similarly a musician must not only sing, but he must sing artfully and expressively in order to move the hearts of the listeners, to arouse their emotions and to allow the music to accomplish its ultimate purpose.

In order to accomplish this, Praetorius says the singer must have a naturally fine voice, a good mind and a thorough knowledge of music. But he must also understand what makes good taste in music, in particular the art of improvisation.

> He must know … where to introduce runs or coloraturas (called *passaggi* by the Italians), that is, not anywhere in a composition, but appropriately, at the right time and in a certain way, in order that the listener may not only be aware of the loveliness of the voice, but also be able to enjoy the art of singing.

The singer who has been gifted with a fine voice, but does not know how to do these things correctly will 'provide little joy for the listeners, particularly those who have some knowledge of the art; on the contrary, it makes them sullen and sleepy.'

---

39 Ibid., 229ff.

Learning the art of beautiful singing, says Praetorius, as in all the other arts, is a matter of Nature, Doctrine and Practice. Regarding Nature, Praetorius says again that the singer must have a beautiful, pleasantly vibrating voice ('not, however, in the manner to which some singers in schools are accustomed, but with moderation'), a smooth round throat (which apparently was thought to aid diminutions), be able to sustain a long tone and find some range in which he can produce a full sound without falsetto. The undesirable qualities in a voice are taking too many breaths, singing through one's nose and keeping the voice in the throat and singing with the teeth closed.

Praetorius mentions two specific sixteenth-century vocal techniques which are quite interesting. The first, *Intonatio*,

> refers to the manner in which a vocal piece is started. Opinions vary about this, some wanting to start the tone on the proper written pitch, some a second below, but in a way that the pitch is gradually raised. Some prefer to begin on the third, some on the fourth, some with a delicate and soft voice. All these methods, for the most part, are designated by the term *accentus*.

The second vocal technique, *Exclamatio*,

> is the proper means of moving the emotions and must be achieved by increasing the voice. It can be employed with all dotted minims and semiminims in descending motion. Especially the following note which moves somewhat fast, arouses the emotions more than the semibreve, which is more frequently used and more effective with a raising and lowering of the voice, and without *exclamatio*.

By Doctrine, Praetorius seems to mean the proper art of embellishment and improvisation. He provides considerable discussion, including musical examples, but we shall only quote his basic definitions. He begins with diminution.

> One speaks of diminution when a longer note is broken up into many other faster and smaller notes. There are different kinds of them [including] accent, tremulo, groppi and tirata.

His examples of 'accent' appear to be single and multiple passing tones, in a variety of rhythmic configurations.

Tremulo 'is nothing but a quiver of the voice over one note; organists call it a mordent.'

Gruppi 'are used in cadences and have to be executed more sharply than the tremuli.' His examples appear as main-note trills.

Tirate 'are long, fast, diatonic runs up or down the keyboard.' The examples, in each case, fill an octave diatonically.

Trills, although he provides numerous configurations in which a trill may be found, he finds more difficult to explain.

These can only be learned through live demonstration and the efforts of a teacher. Then one may learn from the other just as one bird learns by watching another.

Passaggi 'are fast runs which are employed over longer notes, both diatonically and in skips of any size, ascending as well as descending.' In other words, improvisation.

Regarding the third essential, Practice, Praetorius says it would take too long to discuss—better to just study everything he has provided in this volume!

On Thorough-bass

An idea new to the sixteenth century, but one which would of course become familiar in the Baroque, was the thorough-bass. The discussion of this new idea by Praetorius[40] is interesting not only because it permits us to observe an early contemporary reaction, but for how he discusses its use in actual practice.

> To be sure, the thorough-bass was not invented for the benefit of negligent or unwilling organists who dislike preparing their scores ...
>
> In my humble opinion the greatest advantage of the thorough-bass lies in the fact that it furnishes a fine summary for the benefit of a Kapellmeister or other music director. When several copies are made of such a thorough-bass, especially in concerti for several choirs, these can then be distributed among the organists and lutenists of each choir ... marking in red ink the passages they are to play. The conductor should keep one copy for himself, in order to have the entire composition before him, not only because of changes in the *tactus*, to *tripla* and other kinds of time, but also in order to be able to cue the individual choirs.

Before continuing his discussion of thorough-bass, Praetorius digresses to discuss the player who will most use this new form of notation, the organist.[41] The organist, he says, must have three qualifications:

1. He must know counterpoint or at least be able to sing reliably, recognize proportions and the tactus or mensuration correctly, know how to resolve dissonances into consonances on any degree ...
2. He has to have a good grasp of the score and be well practiced in handling the keys, keyboards, or stops on the neck of his instrument, be it organ, regal, lute, theorbo or a similar fundamental instrument, so that he does not have to grope for the intervals ... For he knows that the eye has to be turned toward the score, and the motet, concerto, madrigal, or canzona before him at all times and therefore he can divert little attention to the keyboard ...

---

40 Ibid., 144 (124) ff.
41 Ibid., 145 (125) ff.

Here he adds, in passing, that since most German organists are accustomed to playing from tablature, they should first write out the score to see how thorough-bass works.

3. He has to have a good ear and be able to follow the singers.

Since we are seeing the thorough-bass practice at its birth, at least so far as Praetorius knows, it is interesting to find that the Italian composers were as yet only sporadically using the numeric symbols. Praetorius is quick to say that if this system is going to work, the numbers must be used all the time. To illustrate the potential problem, Praetorius quotes from a new score he has just received by Bernardo Strozzi:

> Therefore I must not fail to demonstrate clearly and conclusively that such figures are absolutely necessary, no matter what others may say, especially since no organist can know or guess the intentions of the composer. For when the organist would assume the composer had put a fifth in a certain place, it might well have been a sixth ... Anyone with a discriminating ear can reflect how pleasant a performance will sound when the organist decides to play a fifth while the singer sings a sixth ...
>
> Some say indeed, that one should indulge one's ear and move one's fingers according to what one hears. To those I reply that this will bring no good results. For once the keyboard is struck, a sound is immediately produced, and though one may want to remove one's finger quickly, it has accomplished its task and the dissonance has been heard.

To this Praetorius adds,

> If he were deaf or would not hear very well and had to be constantly afraid of playing a fifth instead of a sixth ... he would with all his fear hardly be able to pay much attention to the thorough-bass. While looking for the sixths and sevenths which he hears, he would skip notes and get off the track completely.

Interestingly, he also has observed that organists, who had not yet mastered reading this new notation, and thus encountered problems in performance, would simply begin improvising to hide the problems!

> But when they heard their own mistakes, they would quickly start with diminutions and runs until finally they managed to calm down. But in this way they would often disturb the [improvisation] of the singers.

In the end, as Praetorius sees it, the real value of the thorough-bass numbers is to help the organist, to prevent errors which might embarrass him.

> Without these figures one would rather have to regard him as a fool whose lot it is, among other things, to have to guess all kinds of foolishness and stupidity. When the organist thus dares to guess and anticipate the ideas in the composer's mind, he will come to grief and appear like a clumsy idiot. Therefore one immediately says that the organist is crazy and has lost his head.

Another advantage of this new invention, especially to Praetorius, an organist himself, was that one only had to keep the thorough-bass parts themselves and not the entire scores. Why, he says, if one had to keep in books of tablature just the music played in one church in Rome during a single year, 'the organist would have to have a bigger library than a doctor at laws.'

ON CHURCH MUSIC

In Praetorius' discussion of the Church Concerto, he clearly follows the arguments of the Church that the emphasis must be on the words. He mentions that Viadana reports he has found this violated in performances he has heard in which, for lack of singers, some parts are simply left out. Viadana had even heard,

> a motet for five, six or more voices sung to the organ, when there were no more than two or three singers present, particularly in monasteries. The absence of the other voices would considerably impair the loveliness and charm of the ensemble, the more so since the missing parts would be full of imitations and cadences, etc. Thus, after long rests [caused by the missing voices] the text would be mutilated, the listeners much annoyed and the singers burdened with extra work and trouble.[42]

Further significance in the importance given to the text can be seen in a quotation which Praetorius provides following his discussion of thorough-bass, a new system he valued as a practical musician. But there were detractors, no doubt from among the Scholastic 'speculative' musicians, who pointed out that this new thorough-bass could not effectively be used in new editions of the older polyphonic church music. The answer of Praetorius is enlightening because it confirms, as we have documented so abundantly in these volumes, that many people actually living in the sixteenth century considered the polyphonic Church music old-fashioned and archaic. Nothing could be further from the impression left by modern music history texts than what Praetorius describes here. All the more interesting is the fact that he is quoting a contemporary Italian, Agostino Agazzari.

> If someone told me that the bass is not sufficient in the case of the old motets and pieces which are full of imitations and counterpoints I would reply that we no longer make use of such compositions of their kind, because of the confusion and the garbling of the text and words which result from the long and interwoven fugues. Besides, they really give no pleasure and lack charm, for when all voices are sung one hears neither sentence nor sense, since everything is interrupted by frequent imitations and all voices sing different words at the same time, which displeases discerning listeners who pay attention to this. For these reasons and little more a certain pope would have banned music entirely from the Church had not Palestrina taken matters in hand and proved that the fault lay with the composers and not with the art of music. In order to demonstrate this he composed a mass called '*Missa Papae Marcelli*.' For while such

---

42   Ibid., 4.

compositions may be good according to the rules of counterpoint, they are not good according to the precepts of good and true music.[43]

ON THE PERFORMANCE OF CHURCH CONCERTI

Although the fact is scarcely mentioned in music history texts, instruments were used regularly with the voices in both Catholic and Lutheran churches throughout the sixteenth century. We have given numerous examples of documentation for this in the previous chapter and Praetorius also makes a reference, in passing, to this being a common practice. He is speaking of the possibility of doubling a voice part either at the unison or octave, when he pauses to mention,

> This will hardly annoy anyone who has had experience in princely and other chapels, nor town musicians, if they stop to consider that in their own church choirs they put a cornett or trombone player next to the choir boys with whom they play in unison and octaves.[44]

While such doubling must have been fairly common during the sixteenth century, the Italians extended this idea into the realm of original composition in their famous repertoire of polychoral works known as Church Concerti. One of the most striking revelations about sixteenth-century performance found in the third volume of *Syntagma Musicum* deals with the performance of such compositions. Praetorius clearly suggests that these compositions were not intended to be performed as written, but were thought of as a kind of 'source material' from which the conductor or choir master could extract from, add to or enlarge at will. We see this freedom in application distinctly when he defines the origin of the word *capella*, or one of the choirs which make up a polychoral composition in the Italian style.

> In my opinion the Italians originally used *capella* to designate an additional separate choir, extracted from several different choirs with various kinds of instruments and voices, as they are employed at the larger imperial, Austrian or other Catholic musical establishments ... In every concerto one, two or three such *capellae* can be extracted and set up in different parts of the church, each of them consisting only of four persons, or more if available. In case there is a lack of performers, they can be left out entirely.[45]

Praetorius, an experienced Church conductor, devotes a significant portion of this volume to explaining the perimeters, possibilities and problems in such reassembling and reorchestrating of the original music. While our purpose here will be to simply outline his

---

43 Ibid., 150.
44 Ibid., 138 (118).
45 Ibid., 133 (113).

major suggestions, it will soon become apparent to the reader how pale in comparison are our performances today of the works of composers such as Giovanni Gabrieli.

Praetorius begins with some observations regarding the vocal parts alone.[46] The reader must keep in mind that Praetorius is thinking here of a work, let us say, which appears on paper for *two* four-voice choirs, one of four voices of singers and one of four voices of instruments, which might be performed as *five or more* four-voice choirs, spread throughout the church. The additional, newly created choirs, consist of material taken from the original version of the composition.

The soprano part, 'sung by light and delicate voices of small boys,' he recommends doubling to the extent that it can be heard by all the other choirs. We get our first indication of what Praetorius means by 'doubling' when he speaks in general of the middle vocal parts.

> The middle voices, such as alto and tenor, may similarly move in unison in all choirs. For in such a case it sounds no different than when eight, nine or ten boys—if there are enough singers available—are put on a single part next to one another, sometimes along with an instrumentalist, on trombone, cornett or violin. When one separates the various choirs and puts one here, one there, the third still further off, and so on, it is surely best if all the middle parts in each choir continue throughout a composition. This will allow the harmony to resound more fully and to be more clearly heard throughout the entire church.

The handling of the bass part was a very sensitive issue with Praetorius, for purposes of harmony and acoustics. There is what he calls a 'foundation bass' in every composition, which would be the true bass line in a modern analytical sense. But in polychoral compositions this is (on paper) found at the bottom of only one choir, the remaining or other choirs having parts labeled 'bass,' but which are not in fact the true bass. These other basses, Praetorius calls middle basses. The problem is that if a given listener in the church happens to be seated near a choir which does not have the true bass, and is seated too far away to hear the true, or foundation, bass, wherever that choir is located, the listener hears harmonies in incorrect inversions, etc. There are two immediate solutions. If the church has an organ, then the organist plays 'the lowest bass for a foundation,' presumably loud enough to serve as the true bass for the listener. If there is no organ, the conductor or choir master extracts the true bass and spreads it around to the other choirs, thus,

> making the foundation bass heard everywhere and therefore doubling it in each choir is particularly necessary in schools and municipal churches, where one cannot have an organist, regal or positive with every choir as in princely and other chapels.[47]

Having made these suggestions regarding the vocal parts, Praetorius turns to the production at large. He begins by stating that from his experience in the performances he has heard,

---

46 Ibid., 91ff.
47 Ibid., 92.

there are 'three general kinds of flaws frequently heard in concerti.' The first objection is directed toward those who perform the composition as it is written.

1. The discrimination of the performers does not always go far enough to explore and grasp the potential of the artfulness of the written composition.
2. That the instruments are not selected according to the type of concerto, or do not agree with the voices and form discords with them.
3. They put the lowest bass in one choir only.

With regard to the third 'flaw,' Praetorius again recommends that in tuttis the forces be rearranged so that *all* the basses are given the true bass in unison. He quotes an unnamed musician in this regard:

> When the choirs are far separated, the real bass or lowest voice in motets of eight, ten, twelve, sixteen, or more voices should be retained in all choirs whenever they sing together; particularly at the end it should be heard clearly above all others. Otherwise, with no foundation underneath, cacophony results, as both [score] and experience prove.[48]

Now, regarding the distribution of the music in the 'new' choirs which one might create, Praetorius offers some general rules. This discussion,[49] which includes creating new doublings several octaves higher and lower than the original music, is so enlightening we feel obligated to quote it in full.

> Unison doubling can be used throughout a composition without hesitation in high, low and middle voices as well as by instruments.
>
> Octave doubling can be permitted in all voices, provided one part is sung while the other part is played. In arranging a concerto it is quite customary in the case of a low choir, in which the soprano is to be sung by an alto with three trombones or three bassoons, to double the alto with a violin. The instrumentalist then must play the alto part an octave higher. In tuttis—also when only a few choirs join in together—one can quite fittingly have the alto part of the vocal choir transposed one octave higher and use it with the instrumental choir.
>
> The same thing may be done in all voices, and it does not offend the ear when the part of the singer in a choir is played an octave higher or lower by cornetts, violins, recorders, trombones, or bassoons. For some melody instruments, especially recorders are to be played one or two octaves higher than written. This compares with the practice of combining many different stops on an organ in unisons, octaves, super-octaves and sub-octaves and contrabasses.
>
> Provided enough players are available, quite a splendid sound is produced in tuttis if one assigns to a bass part—at the regular pitch—a common or a bass trombone, a chorist-bassoon, or pommer; in addition a double bass trombone, double bassoon, or large double pommer, and double bass, which all sound an octave lower, like the sub-basses on organs. This is particularly common in contemporary Italian concerti and can be sufficiently justified.

---

48 Ibid., 94ff.
49 Ibid., 95ff.

After giving several more examples of doubling, taken from his own experience, Praetorius addresses the principal objection which one might have to this freedom of doubling, which is that it creates parallel octaves. For Praetorius this was a question not of theory but rather a question of the ear responding to the acoustics of the specific performance.

> If someone should have a concerto with only two choirs—one high and one low, positioned at opposite ends—performed at a church or a large hall and should remain standing with the higher choir, he will scarcely hear the lower choir in tuttis when both choirs join in together. He will find then that he can hear no foundation with the higher choir; but in absence of the lower fifths—formed by the foundation bass against the bassett or tenor of the higher choir—dissonant fourths will be heard for the most part, especially if there is no fundamental instrument present, such as a positive or regal. Someone wrote me recently from Venice that,
>> the leading musicians in Italy make frequent use of unisons and octaves in tuttis. For they know from their own experience that in large churches, where the choirs are far apart, a much fuller sound is achieved in tuttis when the choirs move in unison or octaves with one another than when they are arranged in such a way that unisons and octaves are carefully avoided, with the result that a perfect and full harmony can no longer be heard.
>
> I could name a number of very excellent older theorists and practical musicians who would not allow me to do this at first. But later, when they had tried it themselves and further reflected upon the matter they had to approve of it and agree with me that having previously considered it very bad, almost like a deadly sin, they themselves now found that unisons as well as octaves in the basses could not be avoided if in all choirs a complete harmony were to be maintained.

Praetorius also quotes the Italian composer Viadana in this regard.

> In concerti for several choirs one can without danger of confusion extract various capellae at one's pleasure. It does no damage then if there are octaves and unisons between the choirs, since one can hardly hear them, the choirs being placed far apart from one another.[50]

After arguing for freedom in unisons and octaves, Praetorius adds that parallel fifths are not allowed in any circumstances. He says, however, that he sees frequent diminished fifths in Italian music as well as improvisation [diminution] which 'helps to excuse and cover up a great deal.'[51]

Praetorius devotes extensive discussion to the possible choirs of instruments which may be used to augment concerti. Perhaps the most interesting of his review of these consorts is his discussion of one evidently new, the string consort.[52]

---

50 Ibid., 99.

51 Ibid., 100.

52 The reader is reminded that, in general, the 'professional' player was a wind player until after the middle of the sixteenth century.

I have come to the conclusion that there is some need for such a capella. For some among us Germans are still unaccustomed to the new Italian invention, according to which sometimes only one, sometimes two or three *Concertat-Stimen* sing to the accompaniment of organ or regal, and do not like this style very well; they are of the opinion that it sounds too empty and is not particularly pleasing and agreeable to those who know nothing about music. Therefore I have had to think of a way to add a choir in four parts which could at all times join in with trombones or *Geigen*.

Since such an ensemble, when used in church, makes for a richer sound, I soon achieved public acclaim …

It is to be noted here that this capella I have called *fidicinia* because it is better to have it made up of string instruments such as *Geigen*, lutes, harps, and especially viola da gamba, where these are available, and viols da braccio. For the sound of viols and *Geigen* has particular delicacy and is continuous, without the breathing necessary on trombones and other wind instruments.[53]

But, he admits, the idea of a string consort is a new one and not everyone will like it.

But it is up to anyone's pleasure to use this capella, or leave it out. For, as mentioned above, I have only added it because of the approbation of certain listeners and would not otherwise have deemed it very important.

But if one would wish to compose or arrange for such a *capella fidicinia* … one would attract those listeners in Germany who still do not know what to make of the new style, and once having roused their interest one would undoubtedly succeed in giving them great pleasure and satisfaction.

Praetorius mentions the string choir again in association with the cornett choir,[54] both being recommended for high choirs. If the part is very high, he prefers the violin,[55] 'unless a good cornett player having complete control of his instrument is available.' For the lower parts he recommends a trombone or a *Tenorgiege*, since the lower cornets [known also as 'serpents'] sound 'as unpleasant as a cowhorn.'

He makes his recommendations on the basis of the clef seen in the original music, but also on the basis of mode. Thus for the transverse flute choir we read,

On the transverse flute one generally plays the tenth mode, Hypoaeolian, one tone lower. None of the modes are better fitted for these instruments than Dorian, Hypodorian and Hypoaeolian taken down a tone.[56]

He mentions that the lower parts of such a flute choir cannot be heard well on flute and recommends trombone or *Tenorgeige*. However, he says, such a part could be played by a

---

53 Ibid., 136 (116) ff.
54 Ibid., 154.
55 Praetorius always uses *Geigen*.
56 Ibid., 156.

flute an octave higher, 'along with all kinds of other instruments, if no other transverse flutes are involved.'

The recorder choir is of such a range that Praetorius points out such parts can be just as effective with voices or viols da gamba.[57] In the case of a vocal choir, he mentions that boys can learn to sing high A 'provided one would take the pains with them and not mind the trouble to teach them.' He adds that it is sometimes nice if a boy sings the tenor part an octave higher. If a choir of recorders is used, 'I find it better to give the bass part to a bass trombone, or even better a bassoon.' In general, he recommends,

> If one wishes to use recorders alone without any other instruments, in a canzona, motet or concerto for several choirs, one can effectively use the entire consort of recorders, particularly the five sizes beginning with the largest—because the small ones make too much noise—which produce a very pleasant, soft and delicate harmony. They are especially effective in smaller rooms; in the church, however, the large bassett and bass recorders cannot be heard very well.

Regarding the trombone and bassoon choirs, Praetorius is primarily concerned with warning the reader of their limited upper ranges.[58] No trombonist, he says, can play a high G, and bassoons and pommer should be limited to the D above middle C, although 'some players are getting to the point now where they can play four, five and more tones higher with good intonation, provided they are quite skillful and have particularly good reeds.' He concludes with a comment on modes.

> It should be noted here that for such large and low bass instruments as pommers, bassoons or dulcians, and trombones, no compositions are better fitted than those written in Hypodorian (in our usage the second mode) and Hypoionian, which we call the twelfth mode, otherwise called the fifth or sixth mode.

The crumhorn choir presented a difficulty in the fact that the instrument known to Praetorius had a range of only six notes.[59] For them he recommends Mixolydian transposed down a fourth or Hypomixolydian.

Although the shawm choir was a basic sixteenth-century consort, Praetorius finds them difficult to use as an optional choir in a concerto because they are constructed a fifth apart and hence exceed the ranges of the music.[60] He warns that the higher, or smaller, the shawms are, the more intonation problems there are. In particular, it is best 'to leave the squeakey discant shawm alone.'

The final consort Praetorius discusses is the lute choir, by which he means an ensemble consisting of harpsichords or spinets, theorbos, lutes, pandoras, *Orphoreon*, cithers, a large

---

57 Ibid., 157.
58 Ibid., 159ff.
59 Ibid., 165.
60 Ibid., 166.

bass lyra, or 'whatever fundamental instruments of this kind one may be able to gather together,' a mixture he associates with the English.[61] He adds an interesting example from his own experience.

> I once arranged to have the magnificent, immeasurably beautiful motet by de Wert, 'Egressus Jesus,' in seven voices, performed by 2 theorbos, 3 lutes, 2 cithers, 4 harpsichords and spinets, 7 viols, 2 transverse flutes, two boys and an alto singer and large bass viol. This produced a brilliant and magnificent resonance.

In addition to this discussion of the various consorts used in concerti, Praetorius also comments on the proper style of playing the fundamental organ part. This discussion is very important because it reveals, in passing, the extent to which improvisation was also a part of the performance tradition of such works as the familiar concerti of Gabrieli. He begins by quoting Viadana.[62]

> The organist should play from the thorough-bass part, or score, in a very plain style and as cleanly and correctly as possible just as the notes follow one another, without using many runs, especially in the left hand which carries the foundation. But if he wishes to employ some faster movement in the right hand, as in agreeable cadences or similar figures, he has to do this with particular moderation and restraint. Otherwise the singers are impeded and confused, and their voices covered up and drowned out.

Praetorius, in adding his own observations, reveals that the voices as well were engaging in improvisation.

> I have been told by discriminating music lovers of high and noble rank that there are outstanding organists in Italy and elsewhere who, in such concerti, use neither diminutions, nor groppi in cadences, nor mordents. They simply play one chord after another as indicated in the thorough-bass so that the motion of the hands is hardly noticeable.
>
> I rather like the idea that no black notes are used. [But] it does not seem so inappropriate to me if in some concerti the organist observes carefully where the singer makes his diminutions and passaggi and then plays in a plain style, moving stepwise from one key to the next. But as the singer, after completing many varied passaggi, beautiful diminutions, groppi, tremoletti, and trilli, becomes tired and sings the following notes without elaboration, the organist may introduce agreeable diminutions, etc., but only in the right hand—and attempt to imitate the singer's figures, diminutions, variations, etc. Thus the two collaborate, as it were, in producing an echo, until the singer recovers and again proceeds to display his artful embellishments. In my humble opinion, one should not omit all mordents and tremoletti when no diminution or similar figures are employed; for they will not disturb the singer's voice at all, or not nearly as much as all sorts of runs and diminution.

---

61 Ibid., 168.

62 Ibid., 137ff.

Moving to new points, Praetorius says it is not possible for the organist to perform all concerti bass parts at sight. Therefore he should look over the composition, to determine the style and to plan his progressions more perfectly. During tuttis in concerti, the organist should 'use both manual and pedal simultaneously.' However, Praetorius advises, that is enough.

> But one should not add other stops, for the delicate and soft tone of the singers would otherwise be smothered by the heavy noise of the many organ stops and then the organ would be more prominent than the singers.

Praetorius also mentions the well-known tradition of having one or more string instruments double the fundamental organ line. In his discussion of the various instruments appropriate to this function, we are most interested in his reference once again to frequency of improvisation. Here, as in all cases Praetorius has mentioned, he means by 'improvisation' what the player does with the part in front of him. In this light the following is rather extraordinary.

> He who plays the lute (which is the noblest instrument of them all) must play it nobly, with much invention and variety, not as is done by those who, because they have a ready hand, do nothing but play runs and diminution from beginning to end, especially when playing with other instruments which do the same, in all of which nothing is heard but babel and confusion, displeasing and disagreeable to the listener. Sometimes, therefore, he must use gentle strokes and repercussions, sometimes slow *passaggi*, sometimes rapid and repeated ones, sometimes something played on the bass strings, sometimes beautiful conceits, repeating and bringing out these figures at different pitches and in different places; he must, in short, so weave the voices together with long *Gruppen*, trills, and accents, each in its turn, that he gives grace to the consort and enjoyment and delight to the listeners, judiciously preventing these embellishments from conflicting with one another and allowing time for each.[63]

The new violin also appears on the scene playing in the same fashion.

> The discant Geige, known as Violono, must also play beautiful *passaggi*, distinct and long, with playful figures and little echoes and imitations repeated in several places, passionate accents, mute strokes of the bow *Gruppi*, trills, etc.[64]

Having given the reader his views on the individual characteristics of the various consorts which might serve as additional choirs in the performance of the Church concerti, he now devotes a lengthy section to the art of doing this in practice, with particular reference to his own compositions.[65] Again, we can only briefly outline his extensive proposals.

---

63 Ibid., 146ff.
64 Ibid., 148.
65 Ibid., 169ff.

The First Art he calls *Tubiciniae and Tympanistriae*, in which one employs the aristocratic trumpet corps.[66] The problem here is that these trumpet corps often did not read music and performed only memorized 'concert' works, often called sonatas. But Praetorius found that if the trumpets were, let us say, in D, if he wrote a Church concerto in D they could simply join in, playing their memorized pieces, and it would sound OK—provided the Church choir master took their tempo!

> One thing should be remembered here: since the trumpeters are in the habit of rushing, because the trumpet requires a good deal of breath which cannot be sustained very well at a slow pace, one should accelerate the beat when the trumpeters enter, otherwise they always finish their sonatas too soon. Later the beat may be lengthened, until the trumpeters start in again.

And if, due to some greater need by the duke, the trumpeters do not show up, you can perform the composition anyway.

> But if one cannot, will not, or must not use the trumpeters and timpanists, such compositions can nevertheless be performed quite well in town churches without trumpeters.

The Second Art consists of having four boys placed in separate locations in the church, with three of the boys joined by various instruments and the fourth by the full choir. The special effect occurs with,

> each of them singing what is found in his part, cleanly and with animation, clearly and distinctly as if reciting the notes. Thereupon the entire vocal and instrumental ensemble and organ respond, in a style which the Italians call *concerti ripiani* …
>
> It is also quite delightful, and the words of the text can be heard better, if at the beginning the first verse is sung by the boys alone to the accompaniment of a soft and delicate stop on the organ, the *Geigen* and lutes being omitted entirely …
>
> If one or two discant parts are blown on instruments and not sung, one can nevertheless easily guess the preceding texts and rhymes of the first and third discants from the parts of the second and fourth discants which respond to the former like an echo.
>
> On some organs there are *Cymbel-Glöcklein* which, added to the full choir, sound quite delightful and attractive. If they are not too loud, they may sometimes be used even when the boys sing alone.

The Third Art is what we would call today a small church concerto,[67] familiar in such compositions by Schütz, for example, for one singer and three trombones. In a word, it was a kind of chamber concerto. Praetorius discusses this type extensively, with respect to

---

66 At the end of this volume [Ibid., 224] Praetorius lists his books. Among these is a now lost work entitled, *Instruction in the use of trumpets and timpani with full ensemble in electoral and princely chapels, also in other churches, depending on time and place, without producing confusion or drowning out the other vocal and instrumental parts.*

67 Although music history texts do not discuss it, there were at this time four general kinds of concerti: a large and small church concerto and a large and small concerto da camera.

instrumentation and placement. One may have two, three or four singers standing with or apart from an organ; or one may have choirs with solo singers and instruments; or one can alternate singers and instruments, as in the case of a psalm. Another 'manner,' as he calls it, is to have choirs with the discant parts improvising.

One may have a string choir double the organ, 'good for inexperienced organists.' The reader gains the impression here that the current string playing must have been rather robust, for Praetorius warns,

> It must be noted here that in small churches, chapels, and rooms, when one, two or a few more voices alone are singing and a regal or other fundamental instrument is available, the string choir must play quite delicately and softly or must be omitted entirely. Otherwise the voices cannot be heard properly because of the sound of the instruments. But in large churches, where the string choir can be separated a little further from the voices and placed by itself, it must not be left out; on the contrary it is highly necessary in order to provide a richer sound.

Another manner of the Third Art is to have a full chorus, with instruments, which enters in the middle or at the end of a composition. An alternative manner is to have two instrumental choirs, carrying the inner parts, but positioned in a separate location. He adds that the further away the instruments are from the singers, the better the individual voices can be heard. Another manner related to these is to have the two discants improvising, with instrumental choirs used in alternation.

The Fourth Art is a polychoral work in which an entirely different chorale is sung between the verses of the original composition, with the penultimate verse sung in unison with the congregation. Similarly, the Fifth Art is the insertion of a 'Hallelujah' or 'Gloria' fragment 'at the beginning, in the middle and at the end of a composition.' This, he says, may be thought of as a kind of ritornello and he mentions that he got the idea from an Italian composition, by Fattorini, in which the composer had inserted some Latin phrases in this manner. Praetorius found this style to be very pleasing[68] and he mentions that he thought of writing out a separate 'Hallelujah' or 'Gloria' in every mode so they could be published and made available for this purpose. But, he moans, in his previous efforts which have been published there were 'so many errors that the mere thought of it makes me break out in a cold sweat.'

The Sixth Art follows in the same manner, but with an instrumental sinfonia played as a kind of prelude at the beginning of the choral work. An alternative might be to perform a 'pavan, mascherada, or ballet in place of the sinfonia,' but one must make sure the piece has a full harmony. Here again, ritornelli may be inserted in the middle of the choral work and astonishingly he recommends,

> a galliard, saltarello, courante, volta, or similarly gay canzonette, which, however, must not be too long. I have found that quite a few people have liked this very well.

---

68 The repeating ritornello was one of the important steps toward later 'architectural forms,' which are found pleasing by the right hemisphere of the brain.

In the Seventh Art,

> The chorale is sung by one voice while the other parts, be it two, three, four, five or more, play on instruments alone, producing harmony, but also fantasies and imitations against the chorale.

Four more 'Arts' follow which involve various combinations of the previous recommendations. The Twelfth Art, and final one, involves the use of echo effects.

Praetorius, at the end of this volume, lists a number of his own compositions which demonstrate these varied concerti techniques. Some of these have as many as 35 separate voices in 9 choirs! We can only say again, how pale in comparison are our performances today of the Italian polychoral compositions.

Finally, putting everything together, Praetorius deals with an essential problem in the performance of large-scale concerti, and that is tuning. His first suggestion is that it would be nice if the organist could play a little prelude to the concerto, for then the players could simultaneously be tuning.

> In conclusion I must kindly suggest to all organists that they should generally make use of an appropriate introduction when attempting to perform a concerto with several choirs in church or at a banquet. Although it may not belong to the main work, it would serve to make the audience favorably disposed, receptive and attentive, and thus entertain them better—just as excellent orators do who intend to hold forth extensively on important matters. Using their preludes at the beginning they should thus call the listeners and the entire ensemble of musicians together, as it were, so that they may look for their parts and tune their instruments properly and that way prepare themselves for the start of a good and well-sounding performance.[69]

That is theory; practice is something else! Praetorius suddenly remembers his own experience, when, as he was playing an organ prelude, the instruments suddenly ruined his performance by beginning to tune for the following concerto. Being an organist, he cannot understand why all those players can't tune their instruments and 'warm-up' at home, before they come to perform!

> But it creates great confusion and din if the instrumentalists tune their bassoons, trombones, and cornetts during the organist's prelude and carry on loudly and noisily so that it hurts one's ears and gives one the jitters. For it sounds so dreadful and makes such a commotion that one wonders what kind of mayhem is being committed. Therefore everyone should carefully tune the cornett or trombone in his lodging before presenting himself at the church or elsewhere for performance and he should work up a good embouchure with his mouthpiece [at home] in order that he may delight the ears and hearts of the listeners rather than offend them with such cacophony.

---

69 Ibid., 151.

Praetorius returns to the problem of pitch in the performance of concerti in another place, now as it is affected by personalities of the performers.

> This point above all must be carefully kept in mind in all concerti, by instrumentalists as well as singers. No one must cover up and outshout the other with his instrument or voice, though this happens very frequently, causing much splendid music to be spoiled and ruined. When one thus tries to outdo the other, the instrumentalists, particularly cornett players with their blaring, but also singers through their screaming, they cause the pitch to rise so much that the organist playing along is forced to stop entirely. At the end it happens then that the whole ensemble through excessive blowing and shouting has gone sharp by a half, often indeed a whole tone and more.[70]

ENTERTAINMENT MUSIC

One of the performance practices which followed the universal adoption of the consort principle during the sixteenth century was the changing of consorts for each composition during banquet music, thus creating variety in instrumental color. It was, in a sense, the birth of orchestration. Praetorius provides an illustration of how this might work in a typical banquet, but he arrives at this topic by first giving several definitions of *ritornello*. In the last of these, he mentions a work by Monteverdi for voices and instruments where in some places there is no text and the word *ritornello* appears. This, says Praetorius, means only the instruments play, and the purpose implied is variety of tonal color. He then mentions that the term *sinfonia* is also sometimes found in such places and he finds some composers make no clear distinction between *ritornello* and *sinfonia* in such cases. Praetorius, however, recognizes a difference in style.

> A sinfonia is not unlike an agreeable pavan or stately sonata. A ritornello, however, is like a galliard, courante, volta or canzoni, full of faster note values.[71]

In any case, he describes these as relatively brief instrumental interludes and he adds that they are not unlike the *intermedio* which are performed between the acts of Italian comedies, 'to enable the actors to change costumes and catch their breath.'

> One can proceed in a similar manner when trying to arrange some good music for banquets of noblemen and other joyful gatherings. Thus after one has had two or more boys sing with a harpsichord, regal or similar fundamental instrument, one immediately begins to play something else with lutes, pandoras, violins, cornetts, trombones and the like, with instruments alone and no voices. Then one has the voices start again, thus instruments and voices alternating by turns. Similarly after a concerto or a splendid motet a gay canzona, galliard, courante, or the like can be

---

70 Ibid., 148ff.

71 Ibid., 129 (109).

presented with instruments only. This can also be done by a single organist or a lutenist. Playing at banquets he may after performing a motet or madrigal quite slowly and gravely continue with a gay allemande, intrada, branle, or galliard, to be followed again by another motet, madrigal, pavan or artful fugue.

8 SIXTEENTH-CENTURY ENGLAND

With respect to the aesthetic and social recognition given music in the English-speaking world, the late sixteenth century must in retrospect be viewed as an unfortunate turning point. In spite of the extraordinary example set by both Henry VIII and Elizabeth I, as members of the highest class who were active musicians, the view that nobles should be performing musicians was clearly changing. There seem to us two significant reasons for this change in attitude.

First, the obvious growth in intellectual self-confidence, so apparent in the development of sixteenth-century literature, led to a certain insular isolation.[1] We will let an anonymous poem of 1600 represent many contemporary references to the general problem.

> A Painter lately with his pencil drew
> The picture of a Frenchman and Italian,
> With whom he placed the Spaniard, Turk, and Jew;
> But by himself he sat the Englishman.[2]

This self-imposed isolation is especially evident in the frequent ridicule of English students going to Italy for further study, for whom there was a commonly used term of contempt, the 'Italianate Englishmen.' Unfortunately this attitude blinded English high society to the most important insights of humanism.[3] What was sensitive in Italy was called effeminate in England and thus the active interest demonstrated by Italian nobles in promoting high quality music represents an attitude rarely found in England.

Second, the growth in economic power in England during the sixteenth century permitted England to follow the same transition one sees in ancient Rome. That is, music begins in asso-

---

1   Gustave Reese, in *Music in the Renaissance* (New York: Norton, 1959), 763, dates this isolation in music even earlier, to the latter part of the fifteenth century. That this was widely recognized, Reese points to Tinctoris' observation, which we have quoted in Volume Three, regarding the 'wretched poverty of invention' in English music.

2   Anonymous, 'Tom Tel-Troths Message,' (1600) in Frederick Furnivall, ed., *Miscellaneous*, Series VI, Shakespere's England, Nr. 2 (Vaduz: Kraus Reprint, 1965), 122. We have modernized the English in all these sixteenth-century texts.

3   One who misunderstood the Italians was Sir Philip Sidney. In a letter to his brother, quoted in *The Prose Works of Sir Philip Sidney*, ed. Albert Feuillerat (Cambridge: Cambridge University Press, 1962), III, 127, he writes,

> And for the men you shall have there, although some indeed be excellently learned, yet they are all given to such counterfeit learning, as a man shall learn of them more false grounds of things, than in any place else that I do know ... In certain fine qualities, such as Horsemanship, Weapons, Vaulting, and such like, they are better than in those other countries.

ciation with the highest levels of society, but as society becomes wealthy, music becomes the activity of slaves. We can see this very clearly in Thomas Nashe's *The Anatomie of Absurditie* (1589). In his preface he describes a group of 'extraordinary Gentlemen' discussing the 'qualities required in Castiglione's *Il Cortigiano*' (The Courtier). One of the gentlemen mentions the importance of being able to perform on the Citterne and Lute. But another gentleman, who believed that 'the only adjuncts of a Courtier were scholarship and courage,' dismisses the idea of a noble performing music. Leave it, he says,

> to the birthright of every six-penny slave.[4]

Of course, we acknowledge there were fine performers and composers in England at the end of the sixteenth century, but they were not nobles, they were slaves, or if you prefer, servants to high society. In terms of social status, and pay, can anyone pretend that this regrettable model has not remained in place in the English-speaking world until the present day?

On the Changing Manners of Gentlemen

Many people tend to think of the 'Renaissance Man' as that well-rounded gentleman who was, among many other things, an amateur musician. Thomas Whythorne, writing about 1575, believed that at this time this was indeed the case in England.

> Those who learn [music] ... for the love they have for the science and not to earn a living by ... are to be accounted among the number of those who the book called the 'Institution of a Gentleman' doth allow to learn music, and also which the book called 'The Courtier' doth ... for they would have the great gentlemen and the courtiers to learn music ... Which counsel ... the nobility and the worshipful do much follow in these days, for many of those estates have schoolmasters in their houses to teach their children both to sing [counterpoint] and also to play on instruments.[5]

However, by the end of the century, Thomas Morley creates a fictional young gentleman who is embarrassed because he is unable to sight-sing.

> Supper being ended and music books (according to the custom) being brought to the table, the mistress of the house presented me with a part earnestly requesting me to sing; but when, after many excuses, I protested unfeignedly that I could not, everyone began to wonder; yea, some whispered to others demanding how I was brought up.[6]

---

4   Thomas Nashe, *The Anatomie of Absurditie* (1589), in *The Works of Thomas Nashe*, ed., Ronald McKerrow (Oxford: Blackwell, 1966), I, 7. One can also see in this work [Ibid., 11ff.] an example of extraordinary denigration of women, again a fundamental change in perspective from the early Renaissance. Nashe (1567–1601) is best known as the author of *The Unfortunate Traveller*, which some consider the first English novel.

5   Craig Monson, 'Elizabethan London,' in *The Renaissance*, ed. Iain Fenlon (Englewood Cliffs: Prentice Hall, 1989), 333.

6   Thomas Morley, *A Plain and Easy Introduction to Practical Music*, ed. R. Alec Harman (New York: Norton, n.d.), 9.

We believe these two quotations serve to frame a change which had taken place in the manners of the gentleman. What was the philosophy which encouraged this?

The writings of Henry Peacham and Roger Ascham, a tutor to queen Elizabeth, summarize the qualities needed by the ideal noble and are in many ways the English counterparts of Baldassare Castiglione's more famous *Il Cortigiano* (The Courtier). In *The Schoolmaster* (1570), Ascham begins by revealing a curious attitude toward intellectual brilliance which we believe may have been shared by many English nobles.[7] He has observed that 'those which be commonly the wisest, the best learned, and best men' when young, seem to lose their 'quickest of wit' when older. The explanation, he believes, must be something like a sharp knife which becomes dull. Thus such brilliant young men tend to be unable to concentrate on a single field and never excel in 'hard sciences.' 'The quickest wits,' he concludes may make the best poets, but not the best orators.

Perhaps of more consequence in Ascham's view, was that those with 'quickest wit' lack important characteristics appropriate to noble society.

> Also, for manners and life, quick wits commonly be in desire [of the] newfangled, in purpose unconstant; light to promise anything, ready to forget everything, both benefit and injury, and thereby neither fast to friend nor fearful to foe; inquisitive of every trifle, not secret in greatest affairs; bold with any person, busy in every matter; soothing such as be present, nipping any that is absent; of nature, also, always flattering their betters, envying their equals, despising their inferiors; and by quickness of wit very quick and ready to like none so well as themselves.

In addition, he finds 'quick wits' tend to be 'overquick, hasty, rash, heady, brainsick,' and with a tendency towards light company.

All of this seems to suggest a perceived danger in extended study and, indeed, Ascham specifically points to the ill effects of the extended study of music.

> Some wits, moderate enough by nature, be many times marred by overmuch study and use of some sciences, namely, music, arithmetic and geometry. These sciences, as they sharpen men's wits overmuch, so they change men's manners oversore, if they be not moderately mingled and wisely applied to some good use of life. Notice all mathematical heads which be only and wholly bent to those sciences, how solitary they be themselves, how unfit to live with others, and how unapt to serve in the world.

He quotes the early medical writer, Galen (second century AD), as saying 'Much music marreth men's manners,' and then concludes that 'overmuch quickness of wit,' whether by nature or by study, does not result in the 'greatest learning, best manners, or happiest life.'

In another book, a treatise on long bow shooting called *Toxophilus*, Ascham elaborates on the dangers of music. In this dialog, Toxophilus has been explaining the many virtues of

---

[7] Roger Ascham, *The Schoolmaster* (1570), ed. Lawrence Ryan (Ithaca: Cornell University Press, 1967), 21ff. Ascham (1515–1568) was a tutor to the young Elizabeth I and later served in her court as her Latin Secretary.

shooting, when Philologus introduces the subject of music by observing that it is a common recreation for scholars. Toxophilus answers,

> I cannot deny that some music is fit for learning, and I trust you cannot choose but grant that shooting is also fit ... But as concerning which of them is most fit for learning and scholars to use, you may say what you will for your pleasure; [but] this I am sure, that Plato and Aristotle ... do mention music and all kinds of it; wherein they both agree, that music used amongst the Lydians is very ill for young men which be students for virtue and learning, for a certain nice, soft, and smooth sweetness of it, which would rather entice them to naughtiness than stir them to honesty.
> Another kind of music, invented by the Dorians, they both wonderfully praise, allowing it to be very fit for the study of virtue and learning, because of a manly, rough, and stout sound in it, which should encourage young stomachs to attempt manly matters. Now whether [today's] ballads and rounds, these galliards, pavanes, and dances, so nicely fingered, so sweetly tuned, be more like the music of the Lydians or the Dorians, you may judge for yourself.[8]

Toxophilus then quotes the same Galen comment above, that 'Much music marreth men's manners,' and elaborates on its meaning.

> Although some men will say that it is not so, but rather recreateth and maketh quick a man's mind; yet, methink, by reason it doth as honey doth to a man's stomach, which at the first receiveth it well, but afterward it maketh it unfit to abide any good strong nourishing meat, or else any wholesome sharp and quick drink. And even so in a manner these instruments make a man's wit so soft and smooth, so tender and queasy, that they be less able to brook strong and tough study. Wits be not sharpened, but rather dulled and made blunt, with such sweet softness, even as good edges be blunter which men whet upon soft chalk stones.

Toxophilus then quotes an often repeated anecdote which maintains that Cyrus, after conquering the Lydians and desiring to keep them peaceful, arranged for,

> every one of them should have a harp or a lute, and learn to play and sing. Which thing if you do ... you shall see them quickly of men made women. And thus luting and singing take away a manly stomach, which should enter and pierce deep and hard study.

Toxophilus concludes by questioning whether Aristotle and Plato knew what they were talking about.

> Therefore either Aristotle and Plato know not what was good and evil for learning and virtue, and the example of wise histories be vainly set before us, or else the minstrelsy of lutes, pipes, harps, and all other that standeth by such nice, fine, minikin fingering (such as the most part of scholars whom I know use, if they use any), is far more fit, for the womanishness of it, to dwell

---

8   *Toxophilus*, in *The Whole Works of Roger Ascham*, ed. Rev. Giles (London: John Russell Smith, 1864), II, 25ff. Ascham explains at length why shooting is the ideal exercise for the student—such things as tennis and bowling being too 'vehement.'

in the Court among ladies, than for any great thing in it, which should help good and sad study, to abide in the University among scholars.

Now Philologus agrees 'to say the truth, I never thought myself these kinds of music fit for learning.' Nevertheless he attempts to come to the defense of music, although his arguments, while interesting, are all of secondary values.

> That milk is no fitter or more natural for the bringing up of children than music is, both Galen proveth by authority, and daily use teacheth by experience. For even the little babes lacking the use of reason, are scarce so well stilled in sucking their mother's pap, as in hearing their mother sing. Again, how fit youth is made by learning to sing, for grammar and other sciences, both we daily do see ... The godly use of praising God, by singing in the church, needeth not my praise, seeing it is so praised through all the scripture ...
>
> Beside all these commodities, truly two degrees of men, which have the highest offices under the King in all this realm, shall greatly lack the use of singing, preachers and lawyers, because they shall not, without this, be able to rule their breasts for every purpose. For where is no distinction in telling glad things and fearful things, gentleness and cruelness, softness and vehementness, and such-like matters, there can be no great persuasion ... But when a man is always in one tune, like a humble bee, or else now in the top of the church, now down, that no man knoweth where to have him; or piping like a reed, or roaring like a bull, as some lawyers do, which thing they do best when they cry loudest, these shall never greatly move, as I have known many well-trained have done, because their voice was not stayed afore with learning to sing. For all voices, great and small, base and shrill, weak or soft, may be helped and brought to a good point by learning to sing.
>
> Whether this be true or not, they that stand most in need can tell best; whereof some I have known, which, because they learned not to sing when they were boys, were fain to take pain in it when they were men ...
>
> TOXOPHILUS. It were pity truly, Philologus, that the thing should be neglected; But I trust it is not as you say.
>
> PHILOLOGUS. The thing is too true; for of them that come daily to the University, where one hath learned to sing, six hath not.

Henry Peacham, in his *The Complete Gentleman*, has similar doubts about the appropriateness of a gentleman becoming too involved in music. He first discusses the general nature of nobility, discussing whether it is affected by loss of faith, unexpected poverty, engagement in commerce, etc. In such conditions he is usually able to explain the circumstances as not changing one's noble status. But, when he comes to issues 'touching mechanical arts and artists,' he is adamant.

> Whosoever labor for their livelihood and gain have no share at all in nobility or gentry, as painters, stageplayers, tumblers, ordinary fiddlers, innkeepers, fencers, jugglers, dancers, mountebanks and bearwards …[9]

Unlike Italy, where nobles continued to take pride in being actual performers of music, we see in Peacham clear evidence of a trend in England which would become more strongly evidenced in the following century, namely that the noble might well study music, but not practice it to the extent that he becomes a 'master' or to the extent that it interferes with important duties.

> I might run into an infinite sea of the praise and use of so excellent an art, but I only [touch on it] because I desire not that any noble or gentleman should, save at his private recreation and leisurable hours, prove a master in the art or neglect his more weighty employments.[10]

Proving that one was 'a master in the art' presumably included demonstration of technical proficiencies. We have seen in our discussion of sixteenth-century Italy, that Castiglione gives abundant evidence that the gentleman should appreciate listening to music, and even be able to perform, but being a *skilled* performer was quite another matter. Reflecting what seems to have been a basic attitude of nobles nearly everywhere, Castiglione, as well as Peacham here, believed the gentleman should display a certain nonchalance about all skills and should not be expected to apply himself in any form of hard labor which might result in excellence in any skill. This idea may also have formed the background for a comment by Robert Greene. In his greeting 'To the Gentlemen Readers,' of his *Carde of Fancie* (1587), he begins with an anecdote about the god, Pan, which has no relationship with the Romance which follows.

> Pan blowing upon an oten pipe a little homely music, and hearing no man dispraise his small cunning, began to play so loud, and so long, that [the listeners] were more weary in hearing his music, than he in showing his skill, till at last to claw him and excuse themselves, they said his pipe was out of tune.[11]

In addition, Castiglione had specified that one only performs before private gatherings of friends, never before the common masses. Peacham goes even further, saying that the noble does not perform before anyone else.

---

9 Henry Peacham, *The Complete Gentleman*, ed., Virgil Heltzel (Ithaca: Cornell University Press, 1962), 23. Although this work was not published until 1622, we regard it as a reflection of the end of the sixteenth century. Peacham (1576–1643) was born to a literary family and graduated from Cambridge. He thought of himself as a scholar, but he was apparently also a musician, painter and mathematician.

10 Ibid., 111.

11 Robert Greene, *Carde of Fancie* (1587), Prologue, in *The Life and Complete Works of Robert Greene*, ed. Alexander Grosart (New York: Russell & Russell, 1964), IV, 8. Greene (1560–1592) graduated from Cambridge and traveled in Italy and Spain. Although his personal life was perhaps the most sordid of all these writers, little influence of it can be found in his writing. His romance, *Pandosto* (1588), was the source of Shakespeare's *Winter's Tale*.

I desire no more in you than to sing your part sure and at the first sight withal to play the same upon your viol or the exercise of the lute, privately, to yourself.[12]

John Lyly has composed a poem which speaks of the education of the nobleman and he includes music among a list of subjects which may not be 'unfit,' but nevertheless have nothing to do with virtue.

> Some teach their youth to pipe, to sing and dance,
> To hawk, to hunt, to choose and kill their game.
> To blow their [hunting] horn, and with their horse to prance,
> To play at tennis, set the lute in frame,
> Run at the ring, and use such other games:
> Which feats although they be not all unfit,
> Yet cannot they the mark of virtue hit.[13]

Manners as Influenced by the Religious Right

In the second half of the sixteenth century, one finds a number of hostile and negative characterizations of music written by men who were harbingers of the conservative religious right, which was rapidly moving toward the extreme Puritan beliefs of the seventeenth century. The first of these books was written immediately after the first professional theater opened in London, in 1576, and published the following year. This was *A Treatise Against Dicing, Dancing, Plays, and Interludes with other Idle Pastimes*, by a minister named John Northbrooke. Northbrooke admits that some recreation is appropriate, but his initial premise is that there are two inherent dangers. The first is that we abuse recreation 'through too great pleasure which we take in them.'[14] The second danger is that recreation might be used for purposes other than true recreation, as we see in this dialog between 'Youth' and 'Age.'

> YOUTH. Then, I perceive by you that honest recreations, pastimes, and plays are tolerable unto men, and that they may use and frequent it without fault, or offending God, or hurt to the profession of a true, faithful Christian.
> AGE. If it be, as I have said, moderately taken, after some weighty business, to make one more fresh and agile, to prosecute his good and godly affairs, and lawful business …[15]

---

12 Peacham, *The Complete Gentleman*, 112.
13 John Lyly, in *The Complete Works of John Lyly*, ed. Warwick Bond (Oxford: Clarendone Press, 1967), III, 449ff.
14 John Northbrooke, *A Treatise Against Dicing, Dancing, Plays, and Interludes* (1577) (London: The Shakespeare Society, 1843), 52.
15 Ibid.

The antithesis of this proper recreation of the Christian was, for Northbrooke, idleness. Idleness leads to sin and Northbrooke complains that the laws already on the books were not being upheld.

> If these and such like laws were executed justly, truly, and severely (as they ought to be), without any respect of persons, favor, or friendship, this dung and filth of idleness would easily be rejected and cast out of this commonwealth; there would not be so many loitering, idle persons, so many ruffians, blasphemers, and swing bucklers, so many drunkards, tosspots, whoremasters, dancers, fiddlers, and minstrels, dice players and maskers, fencers, thieves, interlude players, cutpurses, cosiners, masterless servants, jugglers, rouges, beggars, counterfeit Egyptians, etc., as there are.[16]

Having given us his general perspective, Northbrooke now turns to a discussion of music.

> YOUTH. What say you to music, and playing upon instruments? Is not that a good exercise?
> AGE. Music is very good, if it be lawfully used, and not unlawfully abused.[17]

Northbrooke begins his discussion by defining what 'lawful' music is, and this consists of examples of the use of music in the Bible. He praises the examples found there of music for the praise of God, for the praise of the good deeds of nobles, the celebration of joy and for weddings.

> And undoubtedly poetry had its beginning here, and it cannot be denied that it is an excellent gift of God; yet this ought to be kept pure and chaste among men, because certain lascivious men have and do filthily defile it, applying it to wantonness, wicked lusts, and every filthy thing.

Now the question is raised, how does one explain the power of music? Northbrooke's answer, as we would say today, is that music satisfies both the left and right hemispheres of the brain.

> YOUTH. Why doth music so rapt and ravish men in a manner wholly?
> AGE. The reason is plain: for there are certain pleasures which only fill the outward senses, and there are others also which pertain only to the mind or reason; but music is a delectation so put in the middle, that both by the sweetness of the sounds it moveth the senses, and by the artfulness of the number and proportions it delighth reason itself: and that happens then chiefly, when such words are added unto it whose sense is both excellent and learned.

Northbrooke here reviews several of the anecdotes of music in ancient literature and then turns to Church music. He reviews some early Christian music practice and especially focuses on St. Augustine's concept that it is the words, not the music, which is important in church music. Thus, one 'when he sang he should but little alter his voice, so that he should be like rather unto one that readeth, than unto one that singeth.'

---

16 Ibid., 76.
17 Ibid., 108ff.

> YOUTH. Let me hear, then, what is to be done and observed, to the end music may lawfully and fruitfully be used in the church.
>
> AGE. First we must take heed that in music be not put the whole sum and effect of godliness, and of the worshiping of God, which among the papists they do almost everywhere think, that they have fully worshiped God, when they have long and much sung and piped. Further, we must take heed that in it be not put merit or remission of sins. Thirdly, that singing be not so much used and occupied in the church, that there be no time, in a manner, left to preach the word of God and holy doctrine; whereby it comes to pass that the people depart out of church full of music and harmony, but yet hungering and fasting for heavenly food and doctrine. Fourthly, that rich and large stipends be not so appointed for musicians, that either very little, or in a manner nothing, is provided for the ministers ... Fifthly, neither may that broken and quavering music be used, wherewith the listeners are so [overwhelmed], that they cannot understand the words ... Lastly, we must take heed, that in the church nothing be sung without choice, but only those things which are contained in the holy scriptures, or which are by just reason gathered out of them, and do exactly agree with the word of God.

Northbrooke concludes by correctly noting that there is no mention of music in the church service in the New Testament and therefore if some church elects not to have music it should not be criticized. Now a final topic is addressed.

> YOUTH. What say you of minstrels, that go and range abroad, and thrust themselves into every man's presence and company, to play some mirth unto them.
>
> AGE. These sort of people are not sufferable, because they are loiterers and idle fellows; and are, therefore, by the laws and statues of this realm, forbidden to range and roam abroad, counting them in the number of rouges, and, to say the truth, they are but defacers of music.

Northbrooke mentions music again with respect to dancing. As the reader can no doubt guess, Northbrooke considers dancing a fundamental evil, calling it, among other things, wicked and filthy.[18]

> Concupiscence is inflamed by dancing with the fire of lust and sensuality; it gives occasion to whoredom and adultery; it makes men forget and neglect their duties and services ...
>
> We now in Christian counties have schools of dancing, howbeit that is no wonder, seeing also we have houses of bawdy. So much the Pagans were better and more sad than we be, they never knew this new fashion of dancing of ours; and unclean handlings, gropings, and kissings, and a very kindling of lechery, whereto serveth all that bussing, as it were, pigeons, the birds of Venus ...
>
> Yea, and further, the ballads that they sing be such, that they would kindle up the courage of the old ... And when the minstrels do make a sign to [stop], then, if you do not kiss her that you are leading by the hand and did dance with, then you are taken for a peasant and one without good manners and nurture.

---

18 Ibid., 145ff.

Music by itself, he says, cannot be condemned. It is the abuse of music through its association with dancing which renders it objectionable.

> Music of itself cannot be condemned; for as much as the world doth almost always abuse it, we ought to be so much the more circumspect: we see at this day that they which use music do swell with poison against God; they become hard hearted; they will have their songs, yea, and what manner of songs? Full of villainy and ribaldry; and afterward they fall to dancing, which is the chief mischief of all, for there is always such unchaste behavior in dancing, that of itself, as they abuse it (to speak the truth in one word) it is nothing but an enticement to whoredom …
>
> To music belongs the art of dancing, very acceptable to maidens and lovers; which they learn with great care, and without deviousness do prolong it until midnight, and with great diligence do devise to dance with framed gestures, and with measurable paces to the sound of the cymbal, harp, or flute, and do, as they think, very wisely, and subtly, the fondest thing of all other, and little differing from madness; which, except it were tempered with the sound of instruments... there would be no sight more ridiculous … than dancing.[19]

We find it rather charming that Northbrooke concludes his book by revealing that no one is paying much attention to such strong condemnation as we have read.

> YOUTH. Truly, good father, I see that as they used Lot so are the preachers now used; for the more they call them back from playing and dancing, the faster they run forward, the harder they cry, the deafer they are, the more they love them, the worse they hate them.
> AGE. That is lamentable that the preachers are becoming their enemies for telling them truth, and their foes for helping them …
> YOUTH. There was never more preaching and worse listening, never more talking and less following …
> AGE. You must not, nor ought not, to impute it unto the preaching of God's word, but unto the wickedness and perverse nature of man's corruption.

The most influential of the radical religious books which attacked music was Stephen Gosson's *The Schoole of Abuse* of 1579. He begins his discussion of music with a few references to the commendable uses of music by the ancient Greeks, but finds these virtues are unobtainable in contemporary music.

> Do you think those miracles could be wrought with the playing of dances, *Dumpes*, Pavanes, Gallliards, *Measures Fancyes*, or new strains? They never came where this grew, nor knew what it meant.[20]

---

19 This last paragraph is taken almost word for word from the German philosopher, Henry Agrippa's *On the Vanitie and Uncertaintie of Arts and Sciences*. See Catherine Dunn (Northridge: California State University, Northridge Press, 1974), 69.

20 Stephen Gosson, *The Schoole of Abuse* (1579), ed. Edward Arber (London, 1868), 26.

At this point, we must remind the reader that for more than a thousand years scholars had stressed the so-called 'speculative' form of music, the theoretical, with very little reference to the 'practical,' or performance. Only in the sixteenth century did most universities begin giving performance more respectability. Thus, in the following, Gosson's point is that the student must forget performance and return to the study of 'speculative' music and to the concept of Harmony used by the Greeks to represent the order of the world. First, he quotes Pythagoras, in something the philosopher surely never said, as 'condemning as fools, anyone who judges Music by sound and by ear.' Then, to the point he wishes to make,

> If you wish to be good Scholars, and to profit from the Art of Music, shut your fiddle cases, and look up to heaven: the order of the Spheres, the infallible motion of the Planets, the just course of the year, and variety of seasons, the concord of the elements and their qualities, Fire, Water, Air, Earth, Heat, Cold, Moisture and Drought concurring together to the constitution of earthly bodies and sustenance of every creature.[21]

Furthermore, instead of those distinguished poet-musicians of ancient Greece, today most musicians are beggars.

> We have infinite Poets, and Pipers, and such peevish chattel among us in England, that live by merry begging, maintained by alms, and privately encroach on every man's purse.

And, instead of those noble and simple instruments of antiquity, what would Pythagoras say, if he were alive today, and saw,

> how many frets, how many strings, how many stops, how many keys, how many clefs, how many modes, how many flats, how many sharps, how many [lines], how many spaces, how many notes, how many rests, how many quirks, how many corners, what chopping, what changing, what tossing, what turning, what wresting and wringing is among our Musicians?[22]

Gosson also condemns music for its role in the theater, noting that as poetry and music are 'German cousins,' so music and acting have great affinity, and all three are 'chained links of abuse.'[23] Indeed, he quotes Maximus Tyrius as saying that the introduction of musical instruments to theaters and drama 'was the first cup that poisoned the commonwealth.' He now makes the ancient observation that music is the most dangerous of the arts, because it reaches the heart.

> Cooks have never shown more craft in their junkets to vanquish the taste, nor Painters in shadows to allure the eye, than Poets in Theaters to wound the conscience.

---

21 Ibid., 26.
22 Ibid., 28.
23 Ibid., 28ff.

> There set they abroache strange consorts of melody, to tickle the ear; costly apparel, to flatter the sight; effeminate gesture, to ravish the sense; and wanton speech, to whet desire to inordinate lust. Therefore of both barrels, I judge Cooks and Painters the better hearing, for the one extendeth his art no farther than to the tongue, palate, and nose, the other to the eye; and both are ended in outward sense, which is common to us and the brute beasts. But these by the private entries of the ear, slip down into the heart, and with gunshot of affection gall the mind, where reason and virtue should rule the roost.[24]

Music, in Gosson's view, is largely responsible for the decay of the English man, from that strong, naked man who ate roots and bark and could suffer any hardship. Early English man found his recreation in shooting, running, wrestling, etc.,

> But the exercise that is now among us, is banqueting, acting, music and dancing, and all such delights as may win us to pleasure, or rock us asleep.
> Oh what a wonderful change is this? Our wrestling at arms, is turned to wallowing in Ladies laps, our courage to cowardice, our running to riot ... We have robbed Greece of gluttony, Italy of wantonness, Spain of pride, France of deceit and Germany of drinking.[25]

As one can imagine, there was considerable reaction to this conservative religious attack on the arts. Soon Gosson published *An Apologie of the Schoole of Abuse*, in answer to some of his critics. Some musicians had responded by saying that both the instruments and the music today are better than they had ever been before, but Gosson simply answers, 'who is to judge?'[26] Then he challenges the musicians further.

> Because I would have Dionysius followed, let them not think I abhor Music: if they put on their spectacles, or take their eyes in their hands, and look better in the *Schoole of Abuse*, they shall find that with Plutarch I accuse them for bringing their cunning into theaters: that I say, they have willfully left, or with ignorance lost, those warlike tunes which were used in ancient times, to stir up in us a manly motion, and sound out new descant with the dancers of Sybaris, to rock us to sleep in all ungodliness. If they had any wit, any learning, or experience, they might know that *Excellens fensible laedit fensum*, their dainty consorts will make us wantons. Aristonicus the musician, for his memory with all posterity, had a brazen idol erected to him by Alexander the Great, and was wonderfully honored for his art. This was not done for playing 'Les guanto Spagniola,' or inventing sweet measures, or coining new dances, but for kindling his soldiers courage, and heartening them all to take armor ... Which of our musicians that are so perfect, is able with his instrument to make a fresh water soldier run to his weapons, or force dolphins in the sea to save his life, if he suffer shipwreck? Which of all their instruments that are so absolute, can perform that which others have done before? If ancient musicians have gone beyond

---

24 Ibid., 32.

25 Ibid., 34.

26 Stephen Gosson, 'An Apologie of the Schoole of Abuse,' in *The Schoole of Abuse* (1579), ed., Edward Arber (London, 1868), 68ff.

us, where is our cunning? If their instruments have passed ours, where is the perfectness that our Pipers imagine? ...

Yet I do not forbid our new found instruments, so long as we handle them as David did, to praise God; nor bring them any more into public theaters, to please wantons.

One of the many books inspired by Gosson was the *Anatomy of the Abuses in England* (1583) by Philip Stubbs, written in support of Gosson. Stubbs, in fact, begins his lengthy condemnation of the abuses of music by plagiarizing much of Gosson's work. Then, proceeding on his own in a dialog between Spudeus and Philoponus, Stubbs writes,

> SPUDEUS. I have heard it said (and I thought it very true) that Music dooth delight both man and beast, reuniteth the spirits, comforteth the heart, and maketh it apter to the service of God.
> PHILOPONUS. I grant Music is a good gift of God, and that it delighteth both man and beast, reuniteth the spirits, conforteth the heart and maketh it readier to serve God; and therefore did David both use music himself and also commend the use of it to his posterity (and being used to that end, for man's private recreation, music is very laudable).
>
> But being used in public assemblies and private conuenticles as directories to filthy dancing, through the sweet harmony and smooth melody thereof, it estrangeth the mind, stireth up filthy lust, womannisheth the mind, ravisheth the heart, enflameth concupiscence and bringeth in uncleanness. But if music openly were used (as I have said) to the praise and glory of God, as our Fathers used it, and as was intended by it at the first, or privately in a man's secret chamber or house, for his own solace or comfort to drive away the fantasies of idle thoughts, solicitude, care, sorrow, and such other perturbations and molestations of the mind, the only ends whereto true music tends, it were very commendable and tolerable. If music were thus used it would comfort man wonderfully, and move his heart to serve God the better; but being used as it is, it corrupteth good minds, maketh them womanish, and inclined to all kinds of whordom and mischief ...
>
> Wherefore, if you would have your son become womanish, unclean, smooth mouthed, affected to bawdy, scurrility, filthy thymes, and unseemly talking; briefly, if you would have him, as it were, transformed into a woman, or worse, and inclined to all kinds of whordom and abomination, send him to dancing school, and to learn music, and than shall you not fail of your purpose. And if you would have your daughter whorish, bawdy, and unclean and a filthy speaker, and such like, bring her up in music and dancing, and, my life for your's, you have won the goal.[27]

During the Middle Ages there were traditions involving civic dancing in the church yard, in part because it was the largest open space in the small villages. Church officials issued

---

27 Philip Stubbs, *The Anatomy of the Abuses in England* (1583), ed. Frederick Furnivall (London: The New Shakespeare Society, n.d.), 169ff.

many edicts against this practice during the later Middle Ages, but apparently the practice continued.[28] Stubbs, in particular, was alarmed to see minstrels playing for the 'devil's dance.'

> Then they have their hobbyhorses, dragons and other Antiques, together with their bawdy Pipers and thundering Drummers to strike up the devil's dance. Then march these heathens toward the Church and Church-yard, their pipers piping, their drummers thundering, their stumps dancing, their bells ringing, their handkerchiefs swinging about their heads like madmen, their hobbyhorses and other monsters skirmishing along the route. And in this sort they go to the Church (I say) and into the Church (though the minister be at prayer or preaching), dancing and swinging their handkerchiefs over their heads in the Church, like devils incarnate, with such a confused noise that no man can hear his own voice. Then, the foolish people they look, they stare, they laugh, they leer & mount upon pews to see these goodly pageants solemnized in this sort. Then, after this, about the Church they go again and again and so forth into the church-yard, where they have commonly their Summer halls, their bowers, arbors and banqueting houses set up, wherein they feast, banquet and dance all that day and all the night too.[29]

There were also important publications in opposition to Gosson and in support of the Arts. One of the most important of these was Thomas Lodge's *A Defence of Poetry, Music and Stage-plays* (1580). Lodge, obviously a very well-read scholar, quotes extensively and to the point from ancient Greek and Roman literature as he separately defends poetry, music and the theater. His own personal comments, like those of the opposition, are passionate. We present here only his own observations on music, which begin with the ancient Greek notion that the universe, in its perfect organization, must be somehow related with music.[30]

> But another matter calls me and I must not stay upon [poetry] only; there is an easier task in hand for me, and that which if I may speak my conscience, fits my vein best, your Second Abuse Gosson, your dispraise of Music, which you misadvisedly call Piping: that is it well most by you, what so is an overstay of life, is displeasant to your person: Music may not stand in your presence, whereas all the learned philosophers have always had it in reverence … Look upon the harmony of the Heavens? Hang they not by music? Do not the spheres move? Be not they *inferiora corpora* affected *quadam sympathia* and agreement? How can we measure the debility of the patient but by the disordered motion of the pulse? Is not man worse accounted of when he is most out of tune? Is there anything that more affects the sense? Doth there any pleasure more *acuat* our understanding? … O Lord! how it maketh a man to remember heavenly things, to

---

28 A sermon preached by John Stockwood in 1578 included the following observation:

> Insomuch that in some places [the actors] shame not in the time of divine service to come and dance [in] the church, and without, to have naked men dancing in nets, which is most filthy … [Quoted in Northbrooke, *A Treatise Against Dicing*, xiv.]

29 Phillip Stubbs, *The Anatomy of Abuses in England*, 147. Stubbs was opposed to dancing in general, calling it an 'introduction to whordom, a preparation to wantonness.' 'Yea,' he says, people 'are not ashamed to erect schools of dancing, thinking it an ornament to their children to be expert in this noble science of heathen deviltry.' [Ibid., 154ff.]

30 Thomas Lodge, *A Defence of Poetry, Music and Stage-plays* (London: Shakespeare Society, 1853), 17ff. Lodge (1558–1625) was born to a distinguished London merchant, who was in fact Lord Mayor in 1562–1563. Lodge attended Oxford and later became a law student at Lincoln's Inn.

wonder at the works of the Creator. Eloquence can stop the soldier's sword from slaying an orator, and shall not Music be magnified which not only saves the body but is a comfort to the soul? ...

Are not the strains in Music to tickle and delight the ear? Are not our warlike instruments to move men to valor? You confess they move us, but yet they delight not our ears, I pray you whence grew that point of Philosophy? It is more than ever my Master taught me, that a thing of sound should not delight the ear. Perhaps you suppose that men are monsters, without ears, or else I think you will say they hear with their heels: it may be so, for indeed when we are delighted with Music, it maketh our heart to skip of joy, and it maybe perhaps by ascending from the heel to the higher parts, it may move us. Good policy in sooth, this was of your own coining; your mother never taught it you: but I will not deal by reason of philosophy with you for that confound your senses, but I can assure you this one thing, that this principle will make the wiser to mislike your invention. It had been a fitter jest for your howlet in your Play, than an ornament in your book: but since you wrote of Abuses we may license you to lie a little, so the abuse will be more manifest ...

But you cannot be content to err, but you must maintain it too. Pythagoras, you say, allows not that Music is discerned by ears, but he wishes us to ascend unto the sky, and mark that harmony. Surely this is but one [professor's] opinion (yet I dislike not of it) but to speak my conscience, I think Music best pleases me when I hear it, for otherwise the catterwalling of Cats, were it not for harmony, should more delight my eyes than the tunable voices of men. But these things are not the chief points you shout at, there is somewhat else sticking in your stomach, God grant it hurt you not! From the dance you run to the pipe ... Our pleasant consorts do discomfort you much, and because you like not thereof, they are discommendable. I have heard it is good to take sure footing when we travel to unknown countries; for when we wade above our shoe latchet, Appelles will reprehend us for cobblers; if you had been a father in Music and could have discerned of tunes I would perhaps have liked your opinion somewhat where now I abhor it; if you were a professor of that practice I would quickly persuade you that the adding of strings to our instrument makes the sound more harmonious, and that the mixture of Music maketh a better concent. But to preach to unskillful is to persuade the brute beasts. I will not stand long in this point although the dignity thereof require a volume, but how learned men have esteemed this heavenly gift, if you please to read you shall see ... The matter is so plentiful that I cannot find where to end, as for beginnings they be infinite, but these shall suffice, I like not to long circumstance where less do serve, only I wish you to account well of this heavenly concent, which is full of perfection proceeding from above, drawing his original from the motion of the stars, from the agreement of the planets, from the whistling winds, and from all those celestial circles, where is either perfect agreement or any *Sumphonia*.

But as I like Music, so admit I not of those that deprave the same: your Pipers are so odious to me as yourself, neither allow I your harping merry beggars; although I knew you myself a professed play maker, and a paltry actor, since which the windmill of your wit hath been turned so long with the wind of folly, that I fear me we shall see the dog return to his vomit, and the cleansed sow to her mire, and the reformed schoolmaster to his old teaching of folly. Beware it be not so, let not your book be a blemish to your own profession. Correct not Music therefore when it is praiseworthy, lest your worthless misliking betray your madness; weigh the abuse ...

The last word in this battle, at least intellectually, came from Sir Philip Sidney. His *The Defence of Poesie* (1595) is far above the other publications in style of language, cool-headed analysis and above all the fact that his arguments were the correct ones—at least they still seem so four hundred years later.

Sidney's book is primarily a defense of poetry, which includes the dramatic theater, and, unfortunately for our present purposes, he therefore devotes little time to music. Music, however, was still closely associated with poetry, which Sidney mentions with respect to versification—which he says should not be confused with poetry.

> There have been many most excellent Poets that never versified, and now swarm many versifiers that need never answer to the name of Poets.[31]

He returns to this point again, adding that versification, measure, order and proportion gives poetry harmony. This leads him to an observation about the ancient association of poetry and music.

> But lay aside the just praise poetry has, by being the only speech fit for Music (Music I say the most divine striker of the senses).[32]

At the close of his treatise, Sidney mentions music again in relationship to versification in poetry.

> Now of versifying, there are two sorts, one ancient, the other modern. The ancient marked the quantity of each syllable, and according to that, framed his verse: The modern, observing only number, with some regard to accent; the chief life of it, standing in the like sounding of the words, which we call rhyme. Whether of these be the more excellent, would bear many speeches, the ancient no doubt more fit for Music, both words and time observing quantity, and more fit, lively to express diverse passions by the low or lofty sound of the well-weighed syllable. The latter likewise with his rhyme striketh a certain Music to the ear: and in conclusion, since it does delight, though by another way, it obtains the same purpose, there being in either sweetness, and wanting in neither, majesty.[33]

There are additional interesting reflections on music which he makes in passing. In his argument that 'neither Philosophy nor History could at the first have entered into the gates of popular judgments, if they had not taken the passport of poetry,' he speaks of the con-

---

31 Sir Philip Sidney, 'The Defence of Poesie,' (1595) in *The Prose Works of Sir Philip Sidney*, ed. Albert Feuillerat (Cambridge: Cambridge University Press, 1962), III, 10. Sidney (1554–1586) came from a noble family, his father being Deputy of Ireland. After attending Oxford, he traveled as a political representative of the queen to Paris, where he barely escaped the St. Bartholomew Massacre. Further diplomatic duties carried him through Germany and Austria. In 1585 he was about to sail with Drake for America, but the queen prevented him from going. The following year he died from a battle wound received at Zutphen, in the Low Countries.

32 Ibid., 27.

33 Ibid., 44.

temporary importance of poets in countries held in little esteem by the English (Turkey and Ireland), and then makes an interesting reference to the New World.

> Even among the most barbarous and simple Indians, where no writing is, yet they have their poets who make and sing songs which they call *Arentos*, both of their ancestors deeds and praises of their Gods.[34]

Sidney also makes an interesting reference to music in the context of a discussion of the relationship of Art and Nature.

> There is no Art delivered unto mankind that hath not the works of nature for his principal object, without which they could not exist, and on which they so depend, as they become Actors & Players, as it were of what nature will have set forth. So doth the Astronomer look upon the stars, and by them he sees set down what order nature hath taken therein. So doth the Geometrician and *Arithmititian*, in their diverse sorts of quantities. So doth the Musicians of rhythm [*in times*] tell you, which by nature agree, which not.[35]

He returns to the relationship of Nature and Art in an interesting comparison of the courtier to the professor, demonstrating the victory of practice over the academic.

> I have found in diverse small learned courtiers, a more sound style, than in some professors of learning, of which I can guess no other cause, but that the courtier following that which by practice he finds fittest to nature therein, though he does not know [why], doth act according to art, though not by art: where the [professor] uses art to show art and not hide art (as in these cases he should do) fleeing [therefore] from nature and indeed abusing art.[36]

Lacking modern knowledge of split-brain function, Sidney could not know of the unique distinctions which music enjoys for its location in the right hemisphere of the brain, separated from the other rational sciences. He therefore follows the old university and Church misunderstanding by associating music with mathematics, although he calls music 'an admirable delight.' Thus he considers philosophy, mathematics, astronomy and music as being 'serving sciences, having a private end in themselves,'[37] but none sufficient to allow one to 'know thyself.'

A particularly interesting discussion of music comes when Sidney is wondering just what it is that Gosson, and other detractors of the stage, find objectionable. Sidney understood dramatic poetry to include Heroic, Lyric, Tragedy, Comedy, Satire, Iambic, Elegiac, Pastoral, 'and certain others.' In examining these forms, one by one, he arrives at the Lyric.

---

34 Ibid., 5.
35 Ibid., 7.
36 Ibid., 43.
37 Ibid., 11.

Is it the Lyric that most displeaseth, who with his tuned Lyre, and well accorded voice, gives praise, the reward of virtue, to virtuous acts? Who gives moral precepts and natural Problems, who sometimes raises up his voice to the height of the heavens, in singing the laudes of the immortal God? Certainly I must confess my own barbarousness [then], for I never heard the old song of 'Percy and Douglas,' but that I found not my heart moved more than with a trumpet; and yet it is sung by some blind Crowder, with no rougher voice, than rude style: which being so evil appareled in the dust and cobwebs of that uncivil age, what would it work, trimmed in the gorgeous eloquence of Pindar? In Hungary I have seen it the manner at all Feasts, and other such meetings, to have songs of their ancestors valor, which that right soldierly nation thinks one of the chief kindlers of brave courage. The incomparable Lacedemonians did not only carry that kind of Music ever with them into the field, but even at home, as such songs were made, so were they all content to be singers of them ...[38]

ON THE PHYSIOLOGY OF AESTHETICS

After Henry VIII's break with the Roman Church, we find few Englishmen writing about its old dogma. Only Bryskett, born of Italian parents in England, and perhaps closer therefore to the old world views, restates the old positions. In his *Discourse of Civill Life*, he contends that man consists of mind and body and therefore the mind must rule. To be otherwise, he says, would be like the master or father, being careful and prudent, being constrained to obey his son or servant.'[39] It is from the improper pleasures, which spring from the senses of the body,

> that all wicked affections take their beginning, such as angers, furies, fond loves, hatreds, ambitions, lusts, suspicions, jealousies, ill speaking, backbiting, false joys, and true griefs; and finally the consuming of the body and goods, and the loss of honor and reputation.[40]

Sir Philip Sidney found Reason tied to a relationship with speech, which is certainly correct in so far as the left hemisphere of the brain is concerned.

> The speech of the mind is very Reason itself: and look what the speech of the mind reasoneth and debateth, that doth the voice utter, and either of them is the image of the next that went afore. For look what proportion is between the voice or speech of the mouth, and the speech of the mind; the like proportion is between the speech of the mind, and the speech of the understanding.[41]

---

38 Ibid., 24.

39 Lodowick Bryskett, *A Discourse of Civill Life*, ed. Thomas Wright (Northridge: San Fernando Valley State College, 1970), 146. We have converted this to modern English. Bryskett (1546–1612) functioned as a secretary to a variety of English politicians. The *Discourse* began as a translation of Giambattista Giraldi's 'Tre dialoghi della vita civile,' but we regard the views we quote as representative of England.

40 Ibid.

41 Sir Philip Sidney, 'Of the Trueness of Christian Religion,' in *The Prose Works of Sir Philip Sidney*, ed. Albert Feuillerat (Cambridge: Cambridge University Press, 1962), III, 267.

Ascham, as befits a book on long bow shooting, understandably considers sight as the most important of the senses. He extends this, however, to a surprising degree in the way he ties sight with Reason.

> The eye is the very tongue wherewith wit and reason doth speak to every part of the body, and the wit doth not so soon signify a thing by the eye, as every part is ready to follow, or rather prevent the bidding of the eye.[42]

On Education

Sir Thomas More was one of the important voices, along with Erasmus, trying to preserve humanism at a time when it was losing support in both Catholic and Lutheran circles. As a fervent defender of the old Church, it was easy for him to follow the views of many early Churchmen and write that Reason is strengthened and quickened by the study of 'Logic, Philosophy and the other Liberal Arts.'[43] We might mention that we find it curious that in all his writings (except for the *Utopia*), More never discusses music, for we know from the testimony of Erasmus that More took 'pleasure in every kind of music' and that his wife had learned 'to play harp, lute, clavichord and recorders; at her husband's request she plays these instruments daily.'[44]

But for the other Liberal Arts, More was an activist. When he heard that a group of Oxford professors had minimized the study of the Liberal Arts, and especially Greek, and had 'formed a deliberate conspiracy to call themselves Trojans,' More sent a critical letter to the Oxford faculty.[45]

John Knox, in his *The Book of Discipline*, introduced into the Scottish parliament in 1560, presented a comprehensive plan for education from grammar schools through the universities. He called for every church to appoint a school master to teach, at least, grammar and Latin and for towns to establish colleges to teach Logic, Rhetoric and Languages. Music was left to the church schools and was dedicated solely to the improvement of church singing. The children, he says, will be,

---

42 Ascham, *Toxophilus*, II, 161.

43 Thomas More, 'A Dialogue Concerning Heresies,' I, xxiii, in *The Complete Works of St. Thomas More* (New Haven: Yale University Press, 1981), VI, 132.

44 P.S. Allen, *Opus epistolarum Des. Erasmi Roterdami* (Oxford, 1906–1958), V, Ep. 1342 and IV, Ep. 999, quoted in Miller, 'Erasmus on Music,' 347. More's most extensive discussion is a few lines in 'A Dialogue Concerning Heresies,' III, ii, in which he pretends to miss the point when an observation is made relative to Church singers singing so fast, which was a frequent objection among the Lutherans that singing of the professional Church singers was devoid of emotion.

45 See 'Letter to the University of Oxford,' in *The Complete Works of St. Thomas More*, XV, 131ff. More claims that one professor branded as a heretic anyone who studied Greek.

exhorted to exercise thame selvis in the Psalmes, that when the Churche convenith, and dois sing, thai may be the more abill togither with commoun heart and voice to prayse God.[46]

Ascham was perplexed by many aspects of education as he knew it in sixteenth-century England. Most men, he observed, would pay more to the man who cares for their horses than to the man who teaches their children. God in heaven laughs, Ascham says, and allows them,

> to have tame and well-ordered horses but wild and unfortunate children; and therefore in the end they find more pleasure in their horses than comfort in their children.

He was horrified to find the teachers were regularly beating their students and, indeed, he tells us that it was a dinner discussion of this topic by a group of high officials at Windsor which led him to write his book, *The Schoolmaster*.[47] In a book written some twenty years earlier, however, he contends that there are three things which will create excellence in a student: aptness, desire and fear.

> Aptness maketh him pliable, like wax, to be formed and fashioned, even as a man would have him. Desire, to be as good, or better than his fellows; and fear of them whom he is under, will cause him to take great labor and pain with diligent heed in learning.[48]

For the practical man, Ascham placed a greater value on learning than on experience. One year of learning, he says, is worth twenty of experience and, furthermore, 'experience maketh more miserable than wise.'[49]

> An unhappy master he is that is made cunning by many shipwrecks; a miserable merchant, that is neither rich nor wise but after some bankrupts. It is costly wisdom that is bought by experience.

With regard to manners, Ascham was outspoken against a contemporary trend in which families sent children to Italy for further education.

> I know divers that went out of England men of innocent life, men of excellent learning, who returned out of Italy not only with worse manners but also with less learning, neither so willing to live orderly nor yet so able to speak learnedly as they were at home before they went abroad.[50]

---

46 Frederick Eby, *Early Protestant Educators* (New York: McGraw-Hill, 1931), 276ff. John Knox (1505–1572) became a priest after study at St. Andrews University. After coming in contact with Calvin, he converted to the Protestant movement and became an extremely radical leader of that faith.

47 Ascham, *The Schoolmaster*, Preface to the Reader.

48 Ascham, *Toxophilus*, II, 136.

49 Ascham, *The Schoolmaster*, 50.

50 Ibid., 63.

Specifically, they return with,

> a factious heart, a discoursing head, a mind to meddle in all men's matters; for experience, plenty of new mischiefs never known in England before; for manners, variety of vanities and change of filthy living.[51]

......

> They care for no Scripture; they make no count of general councils; they condemn the consent of the church; they pass for no doctors; they mock the Pope; they rail on Luther; they allow neither side; they like none but only themselves; the mark they shoot at, the end they look for, the heaven they desire, is only their own present pleasure and private profit.[52]

Ascham says he himself went to Italy, but 'thank God it was only for nine days!'

Philip Stubbs, in his *The Anatomy of the Abuses in England* (1583), states that the principal problem underlying the poor schools in England was the inadequate pay offered to the teachers.

> But alas, such small pittance is allowed the schoolmasters, that they can neither buy the libraries, nor, which is less, hardly maintain themselves; which thing altogether dissuades them from their books, and is the reason why many a one snores in palpable ignorance all the days of their life.[53]

Bryskett, in his *Discourse of Civill Life*, printed in 1606, reflects admiration only for the study of law, religion and 'Physicke.' Beyond this he observes,

> Of the meaner intentions I will not speak. And too common an error it is in scholars themselves, when they are entered into the Arts, which are called liberal, to spend their time in curious searching of subtilties, frivolous, and to no use.[54]

Regarding higher education, the headmaster of the Merchant Tailors School, Mulcaster, required extensive musical exercises by all students, although this was almost certainly an exception.[55]

Henry Peacham, in *The Complete Gentleman*, believed strongly that 'learning is an essential part of nobility.' Among the illustrations he uses to introduce his discussion of the education of the noble, he mentions a duke of Württemberg visiting in Italy, who became so outraged when he could not join in a discussion being held in Latin, that he struck his tutor who happened to be there.[56]

---

51 Ibid., 67.

52 Ibid., 71.

53 Stubbs, *The Anatomy of the Abuses in England*, II, 20ff.

54 Bryskett, *A Discourse of Civill Life*, 14.

55 Frederick Sternfeld, 'Music in the Schools of the Reformation,' in *Musica Disciplina* (Rome: American Institute of Musicology in Rome, 1948), 121.

56 Peacham, *The Complete Gentleman*, 31.

Peacham was much concerned with the quality of teachers in England, finding that for every discreet and able one there were twenty ignorant and careless. Consequently, he maintains, for every child they make a scholar, they mar ten.[57] In another treatise, Peacham offers an explanation for the poor quality of teachers.

> There is no profession more necessary to erecting the frame of a famous commonwealth than that of schoolmasters, yet none in more disesteem among the common vulgar, yea, and illiterate great ones. I know not the reason of this, except that the greater part of the multitude being ignorant, they are desirous that their children should be so likewise.[58]

Like Ascham before him, Peacham speaks out against teachers who beat their students. In this regard he finds a model in Germany,

> where it is a rare thing to see a rod stirring; yet I heartily wish that our children of England were but half so ready in writing and speaking Latin, which boys of ten and twelve years old will do so roundly and with so neat a phrase and style that many of our masters would hardly mend them, having only for their punishment shame and for their reward praise.[59]

He also lays considerable blame for the results of education on the parents, especially the mother,

> not only for her overtenderness, but in winking at the child's lewd courses, yea, more in seconding and giving them encouragement to do wrong.[60]

Peacham's recommendations for the young nobleman attending the university are centered on his maintenance of his social status. For example,

> For the companions of your recreation consort with gentlemen of your own rank and quality, for that friendship is best contenting and lasting. To be overfree and familiar with inferiors argues a baseness of spirit and begetteth contempt.[61]

Sir Philip Sidney saw the end of education to be the understanding of the grand harmony of all creation, sounding very much like the ancient Greeks for a modern Christian![62] He briefly epitomizes the importance of Grammar, Rhetoric and Logic and then turns to the

---

57 Ibid., 33.

58 Henry Peacham, 'The Truth of Our Times,' in Ibid., 185.

59 Henry Peacham, Ibid., 35.

60 Ibid., 43.

61 Ibid., 51.

62 Sir Philip Sidney, 'On the Trueness of Christian Religion,' in *The Prose Works of Sir Philip Sidney*, III, 222. Later [Ibid., 305] he was careful to clarify his position.

> The Aristotelians have no voice here, because they stand all in commenting upon Aristotle, who gave himself more to the liberal Arts and the searching of Nature, than to looking up to God the maker of all things.

mathematical sciences. Like the old Scholastics, it is here that he includes music, and like them he can describe its essence only in theoretical terms.

> Arithmetic proceeds from unity, Geometry from a prick; and Music from agreement of sounds; and the end of them is to reduce things to one common reason, to one proportion, and to one harmony, all of which are kinds of unity, and their branches are branches of the same.

ON THE PSYCHOLOGY OF AESTHETICS

While the poets and writers of fiction devote much space to the emotions, especially Love, those writers concerned with philosophy rarely discuss feelings. The short-lived and diplomatically engaged Sir Philip Sidney professed not to understand Love at all.

> Alas Love, I would thou couldest as well defend thyself, as thou canst offend others: I would those on whom thou doest attend, could either put thee away, or yield good reason why they keep thee.[63]

It was clear to him, as a philosopher, that the processes of Love and Reason were unconnected.

> Wit is not to be seen, and no Woman takes advice of any in her Loving, but of her own Eyes, or her Waiting Women: nay, what is worse, Wit is not to be felt, and is no good Bedfellow.[64]

On Pleasure and Pain

Sir Thomas More's *Utopia* presents a lengthy passage on the nature of Pleasure and Pain which is clearly more More's philosophy than a fictional description of the Utopians, although he introduces the topic through a description of the religion of the Utopians. More's theory about religion runs thus: [1] God designed people to be happy, [2] happiness is inseparable from the 'rewards for good and virtuous action, and punishments for vice, to be distributed after this life,' and, [3] organized religion has passed these ideas down by tradition. Even Reason, says More, encourages a man to believe this,

> for if these were taken away no man would be so insensible as not to seek after pleasure by all possible means, lawful or unlawful; using only this caution, that a lesser pleasure might not stand in the way of a greater, and that no pleasure ought to be pursued that should draw a great deal of pain after it; for they think it the maddest thing in the world to pursue virtue, that is a

---
63 Sir Philip Sidney, 'The Defence of Poesie,' (1595) in Ibid., III, 30.
64 Sir Philip Sidney, 'Valour Anatomized in a Fancie,' in Ibid., III, 309.

sour and difficult thing; and not only to renounce the pleasures of life, but willingly to undergo much pain and trouble, if a man has no prospect of a reward. And what reward can there be for one that has passed his whole life, not only without pleasure, but in pain, if there is nothing to be expected after death? Yet they do not place happiness in all sorts of pleasures, but only in those that in themselves are good and honest.[65]

More concludes this argument by observing,

> A life of pleasure is either a real evil, and in that case we ought not to assist others in their pursuit of it ...; or if it is a good thing, so that we not only may, but ought to help others to it, why, then, ought not a man to begin with himself?[66]

More then begins to make a few specific definitions regarding the nature of Pleasure and Pain, again attributing them to the Utopians. First, Pleasure should be nature-based and of an essence which does not harm others.

> Thus [the Utopians] cautiously limit pleasure only to those appetites to which nature leads us; for they say that nature leads us only to those delights to which reason as well as sense carries us, and by which we neither injure any other person nor lose the possession of greater pleasures, and of such as draw no troubles after them; but they look upon those delights which men by a foolish though common mistake call pleasure, as if they could change easily the nature of things as the use of words; as things that greatly obstruct their real happiness, instead of advancing it, because they so entirely possess the minds of those that are once captivated by them with a false notion of pleasure, that there is no room left for pleasures of a truer or purer kind.[67]

Among foolish pleasures, More includes games with dice and hunting. What, for example, can be the pleasure in hunting? If it is in watching dogs run, that can be done without hunting,

> but if the pleasure lies in seeing the hare killed and torn by the dogs, this ought rather to stir pity, that a weak, harmless and fearful hare should be devoured by strong, fierce, and cruel dogs.[68]

Pleasure, he concludes, are 'those things which create some tickling in the senses (which seems to be a true notion of pleasure).'[69]

After mid-century, the influence of the growing conservative religious right began to become noticeable in publications. These works show a disdain for pleasure which forecasts the forthcoming Puritan period. In 1580 an anonymous supporter of Gosson's *Schoole of Abuse* published *A Third Blast of Retrait from Plaies and Theaters,* in which we find a typical example of this trend.

---

65 Henry Morley, *Ideal Commonwealths* (Port Washington: Kennikat Press, 1968), 56.
66 Ibid., 57.
67 Ibid., 58ff.
68 Ibid., 60.
69 Ibid., 61.

O my dear brethren, let not your affections carry you to wickedness; it behooves you to be very wary, and circumspect how you thrust yourselves into public assemblies of profane plays, since there be so many enticements into looseness, and so many means to train you to unthriftiness there, as wonder it is, if you haunt them but your souls will be grievously hurt.

Pleasure their captain is so politique an enemy, that he knows how to train you into danger. But when you are once within his lap, hard will it be for you to escape.[70]

ON THE PHILOSOPHY OF AESTHETICS

Ascham, in his *Toxophilus*, states that some things have no other end than pleasure and he gives the example of painting and dancing.[71]

On Poetry

Stephen Gosson, reflecting the increasingly conservative Church influence, reaches back to the old Catholic idea that the poet is a dishonest person, as he deals in fables.

I must confess that Poets are the whetstones of wit, notwithstanding that that wit is dearly bought: where honey and gall are mixed, it will be hard to sever the one for the other.[72]

Take away the masks they hide behind, he says, and you find reproach, vanity, wantonness and folly.

Gosson attempts to suggest this association was a very ancient one by producing an anecdote we have not seen elsewhere. The sixth century BC philosopher Anacharsis supposedly asked a Greek from Scythia if they had musical instruments or schools of poetry in that country. The answer, 'yes, and without vice,' meant, according to Gosson, that vice and poetry were considered inseparable. In another illustration of his thesis, he reminds us that all early poetry was sung, as he describes the famous poetess Sappho 'a good singer, but a whore.'

Believing he has thus revealed the evil nature of poetry, this Puritan now warns, on the basis of his own personal experience as a student in this particular 'School of Abuse,' that writing poetry is the first step in a dramatic decline which takes one from poetry to music to theater to pleasure to sloth to sleep to sin to death, and finally, to the devil![73]

---

70 Anonymous, in *A second and third blast of retreat from plays and theatres* (1580) (New York: Johnson Reprint Corporation, 1972), 71.
71 Ascham, *Toxophilus*, II, 138.
72 Stephen Gosson, *The Schoole of Abuse*, 20.
73 Ibid., 24.

Gosson's book was followed by a number of publications, representing the views of those for and against his attack on poetry, music and theater. One such publication which supported him was an anonymous treatise called *A Third Blast of Retrait from Plaies and Theaters, showing the abhomination of them in the time present*. This author reflects the old Catholic view of the poet.

> The writers of our time are so led away with vainglory, that their only endeavor is to please the humor of men; and rather with vanity to content their minds, than to profit them with good example. The most notable liar is become the best Poet.[74]

On the relationship of poetry and the most melancholic of emotions, George Puttenham writes in 1589,

> Lamenting is altogether contrary to rejoicing, euery man saith so, and yet is it a piece of joy to be able to lament with ease, and freely to poure forth a mans inward sorrowes and the greefs wherewith his mind is surcharged. This is a very necessary devise of the Poet, and a fine [thing], besides his poetrie to play also the Phisitian, and not only by applying a medicine to the ordinary sicknes of mankind, but by making the very greef it selfe [the] cure of the disease.[75]

Peacham, in his recommendations to young nobles attending the university, approves of poetry as an appropriate form of recreation.

> To sweeten your severer studies by this time vouchsafe poetry your respect, which howsoever censured and seeming fallen from the highest stage of honor to the lowest stair of disgrace ...[76]

Later he offers his explanation why poetry has fallen into disrespect.

> But some may ask me how it falleth out that poets nowadays are of no such esteem as they have been in former times. I answer, because virtue in our declining and worser days generally findeth no regard.[77]

Sir Philip Sidney, in his *Defence of Poesie*, begins by recognizing a decline in poetry in England, 'from almost the highest estimation of learning, to become the laughing stock of children.'[78] His eventual answer for why this was the current state of affairs had mostly to do with the quality of the poetry itself and the short-term goals of poets writing for money, rather than from inspiration.

---

74 Anonymous, in *A second and third blast of retreat from plays and theatres* (1580) (New York: Johnson Reprint Corporation, 1972), 104.

75 George Puttenham, *The Arte of English Poesie* (1589), ed. Edward Arber (London, 1869), XXIII, 61.

76 Peacham, *The Complete Gentleman*, 90.

77 Ibid., 94.

78 Sir Philip Sidney, 'The Defence of Poesie,' III, 4.

Sidney is particularly effective in addressing the old Church charge that poets, because of their fables, are liars. He points out that poets do not aspire to tell the truth, rather their free imagination. They do not want, for example, to picture Cyrus as he really was, but in the ideal of what he might have been.[79] History, he also points out, cannot tell the truth, for not only is the real truth unknown of the distant past, but the historian cannot account for the influences of what we call 'fortune.'

He accepts Aristotle's definition of the purpose of poetry being to imitate and to delight, but he adds a strong emphasis on education.

> [Poets] indeed do merely make to imitate, and imitate both to delight and teach, and delight to move men to take that goodness in hand, which without delight they would flee as from a stranger; and teach to make them know that goodness whereunto they are moved; which being the noblest scope to which any learning was ever directed, yet not without idle tongues to bark at them.[80]

On the Theater

As we have said above, the first published attack against the theater came in the very year the first professional theater was constructed in London, in John Northbrooke's *A Treatise Against Dicing, Dancing, Plays, and Interludes*. The discussion begins with 'Youth's' question.

> YOUTH. Seeing that we have somewhat largely talked and reasoned together of idle plays and vain pastimes, let me crave your further patience, to know your judgment and opinion as touching on plays and players, which are commonly used and much frequented in most places in these days, especially here in this noble and honorable city of London.[81]

After giving an extensive history of the theater from Roman times, Northbrooke eventually offers his judgment on the Elizabethan theater.

> I am persuaded that Satan hath not a more speedy way, and fitter school to work and teach his desire, to bring men and women into his snare of concupiscence and filthy lusts of wicked whoredom, than those places, and plays, and theaters are; and therefore necessarily those places, and players, should be forbidden, and dissolved, and put down by authorities as brothel houses and stewes are.

---

79 Sidney makes this point again in a letter to his brother, quoted in *The Prose Works of Sir Philip Sidney*, III, 131.

> A Poet in painting forth the effects, the motions, the whisperings of the people, which though in disputation one might say were true, yet who will mark them well shall find them taste of a poetical vein, and in that kind are gallantly to be marked, for though perchance they were not so, yet it is enough that they might be so.

80 Ibid., 10.

81 Northbrooke, *A Treatise Against Dicing*, 82ff.

But, observes his young participant in this dialog, I see many important people, both men and women going to the theater.

> The more is the pity, and greater is their shame and pain, if they repent not and leave it off. Many can tarry at a vain play two or three hours, when as they will not abide scarce one hour at a sermon. They will run to every play, but scarce will come to a preached sermon …
>
> If you wish to learn how to be false and deceive your husband, or husbands their wives, how to play the harlot, to obtain one's love, how to ravish, how to beguile, how to betray, to flatter, lie, swear, forswear, how to allure to whoredom, how to murder, how to poison, how to disobey and rebel against princes, to consume treasures prodigally, to move to lusts, to ransack and spoil cities and towns, to be idle, to blaspheme, to sing filthy songs of love, to speak filthily, to be proud, how to mock, scoff, and deride any nation, shall you not learn, then, at such interludes how to practice them?

The influential *The Schoole of Abuse*, by Stephen Gosson, which appeared in print shortly afterward, also saw the theater as the devil's playground.

> The Carpenter raises not his frame without tools, nor the Devil his work without instruments: were not Actors the mean, to make these assemblages, such multitudes, would hardly be drawn in so narrow a room. They seek not to hurt, but desire to please: they have purged their Comedies of wanton speeches, yet the Corn which they fell is full of Cockle: and the drink they draw, overcharged with dregges. There is more in them than we perceive, the Devil stands at our elbow when we see not, speaks when we hear him not, strikes when we feel not, and woundeth fore when he raises no skin … In those things, that we least mistrust, the greatest danger often lurks.[82]

He goes on to say that the public would not support attempts by the court to censor the theaters and he admits there are some actors who are 'sober, discreet, properly learned honest householders and Citizens well thought of by their neighbors.' Nevertheless, he concludes,

> Let us but shut up our ears to Poets, Musicians and Actors, pull our feet back from resort to Theaters, and turn away our eyes from beholding of vanity, the greatest storm of abuse will be overblown, and a fair path trodden to amendment of life. Were not we so foolish to taste every drug, and buy every trifle, Actors would shut their shops and carry their trash to some other Country.[83]

After Gosson's attack created considerable public response, he soon published *An Apologie of the Schoole of Abuse*, in which he reaffirms his views on the evils of the theater. Again he says we do not recognize the dangers, that 'plays are venomous arrows to the mind.'[84]

---

82 Gosson, *The Schoole of Abuse*, 37.
83 Ibid., 44.
84 Stephen Gosson, 'An Apologie of the Schoole of Abuse,' in Ibid., 71ff.

> He that thinks wanton plays are a meete recreation for the mind of man, is as far from the truth as the foolish gentiles, which believed that their gods delight in toys; and we which carry our money to actors to feed their pride, may be well compared to the bath keepers ass which brought him wood to make his fire and was contented with the smell of the smoke.
>
> It is a great folly in us to seek to live in those places that are healthy to the body, but not flee from those that are hurtful to the soul; and as hard a matter for him to be cured, that knoweth not the grief wherewith he is troubled.

In 1583 Philip Stubbs, another member of the conservative right, added his book on the abuses in England and included an attack on the theater.

> There is no mischief which these plays do not maintain. For do they not nourish idleness? and *otia dant vitia*, idleness is the Mother of vice. Do they not draw the people from hearing the word of God, from Godly lectures and sermons? For you shall have them flock thither, thick & threefold, when the church of God shall be bare and empty ... Do they not induce whordom and uncleanliness? Nay, are they not rather plain devourers of maidenly virginity and chastity? For proof whereof, notice the flocking and running to theaters and curtains, daily and hourly, night and day, time and tide, to see plays and enterludes; where such wanton gestures, such bawdy speeches, such laughing and leering, such kissing and bussing, such clipping and culling, such winking and glancing of wanton eyes, and the like, is used, it is wonderful to behold. Then, these goodly pageants being done, every mate sorts to his mate, every one brings another home, on their way very friendly, and in their secret conclaves (covertly) they play *the Sodomits*, or worse.[85]

Stubbs was particularly concerned that the lessons learned in the theater would carry over into real life and that seeing such things as treason, for example, would lead to actual treason.

Sir Philip Sidney's *The Defence of Poesie* was intended to be primarily a defense of stage plays, although most of his discussion centered on poetry in a broader sense. He returns to the accusation that poets are liars when he reminds the readers that 'Tragedy is tied to the laws of Poetry and not to History.'[86] With respect to Comedy, he too was concerned by the quality of what he had seen on the London stage.

> But our comedians think there is no delight without laughter, which is very wrong, for though laughter may come with delight, yet it comes not of delight ... Delight has a joy in it either permanent or present. Laughter has only a scornful tickling. For example, we are ravished with delight to see a fair woman, and yet are far from being moved to laughter.[87]

---

85 Stubbs, *The Anatomy of the Abuses in England*.
86 Sir Philip Sidney, 'The Defence of Poesie,' III, 39.
87 Ibid., 40.

ON THE AESTHETICS OF MUSIC

The important Church philosopher, Richard Hooker, begins his discussion of Church music with an eloquent testimonial to music which is also, for the sixteenth century, a remarkable definition of aesthetics in music.

> Touching musical harmony whether by instrument or by voice, it being but of high and low in sounds a due proportionable disposition, such notwithstanding is the force thereof, and so pleasing effects it hath in that very part of man which is most divine, that some have been thereby induced to think that the soul itself by nature is or hath in it harmony. A thing which delighteth all ages and beseemeth all states; a thing as seasonable in grief as in joy; as decent being added unto actions of greatest weight and solemnity, as being used when men most sequester themselves from action. The reason hereof is an admirable facility which music hath to express and represent to the mind, more inwardly than any other sensible means, the very standing, rising, and falling, the very steps and inflections every way, the turns and varieties of all passions whereunto the mind is subject; yea so to imitate them, that whether it resemble unto us the same state wherein our minds already are, or a clean contrary, we are not more contentedly by the one confirmed, than changed and led away by the other. In [music] the very image and character even of virtue and vice is perceived, the mind delighted with their resemblances, and brought by having them often iterated into a love of the things themselves. For which cause there is nothing more contagious and pestilent than some kinds of [music]; then some nothing more strong and potent unto good. And that there is such a difference of one kind from another we need no proof but our own experience, inasmuch as we are at the hearing of some more inclined unto sorrow and heaviness; of some, more mollified and softened in mind; one kind more apt to stay and settle us, another to move and stir our affections; there is that draweth to a marvelous grave and sober mediocrity, there is also that carrieth as it were into ecstasies, filling the mind with an heavenly joy and for the time in a manner severing it from the body. So that although we lay altogether aside the consideration of the text of a song [ditty] and substance [matter], the very harmony of sounds being framed in due sort and carried from the ear to the spiritual faculties of our souls, is by a native puissance and efficacy greatly available to bring to a perfect temper whatsoever is there troubled, apt as well to quicken the spirits as to allay that which is too eager, sovereign against melancholy and despair, forcible to draw forth tears of devotion if the mind be such as can yield them, able both to move and to moderate all affections.[88]

Roger Ascham, in his *Toxophilus*, quotes the medieval medical writer, Galen, as observing that the lower crafts man learned by observing animals, such as learning weaving by watching spiders. However, the higher arts man learned from the gods, such as shooting and music from Apollo.[89]

---

[88] Richard Hooker, *On the Laws of Ecclesiastical Polity*, V, xxxviii, in *The Works of Mr. Richard Hooker* (Oxford: Clarendon Press, 1888), II, 159. Hooker (1553–1600) was one of the important moderate voices which tried to counter the arguments of the radical Puritans.

[89] Ascham, *Toxophilus*, II, 19.

Sir Thomas More, *Utopia* (1515)

While this famous work pretends not to comment on contemporary society, it obviously does. It is of interest to us as a document which outlines what a sixteenth-century thinker thought aesthetic standards *should* be.

More's Utopians were permitted a rather limited choice of entertainment, in a day which began with public lectures before daybreak. No 'foolish games' were played, only those which included some form of intellectual stimulation. It is in this context where More first mentions musc. After dinner, an hour was set aside 'where they entertain each other, either with music or discourse.'[90] Later he suggests that the purpose of the music at meal time was to 'cheer up their spirits.'

> They despatch their dinners quickly, but sit long at super; because they go to work after the one and are to sleep after the other ... They never sup without music ... while they are at table, some burn perfumes and sprinkle about fragrant ointments and sweet waters: in short, they [lack] nothing that may cheer up their spirits.[91]

After a lengthy discussion of his philosophy of pleasure, More appends music as a separate category. In the course of discussing how music affects man, we find it especially interesting that he emphasizes something of great importance to the ancient Greeks, but little mentioned in the Christian era, the fact that music is the only art which cannot be seen.

> There is another kind of pleasure that arises neither from our receiving what the body requires, nor its being relieved when overcharged, and yet by a secret, unseen virtue affects the senses, raises the passions, and strikes the mind with generous impressions; this is the pleasure that arises from music.

More returned to the subject of how music affects, during a brief discussion of the church music of the Utopians. In general, More says they sing hymns accompanied by instruments and that the music of the hymns is 'much sweeter than ours.' The main point which he wished to make, and clearly it is a criticism of the English Church music he knew, is that the music of the Utopians has a strong, and precisely directed, emotional quality.

> Yet in one thing they very much exceed us; all their music, both vocal and instrumental, is adapted to imitate and express the passions, and is so happily suited to every occasion, that whether the subject of the hymn be cheerful or formed to soothe or trouble the mind, or to express grief or remorse, the music takes the impression of whatever is represented, affects and kindles the passions, and works the sentiments deep into the hearts of the listeners.[92]

---

90 In Morley, *Ideal Commonwealths*, 41.
91 Ibid., 49.
92 Ibid., 94.

Lodowick Bryskett (1546–1612), *A Discourse of Civill Life*

Bryskett, to whom we have referred above, in the context of reviewing a number of ancient Greek philosophers and their philosophies, provides an extensive summary of other purposes and virtues of music.[93] He begins by reviewing the Greeks' use of music in education, in which Bryskett incorrectly understands that the main point was that the education of music and gymnastics were inseparable. He quotes Aristotle as saying that the study of music alone would produce a 'soft minded and effeminate' man. He reviews the use of music by the Greeks in battle and adds the observation that he finds in his time only the German and the Swiss effectively use music with their troops.

Now Bryskett turns his attention to sixteenth-century music. He says that while many examples of corruption in his time could be pointed to,

> one of the principal ones, in the judgment of wise men, may well be the quality of that corrupted music which is most used today; carrying with it nothing but a sensual delight to the ear, without working any good to the mind at all. Nay, would God that it did not greatly hurt and corrupt the mind. For as music well used is a great help to moderate the disorderly affections of the mind: so being abused it expels all manly thoughts from the heart, and so 'effeminateth' men, that they are little better than women: and in women breeds such lascivious and wanton thoughts, that often them forget their honesty, without which they cannot be worthy of the name of women. Not that I would infer that music generally is not liked, or unfit for women also: but my meaning is of this wanton and lascivious kind of music, which is today most pleasing.[94]

The kind of music we *should* have, he points out, is also found in the writings of the ancient Greeks. It should be grave, with learned and grave verses by excellent poets, and should create magnificent and noble desires in the minds of the listeners. Such music enters,

> like lively sparks into men's minds, to kindle in them desires of dignity, greatness, honor, true praise and commendation, and to correct whatsoever is in them of base and vile affection.[95]

Young men today, he advises, must be very selective of what they listen to.

> Let it suffice that young men are to take great account of that part of music which bears with it grave melodies, fit to compose the mind to good order by virtue of the rhythms and sound … But those which by variety in tunes, and warbling variations, confounds the words and melodies, and yields only a delight to the exterior sense, and no fruit for the mind, I wish them to neglect and not to esteem.
>
> Indeed … our music is far different from the ancient music and while it may well serve to please the ear, I say that it 'effeminateth' the mind and diverts it from bliss and felicity.[96]

---

93 Bryskett, *A Discourse of Civill Life*, 107ff.
94 Ibid., 109ff.
95 Ibid., 110.
96 Ibid., 113.

Thomas Morley, *A Plain and Easy Introduction to Practical Music* (1597)

Contrary to its title, Morley's book is primarily devoted to the theoretical aspects of music. Nevertheless, it does bear witness to the gradual swing from emphasis on the theoretical toward performance which occurs during the Renaissance, in so far as he recognizes that to be pleasing a musician's performance must both 'please the ears of other men' as well as be capable of being 'defended by reason.'[97] He clearly recognizes and accepts improvisation in Church music and his definitions of consonance (that which gives 'delight to the ear') and dissonance ('sounds naturally offending the ear') are no longer based on mathematics.[98]

At the end of his book, Morley briefly speaks more directly on matters of aesthetics. In composing music to poetry, he makes the point so often stressed by sixteenth-century Italian humanists that the emotions of the music must match those of the words.

> You must therefore, if you have a grave matter, apply a grave kind of music to it; if a merry subject you must make your music also merry, for it will be a great absurdity to use a sad harmony to a merry matter or a merry harmony to a sad, lamentable, or tragical [text].
>
> You must then when you would express any word signifying hardness, cruelty, bitterness, and other such like make the harmony like unto it, that is, somewhat harsh and hard, but yet so that it offends not.[99]

Failing to do this he calls 'barbarism.'

Also Morley makes a point of saying that even though the emotions of the words are clearly mirrored in the music, the words still carry the meaning and thus cannot be left out.

> But I see not what passions or motions it can stir up being sung as most men do commonly sing it, that is leaving out the [text] and singing only the bare notes, as it were a music made only for instruments, which will indeed show the nature of the music but never carry the spirit and, as it were, that lively soul which the [text] giveth.[100]

It is curious that Morley speaks of 'the nature of the music,' apart from the emotions. This is, unfortunately, only a remnant of the old Scholastic, mathematics concept of music, where the art of composition has to do with observing rules and feelings are almost never mentioned. He seems to confirm his old fashioned concept when he speaks of the instrumental form, the Fantasy, again defining the 'art' without reference to emotions.

---

97 Morley, *A Plain and Easy Introduction to Practical Music*, 136. In another place he says the goal must be to both please the ear and display the art of composition. [Ibid., 217]

98 Ibid., 141.

99 Ibid., 290.

100 Ibid., 293.

In this [form] may more art be shown than in any other music because the composer is tied to nothing, but that he may add, diminish, and alter at his pleasure.[101]

Morley also addresses aesthetics with reference to several other forms. Under the general label 'Motet style' he includes 'all grave and sober music.' He seems to mean by this primarily church music and he advises such music must have majesty and be mostly in longer note values, as 'quick motions denote a kind of wantonness.'[102] He observes that this style of music, while the highest art, is now little esteemed. The preference for 'light music' he finds not just prevalent in England, but throughout Europe. He quotes one unnamed writer as complaining that,

> the musicians of this age, instead of drawing the minds of men to the consideration of heaven and heavenly things, do by the contrary set wide open the gates of hell, causing such as delight in the exercise of their art tumble headlong into perdition.

What is this 'light music' which is opening the gates of Hell? The highest form of light music, for Morley, is the madrigal. The madrigal, he says, would be nice music, if it were not for the words.

> This kind of music were not so much disallowable if the poets who compose the [text] would abstain from some obscenities which all honest ears abhor, and sometime from blasphemies such as *ch'altro di te iddio non voglio* ['I wish no other god but thee'], which no man, who has any hope for salvation, can sing without trembling. As for the music it is, next to the Motet, the most [artful] and, to men of understanding, most delightful. If therefore you will compose in this kind you must possess yourself with an amorous humor (for in no composition shall you prove admirable except you put on and possess yourself wholly with that vein wherein you compose), so that you must in your music be wavering like the wind, sometimes wanton, sometimes drooping, sometimes grave and staid, otherwhile effeminate ...[103]

Aesthetically, the next lower categories of 'light music' are canzonets, Neapolitans and Villanelles. The latter is 'the [lowest] degree of gravity,' being country songs. 'Balletts,' he considers 'but a slight kind of music, devised to be danced to voices.'

The very lowest category of music, 'if they deserve the name of music,' are drinking songs (Vinate), Giustinianas, 'a wanton and rude kind of music' and Passamezzos, 'tedious and superfluous.'

---

101 Ibid., 296.

102 Ibid., 293ff.

103 Ibid., 294ff. His reference to the composer putting himself into the mood of the text before composing ('possess yourself wholly with that vein wherein you compose') reminds us of a similar, and more elegant, comment by William Byrd in the dedication to his *Gradualia* (1605).

> In these words, as I have learned by trial, there is such a profound and hidden power that to one thinking upon things divine and diligently and earnestly pondering them, all the fittest [notes] occur as if of themselves and freely offer themselves to the mind which is not indolent or inert.

Henry Peacham (1576–1643), *The Complete Gentleman*

Henry Peacham, in discussing the education of the noble, includes music as an important subject for study.[104] He begins, however, with a little attack on the Italians, quoting a current proverb 'Whom God loves not, that man loves not music.'

> But I am verily persuaded that they are by nature very ill-disposed and of such brutish stupidity that scarce anything else that is good and favorable to virtue is to be found in them.[105]

His most specific praise of the purposes of music has to do with music therapy.

> The physicians will tell you that the exercise of music is a great lengthener of the life by stirring and reviving of the spirits, holding a secret sympathy with them. Besides, the exercise of singing openeth the breast and pipes. It is an enemy to melancholy and dejection of the mind … Yea, a curer of some diseases … Besides the aforesaid benefit of singing, it is a most ready help for a bad pronunciation and distinct speaking, which I have heard confirmed by many great divines. Yea, I myself have known many children to have been helped of their stammering in speech only by it.

But Peacham finds many other purposes of music, including value in the 'speculative,' or theoretical form of music.

> Infinite is the sweet variety that the theoric of music exerciseth the mind withal, as the contemplation of proportion, of concords and discords, diversity of moods and tones, infiniteness of invention, etc. But I dare affirm there is no one science in the world that so affecteth the free and generous spirit with a more delightful and inoffensive recreation, or better disposeth the mind to what is commendable and virtuous …
> Yea, in my opinion, no rhetoric more persuadeth or hath greater power over the mind …
> How doth music amaze us, when of sound discords she maketh the sweetest harmony! And who can show us the reason why two basins, bowls, brass pots, or the like of the same bigness, the one being full, the other empty, shall, stricken, be a just diapason in sound one to the other, or that there should be such sympathy in sounds that two lutes of equal size being laid upon a table and tuned unison … the one stricken, the other shall answer it?[106]

He concludes his discussion of the purposes of music with those more frequently mentioned in earlier literature.

> If all arts hold their esteem and value according to their effects, account this goodly science not among the number of those which Lucian placeth without the gates of hell as vain and unprofit-

---

104 Peacham, *The Complete Gentleman*, 108ff.

105 Of the French, he says,
> They delight for the most part in horsemanship, fencing, hunting, dancing, and little esteem of learning and gifts of the mind … [Ibid., 163]

106 Ibid., 115ff.

able, but of such which are ... the fountains of our lives' good and happiness. Since it is a principal means of glorifying our merciful Creator, it heightens our devotion, it gives delight and ease to our travails, it expelleth sadness and heaviness of spirit, preserveth people in concord and amity, allayeth fierceness and anger, and lastly, is the best physic for many melancholy diseases.[107]

Peacham also recommends the composers he regards as most worthy of study, beginning with William Byrd, 'whom in that kind I know not whether any may equal.' Byrd is followed by Victoria, Lassus, Marenzio and Ferrabosco, the father, among many others.[108]

Finally, we find a few additional reflections on the purposes of music, beginning with its traditional ability to soothe the listener.

Coperario's *Funeral Tears for the Earle of Devonshire* (1606), expresses the interesting thought that while music soothes, it does not replace or eliminate the original emotion.

> Musicke though it sweetens paine
> Yet no whit impaires lamenting ...

Another writer, John Case, in *The Praise of Musicke* (1586), attempts to identify more precisely how music soothes a listener under such emotions.

> With musick no times are amisse. For we know that life is, as it were, put into the dead'st sorrows by inflection and modulation of the voice. And they whose heartes even yearne for very greefe sometimes fall on singing, not to seek comfort therein (for the best seeming comfort in such cases is to be comfortless) but rather to set the more on float that pensiveness wherewith they are perplexed.[109]

One of the most commonly observed instances where music soothes is the lullaby, as is often mentioned in all early literature. Bryskett, in his *A Discourse of Civill Life*, provides a curious explanation for how this happens.

> Here may also be added the singing of nurses, whereby they commonly still [children], using [music], as taught by nature only: which some men think comes to pass, by reason that the soul is (as they say) composed of harmony, and therefore is delighted with that which is proper and natural to it. Others (happily of better judgment) say, that children are stilled by the singing of their nurses, because one contrary expels and drives away another, when it is the stronger: so as the nurse's singing is louder than the child's crying, therefore it prevails. But the most effectual reason is, that the vegetative power or faculty being of most force in that age, and it taking pleasure in things delightful, and abhorring those that are displeasing and noisome; when with

---

107 Ibid., 116.

108 Ibid., 112ff. His judgment has been confirmed by Time.

109 Quoted in Charles Sayle, *In Praise of Music* (London, 1897), 85.

crying it finds itself annoyed, it more willingly admits the nurse's singing, and becomes calm and still by hearing the numbers and sweetness of the voice delighting them.[110]

Occasionally we read of a rare example where music fails to soothe the listener. A vivid example is found in the anonymous *The Passionate Morrice* of 1593. Here an unhappy lady falls on her knees and cries.

> And after that, being indeed in her right mind,[111] she took her lute, singing to her fingering this sonnet:
>
>> What booteth love, that liking wants his joy?
>> Grievous that joy which lacks his heart's content …
>
> Which music would be so metamorphofed, as, in truth, her singing would turn to sighing, and her playing to complaining, when, in a rage, she would throw her lute down, beginning to dilate on her love's unkindness, that could be so cruel as to stay four and twenty hours from her.[112]

Another anonymous work of 1600, 'Tom Tel-Troths Message,' devotes a stanza of poetry to each of the Liberal Arts. While most simply define the science, the one for Music seems again to reflect a singer who is not soothed by music.

> *Musicke*, I much bemourne thy miserie,
> Whose well-tuned notes delight the Gods above,
> Who, with thine ear-bewitching melody,
> Doest unto men and beasts such pleasure move:
> Though wailing cannot help, I wail thy wrong,
> Bearing a part with thee in thy sad song.[113]

On Church Music

Church music in England had long been enriched by the addition of instruments, a tradition which can be documented well before most other countries. One scholar dates this practice from 1306, when a Te Deum was performed at the end of the vigil preceding the knighthood of the Prince of Wales.

---

110 Bryskett, *A Discourse on Civill Life*, 42ff.

111 This familiar phrase refers, unconsciously, to the fact that the 'real us' is the 'right mind,' or the right hemisphere of the brain.

112 Anonymous, 'The passionate Morrice,' in *Miscellaneous*, Series VI, Shakespeare's England, Nr. 2, ed. Frederick Furnivall (Vaduz: Kraus Reprint, 1965), 78.

113 Anonymous, 'Tom Tel-Troths Message,' in *Miscellaneous*, Series VI, Shakespere's England, Nr. 2, ed. Frederick Furnivall (Vaduz: Kraus Reprint, 1965), 116.

Matthew of Westminster remarks that the noise of trumpets and shawms, and the raising of voices was so loud that the 'shout of praise' [*iubilatio*] with which the choir entered could not be heard.[114]

One reads of Henry VIII and Cardinal Wolsey attending Mass at St. Paul's, in 1525, after which 'the quere sang Te Deum, and the mynstrelles plaied on every side.'[115] This reference and a similar one of 1527, mentioning the 'King's trumpetts and shalmes' again in St. Paul's,[116] follow a familiar pattern of the use of royal or civic wind bands within the church on special occasions.

Canterbury Cathedral, on the other hand, seems to have been an early example of a major church which maintained its own small wind band from an early date. As early as 1532, a cathedral statute calls for the employment of '2 sackbutteers and 2 cornetteers.'[117]

Henry VIII's break with the Church of Rome, in 1534, ushered in a period of some chaos in traditional Church music. When he closed the monasteries, eliminating the traditional singing schools, not only were professional Church musicians suddenly out of work, but the link with the Roman church music was broken. On the other hand, Henry VIII also had no desire to promote Luther and his Church, thus he banned some of the early Church music from that source.[118] Some composers, at this point, appear to have explored the possibility of sales in the private sector. Tye's *Actes of the Apostles* (1553) included music for solo singer and a part for lute, 'very necessary for students after their study.'[119]

To complicate matters further, the Puritans were, at first, inclined toward having no music at all in the church. They apparently felt that any large-scale musical performances in church were to be regarded as a remnant of Catholicism, as we can see in John Field's *An Admonition to Parliament* (1572).

> In all their order of service there is no edification, according to the rule of the Apostles, but confusion; they toss the Psalms in most places like tennis balls ... As for organs and curious singing, though they be proper to popish dens, I mean to Cathedral churches, yet some others also must have them. The queen's Chappell, and these churches which should be spectacles of Christian reformation, must be patterns and precedents to the people, of all superstitions ... We should be too long to tell your honours of Cathedral churches, the dens aforesaid of all loitering lubbers, where master Dean, master Vicedean ... the chief chanter, singingmen ... squeaking

---

114 Richard Rastall, 'Some English Consort-Groupings of the Late Middle Ages,' *Music & Letters* 55, no. 2 (April 1974): 194, http://www.jstor.org/stable/733853.

115 Edward Hall, *Chronicle* (London, 1809), 693.

116 William Dugdale, *The History of Saint Paul's Cathedral* (London, 1818), 433.

117 Walter Woodfill, *Musicians in English Society* (Princeton, 1953), 149.

118 Reese, *Music in the Renaissance*, 781.

119 A similar work by Richard Alison, the *Psalmes of David* (1599), indicates in its preface,

> The plain song being the common tune to be sung and played upon the Lute, Orpharyon, Citterne or Bass Viol, severally or altogether, the singing part to be either Tenor or Treble to the Instrument, according to the nature of the voice or for four voices. [Reese, Ibid., 808]

choristers, organ players ... live in great idleness ... If you would know whence all these came, we can easily answer you, that they came from the Pope, as out of the Trojan horse's belly, to the destruction of God's kingdom.[120]

Under their influence, in the years after the death of Henry VIII more than '100 pairs of organs were pulled down.'[121]

During this period when Puritan forces were calling for the elimination of all music in the church, the important Church philosopher, Richard Hooker, whose eloquent testimonial to the power of music we have quoted above, was one of those speaking against this radical movement. Nevertheless, Hooker had his own aesthetic ideals for Church music.

In church music curiosity and ostentation of art, wanton or light or unsuitable harmony, such as only pleaseth the ear, and doth not naturally serve to the very kind and degree of those impressions, which the matter that goeth with it leaveth or is apt to leave in men's minds, doth rather blemish and disgrace that we do than add either beauty or furtherance unto it. On the other side, these faults prevented, the force and efficacy of the thing itself, when it drowneth not utterly but fitly suiteth with matter altogether sounding to the praise of God, is in truth most admirable, and doth much edify if not the understanding because it teacheth not, yet surely the affection, because therein it worketh much. They must have hearts very dry and tough, from whom the melody of psalms doth not sometime draw that wherein a mind religiously affected delighteth.

He mentions the very simple chant of the original Christians, which was always discussed by those who objected to contemporary Church music. Hooker's argument was that the simple chant was appropriate for the early simple Christians, but for the 'grosser and heavier minds' of sixteenth-century men, 'the sweetness of melody might make some entrance for good things.'[122]

More elaborate Church music began to appear with the reign of Elizabeth I. It was clearly her preference, for many accounts exist which describe services such as that in 1575 when she visited Worcester Cathedral and heard 'a great and solemn noise of singing of service in the quire both by note and also playing with cornetts and sackbutts.'[123] Even at home in more private circumstances, accounts speak of a surprising number of instruments participating in her services. A secretary of the visiting Duke of Württemberg, who attended a service in 1592, records,

This Castle stands upon a knoll; in the outer or first court there is a very beautiful and immensely large church, with a flat even roof, covered with lead, as is common with all churches in this kingdom. In this church his Highness listened for more than an hour to the beautiful music, the usual ceremonies, and the English sermon. The music, especially the organ, was exquisitely

---

120 Quoted in Monson, 'Elizabethan London,' 307.
121 Ibid., 315.
122 Richard Hooker, *The Works of Mr. Richard Hooker*, II, 161ff.
123 Woodfill, *Musicians in English Society*, 149.

played; for at times you could hear the sound of cornetts, flutes, then fifes and other instruments ... After the music, which lasted a long time, had ended ...[124]

A similar account of services at Whitehall in 1597 speaks of 'voices, organs, cornetts, and sackbutts, with other ceremonies and music.'[125]

Beyond this, it is clear that Elizabeth used Church music, to some degree, for political purposes, in particular to impress foreign diplomats that religion had not ended in England with Henry VIII. We can see this clearly in the report of a visiting Italian diplomat in 1589.

> Seeing him [the archbishop] upon the next Sabbath day after in the Cathedral Church of Canterbury, attended upon by his Gentlemen, and servants ... also by the Deane, Prebendaries, and Preachers in their Surplesses, and scarlet Hoods, and heard the solemne Musicke with the voyces, and Organs, Cornets, and Sagbutts, hee was overtaken with admiration, and tolde an English Gentleman of very good qualitie, 'That they were led in great blindness at Rome, by our own Nation, who made the people there believe, that there was not in England, either Archbishop, or Bishop, or Cathedral, or any Church or Ecclesiastical government; but that all was pulled down to the ground, and that the people heard their Ministers in the Woods, and Fields, amongst Trees, and brute beasts; but, for his own part, he protested, that (unless it were in the Popes Chappell) he had never saw a more solemne sight, nor heard a more heavenly sound.[126]

Another eyewitness account by a visitor at this time makes a similar comparison with Rome.

> The altar was furnished with rich plate, with two gilt candlesticks, with lighted candles, and a massy crucifix in the midst; and that the service was sung not only with organs, but with the [artful] music of cornets, sacbuts, etc., on solemn festivals ... That, in short, the service performed in the queen's Chapel, and in sundry cathedrals, was so splendid and showy, that foreigners could not distinguish it from the Roman, except that it was performed in English.[127]

---

124 Jacob Rathgeb, *A True and Faithful Narrative* ... (Tübingen, 1602), quoted in *England as seen by Foreigners,* ed. William Rye(New York: Blom), 115ff. Elizabeth is here mentioned in the masculine form as was the custom at this time for all female rulers.

125 George Harrison, ed., *The Elizabethan Journals* (New York: MacMillian), 184.

126 G. Paule, *The Life of the most reverend and religious prelate John Whitgift Lord Archbishop of Canterbury* (London, 1612), 79.

127 Quoted in Edmondstoune Duncan, *The Story of Minstrelsy* (London: Walter Scott, 1968), 177.

9 ROYAL MUSIC OF SIXTEENTH-CENTURY ENGLAND

The primary purpose of this chapter, and the following one, is to provide the reader with some indication of the wider world of music making which existed in sixteenth-century England than that which is reflected in general music history texts.

HENRY VIII (1509–1547)

From all appearances, Henry VIII, among all other things, was the most musical king in English history. The Venetian ambassador mentions some of the instruments he played.

> His Majesty is the handsomest potentate I ever set eyes on; above the usual height, with an extremely fine calf to his leg, his complexion very fair and bright, with auburn hair combed straight and short … He speaks French, English, and Latin, and a little Italian, plays well on the lute and harpsichord, sings from book at sight, draws the bow with greater strength than any man in England, and jousts marvelously.[1]

We know he played the flute, and owned no fewer than 154 of them when he died, in addition to a large number of keyboard instruments, fifty strings and another hundred crumhorns, shawms and bassoon-types.[2] So perhaps Erasmus was correct when he said of him, 'there is no kind of music in which he is not more than moderately proficient.'[3] In addition, Peacham, writing later in the century, quotes Erasmus as having knowledge of Henry's long-rumored activity as a composer.

> King Henry the Eighth could not only sing his part sure but of himself compose a service of four, five and six parts, as Erasmus in a certain epistle testifieth of his own knowledge.[4]

---

1 Letter dated 1515, by Piero Pasqualigo, quoted in Sebastian Giustinian, *Four Years at the Court of Henry VIII* (London, 1854), I, 83. Perhaps he improvised on the lute, for there is no extant English lute music from this period. See Gustave Reese, *Music in the Renaissance* (New York: Norton, 1959), 842.

2 Entirely missing in his personal collection are the ceremonial trumpets, fifes and percussion instruments.

3 P.S. Allen, *Opus epistolarum Des. Erasmi Roterdami* (Oxford, 1906–1958), VIII, Ep. 2143 , quoted in Miller, 'Erasmus on Music,' 347.

4 Peacham, *The Complete Gentleman*, 111.

Henry's coronation service in June 1509 included a consort of nine 'Styll shalmes,' a consort of four shawm and sackbuts and fourteen trumpets.[5] On the following day there was a great allegorical tournament, on the theme of Pallas and her relationship to both War and Wisdom. There was a wagon constructed in the form of a mountain, drawn by a 'lyon made of Glyteryng gold.' The challengers rode onto the field to the sound of trumpets and 'Dromes and Fifes a greate nombre.'[6] On the fourth day a hunting pageant was held, with eight knights announced by 'a greate nombre of hornes blowen' by men dressed as foresters. A deer was let loose to be killed by the dogs. The ensuing combat display got out of hand and became so violent that Henry was forced to call out the guard and halt the proceedings.

The early years of Henry's reign are characterized by such allegorical productions in which the nobles could participate in elaborate disguises. One of the most important was held in February, 1511, to celebrate the birth of the king's son. A banquet for the foreign ambassadors, following this pageant, included a performance by the singers of the Chapel Royal. During the banquet a large float was rolled into the hall on which rode six children singers of the Chapel, six richly clad ladies, the principal challengers of the tournament held earlier in the day[7] and eight minstrels 'with strange instruments.'[8] After the banquet the minstrels provided music for dancing and it was said that the minstrels themselves joined in the dancing so 'that it was a pleasure to behold.'

A 'disguising' was an allegorical event on a smaller scale and a typical one occurred on 1 May 1515, when the king and his company while out for a ride were surprised by 'Robin Hood' and his men.

> Then Robyn hood desyred the kynge and quene to come into the grene wood, & to se how the outlawes lyve. The kyng demaunded of ye quene & her ladyes, if they durst adventure to go into the wood with so many outlawes ... The hornes blewe ... there was an Arber made of boowes with a hal, and a great chamber and an inner chamber very well made & covered with floures & swete herbes, whiche the kyng muche praysed.[9]

The king and his guests were served a breakfast of venison, accompanied by music of organs, flutes and a lute. One of the guests, a Venetian, describes the return home.

---

5   Henry Cart de LaFontaine, *The King's Musik* (London, 1909), 4.

6   Descriptions taken from Edward Hall, *Hall's Chronicle* (London, 1809), 508 and I. D. Thornley, *The Great Chronicle of London* (London: G. W. Jones, 1938), 341ff.

7   A manuscript volume called the *Great Tournament Roll*, housed at the College of Arms, contains illustrations of this tournament. One sees here a rare black trumpet player, who is identified in the accounts as 'John Blanke.'

8   This wagon was so heavy that when it was under construction at the bishop of Harford's palace it fell through the floor.

9   Hall, *Chronicle*, 582.

> Proceeding homewards, certain tall paste-board giants being placed on carts, and … [we] were conducted with the greatest order to Greenwich, the musicians singing the whole way, and sounding trumpets and other instruments, so that, by my faith, it was an extremely fine triumph.[10]

After about 1516 the large scale allegorical pageants were no longer held, although court entertainments continued to be richly adorned. A joust in honor of the Flemish ambassadors in 1517 included harnesses for the horses made of pure silver. An eyewitness, Chieregato, reports that this required all the smiths in London to work on nothing else for four months before the joust.[11]

Cardinal Wolsey maintained his own private minstrels and we read of their appearance at a mumming[12] he gave for the French ambassadors in October 1518.

> And when the banquet was done, in came six minstrels, richly disguised, and after them followed three gentlemen in wide and long gowns of Crimson satin, everyone having a cup of gold in their hands, the first cup was full of Angels and royals, the second had diverse balls of dice, and the third had certain pairs of cards. These gentlemen offered to play at monchaunce, and when they had played a length of the first board, then the mynstrels blew up, and then entered into the chamber twelve ladies disguised …[13]

Another contemporary account describes an appearance by the cardinal's wind band, during a banquet given for the king, and it hints rather darkly of possible foul play in the sudden death of one of the shawm players.

> There was not only plenty of fine meats, but also much mirth and solace, as well in merry communication as with the noise of my Lord's minstrels, who played there all that night so cunningly, that the king took therein great pleasure; insomuch that he desired my Lord to lend them unto him for the next night, and after supper their banquet finished, the ladies and gentlemen fell to dancing, among whom, one Madame Fontaine, a maid, had the prize. And thus passed they the most part of the night ere they departed. The next day the king took my Lord's minstrels, and rode to a nobleman's house where there was some image to whom he vowed a pilgrimage, to perform his devotions. When he came there, which was in the night, he danced and caused others to do the same, after the sound of my Lord's minstrels, who played there all night, and never rested, so that whether it were with extreme labor of blowing, or with poison (as some

---

10 Letter of Nicolò Sagudino, quoted in Sebastian Giustinian, *Four Years at the Court of Henry VIII*, I, 80.
11 Sydney Anglo, *The Great Tournament Roll of Westminster* (Oxford: Clarendon, 1968), 65.
12 A mumming consisted of the appearance of masked persons who invited the guests to games of dice, fixed so that the guests always won.
13 Hall, *Chronicle*, 595.

judged) because they were commended by the king more than his own, I cannot tell, but the player on the shawm (who was very excellent on that instrument) died within a day or two after.[14]

Henry was in fact, at this time, looking for fine musicians to add to his musical household. He was particularly interested in foreign musicians and the results of one recruiting effort are reported in a letter from Chamberlain, Court-Master of the English merchants in Antwerp, to Paget, First Secretary of the court. He reports that with the help of local merchants he has found five musicians, one of whom can make all sorts of instruments. Four of the musicians are young and would like to join the king's service, but own no instruments. The fifth, who owns the instruments, has with some difficulty been persuaded to go with them. If paid wages and expenses in advance they agree to stay in England until the new year. We can see typical evidence of the preference for wind instrument players at this time in Chamberlain's report that there are some Italians in town, but they can only play the viols, and therefore 'are no musicians.'[15]

One of the foreign musicians hired by Henry VIII was Philip van Wilder, a lute player and 'keeper of the king's instruments.' A document addressed to him reveals that sometimes the wind band also played in more intimate circumstances.

> … paied to phillip of the pryvat chambre for 2 sagbuttes, 2 tenor shalmes and 2 treble shalmesse. 10.10s.[16]

As Henry's reign progressed, the elaborate disguisings and tournaments became more and more rare. Most accounts which describe actual performances now are associated with distinguished visitors. For the arrival of Charles V in 1522 there was a procession which included a mechanical dragon and two great bulls, 'whiche beastes cast out fyer continually,' and a great arch which held trumpets in one tower and shawms and sackbuts in another.[17]

Henry VIII arranged an especially elaborate reception for the arrival of his second wife, Anne Boleyn, as part of his attempts to gain support for her on the part of the public—after all she had cost him a split with the pope and she was six months pregnant. First, there was a great water procession which included a mechanical dragon in the river and a group of 'terrible monsters and wylde men castyng fyer, and makyng hideous noyses.' Music was provided by the mayor's barge, which contained shawms, sackbuts 'and diverse other instru-

---

14 Stow's Annals, quoted in Duncan, *The Story of Minstrelsy*, 139. One of Wolsey's biographers, Cavendish, tells a somewhat different version of the same tale. He says that when Wolsey was visiting the French court in Paris, in 1527, with his wind band in tow, the king of France, François I, who was always on the lookout for good wind players, stole one of Wolsey's shawms. The implication here is that Wolsey, in retribution, was somehow responsible for the death of the shawm player. [George Cavendish, *The Life and Death of Cardinal Wolsey*, ed. Richard Sylvester (London, 1959), 60] See also, Joycelyne Russell, *The Field of Cloth of Gold* (New York, 1969), 163.

15 John Stevens, *Music & Poetry in the Early Tudor Court* (London: Methuen), 308.

16 Ibid., 307.

17 Hall, *Chronicle*, 638.

ments, which continually made goodly harmony,' and forty-eight additional boats, each with musicians, representing various guilds of London, 'their minstrels continually playing.'[18]

The following day there was the official procession of the new queen into London and among the many descriptions of ceremonial music we are attracted especially to one which reads,

> [In a tower] was suche several solemne instrumetes, that it seemed to be an heavenly noyse, and was muche regarded and praised.[19]

For the following queens, due to their rapid succession, it was deemed that such pomp was inappropriate.

The accounts of the funeral of Henry VIII list the participation of twenty-nine singers, eight string and forty-two wind and percussion players. Among the latter were twenty-one trumpets, a consort of seven players called 'Mynstrells,' a five-member consort called 'Musytyans' (all with the family name of Bassani), a four-member sackbut consort, a five-member flute consort, and one each of fife, drum and bagpipe.[20]

EDWARD VI (1547–1553)

The most extensive accounts of music under Edward VI, who became king at age ten, are those describing his coronation in 1548. Among the many pageants which the coronation procession passed in the streets of London, we should particularly like to mention one which was given by a group of actors, 'richly apparelled like ladyes.' They represented the seven Liberal Arts and our attention is drawn to the fact that the purpose of Music is given as only a pastime. The actors made the following speeches:

Grammar
I, Grammar, with the silver key unlock the door to science every way.

Logic
And I, Logic, directly discuss all things uprightly.

Rhetoric
And I, the adorned Rhetoric, to beautify speeches is much politic.

Arithmetic
And I, Arithmetic, through exercise in numbering make men wise.

Geometry
I, Geometry, ordained for measuring, and as necessary for building.

---

18 Ibid., 798ff.
19 Ibid., 802.
20 LaFontaine, *The King's Musik*, 7ff.

Music
Yet I, pleasant Music, for king's pastime am most liked.

Astronomy
I, prudent Astronomy, describe of planets the mystery.[21]

We gain some insight into the nature of the regular musicians employed by Edward VI in an extant document regarding payments to the entire household in 1553. Included here are payments to the king's trumpets, the king's 'drumslades,' the 'still mynstrelles' [shawms], the sackbuts and to the five Bassiam family members called 'mynstrelles' and to another group of three minstrels.[22]

MARY TUDOR (1553–1558)

Mary already at age six had a substantial number of musicians in her personal employ, music being an accepted means of whiling away the days for a single lady with no expectation of ever playing an important role in society.[23] These, combined with the court musicians remaining from Henry VIII's reign, supplied the typical ceremonial music for her coronation.

The following year, 1554, Philip of Spain came to do his duty in trying to produce an heir for Mary and England. Since Mary and Philip shared no language, there may have been more music than usual to fill the silence—at least accounts speak of their days being filled with 'minstrels all playing.'[24] Some of the entertainments for Philip which were regarded as remarkable included a Spanish game on horses, a 'cane game,' played to the music of 'drums made of Ketylles and trumpets,' and minstrels dressed as apes, sitting in a row playing bagpipes.[25]

---

21 John G. Nichols, ed., *Literary Remains of King Edward the Sixth* (London, 1857), I, cclxxviiiff.

22 Ibid., I, cccxiii. Edward must have had some reputation for knowledge in music for a play by Rowley, *When You See Me You Know Me* (1605) attributes this speech to him regarding the composer Christopher Tye:

> Doctor, I thank you and commend your cunning.
> I oft have heard my Father merrily speak
> In your high praise and thus his Highness said,
> England one God, one Truth, one Doctor has
> For Music's Art and that is Doctor Tye.

23 Gerald Hayes, *King's Music* (Oxford, 1937), 52.

24 Hilda F. M. Prescott, *A Spanish Tudor* (New York, 1940), 351.

25 Ibid., 355 and Daniel Henderson, *The Crimson Queen* (New York: Duffield and Green, 1933), 227.

ELIZABETH I (1558–1603)

As with Mary, no one expected Elizabeth would ever be a public figure, so her youth was spent being provided education in history, languages, dance and music. No male royal figure in English history, with the possible exception of Victoria's consort Albert, was ever so well educated and it contributed fundamentally to the success of her forty-five year reign. Her private tutor, Roger Ascham, observed of her,

> It is to your shame (I speak to you all, you young gentlemen of England) that one maid should go beyond you all in excellency of learning and knowledge of divers tongues. Point forth six of the best-given gentlemen of this court, and all they together show not so much good will, spend not so much time, bestow not so many hours, daily, orderly, and constantly, for the increase of learning and knowledge as doth the Queen's Majesty herself. Yea, I believe that, beside her perfect readiness in Latin, Italian, French, and Spanish, she readeth here now at Windsor more Greek every day than some prebendary of this church doth read Latin in a whole week. And that which is most praiseworthy of all, within the walls of her privy chamber she hath obtained that excellency of learning, to understand, speak, and write, both wittily with head and fair with hand, as scarce one or two rare wits in both the universities have in many years reached unto.[26]

Elizabeth took all of this in her stride, making perhaps her most often quoted single statement, 'it is no marvel to teach a woman to talk; it is far harder to teach her to hold her tongue.'

Her musical abilities have also been well documented. She told the ambassador, de Maisse, that she played at least a pavan every day on the virginal.[27] In a frequently quoted passage from the memoirs of Sir James Melville, he recalls hearing her play.

> The same day, after dinner, my Lord Huntsdean drew me up to a quiet gallery that I might hear some music (but he said he durst now avow it), where I might hear the Queen play upon the virginals. After I had hearkened a while, I took by the tapestry that hung before the door of the chamber, and, seeing her back was towards the door, I entered within the chamber, and stood a pretty space, hearing her play excellently well; but she lift off immediately so soon as she turned her about, and came forward, seeming to strike me with her hand, alleging, she was not used to play before men, but only when she was solitary to shun melancholy.[28]

Elizabeth's interest in music continued throughout her reign as she developed a broad and large musical establishment.[29] Incomplete accounts make it difficult to trace these musicians in some cases, but it is clear she had large numbers of trumpets, a six-member trombone consort (until ca. 1593) and a consort of eight string players. Missing in the official records

---

26 Roger Ascham, *The Schoolmaster* (1570), ed. Lawrence Ryan (Ithaca: Cornell University Press, 1967), 56.

27 Harrison, *The Elizabethan Journals*, II, 242.

28 Quoted in John Nichols, *The Progresses and Public Processions of Queen Elizabeth* (London, 1788, 1805), III [these volumes carry no page numbers].

29 Her attention to this is evidenced by the fact that when Bull was once traveling on the continent, Elizabeth ordered him home, fearing he might be hired by a foreign court. [Reese, *Music in the Renaissance*, 809]

are the shawms and cornetts, which, as they are documented in other literature, must have been present. One fact which is clear is that a majority of the musicians were foreign born. Many of these had come on their own to England for religious reasons, but some have suggested that there was a shortage of skilled musicians in England as a consequence of Henry VIII closing the monasteries and Church schools. This is one of the observations Nichols makes, writing in 1788.

> This Matthew Gwin was a Fellow of St. John's College, studied physic, poetry, chemistry, etc., and made a great figure in almost every part of learning. He was chosen Music Professor of Oxford University in 1582, though he understood not a title either of the theory or practice of that science ... The greatest wound, which music ever received in England, was from the suppression of the monasteries; after which the Puritans often made it their business to run it down as a relic of popery. For both these reasons, very few Englishmen regarded it in Queen Elizabeth's time. Her own band of musicians were many of them foreigners (Venetians).[30]

Elizabeth was particularly skillful in using her musicians for political purposes. One German visitor in 1598 was impressed, but not fooled.

> During the time that this guard, which consists of the tallest and stoutest men that can be found in all England, 100 in number, being carefully selected for this service, were bringing dinner, twelve trumpets and two timpani made the hall ring for half-an-hour together.[31]

She must have made sure that more musically sophisticated impressions were made as well. A guest of another banquet recalls that after the third course,

> had been served and taken away, the Queen's musicians appeared in the Chamber with their trumpets and shawms, and after they had performed their music, everyone withdrew, bowing themselves out just as they had come in.[32]

Similarly, Albertus Alasco, Palatine of Siradia [Poland] was welcomed in 1583, by,

> a consort of musicians, who, over a long space, made very sweet harmony, which could not but move and delight.[33]

For politically sensitive visitors Elizabeth was capable of arranging for elaborate entertainments, as when for the visit of the French ambassador in April 1581 she had erected for the occasion a banquet hall 332 feet long with 292 windows.[34] An allegorical tournament

---

30 Nichols, *The Progresses and Public Processions of Queen Elizabeth*, II.
31 Paul Hentzner, 'Travels in England,' in *England as seen by Foreigners* (London, 1865), 106. This visitor complained of the general noise pollution in London and claims citizens liked to get drunk and go ring church bells just for exercise.
32 Ian Dunlop, *Palaces and Progresses of Elizabeth I* (London, 1962), 109.
33 Nichols, *The Progresses and Public Processions of Queen Elizabeth*, II.
34 G. W. Thornbury, *Shakespeare's England* (London, 1856), II, 372ff.

was given, with four of Elizabeth's nobles serving as the principal challengers, disguised as the 'Four Children of Desire.' These four entered the field, with their personal trumpets, and approached a 'fortress' rolling on wheels, with 'divers kinds of most excellent music' hidden inside. When it stopped, a boy sang, accompanied by cornetts, presumably the hidden musicians,

> Yield, yield, O yield, you that this fort do hold,
> Which seated is in spotless honors field …

Then two imitation cannons shot perfumed powder and water, the sound of the cannons being supplied by 'excellent melodie.' Scaling ladders were applied to the walls of the fortress and 'missiles' of flowers and love letters were thrown inside. At another time, the Four Children of Desire appeared again with a 'curiously decked' chariot.

> In the [middle] of the charriot was conveied roome for a full consort of musike, who plaied still very doleful musike as the charriot mooved.[35]

Elizabeth's Progresses

Soon after her coronation, Elizabeth began the custom of making extended travels, known as 'Progresses,' throughout her realm during the summer. Her purpose was partly to come to know the country she had unexpectedly become queen of, partly to keep an eye on her powerful vassal lords and partly to escape the discomfort, and plagues, of London. She traveled in style, with large numbers of her court, her personal belongings and even furniture. This, combined with the extravagant entertainments her hosts knew she would expect, caused many lords to pray she would not honor them with a visit.

The first of these extended summer visits for which there is considerable first-hand information regarding the music heard, was her visit in 1575 to the Kenilworth Castle of the Earl of Leicester. Her entrance to the castle property was greeted by six giant statues ['made up'] of trumpet players, behind which real trumpet players played. One eyewitness, Robert Laneham, thought they were real and was duly impressed.

> The porter cauzed his Trumpetoourz that stood upon the wall of the gate thear, too soound up a tune of welcum: which, besyde the noble noyz, was so mooch the more pleazaunt too behold, becauz theez Trumpetoourz, beeing sixe in number, were every one an eight foot hye, in due proportion of person besyde, all in long garments of silk suitable, each with his silvery Trumpet of a five foot long, formed taper wise, and straight from the upper part to the neather end: where the diameter was a 16 inch over, and yet so tempered by art, that being very eazy too the blast, they cast foorth no greater noyz nor a more unpleazaunt soound for time and tune, than any

---

35 Nichols, *The Progresses and Public Processions of Queen Elizabeth*, II.

oother comon Trumpet, be it never so [artfully] formed. These harmonious blasterz, from the foreside upon the wallz, untoo the inner; had this muzik maintained from them very delectable, while her Highness all along this Tylt-yard rode.[36]

As Elizabeth passed the outer walls into the tournament field she came upon an artificial lake which had been constructed for her visit. Now a pageant based on the 'Lady of the Lake' was given, which began with a mechanically propelled 'floating island' which drifted toward the shore where the queen waited. The island, blazing with torches, supported two Nymphs who addressed the queen in poetry regarding the history of the castle and its owners. This was followed by a performance by a large wind band.

> This Pageaunt was cloz'd up with a delectable harmony of Hautboiz, Shalmz, Cornets, and such oother looud muzik, that held on while her Majestie pleazauntly so passed from thence toward the Castl gate.

The bridge into the castle was decorated with gifts from various Greek gods. Two virtues of music were noted relative to the gifts presenting Phoebus [Apollo] there,

> were thear placed too saer Bay braunchez of a four foot hy, adourned on all sides with lutes, viollz, shallmz, cornets, flutes, recorders, and harpes, az prezents of Phoebus, God of Musik for rejoycing the mind, and of phizik for health to the body.

Finally, before entering the castle, Elizabeth paused to hear a flute consort ['a fresh delicate armony of Flutz'].

The following day, Sunday, the queen and her party attended church and then spent 'the afternoon in excellent muzik of sundry swet instruments, and in dauncing,' followed by fireworks in the evening. On Monday there was hunting, followed by an evening entertainment featuring a 'wild man' ['Hombre Salvagio'] accompanied by fauns and Nymphs. Tuesday featured more musical performances, including one performed on a boat on the artificial lake:

> where it pleased her to stand, while upon the pool oout of a barge fine appoynted for the purpoze, too hear sundry kinds of very delectabl muzik ...

On Monday of the second week of her visit, Elizabeth was treated to one of the most extraordinary pageants of the sixteenth century. Returning from a hunt, as she came to the artificial lake she encountered a mechanical mermaid, eighteen feet long, swimming along with Triton and his trumpet on its back. Following this came a mechanical dolphin, large enough to contain a complete consort of musicians hidden in its belly. Sitting on top of this twenty-four foot long dolphin was the god, Arion (or, Protheus, by one account). Upon reaching Elizabeth the god began to sing, although one eyewitness found his voice 'horse and

---

36 The eyewitness descriptions are taken from Nichols, *The Progresses and Public Processions of Queen Elizabeth*, I.

unpleasant, yet he could order his voice to an instrument exceedingly well.' Accompanied by the musicians in the belly of the dolphin, the god sang,

> O Noble Queen, give ear to this my floating Muse;
> And let the right of ready will my little skill excuse.
> For herdsmen of the seas sing not the sweetest notes;
> The winds and waves do roar and cry, where Phoebus seldom floats;
> Yet, since I do my best …

The reaction of one of the eyewitnesses to this performance, Robert Laneham, is extant.

> The God beegan a delectabl ditty of a Song well apted to a melodious noiz; compounded of six severall instruments, al coovert, casting soound from the Dolphin's belly within; Arion, the seaventh, sitting thus singing without. Noow, Syr, the ditty in meter so aptly endighted to the manner, and after by voice so delicioously delivered; the Song by a skilful artist into his parts so sweetlie sorted; each part in hiz instrument so clean and sharpely toouched; every instrument again in hiz kind so excellently tunabl; and this in the evening of the day, resoounding from the calm waters, where prezens of her Majesty, and longing to listen, had utterly damped all noyz and dyn; the whole harmony conveyd in tyme, tune, and temper thus incomparably melodious; with what pleazure … with what sharpnes of conceyt, with what lyvely delighte, this az ye may; for, so God judge me, by all the wit and cunning I have, I cannot express, I promis yoo … Ah, muzik iz a nobl art!

Another well-documented 'Progress' by Elizabeth was her visit to Norwich in 1578.[37] At the town gate she was welcomed by the Norwich civic wind band, together with a chorus made up of 'the best Voyces in the Citie.'

> The dew of heaven drops this day
> On dry and barren ground,
> Wherefore at fruitful hearts I sing
> Of drum and trumpet sound.
> Yield that is due, show what is meet,
> To make our joy the more,
> In our good hope and her good praise,
> We never saw before …

During her procession into the city, Elizabeth came to a stage where a child actor, richly dressed, addressed the queen after a performance by another wind band.

> … which boy was not seene till the Queene had a good season marked the musicke, whiche was marvellous sweete and good, albeit the rudeness of some ringer of belles did somewhat hinder the noyse and harmonie: and as soone as the musike ended, the boy stepped forth….

---
37 The eyewitness accounts are quoted in Nichols, Ibid., II.

After the boy's speech, the queen remained to hear this wind band perform some more.

> Then the noyse of musicke beganne agayne; to heare the which, the Queene stayed a good while.

Another pageant presented five actors dressed as famous women. A wind band performed as the queen approached.

> At the first sight of the Prince,[38] and till her Majesties comming to the pageant, the musitians, whiche were close in the chambers of the saide pageant, used their loude musicke, and then ceassed.

After speeches by the 'famous women,' the queen continued on while the 'musitions within the gate, upon their softe instruments, used broken musick, and one of them did sing this dittie:'

> From slumber softe I fell asleepe,
> From sleepe to dreame, from dreame to depe delight,
> Eche jem the Gods had given the world to keepe
> In princely wise came present to my sight:
> Such solace then did sincke into my minde,
> As mortall man on molde could never finde.

After several days of music, dinners and masques, there was another extraordinary pageant. This consisted of a great hole dug in the ground and covered by canvas, the canvas painted to look like a cave could be drawn back by a rope. Buried in this 'cave' was an ensemble of musicians and twelve Nymphs.

> And in the same cave was a noble noyse of musicke of al kind of instruments, severally to be sounded and played upon; and at one time they shoulde be sounded all togither, that mighte serve for a consorte of broken musicke ... which wure had bin a noble hearing; and the more melodious for the varietie thereof, and bycause it should come secretely and strangely out of the earth. And when the musicke was done, then shoulde all the twelve Nymphes have issued togither, and daunced a daunce with timbrels that were trimmed with belles, and other jangling things; which timbrels were as brode as a seeve, having bottoms of fine parchment; and being sounded, made such a confused noyse and pastime, that it was to be wondered at; besides, the strangenesse of the timbrels (yet knowen to oure fore-fathers) was a matter of admiration to such as were ignorante of that new-founde toy, gathered and borrowed from our elders.

Another source adds,

> Unhappily, a terrible great cloud-burst rather spoiled the intended effect and half-drowned the subterranean musicians.[39]

---

38 Elizabeth, together with other women leaders, was addressed in the masculine tense!
39 Elizabeth Burton, *The Pageant of Elizabethan England* (New York: Scribner, 1958), 198.

Regarding a Progress to visit to Lord Montecute in Sussex, in 1591, we only call attention to a day of hunting she enjoyed there. Extraordinarily enough, in a 'delicate Bower' her personal musicians performed with a singer while she shot deer![40]

In the same year, Elizabeth visited the Earl of Hertford. The preparations for the arrival of Elizabeth in this case included the construction of an artificial lake in the perfect figure of a half moon. In the lake were three large boats representing pageants, one a hundred feet in length, in addition to 'diverse boats prepared for music.'[41]

The first day's entertainment included the performance of a six-part song by 'six virgins.'

> With fragrant flowers we strew the way
> And make this our chief holiday ...

The entertainment of the second day included a number of pageants on the artificial lake, among which we find,

> In the pinnace [of one boat] were three Virgins, which with their cornetts played Scottish Gigs, in three-parts. There was also in the said pinnacle another Nymph of the sea, named Neaera, the old love of Sylvanus, a God of the woods. Near to her were placed three excellent voices to answer by manner of an Echo: after the pinnace, and two other boats, which were drawn by Sea-gods, the rest of the train followed breast high in water, all attired in ugly marine suits, and every one armed with a huge wooden squirt in his hand ... In their marching towards the pond, all along the middle of the current, the Tritons sounded one half of the way, and then ceasing, the cornetts played their Scottish gigs. The melody was sweet and the show stately.

After an oration addressed to her majesty, 'three voices sung a song to the lute with excellent divisions, and the end of every verse was answered by lutes and voices in the other boat somewhat far off, as if they had been echoes.'

> On the morning of the third day of her visit, Elizabeth opened her window to find, three excellent musicians, who, being disguised in ancient country attire, greeted her with a pleasant song of Coridon and Phylida, in three-parts. The song, as well as the worth of the poetry, and for the appropriateness of the music applied to it, pleased her Highness. After it had been sung once, she commanded that it be sung again.

> In the merry month of May,
> In a morn, by break of day,
> Forth I walked by the wood side ...

---

40 The original account of this Progress is quoted in *The Complete Works of John Lyly*, ed. Warwick Bond (Oxford: Clarendon Press, 1967), I, 422ff.

41 The original account of this Progress is quoted in Ibid., I, 433ff. Nichols, *The Progresses and Public Processions of Queen Elizabeth*, II, calls these three 'islands,' one in the shape of a snail and another in the shape of a boat. He also adds, regarding the fourth day of her visit,

> On Thursday morning, her Majestie was no sooner readie, and at her gallerie window looking into the garden, but there began three cornets to play certaine fantasike dances ...

On the fourth day, after another speech,

> the Fairy Queen and her maids danced about the garland, singing a song in six-parts, with the music of an exquisite consort; wherein was the lute, bandora, base-viol, citterne, treble-viol, and flute … This spectacle and music so delighted her Majesty, that she desired to see and hear it twice over.

Upon her departure, 'there was a consort of musicians hidden in a bower, playing the song "Come again," with excellent divisions, by two, that were cunning.'

> O come againe, worlds starbright eye,
> Whose presence doth adorne the skie.
> O come againe, sweet beauties sunne:
> When thou are gone, our joyes are done.[42]

According to Nichols, there was also music to accompany Elizabeth on her final 'Progress.'

> In the hour of her departure, she ordered her musicians into her chamber; and died while hearing them.[43]

---

42 Text of song given in Nichols, Ibid.
43 Nichols, Ibid., III.

10 CIVIC MUSIC OF SIXTEENTH-CENTURY ENGLAND

THE MINSTRELS

The long medieval tradition of the wandering minstrel was rapidly drawing to a close during the sixteenth century. It seems a pity, after they were so welcome for so many centuries, and after they had contributed so much to the creation of a unified musical language in Western Europe, to see them now so unwelcome.

Before their virtual demise in England, there is one final and curious chapter. London was one of few cities at this time in which there was sufficient work, beyond that taken by the civic wind bands and the aristocratic ensembles, for independent minstrels to see the hope for sustaining themselves.[1] Their opportunity to make a living rested in their success in obtaining the remaining available work in place of the true wandering minstrels. To accomplish this they formed a rather rare Minstrels Guild, modeled after the numerous civic music guilds throughout Europe. They received a charter in London in 1500, took as their patron saint St. Anthony and swore to guard against improper language. In their request for this charter they mentioned,

> The continual recourse of foreign minstrels, daily resorting to this City out of all the countries of Europe and enjoying more freedom than the freemen, causes the Minstrels of the City to be brought to such poverty and decay that they are not able to pay 'lot and scot' and do their duty as other freemen do, since their living is taken from them by these foreigners.[2]

In particular, they accused the foreign, or wandering, musicians of outrageous behavior, appearing,

> uninvited, sometimes as many as five or six at a time crowding to the end of the tables, playing without skill and causing great pain and displeasure to the Citizens and to their honest friends and neighbors.[3]

---

[1] At the beginning of the sixteenth century 75% of the population was rural and only four cities in Western Europe had more than 100,000 inhabitants: Paris, Venice, Naples and Milan.

[2] H. A. F. Crewdson, *The Worshipful Company of Musicians* (London: Knight, 1971), 28.

[3] Ibid.

By the time Henry VIII began his reign, the Minstrel Guild had become more organized, limiting the appearances of apprentices and establishing proficiency examinations. By mid-century, however, the pressure of competition sent the Guild back to court in an attempt to gain new restrictions against the wandering minstrels. The City Corporation complied, noting that competition was causing 'hinderaunce of the gaines and profitts of the poore minstrels being freemen of the Cytie.' The wandering minstrel was now forbidden to sing or play in public halls, taverns, etc., or to take apprentices and neither minstrels, freemen nor 'foreign musicion' could teach dancing.[4] Further, since there were other freemen, members of other guilds, who engaged in part-time music making, this ordinance of 1554 attempted to place some restrictions on their work as well. These part-time musicians,

> leaving the use of their crafts and manual occupations and giving themselves wholly to wandering about riot vice and idleness do commonly use nowadays to sing songs called 'Three Men's Songs' in taverns, at weddings, etc … to the great loss of the poor fellowship of minstrels, it is enacted that such conduct is to cease.

By mid-century other towns in England were passing local ordinances in an attempt to control the wandering minstrels. A civic code in Beverly, passed in 1555, forbids any part-time musician to play outside his parish.[5] In York an ordinance of 1561 specifies that 'no manner of foreigner' be allowed to practice any form of minstrelsy,

> singing or playing upon any instrument within any parish within this city or franchise thereof upon any church holidays or dedication days hallowed or kept within the same parish, or any brotherhood's or freeman's dinner or dinners.[6]

All these ordinances reflect an increasingly modern urban society concerned over beggars, peddlers, vagabond and rouges. A national law had been passed in 1547 which defined a vagabond as any able-bodied person without an income sufficient to support him who was found,

> either like a serving man wanting a master or like a beggar, [wandering and] not applying himself to some honest and legal art, science, service or labor … for three days or more.[7]

A justice of the peace was empowered to decide, in the case of an independent minstrel, for example, if he were following an 'allowed art,' or was a vagabond. The penalties were rather serious: branding with a 'V,' enslaving for two years, whipping until bloody, or the loss of ears, to name a few! An ordinance of 1572 goes further, for now a person traveling without

---

4   Ibid., 36ff.

5   Edmondstoune Duncan, *The Story of Minstrelsy* (London: Walter Scott, 1907), 217.

6   Walter Woodfill, *Musicians in English Society from Elizabeth to Charles I* (Princeton, 1953), 111ff. Another ordinance in York requires the freemen musicians to instruct their apprentices in the art of conversation, in addition to just music, so that 'he may be well thought of.'

7   Ibid., 56.

a patron or proper traveling papers could be 'grievously whipped, and burnt through the gristle of the right ear with a hot iron of the compass of an inch about' on first conviction and death on the third conviction![8]

At about this time the religious right, the early Puritans, also began to attack the wandering minstrels. Stephen Gosson, in his famous *The Schoole of Abuse* (1579), wrote,

> If any part of Music has suffered shipwreck, and been ruined by fortune at their finger tips, with show of gentility they take up in fair houses, receive lusty lasses at a price for boarders, and pipe from morning to evening for wood and coal. By the brothers, cousins, uncles, great grandfathers and such acquaintances of their guests, they drink of the best, they sit rent free, they have their own table spread to their hands, without wearing the strings of the purse ... If their houses be searched, some instruments of Music is laid in sight to dazzle the eyes of every Officer, and all that are lodged in the house by night, or frequent it by day, come thither as pupils to be well schooled.[9]

The public response to this conservative religious attack prompted Gosson to issue soon after *An Apologie of the Schoole of Abuse*. Here again he attacks the wandering minstrels.

> London is so full of unprofitable Pipers and Fidlers, that a man can no sooner enter a tavern, but two or three of them land at his heals, to give him a dance before he departs; therefore let men of gravity examine the case, and judge uprightly, whether the sufferance of such idle beggars be not a grievous abuse in a commonwealth.[10]

One of the books inspired by Gosson's attack on the arts was the *Anatomy of the Abuses in England* (1583) by Philip Stubbs. In this work, a dialogue between the speakers, Spudeus and Philoponus, Stubbs presents an unusually strong attack on the minstrel class, warning them to repent and stop playing, or go to Hell.

> SPUDEUS. What say you, then, of musicians and minstrels, who live only upon music?
> PHILOPONUS. I think that all good minstrels, sober and chaste musicians (speaking of such drunken sockets and bawdy parasites as range the country, rhyming and singing unclean, corrupt, and filthy songs in taverns, ale-houses, inns and other public assemblies) may dance the wild Morris through a needle's eye. For how should they have chaste minds, seeing that their exercise is the pathway to all uncleanliness. There is no ship so balanced with massive matter, as their heads are fraught with all kinds of bawdy songs, filthy ballads and scurvy rhymes, serving for every purpose, and for every company.
> Who be more bawdy than they? who uncleaner than they? who more licentious and loose minded? who more incontinent than they? and, briefly, who more inclined to all kinds of insolence and lewdness than they? ...

---

8   Ibid., 57.
9   Stephen Gosson, *The Schoole of Abuse* (1579), ed. Edward Arber (London, 1868), 36.
10 Stephen Gosson, 'An Apologie of the Schoole of Abuse,' in Ibid., 70.

And yet, notwithstanding, it is better (with respect of acceptance) to be a Pyper, or bawdy minstrel, than a devil, for the one is loosed for his ribaldry, the other hated for his gratuity, wisdom and sobriety.

Every town, city, and country, is full of these minstrels to pipe up a dance to the Devil; but of those [understanding arithmetic] there are so few they can hardly be seen.

But some of them will reply, and say, what, Sir! we have licenses from Justices of the Peace to pipe and use our minstrelsy to our best commodity. Cursed be those licenses which license any man to get his living with the destruction of many thousands!

But have you a license from the Arch-justice of Peace, Christ Jesus? If you have so, you may be glad; if you have not (for the Word of God is against your ungodly exercises, and condemeth them to Hell), then may you as rogues, extrauagantes, and stragglers from the Heavenly Country, be arrested of the high Justice of Peace, Christ Jesus, and be punished with eternal death, notwithstanding your pretended licenses of earthly men. Who shall stand between you and the Justice of God on the day of Judgment? Who shall excuse you for drawing so many thousands to Hell? shall the Justices of Peace? shall their licenses? Oh, no: For neither ought they to grant any licenses to any to do hurt withal; neither (if they would) ought any to take them.

Give over, therefore, your occupations, you pipers, you fiddlers, you minstrels, and you musicians, you drummers, you Tabretters, you flutists, and all other of that wicked brood; for the blood of all enticing allurements, shall be poured upon your heads at the day of judgment.[11]

THE WAITS

The civic wind bands in England went under the name 'Waits,' a word whose etymology is uncertain. The sixteenth century was the highest point of development for these official civic bands and nearly every town had one. London, in addition to its official wait band, also had wait bands in all the major wards of the city, in Finsbury, Southwark, Blackfriars, Tower Hamlets and the City of Westminster. While the official size of these bands was still only four or five players, they were allowed to include their apprentices in performances. Thus, the actual performing band often had as many as twelve players before mid-century and as many as eighteen afterwards.[12]

There are numerous civic records throughout England during the sixteenth century concerned with the purchase of instruments for the civic waits, or inventorying their collections. One we like is an inventory of the Norwich Waits in 1572, which reads,

---

[11] Philip Stubbs, *The Anatomy of the Abuses in England* (1583), ed. Frederick Furnivall (London: The New Shakespeare Society, n.d.), 171ff. In another place Stubbs says of beggars, if they cannot work, should be hanged! [Ibid., II, 42].

[12] Woodfill, *Musicians in English Society*, 33.

2 trumpets; 4 sackbuts, 3 shawms [*haukboyes*]; 5 recorders being a Whole noise [consort of winds]; and one old Lyzardyne.[13]

The wait bands were also provided with official civic uniforms, which were a source of great pride. The pay was meager and was often raised by direct taxation. A new tax voted for Leicester in 1581 read,

> It is agreed that every inhabitant or housekeeper in Leicester (being of reasonable ability) shall be taxed (at the discretion of Mr. Mayor) what they shall quarterly give to the Waytes towards the amending of their living. In consideration whereof the said Waytes shall keep the town, and to play every night and morning orderly, both in winter and summer, and not to go forth of the town to play except to fairs and weddings.[14]

In addition to augmenting their pay by assisting weddings, many of the English wait bands apparently were relatively free to travel to earn money in other towns. In Nottingham in a single year, 1571–1572, bands visited from Wakefield, Derby, Newark, Barton upon Humber, Leicester, Chesterfield, Leeds, Oxford, Ratford and Grantham.[15] On rare occasions some of them had the opportunity to travel abroad. In 1589, the famous Sir Francis Drake was preparing to sail to Portugal, 'to singe the King of Spain's beard,' and made a request to the Norwich Corporation for the loan of their wait band to accompany him at sea.

> This day was read in the Court, a letter sent to Master Mayor and his brethren from Sir Francis Drake, whereby he desires that the Waits of this City may be sent to him, to go on the new intended voyage; whereunto the Waits being here called do all assent, whereupon it is agreed that they should have six cloaks of stemell cloth made ready before they go; and that a wagon shall be provided to carry them and their instruments, and that they shall have 4 lb to buy them, three new oboes and one treble recorder, and x lb to bear their charges; and that the City shall hire the wagon and pay for it. Also that the Chamberlain shall pay Peter Spratt xs.3d. for a sackbut case.[16]

This particular adventure was a military failure and many lives were lost. We regret to report that of the six Norwich waits who made the voyage, only two returned.

The official duties of the civic bands were many and varied. In some towns the old original function of serving as watchmen against fire and theft at night was still required. In Ipswich an order of 1587 states that the Waits shall walk about the town,

---

13 Lilla M. Fox, *Instruments of Processional Music* (London: Lutterworth Press, 1967), 26.

14 J. Bridge, 'Town Waits and their Tunes,' *Proceedings of the Musical Association* (London, 1927), 80.

15 Woodfill, *Musicians in English Society*, 288.

16 Bridge, 'Town Waits and Their Tunes,' 84ff. Upon Sir Francis' death, an inventory of his ship found a 'chest of instrumentes of musicke,' including 'a lute, hobboyes, sagbutes, cornettes, orphorions, bandora and suche like.' See Carl Bridenbaugh, *Vexed and Troubled Englishmen* (New York: Oxford University Press, 1968), 348.

from Michaelmas until our Lady-day ... and shall go thereabout nightly from two of the clock until they have gone throughout the town.[17]

A London order of 1553 forbids anyone to play any instrument in the open streets between ten o'clock at night and five o'clock in the morning in order that their sounds will not be confused with those of the musical-watchmen.

In the Middle Ages the watch-musicians, playing during the night, served the function of a surrogate clock for a town without lights. As the waits had thus become associated with the designation of time, in 1589 the Cornhill Waits were ordered by the city to go to St. Michael's Church to 'take note of a new church bell.' In this case the town band seems to have failed to satisfy the churchwardens for another group of musicians was called in 'to take further note.'[18]

The waits performed for important civic celebrations of all kinds. In London the most famous was the annual Mayor's parade. A London haberdasher, William Smythe, describes part of this procession in 1575.

> Then a consort of hautboys playing ... Then the pageant of Triumph richly decked ... sixteen trumpeters ... the drum and fife of the city ... and after, the waits of the city in blue gowns, red sleeves and caps, every one having his silver collar about his neck.[19]

In towns by the sea, the civic band often welcomed the arrival of ships. In Liverpool the tradition was to wait until the day after the arrival and then play at the door of the homes of the sailors and their families.[20] Welcoming ceremonies were never more festive than when welcoming a member of the royal family. The London Waits, of course, participated in Elizabeth's coronation procession in 1558. One eyewitness reports of this performance,

> Upon the porch of St. Peter's Church door, stood the waites of the citie, which did give a pleasant noise with their instruments as the Queen's majestie did pass by.[21]

We have mentioned in the previous chapter the performance by the Norwich Waits in 1578 when the queen visited. Tradition has it that she was so pleased with this particular performance that she gave each of the five waits a new instrument and a house on King Street as well![22]

Another sphere of major activity by the wait bands was their participation in the performances of theater plays. This association had its roots in the traditional relationship of both

---

17 Woodfill, *Musicians in English Society*, 75.
18 Crewdson, *The Worshipful Company of Musicians*, 174.
19 Woodfill, *Musicians in English Society*, 48.
20 Bridge, 'Town Waits and Their Tunes,' 66, 84ff.
21 John Nichols, *The Progresses and Public Processions of Queen Elizabeth* (London, 1788), I [the volume has no page numbers].
22 Bridge, 'Town Waits and Their Tunes,' 83.

dramatic literature and the waits with the church. For example, early in the century one reads of a minstrel and three waits from Cambridge assisting with the play, *The Holy Martyr St. George* at Basingbourne[23] and in 1517 the household book of the Hickling Priory contains an entry, 'Regiis histrionibus vocatis waytes.'[24] An account from York in 1561 suggests the waits were charged with the responsibility of organizing the church-civic dramas.[25]

The City of Lincoln, in 1565, had the waits actually take speaking roles in a play designed to warn the public about the proper observation of Christmas. The speeches made by the waits were:

> *First Senator*
> The Angels with mirth the shepherds did obey;
> When they sang *Gloria in Excelsis* in tunes mystical;
> The birds with solemn song on every spray,
> And the beasts for joy made reverence in every stall.
>
> *Second Senator*
> Therefore with a contrite heart let us be merry all
> Having a steadfast faith and a love most amiable,
> Disdaining no man of power great or small
> For a cruel oppressor is nothing commendable.
>
> *Third Senator*
> That is the chief cause hither we were sent,
> To give the people warning to have all things perfectly,
> For they that do not, break Mr. Mayor's commandment
> And according to the order, punished must they be.[26]

As we shall see below, the waits also appear to have provided the more complicated music of the later Elizabethan theater.

Finally, the duties of the waits included real public concerts during the sixteenth century. A description of the concerts played by the Norwich Waits is found in a notice by the Mayor's Court in 1553, ruling,

> that the waits of the City shall have liberty and license every Sunday at night and other holidays at night between this and Michaelmas next coming to come to the guildhall, and upon the nether leads of the same hall next the council house shall between the hours of seven and eight of the clock at night blow and play upon their instruments the space of half an hour to the rejoicing and comfort of the hearers thereof.[27]

---

23 Lyndesay Langwill, *The Waits* (London: Hindrichsen, 1952), 173.
24 Bridge, 'Town Waits and Their Tunes,' 81.
25 Ibid.
26 Ibid., 82.
27 Woodfill, *Musicians in English Society*, 81ff.

These concerts continued until at least 1570. In London, in 1571, a tradition began of the waits giving an hour-long concert on Sunday evening from the turret of the Royal Exchange Building. These concerts continued until 1642, when the Puritans prevented Sunday concerts.

Although in Germany the ancient civic wind band tradition would continue and reach its artistic peak during the seventeenth century, in England the wait tradition was clearly in decay by the latter part of the sixteenth century. No doubt several factors brought this about, including changing taste in music. Perhaps the end of the period during which the Church oversaw much of music education, with the closing of the monasteries and the general civil strife which followed, was an influential factor, for it is clear that by mid-century the sense of self-discipline had broken down. In York, in 1561, the town had to warn one member of the town waits that he must,

> respite to learne and applie himself in the instruments and songs belonging to the sayd wayts, and to leave his unthrifty gamyng upon payne to be putte forth of that office.[28]

The same officials dismissed two waits in 1584, charging,

> their evil and disorderly behavior, to the discredit of this city. Viz. for that they have gone abroad, in the country, in very evil apparel, with their hose forth at their heels, also for that they are common drunkards and cannot so cunningly play on their instruments as they ought.[29]

During these proceedings, one of the other wait members testified against one of those dismissed as follows,

> He is become so disordered and distempered and such a person as will be oft drunk and is at diverse times troubled with the falling sickness and his hearing imperfect or almost deaf as that he is not sufficient to serve in his place, and that diverse times he hath so disordered himself in the exercise of his place in playing before the magistrates of this city and others as that he hath made the rest of them by his playing forth of tune and time to be ashamed of themselves and they to be thereby thought of by the hearers to have no such skill as is requisite for their places to their great discredit.[30]

In fact, in a number of instances the entire wait bands were dismissed by the city for reasons of discipline, including the York Waits in 1566 and again in 1572, the Nottingham Waits in 1578, the Ipswich Waits in 1597 and those of Leicester in 1563. In the latter case the dismissal order read,

> The Waits because they cannot agree together are therefore now dismissed from being the Town Waits from henceforth.[31]

---

28 Bridge, 'Town Waits and Their Tunes,' 72.
29 Woodfill, *Musicians in English Society*, 88.
30 Ibid.
31 Bridge, 'Town Waits and Their Tunes,' 73.

Changing tastes was another important factor in the demise of the old tradition. String instruments were beginning to appear and, being preferred for indoor performances, the pure wind bands were being relegated to outdoor ceremonial work. Appointments of civic string players can be documented in Norwich in 1585 and in Exeter in 1602. This transformation is quite evident in the publication of Thomas Morely's *First Book of Consort Lessons* of 1599. Although Morely dedicated this book of Wait repertoire to the Waits of London, he recommends performance by a broken consort of 'Treble Lute, Pandora, Cittern, Base-violl, Flute and Treble-Violl.' His actual dedication is worthy of quoting, for although the period of the civic wind band in England was over he eloquently draws a distinction between this tradition and that of the wandering minstrel.

> ... for I desire not to satisfy babblers, which are baser than brute beasts in reproving excellence, never attain to the first degree of any commendable Science or mystery. But as the ancient custom is of this most honorable and renowned City hath been ever, to retain and maintain excellent and expert Musicians, to adorn your Honors' favors, Feasts and solemn meetings: to those your Lordships Waits ... I recommend the same to your servants careful and skillful handling.[32]

AMATEUR CIVIC MUSIC

Although it is a topic which has never received the attention and research that it deserves, there was a growing economic base which was leading to sponsorship and participation in music performance by individual citizens. Reese devotes only one sentence, in passing, to this movement.

> Wealthy citizens, in town and country, with their liking for instrumental music generally, cultivated music for ensemble, as well as for soloists.[33]

Reese was probably thinking of such extant collections of secular music as the *Psalmes, Sonets, & songs of sadnes and pietie* (1588) by Byrd, which was originally composed for instruments and one voice. But there is also evidence of citizens maintaining their own ensembles, as for example the English merchant, Thomas Kytson, of Hengrave, Suffolk. His household accounts for 1574 contains a payment for 'seven cornetts bought for the musicians.'[34]

---

[32] The expression, 'the Science and mystery,' was an expression used in some form or other for centuries to describe musical performance. Today we should say the expression nicely represents fact: the left and right hemisphere of the musician's brain.

[33] Gustave Reese, *Music in the Renaissance* (New York: Norton, 1959), 867.

[34] Woodfill, *Musicians in English Society*, 263. Upon Kytson's death in 1603 the inventory of his instruments included large numbers of keyboard instruments, several consorts of strings, a case of seven recorders, in addition to four cornetts, two sackbuts, three shawms, two flutes, a curtal and a lysarden.

One group of upper class citizens who frequently sponsored music in London were the Temple lawyers, who held an annual 'Revel' at Christmas. For the Revel of 1562, we have this description of the music accompanying their banquet on Christmas Eve.

> The Prince so served with tender meats, sweet fruits, and dainty delicates ... and at every course the trumpeters blew the courageous blast of deadly war, with noise of drum and fife, with the sweet harmony of violins, sackbutts, recorders, and cornetts, and other instruments of music, as it seemed Apollo's harp had tuned their stroke ...
>
> At the first course the minstrels must sound their instruments, and go before the food ... All which time the music must stand right above the hearth side, with the noise of their music; and face direct toward the highest table: and that done, to return to the buttery, with their music sounding. At the second course, in every respect; which performed, the servitors and musicians are to resort to the place assigned for them to dine at; which is the Valets or Yeoman's table, beneath the screen. Dinner ended, the musicians prepare to sing a song, at the highest table ...

The following day, Christmas Day, the Revel continued with another banquet.

> At the first course is served in a fair and large boar's head, upon a silver platter, with minstrelsy. Two gentlemen in gowns are to attend at supper, and to bear two fair torches of wax, next before the musicians and trumpeters, and stand above the fire with the music, till the first course be served in through the hall. Which performed, they, with the music are to return to the buttery.

The Temple lawyers held another banquet on St. Stephen's Day, now with a more rustic, hunting theme. The featured guest, Lord Dudley, enters the hall dressed in a costume appropriate to the theme,

> arrayed with a fair, rich, complete harness, white and bright, and gilt, with a nest of feathers of all colors upon his crest or helm, and a gilt pole-axe in his hand: to whom his associate the Lieutenant of the Tower, armed with a fair white armor, nest of feathers in his helm, and a like pole-axe in his hand; and with them sixteen trumpeters; four drums, and fifes going in rank before them: with them attendeth four men in white harness ... halberds in their hands ... with the drums, trumpets, and music, go three times around the fire. Then comes in the Master of the Game, appareled in green velvet: and the Ranger of the Forest also ... with either of them a hunting horn about their necks: blowing together three blasts of venery, they pace round about the fire three times ... A huntsman comes into the hall, with a fox and a purse-net with a cat, both bound at the end of a staff; and with them nine or ten couple of hounds, with the blowing of hunting horns. And the fox and cat are by the hounds set upon, and killed beneath the fire.[35]

Thus amidst cheers, after the fox and cat were torn into a thousand bloody bits, dinner was served.

---

35 Dugdale, 'Origines Juridiciales,' in Nichols, *The Progresses and Public Processions of Queen Elizabeth*, I.

There was also some genuine popular music in the sixteenth century of course, even if we know little about it. Among the music of the lower citizen class there was something called freemen's songs, which are even mentioned once in connection with Henry VIII.

> For the King himself being much delighted to sing, and Sir Peter Carewe having a pleasant voice, the King would very often use him to sing with him certain songs they call freemen songs, as namely, 'By the bank I lay,' and 'As I walked the wood so wild,' etc.[36]

At the very bottom of society were the street songs of the peddlers. While the true traditions of such street music is lost to us, these songs were, however, of sufficient interest to sixteenth-century people that Weelkes, Gibbons and Deering all composed vocal ensemble compositions incorporating fragments of these songs.[37]

---

36 *The Lyffe of Sir Peter Carewe*, quoted in Reese, *Music in the Renaissance*, 769
37 Reese, Ibid., 832ff.

11 SIXTEENTH-CENTURY ENGLISH POETRY

WE HAVE SEEN COMPLAINTS by late sixteenth-century writers regarding the decline of the arts in England. England's greatest poet of this period, Edmund Spenser, has dedicated to this topic a substantial poem called 'The Tears of the Muses.' He protects himself by composing a fable about Greek gods, but it is clear that his subject is England. He begins by saying music is not what it was.

> Rehearse to me, ye sacred Sisters nine,
> The golden brood of great Apollo's wit,
> Those piteous plaints and sorrowful sad tine,
> Which late ye powered forth as ye did sit
> Beside the silver Springs of Hellicon,
> Making your music of heart-breaking moan.
>
> For since the time that Phoebus' foolish son
> Thundered, through Jove's vengeful wrath,
> For traversing the chariot of the Sun
> Beyond the compass of his appointed path,
> Of you, his mournful Sisters, was lamented,
> Such mournful tunes were never since invented.[1]

Before finishing his prologue, Spenser makes the charming suggestion that man learned the aesthetic importance of the bass part in a consort by hearing the sound of a stream juxtaposed against other natural sounds, such as birds. Following this brief prologue, the nine Muses make separate speeches on the decline of their arts, beginning with Clio, Muse of History.

> Behold the foul reproach and open shame,
> The which is day by day unto us wrought
> By such as hate the honor of our name,
> The foes of learning and each gentle thought;
> They, not contented us themselves to scorn,
> Do seek to make us of the world forlorn …
>
> It most behooves the honorable race
> Of mighty Peers true wisdom to sustain,

---
1 Edmund Spenser, 'The Tears of the Muses,' lines 1ff. Spenser (1552–1599) spent most of his career in Ireland.

> And with their noble countenance to grace
> The learned foreheads, without gifts or gain;
> Or rather learned themselves behooves to be,
> That is the garland of Nobility.
>
> But (ah!) all otherwise they do esteem
> Of the heavenly gift of wisdom's influence,
> And to be learned it a base thing deem:
> Base minded they that lack intelligence …[2]

Melpomene, the Muse of Tragedy, follows.

> Why then do foolish men so much despise
> The precious store of this celestial riches?
> Why do they banish us, that patronize
> The name of learning? Most unhappy wretches!
> They which lie drowned in deep wretchedness,
> Yet do not see their own unhappiness.
>
> My part it is and my professed skill
> The Stage with Tragic buskin to adorn,
> And fill the Scene with plaint, and outcries shrill
> Of wretched persons to misfortune born;
> But none more tragic matter I can find
> Than this, of men deprived of sense and mind …
>
> So all with rueful spectacles is filled,
> First for Megera or Persephone;
> But I that in true Tragedy am skilled,
> The flower of wit, find nought to busy me:
> Therefore I mourn, and pitifully moan,
> Because that mourning matter I have none.
>
> Then began she woefully to wail, and wring
> Her wretched hands in lamentable wise;
> And all her Sisters, thereto answering,
> Threw forth loud shrieks and dreary doleful cries.[3]

She is followed by Thalia, the Muse of Comedy.

> Where be the sweet delights of learnings' treasure
> That wont with Comic sock to beautify
> The painted Theaters, and fill with pleasure
> The listeners' eyes and ears with melody;

---

2 Ibid., lines 61ff.

3 Ibid., lines 144ff.

In which I late was wont to reign as Queen,
And mask in mirth with Graces well beseen?

O! all is gone; and all that goodly glee,
Which wont to be the glory of gay wits,
Is laid abed, and no where now to see;
And in her room unseemly Sorrow sits,
With hollow brows and grisly countenance,
Marring my joyous gentle dalliance.

And him beside sits ugly Barbarism,
And brutish Ignorance, crept of late
Out of dread darkness of the deep Abyss,
Where being bred, he light and heaven does hate:
They in the minds of men now tyrannize,
And the fair Scene with rudeness foul disguise.[4]

Terpsichore, the Muse of Choral Dance and Song, complains of the level of music being heard.

They to the vulgar sort now pipe and sing,
And make them merry with their fooleries;
They cheerfully chant, and rhymes at random fling,
The fruitful spawn of their rank fantasies:
They feed the ears of fools with flattery,
And good men blame, and losels magnify.

All places they do with their toys possess,
And reign in liking of the multitude;
The schools they fill with fond new fangleness;
And sway in Court with pride and rashness rude....[5]

Next we hear from Erato, Muse of Love Poetry.

For neither you nor we shall anymore
Find entertainment or in Court or School;
For that which was accounted heretofore
The learned's meed is now lent to the fool;
He sings of love, and makes loving songs,
And they him hear, and they him highly praise.[6]

---

[4] Ibid., lines 174ff.

[5] Ibid., lines 318ff.

[6] Ibid., lines 410ff.

Calliope, Muse of Epic Poetry, observes,

> Ne do they care to have the ancestry
> Of the old Heroes memorized anew;
> Ne do they care that later posterity
> Should know their names, or speak their praises do,
> But die forgotten from whence at first they sprung,
> As they themselves shall be forgot ere long ...

> But now I will my golden Clarion rend,
> And will henceforth immortalize no more;
> [Since] I no more find worthy to commend
> For prize of value, or for learned lore:
> For noble Peers, whom I was wont to raise,
> Now only seek for pleasure, nought for praise.

> Their great revenues all in sumptuous pride
> They spend, that nought to learning they may spare;
> And the rich fee, which Poets wont divide,
> Now parasites and sycophants do share ...[7]

Urania, Muse of Astronomy, asks,

> What difference between man and beast is left,
> When the heavenly light of knowledge is put out,
> And the ornaments of wisdom are bereft?[8]

Finally, Polyhymnia, Muse of Sacred Poetry, complains that poets are no longer required to meet the ancient disciplines.

> For the sweet numbers and melodious measures,
> With which I wont the winged words to tie,
> And make a tuneful Diapason of pleasures,
> Now being let to run at liberty
> By those which have no skill to rule them right,
> Have now quite lost their natural delight.[9]

---

7 Ibid., lines 439ff.

8 Ibid., lines 487ff.

9 Ibid., lines 547ff.

Spenser briefly returns to his complaint over the decay of Art in his 'Colin Clouts Come Home Again.'

> No art of school, but Courtiers schoolery.
> For arts of school have there small countenance,
> Counted but toys to busy idle brains;
> And there professors find small maintenance,
> But to be instruments of others gains.
> Nor is there place for any gentle wit,
> Unless to please itself it can apply …[10]

Relative to other contemporary events, we are surprised that, aside from members of the clergy (and Thomas More), that there is surprisingly little commentary among the poets on the forces which were changing the Church. The Catholic poet, John Skelton, took note, however, and made Luther's voice a lute.

> Ye stringed so Luther's lute
> That ye dance all in a suit
> The heretics' ragged ray,
> That brings you out of the way
> Of Holy Church's lay …[11]

This same poet bemoans the closing of the monasteries in his, 'The World Nowadays.'

> So many cloisters closed,
> And priests at large loosed
> Being so evil-disposed,
> Saw I never …
> Sometime we sang of mirth and play
> But now our joy is gone away
> For so many fall in decay,
> Saw I never …[12]

He addresses the same subject again in his 'Colin Clout,' in an attack against cardinal Wolsey.

> How ye brake the deades wills,
> Turn monasteries into water-mills;
> Of an abbey ye make a grange
> (Your works, they say, are strange) …[13]

---

10 Edmund Spenser, 'Colin Clouts Come Home Again,' lines 702ff.

11 John Skelton, 'A Replication,' in *The Complete Poems of John Skelton*, ed. Philip Henderson (London: Dent, 1959), 420. Skelton (1460–1529) was a tutor to the young Henry VIII and was a figure in the court until his satires against Wolsey brought him into disfavor.

12 John Skelton, 'The World Nowadays,' in Ibid., 138.

13 John Skelton, 'Colin Clout,' in Ibid., 262.

The courtier was a much present fixture in sixteenth-century England, as elsewhere, and sprinkled throughout this repertoire of poetry one finds uncomplimentary references to him. Spenser, in describing some courtiers entertaining ladies, suggests that some at least still had performance skills in music.

> Diverse delights they found themselves to please;
> Some sung in sweet consort; some laughed for joy;
> Some played with straws; some idly sat at ease …[14]

Sir Thomas More, on the other hand, has left a poem, 'To a Courtier,' which reminds us of the inherent danger of striving to be near the king.

> You often boast to me that you have the king's ear and often
> Have fun with him, freely and according to your own whims.
> This is like having fun with tamed lions—often it is harmless,
> But just as often there is the fear of harm.
> Often he roars in rage for no known reason,
> And suddenly the fun becomes fatal.
> The pleasure you get is not safe enough
> To relieve you of anxiety.
> For you it is a great pleasure.
> As for me, let my pleasure be less great—
> And safe.[15]

ON THE PHYSIOLOGY OF AESTHETICS

Fulke Greville, in his Romance, 'Caelica,' first seems to discount all books and knowledge, putting his faith in experience and especially in connection with Nature. But he quickly qualifies this by insisting that Reason rule over the emotions.

> I have for books above my head the skies;
> Under me, earth; about me, air and sea;
> The truth for light, and reason for mine eyes,
> Honor for guide, and nature for my way.
> With change of times, laws, humors, manners, right,
> Each in their diverse workings infinite.

---

14   Edmund Spenser, *The Faerie Queene*, Book II, Canto IX, xxxv.
15   More, *The Complete Works*, III, Pt. 2, 205.

> Which powers from that we feel, conceive, or do,
> Raise in our senses through joy, or smarts,
> All forms, the good or ill can bring us to,
> More lively far than can dead books or arts;
> Which at the second hand deliver forth
> Of few men's heads strange rules for all men's worth …
>
> Let him then first set straight his inward sprite,
> That his affections in the serving rooms
> May follow reason not confound her light.[16]

Having discounted the importance of book learning, Greville also questions the value of the information gained by the senses, something long questioned by the medieval Church. In his important philosophical poem, 'A Treatie of Human Learning,' Greville seems to suggest that the judgments we make from the senses are largely matters of our own invention.

> Yet these, racked up by wit excessively,
> Make fancy think she such gradations finds
> Of heat, cold, colors, such variety,
> Of smells, and tastes, of tunes such divers kinds,
> As that brave Scythian never could descry,
> Who found more sweetness in his horse's naying
> Than all the Phrygian, Dorian, Lydian playing.[17]

He continues by saying that whatever the imagination learns from the senses is misunderstood and memory, 'register of sense, and mold of arts,' is corrupted with this 'disguised intelligence.'

Several of the English poets question traditional education. John Skelton satirizes the college graduate who has only a smattering of knowledge. It is interesting that he mentions here the tradition common throughout Western Europe, of the new graduates hiring wind players to parade themselves through the town in celebration.

> How young scholars nowadays enbolned with the flyblown blast of the much vainglorious pippling wind, when they have delectably licked a little of the licorous electuary of lusty learning, in the much studious school-house of scrupulous Philology, counting themselves clerks excellently informed and transcendingly sped in much high cunning, and when they have once superciliously caught
>   A little rag of rhetoric,
>   A less lump of logic,
>   A piece or a patch of philosophy,

---

16 Fulke Greville, 'Caelica,' LXVI, in *Five Courtier Poets of the English Renaissance*, ed. Robert Bender (New York: Washington Square Press, 1967), 523ff. Greville (1554–1628) was active in the Elizabethan court and amassed a large fortune. He began writing poetry in the 1570s.

17 Fulke Greville, 'A Treatie of Human Learning,' IX, in Ibid., 564ff.

> Then forthwith by and by
> They tumble so in theology,
> Drowned in dregs of divinity,
> That they judge themself able to be
> Doctors of the chair in the Vintry
> At the Three Cranes
> To magnify their names:
> But madly it frames,
> For all that they preach and teach
> Is further than their wit will reach.[18]

Sir John Davies questions whether we learn anything at all in school. Indeed, he says, it was the desire of Adam to know which resulted in the 'original sin.' For Davies, only affliction focuses the mind.

> Why did my parents send me to the schools,
> That I with knowledge might enrich my mind?
> Since the desire to know first made men fools,
> And did corrupt the root of all mankind …
>
> What can we know? or what can we discern?
> When Error chokes the windows of the mind,
> The divers forms of things how can we learn
> That have been ever from our birthday blind?
>
> When Reason's lamp, which like the sun in sky
> Throughout Man's little world her beams did spread,
> Is now become a sparkle, which doth lie
> Under the ashes, half extinct and dead …
>
> If aught can teach us aught, Affliction's looks,
> Making us look into ourselves so near,
> Teach us to know ourselves beyond all books,
> Or all the learned Schools that ever were.
>
> This mistress lately plucked me by the ear,
> And many a golden lesson hath me taught;
> Hath made my Senses quick, my Reason clear,
> Reformed my Will and rectified my Thought.[19]

---

18 John Skelton, 'A Replication,' in *The Complete Poems*, 414.

19 Sir John Davies (1569–1626), 'Of Human Knowledge,' from *Nosce Teipsum* in Emrys Jones, ed., *The New Oxford Book of Sixteenth Century Verse* (Oxford: Oxford University Press, 1991), 667ff.

ON THE PSYCHOLOGY OF AESTHETICS

Poems, in all ages, often deal with the emotions, especially that of Love. So it is a rare exception that Michael Drayton begins his cycle of sonnets called 'Idea' by specifically pointing out that if the reader is looking for emotion, he should look elsewhere.

To the Reader of these Sonnets

Into these Loves, who but for Passion looks,
At this first sight, here let him lay them by,
And seek elsewhere, in turning other Books,
Which better may his labor satisfy.
No far-fetch'd Sigh shall ever wound my Breast,
Love from mine Eye a tear shall never wring,
Nor in *Ah-mees* my whining Sonnets dressed,
(A Libertine) fantastically I sing:
My Verse is the true image of my Mind,
Ever in motion, still desiring change;
And as thus to Variety inclin'd,
So in all Humors sportively I range:
My muse is rightly of the English strain,
That cannot long one fashion entertain.[20]

Sir Henry Wotton seems to reflect the old medieval Church attitude when he agrees that strong emotions are bad.

Then first the mind of passions must be free
Of him that would to happiness aspire,
Whether in princes' palaces to be
Or whether to his cottage he retire;
For our desires that on extremes are bent
Are friends to care and traitors to content.[21]

Nevertheless, Love is an emotion frequently discussed in English poetry. Since we know today that the emotions and the experiential aspect of music are both in the right hemisphere of the brain, it is no surprise to find Henry Constable making music a metaphor for his heart.

Whilst Echo cries, what shall become of me,
And desolate my desolations pity,
Thou in thy beauties charrack sitt'st to see
My tragic down-fall, and my funeral ditty.

---

[20] Michael Drayton (1563–1631), 'Idea' (1594), in Richard Sylvester, ed., *The Anchor Anthology of Sixteenth-Century Verse* (Garden City: Anchor Books, 1974), 583.

[21] Sir Henry Totton (1568–1639), 'To John Donne,' in Jones, *The New Oxford Book of Sixteenth Century Verse*, 508.

> No Timbrel, but heart thou play'st upon,
> Whose strings are stretch'd unto the highest key,
> The diapason love, love is the unison,
> In love, my life and labors waste away.[22]

Poets of all earlier periods were quick to observe that there seemed to be some basic conflict between the emotions of Love and with Reason. George Turberville devotes a poem to the idea that Reason and Love are of opposite natures. I'll take Love, he says, and leave Reason to others.

> Shall Reason rule where Reason hath no right
> Nor never had? shall Cupid lose his lands?
> His claim? his crown? his kingdom? name of might?
> No, Friend, thy ring doth will me thus in vain;
> Reason and Love have ever yet been twain.
>
> They are by kind of such contrary mold,
> As one mislikes the other's lewd device:
> What Reason wills Cupid never would;
> Love never yet thought Reason to be wise.
> To Cupid I my homage erst have done;
> Let Reason rule the hearts that she hath won.[23]

Sir Philip Sidney, in love, wonders in this sonnet why he can't get control of his rational thinking and why the senses pay no attention to Reason. Yet, here it is clear he associates wisdom with Reason and not the senses.

> If I could think how these my thoughts to leave,
> Or thinking still my thoughts might have good end;
> If rebel senses would reason's law receive,
> Or reason foiled would not in vain contend;
> Then might I think what thoughts were best to think;
> Then might I wisely swim or gladly sink.[24]

In another sonnet he despairs over the subjugation of his Reason.

> Desire, Desire! I have too dearly bought,
> With price of mangled mind, thy worthless ware;

---

22 Henry Constable (1562–1613), from 'Diana' (1594), in Sylvester, *The Anchor Anthology*, 561ff.

23 George Turberville, 'To his Love, that Sent him a Ring wherein was Graved, *Let Reason Rule*,' in John Williams, ed., *English Renaissance Poetry* (Fayetteville: The University of Arkansas Press, 1990), 128. Turberville (ca. 1540–1595) studied at Oxford and was a secretary to the ambassador to Russia.

24 Sir Philip Sidney, in Bender, *Five Courtier Poets*, 319. Sidney (1554–1586), scholar, poet, diplomat, courtier and soldier, was a key member of Elizabeth's court in its early period.

> Too long, too long, asleep thou hast me brought,
> Who should my mind to higher things prepare.[25]

Finally, in a sonnet from 'Astrophel and Stella,' his view has changed, now he says, in effect, 'Reason, mind your own business!'

> Reason, in faith thou are well served, that still
> Wouldst arguing be with Sense and Love in me;
> I rather wisht thee clime the Muses' hill;
> Or reach the fruit of Nature's choicest tree;
> Or seek heaven's course or heaven's inside to see:
> Why shouldst thou toil our thorny soil to till?
> Leave Sense, and those which Sense's objects be;
> Deal thou with powers of thoughts, leave Love to Will.[26]

In the 'Sixth Song' of his 'Astrophil and Stella,' Sidney seems to argue for a higher recognition of Music, Love and Beauty.

> Love more affected seems
> To Beauty's lovely light;
> And Wonder more esteems
> Of Music's wondrous might;
> But both to both so bent,
> As both in both are spent.
>
> Music doth witness call
> The ear his truth to try;
> Beauty brings to the hall
> The judgment of the eye:
> Both in their objects such,
> As no exceptions touch …
>
> Then Reason, princess high,—
> Whose throne is in the mind,
> Which Music can in sky
> And hidden beauties find,—
> Say whether thou wilt crown
> With limitless renown?[27]

---

25 Ibid., 331.

26 Sir Philip Sidney, 'Astrophel and Stella,' in Alexander Grosart, *The Complete Poems of Sir Philip Sidney* (Freeport: Books for Libraries Press, 1970), I, 18.

27 Ibid., 173ff.

The Churchman Sir Thomas More concluded that one should follow Reason in falling in love.

> What is beauty? Does it not fail in sickness,
> Perish with time? Like a flower in the sun.
> Then, when the bloom leaves her cheek,
> A love secured only by such ties as these
> Breaks free and is gone forever.
> Only a man of intelligence and foresight,
> With reason for his guide,
> Can enter upon true love.[28]

In this joyous English century there was a rather broad discussion of the nature of Pleasure and Pain. Several sixteenth-century English poets had a rather fatalistic view of pleasure, saying, in effect, take pleasure while you can. One of these was an anonymous poet, whose poem was set as a madrigal by Thomas Morley in 1595.

> Sing we and chant it
> While love doth grant it.
> Not long youth lasteth,
> And old age hasteth.
> Now is best leisure
> To take our pleasure.
>
> All things invite us
> Now to delight us.
> Hence, care, be packing!
> No mirth be lacking!
> Let spare no treasure
> To live in pleasure.[29]

Similarly, a poem by Thomas Lodge begins,

> Pluck the fruit and taste the pleasure,
> Youthful lordings, of delight;
> Whilst occasion gives you seizure,
> Feed your fancies and your sight:
> After death, when you are gone,
> Joy and pleasure is there none.[30]

---

28 More, *The Complete Works*, III, Pt. 2, 183.

29 Anonymous, in Jones, *The New Oxford Book of Sixteenth Century Verse*, 619.

30 Thomas Lodge, in Williams, *English Renaissance Poetry*, 238. Lodge (1558–1625) is best known as a playwright, in particular for his *Rosalynde* which was used as a source by Shakespeare for *As You Like It*.

Spenser, on the other hand, advises, 'learn from pleasure's poison to abstain …'[31]

Nearly all early philosophers observe that Pleasure and Pain seem always to be connected. Thomas, Lord Vaux, has written a poem whose very title is, 'No Pleasure Without Some Pain,' which begins,

> How can the tree but waste and wither away
> That hath not sometime comfort of the sun?
> How can that flower but fade and soon decay
> That always is with dark clouds over-run?
> Is this a life? Nay, death you may it call
> That feels each pain, and knows no joy at all.[32]

We find the same thought by Thomas Howell.

> That life is life a Bubble blown, or smoke that soon doth pass,
> That all our pleasures are but pains, our glory brittle glass.[33]

And Thomas Wyatt,

> I trust sometime my harm may be my health,
> Since every woe is joined with some wealth.[34]

The nature of Pleasure and Pain was a subject often discussed with respect to Love. Wyatt found that this pleasure was only a brief one.

> Love is a fervent fire
> Kindled by hot desire,
> For a short pleasure
> Long displeasure …[35]

---

31 Edmund Spenser, *The Faerie Queene*, Book II, Canto II, xlv.

32 Thomas, Lord Vaux, 'No Pleasure Without Some Pain,' in Ibid., 54. Lord Vaux (1510–1556) was educated at Cambridge and spent his life in the court of Henry VIII. He was made a Knight of the Bath in 1533.

33 Thomas Howell, 'H. his deuises, for his owne exercise, and his friends pleasure' (1581), in Norman McClure, ed., *Sixteenth-Century English Poetry* (New York: Harper & Brothers, 1954), 133. Howell (fl. 1568–1581), the author of only three small volumes of poetry, apparently studied at Oxford and was a retainer for the earls of Shrewsbury and Pembroke.

34 Thomas Wyatt, 'That pleasure is mixed with euery paine,' in Hyder Rollins, ed., *Tottel's Miscellany (1557–1587)* (Cambridge: Harvard University Press, 1965), 211. Wyatt (1503–1542) was the model of the well-rounded courtier, active in arms, sports, diplomacy, poetry and literature. Because some of his poems were intended to be sung, he may also have been a musician. He was highly regarded by Henry VIII, but came into difficulty because of a romantic relationship with Anne Boleyn, before it was known the king would marry her.

35 Thomas Wyatt, *Sir Thomas Wyatt, Collected Poems*, ed. Joost Daalder (London: Oxford University Press, 1975), LXXXVII.

Much more frequently discussed, was the pain of Love. Representing many such examples, we point to the passionate Henry Howard,

> When raging love with extreme pain
> Most cruelly distrains my heart;
> When that my tears, as floods of rain,
> Bear witness of my woeful smart;
> When sighs have wasted so my breath
> That I lie at the point of death …[36]

to Thomas Wyatt,

> Behold, Love, thy power how she despiseth!
> My great pain how little she regardeth![37]
>
> ……
>
> Alas the grief and deadly woeful smart,
> The careful chance, shapen afore my shirt,
> The sorrowful tears, the sighes hot as fire,
> That cruel love hath long soaked from mine heart![38]

and to Sir Thomas More.

> Break, sad heart, pitiably engulfed in deepest woe.
> Let this be the end of your punishment.
> Show your mistress your bloody wounds.
> It is she only who will presently part us two.
> Alas, how long shall I in my misery thus weep and complain?
> Come, dreaded death, and release me from such monstrous woes.[39]

In one of Wyatt's most famous poems, a lover has given up in his pursuit and sings one last song. He knows it will do no good, for he might as well sing to a dead person.

> My lute awake! Perform the last
> Labor that thou and I shall waste,
> And end that I have now begun;
> For when this song is sung and past,
> My lute be still, for I have done.

---

36 Henry Howard, 'When raging love' in Bender, *Five Coutier Poets*, 185. Howard (1517–1547), earl of Surrey, being of noble birth was highly educated. He was a close friend of Henry Fitzroy, an illegitimate son of Henry VIII. His life as a courtier included various intrigues and foreign service and ended in his being beheaded at age thirty.

37 Wyatt, *Collected Poems*, I.

38 Ibid., V

39 More, *The Complete Works*, III, Pt. 2, 145.

As to be heard where ear is none,
As lead to grave in marble stone,
My song may pierce her heart as soon.
Should we then sigh or sing or moan?
No, no, my lute, for I have done.

The rocks do not so cruelly
Repulse the waves continually
As she my suit and affection,
So that I am past remedy,
Whereby my lute and I have done …

Now cease, my lute: this is the last
Labor that thou and I shall waste,
And ended is that we begun.
Now is this song both sung and past:
My lute, be still, for I have done.[40]

Another poet, Richard Lynche, also gives up singing when he has lost his love.

But thou my dear sweet-sounding Lute be still,
Repose thy troubled strings upon this moss,
Thou hast full often eased me against my will,
Lie down in peace, thy spoil were my great loss …[41]

ON THE PHILOSOPHY OF AESTHETICS

Insights into the aesthetics of music can often be found in comments about poetry, because in the ancient and medieval world poetry was sung and was often considered as a form of music itself. One sixteenth-century English poet reminds us how close this relationship yet remained.

If Music and sweet Poetry agree,
As they must needs (the Sister and the Brother)
Then must the Love be great, twixt thee and me,
Because thou lov'st the one, and I the other.
Dowland to thee is dear; whose heavenly touch
Upon the Lute, doeth ravish humaine sense:
Spenser to me; whose deep Conceit is such,
As passing all Conceit, needs no defence.

---

40 Wyatt, *Collected Poems*, LXVI.
41 Richard Lynche (fl. 1596–1601), from 'Diella' (1596), in Sylvester, *The Anchor Anthology*, 571.

> Thou lov'st to hear the sweet melodious sound,
> That Phoebus Lute (the Queen of Music) makes:
> And I in deep Delight am chiefly drowned,
> When as himself to singing he betakes.
> One God is God of both (as Poets faigne)
> One Knight loves Both, and Both in thee remain.[42]

Some poetry was still intended to be sung, as we can clearly see in the poem, 'First Song,' in Sir Philip Sidney's Romance, 'Astrophil and Stella.'

> Doubt you to whom my muse these notes intendeth,
> Which now my breast, o'ercharged, to music lendeth?
> To you, to you, all song of praise is due;
> Only in you my song begins and endeth.[43]

Indeed, some poetry was composed to go with pre-existent tunes. In Sir Philip Sidney, for example, we find sonnets written 'To the tune of Wilhelmus van Nassaw' and 'To the tune of The Smokes of Melancholy.'

The Catholic Church had often criticized poets on the basis that they told fables, that is untruths. John Skelton asks, in view of King David in the Old Testament, how can they maintain this?

> Then, if this noble king
> Thus can harp and sing
> With his harp of prophecy
> And spiritual poetry,
> As Saint Jerome saith,
> To whom we must give faith,
> Warbling with his strings
> Of such theological things,
> Why have ye then disdain
> At poets, and complain
> How poets do but feign?[44]

On the contrary he says, now in Latin, poets are rare and divinely inspired.

> Infinite, innumerable are the sophists, infinite, innumerable are the logicians, innumerable are the philosophers and the theologians, infinite in number are doctors, and masters; but poets

---

42 Richard Barnfield (1574–1627), 'Poems: In divers humors' (1598), in Ibid., 575.

43 Sir Philip Sidney, in Bender, *Five Courtier Poets*, 362. Sidney is said to have been a musician as well as poet. The first poem in his 'Pansies from Penshurst and Wilton,' written for a meeting with poets, Dyer and Greville, calls on music to join their hearts and hands.

44 John Skelton, 'A Replication,' in *The Complete Poems*, 426.

are few and rare. Hence all that is precious is rare. I think, then, that poets before all others are filled with the divine afflatus.⁴⁵

Probably more of these poets were inspired by their Lady than heaven. Giles Fletcher found himself unable to compose when his love had left him.

> But when your figure, and your shape is gone,
> I speechlesse am, lyke as I was before:
> Or if I write, my verse is fill'd with moane,
> And blurd with teares, by falling in such store.
> Then muse not if my Muse be slacke,
> For when I wrote, I did thy beautie lacke.⁴⁶

The purpose of poetry, in a more philosophic sense, was addressed by John Skelton, who apparently viewed poetry as a medium, like comedy, in which one could be more truthful than in ordinary speech. This, in spite of the fact that his satires more than once landed him in prison.

> I, calling to mind the great authority
> Of poets old, which full craftily,
> Under as covert terms as could be,
> Can touch a truth and cloak it subtilly …⁴⁷

In a rare reference to painting by these poets, Fulke Greville calls,

> Painting, the eloquence of dumb conceit …⁴⁸

Sir Philip Sidney adds painters to the Church's objection that poets deal in untruths.

> Poor Painters oft with silly Poets join,
> To fill the world with strange but vain conceits:
> One brings the stuff, the other stamps the coin,
> Which breeds nought else but glosses of deceits …⁴⁹

The only sixteenth-century English poet who questioned the ability of the general public to judge matters of art was Thomas More. In a poem called, 'On Fame and Popular Opinion,' he observes,

---

45   Ibid., 429.
46   Giles Fletcher, the elder (1546-1611), from 'Licia' (1593), in Sylvester, *The Anchor Anthology*, 558.
47   John Skelton, 'The Bouge of Court,' in *The Complete Poems*, 37.
48   Fulke Greville, 'Caelica,' XXIV, in Bender, *Five Courtier Poets*, 496.
49   Sir Philip Sidney, *The Countesse of Pembrokes Arcadia* (1590), in *The Prose Works of Sir Philip Sidney*, I, Book II, xiv.

> Most men congratulate themselves if they attain to fame,
> Empty though it is; and, because they are light-minded,
> They are lifted to the stars by the fickle wind of opinion.
> Why do you derive satisfaction from the comments of the populace?
> In their blindness they often interpret what is best as a failing
> And thoughtlessly approve what is very reprehensible.
> You hang everlastingly upon a stranger's opinion
> For fear that some cobbler will retract the praise he has conferred.[50]

ON THE AESTHETICS OF MUSIC

We have mentioned above, Edmund Spenser's 'The Tears of the Muses,' which comments on the decline of the Arts in general in late sixteenth-century England. We also find in the poetry of this period some interesting reflections of where music stood with respect to the other Liberal Arts, which might shed light on this change of attitude. Fulke Greville, in his 'A Treatie of Human Learning,' in two places questions various branches of the Liberal Arts, and other disciplines. Within his rather pessimistic discussions we discover the relatively low value he assigns to music. First, he questions Reason.

> Reason we make an art, yet none agree
> What this true reason is, nor yet have powers
> To level other's reason unto ours.[51]

We are, he adds, no more successful with Nature.

> Nature we draw to art, which then forsakes
> To be herself when she with art combines …

Then he discounts the value of Astrology, Philosophy ('nothing but books of poetry in prose,' meaning fables) and Physicians ('they never helpeth the disease'). Music, he says, teaches the different modes [mathematics], but, he wonders, why can't she teach me to control my emotions?

> Music instructs me which be lyric moods;
> Let her instruct me rather how to show
> No weeping voice for loss of fortune's goods.

---

50 More, *The Complete Works of St. Thomas More*, III, Pt. 2, 175.
51 Fulke Greville, 'A Treatie of Human Learning,' XXVI, in Bender, *Five Courtier Poets*, 568ff.

Regarding all of the above 'arts,' he summarizes,

> Then, if our arts want power to make us better,
> What fool will think they can us wiser make;
> Life is the wisdom, art is but the letter
> Or shell which oft men for the kernel take …

His comments on the value of music are more revealing when he returns to this subject later. Now he ranks the intellectual disciplines in order of their importance, after a discussion of divine wisdom, which, of course, is the highest.[52] Following this, in order of importance, comes Physics, Philosophy, Grammar, Logic and Rhetoric. In reference to the latter, curiously, he unwittingly provides the most important definition of music,

> Because no language in the earth affords
> Sufficient characters to express all things.

Next come Poetry and Music, both of which are of value only for recreation, for idle men. They can move us temporarily, even affect our emotional state, but not really enrich the intellect, which is more important. They are the sauce for the food of life.

> Poesy and music, arts of recreation,
> Succeed, esteemed as idle men's profession,
> Because their scope, being merely contentation,
> Can move but not remove or make impression
> Really, either to enrich the wit,
> Or, which is less, to mend our states by it.
>
> This makes the solid judgments give them place
> Only as pleasing sauce to dainty food,
> Fine foils for jewels, or enamel's grave,
> Cast upon things which in themselves are good,
> Since, if the matter be in nature vile,
> How can it be made precious by a style?

He admits that music has a value in church in helping to 'move thoughts' to God, but he says again Poetry and Music are not really important. Indeed, he finds too much study of Music leads to 'disease of mind.'

> Let therefore human wisdom use both these,
> As things not precious in their proper kind,
> The one a harmony to move, and please,
> If studied for itself, disease of mind,
>   The next [poetry], like nature, doth ideas raise,

---
52 Ibid., XCVIff.

> Teaches, and makes, but hath no power to bind,
> Both, ornaments to life and other arts,
> Whiles they do serve and not possess our hearts.

It is interesting that he has separated music from the next three 'mathematical arts,' to which it had been joined for a thousand years: arithmetic, geometry, and astronomy. Finally, in view of the doubts we have seen him express toward books above, it is not surprising that he stipulates that all these arts must be learned from practice, not from books.

> Again, the active, necessary arts
> Ought to be brief in books, in practice long …
>
> ……
>
> For sciences from nature should be drawn,
> As arts from practice, never out of books …[53]

Sir Walter Ralegh seems to have had a similar general disrespect for the Liberal Arts.

> Tell arts they have no soundness,
> But vary by esteeming;
> Tell schools they want profoundness,
> And stand too much on seeming.
> If arts and schools reply,
> Give arts and schools the lie.[54]

Samuel Daniel, in his Romance 'Musophilus,' also senses a decline in the appreciation of music. He finds late sixteenth-century England more interested in making money. The [singing] poet, he says, can no longer be subtle.

> Now when this busy world cannot attend
> Th'untimely music of neglected [songs].
> Other delights than these, other desires,
> This wiser profit-seeking age requires …
> Besides, so many so confusedly sing,
> As diverse discords have the music marred,
> And in contempt that mystery doth bring,
> That he must sing aloud that will be heard …[55]

---

[53] Ibid., LXVIII, LXXV.

[54] Sir Walter Ralegh, 'The Lie,' in Ibid., 622. Ralegh (1552–1618) was a major figure in the court, due to his personal closeness to Elizabeth. After a romantic indiscretion with one of her maids of honor he fell into disfavor. He and his family spent some years in the Tower, but he was released and sent to capture Guiana from Spain, as a means of restoring himself to favor. When this effort failed, he was beheaded to appease Spain.

[55] Samuel Daniel (ca. 1563–1619), 'Musophilus,' in Jones, *The New Oxford Book of Sixteenth Century Verse*, 519ff.

On the Purpose of Music

In these sixteenth-century English poems, one finds a broad range of references to the purpose of music, beginning with the most universally understood, for the expression of feelings. Wyatt, in a Prologue to Psalm 32, portrays an unusually strong communication of emotions by Kind David.

> Sorrowful David after his languor,
> That with the tears that from his eyes down rolled
> Paused his plaint, and laid adown his harp,
> Faithful record of all his sorrows sharp …
>
> With vapoured eyes he looked here and there,
> And when he hath a while himself bethought,
> Gathering his sprites that were dismayed for fear,
> His harp again into his hand he raught.
>
> Tuning accord by judgment of his ear,
> His heartes bottom for a sigh he sought,
> And therewithal upon the hollow tree
> With Strained voice again thus crieth he …[56]

Another poem by Wyatt which deals with music expressing feelings is particularly interesting. Some medieval writers had maintained that it was the instrument, not the player, which made the music. Here we see the music is in the player. This beautiful poem begins,

> Blame not my lute, for he must sound
> Of this or that as liketh me:
> For lack of wit the lute is bound
> To give such tunes as pleaseth me.
> Then though my songs be somewhat strange
> And speaks such words as touch they change,
>   Blame not my lute.[57]

Curiously, we have found only in this English repertoire examples where poets express doubt regarding the relationship of music and the emotions. Wyatt, for one, complains that the emotions of his songs have been misunderstood, therefore he will now sing only songs without emotion.

> Me list no more to sing
> Of love nor of such thing
> How sore that it me wring,

---

56 Wyatt, *Collected Poems*, CVIII.

57 Ibid., CXV.

> For what I sung or spake,
> Men did my songs mistake.
>
> My songs were too diffuse,
> They made folk to muse.
> Therefore, me to excuse,
> They shall be sung more plain,
> Neither of joy nor pain.[58]

Sometimes the purpose of music is given as purely the delight of music itself. One unusual example is found in Spenser's 'Daphnaïda,' an elegy on the death of Douglas Howard. Here the poet says the Muses should not be called on, for even the saddest music, being music, has a certain delight.

> For even their heavy song would breed delight;
> But here no tunes, save sobs and groans shall ring.[59]

One of the most frequently cited purposes of music in early literature was to soothe the feelings. One such example is found in Arthur Brooke, in his *Romeus and Juliet* (1562),

> Leave of thy woonted song of care
> And now of pleasure sing.[60]

Another example is found in Wyatt.

> All heavy minds
> Do seek to ease their charge,
> And that that most them binds
> To let at large.
>
> Then why should I
> Hold pain within my heart,
> And may my tune apply
> To ease my smart?
>
> My faithful lute
> Alone shall hear me plain,
> For else all other suit
> Is clean in vain.[61]

---

58 Ibid.., CXXX.

59 Edmund Spenser, 'Daphnaïda,' lines 13ff. Additional examples of reference to delight as a purpose in music in Spenser can be found in *The Faerie Queene*, Book I, Canto VIII, xliv, 'Best music breeds delight [even] in loathing ears,' and *Daphnaïda*, lines 321ff, speak of the bagpipe alluring 'the senses to delight'

60 Arthur Brooke, *Romeus and Juliet* (Vaduz: Kraus Reprint, 1965), 676.

61 Wyatt, *Collected Poems*, LXXXIV.

A poem set as a madrigal by William Byrd begs music for solace.

> Come, woeful Orpheus, with thy charming lyre,
> And tune my voice unto thy skilful wire;
> Some strange chromatic notes do you devise,
> That best with morunful accents sympathise;
> Of sourest sharps and uncouth flats make choice,
> And I'll thereto compassionate my voice.[62]

In sixteenth-century literature music's ability to soothe is often aimed at melancholy, as in Spenser's *The Faerie Queene*.

> There many Minstrels make melody,
> To drive away the dull melancholy ...[63]

In some instances the soothing effects of music is tied to heavenly thoughts. Music, Humphrey Gifford says, raises spirits, delights, takes our mind away from earthly things and gives us a taste of heaven. He believes the ancient Greeks were right—harmony holds the world together.

> She with her silver sounding tunes
> Revives man's dulled sprites;
> She feeds the ear, she fills the heart,
> With choice and rare delights.
> Her sugared descant doth withdraw
> Thy mind from earthly toys,
> And makes thee feel within thy breast
> A taste of heavenly joys.
> The planets and celestial parts
> Sweet harmony contain,
> Of which if creatures were deprived
> This world could not remain.
> It is no doubt the very deed
> Of golden melody
> That neighbors do together live
> In love and unity.
> Where man and wife agrees in one,
> Sweet music doth abound;
> But when such strings begin to jar,
> Unpleasant is the sound.[64]

---

62 Anonymous, 'Come, woeful Orpheus,' in Williams, *English Renaissance Poetry*, 271.

63 Edmund Spenser, *The Faerie Queene*, Book I, Canto V, iii. In Book II, Canto VI, iii, a lady sings for this purpose.
> And there sat a Lady fresh and fair,
> Making sweet solace to herself alone.

64 Humphrey Gifford, 'In the praise of music,' in Ibid., 325ff.

Thomas Campion, at the end of his life, no longer finds pleasure in his music, as his thoughts as well are turned to God.

> To music bent is my retired mind,
> And fain would I some song of pleasure sing;
> But in vain joys no comfort now I find:
> From heavenly thoughts all true delight doth spring.
> Thy power, O God, thy mercies, to record,
> Will sweeten every note and every word.[65]

A large number of sixteenth-century English poems deal with the darker side of the emotions. John Lyly has left two poems which focus on music communicating sad feelings, rather than the more usual case of soothing such feelings. First, from a song thought to have been used in his play, *Woman in the Moone*,

> Sorrow was there made fair,
> And passion wise, tears a delightful thing,
> Silence beyond all speech a wisdom rare,
> She made her sighs to sing,
> And all things with so sweet a sadness move,
> As made my heart at once both grieve and love.[66]

An even more remarkable poem of dark emotions by Lyly is one in which he complains that his personal muse was one which was 'out of tune,' causing his songs of woe.

> Some men will say there is a kind of muse
> That helps the mind of each man to write
> And some will say (that often these Muses use)
> There are but Nine that ever used to write
> Now of these nine if I have hit on one
> I muse what Muse 'tis I have hit upon.
>
> Some poets write there is a heavenly hill
> Where Pallas keeps: and it Parnassus hyghte
> There Muses sit for-sothe, and cut the quill
> There being framed doth hidden fancies write
> But all these dames divine conceits do sing
> And all their pens be of a phoenix wing.

---

65 Thomas Campion, 'To Music Bent is my Retired Mind,' in Williams, *English Renaissance Poetry*, 322. Campion (1567–1620) studied at Cambridge for a while, then studied law briefly and finally medicine. He is remembered, however, as a poet and a musician and is the only musician of sixteenth-century England who regularly wrote the accompanying poetry.

66 John Lyly, in *The complete Works of John Lyly*, ed. Warwick Bond (Oxford: Clarendone Press, 1967), III, 471. This poem is found in John Dowland's *Second Booke of Songs* (1600). Lyly (1554–1606) graduated from Oxford in 1569 and aspired to reach a high position in court, although beyond serving in parliament he never reached his goal.

Believe me now I never saw the place
Unless in sleep I dreamed of such a thing
A never viewed fair Pallas in the face
Nor never yet could hear the Muses sing
Whereby to frame a fancy in her kind
Oh no! my muse is of another mind.

From Hellicon? no, no from Hell she came
To write of woes and mysteries: she hyghte
Not Pallas but Atlas her Lady's name
Who never calls for songs of delight.
Her pen is Pain; and all her matter moan
And panting hearts she paints her mind upon.

A heart not Harp is all her instrument
Whose weakened strings all out of tune she [plays]
And then she strikes a dump of discontent
Till every string be plucked in two with pains
Then in a rage she shuts it up in Case:
That you may see her instrument's disgrace.

Her music is in sum but sorrow in song
Where discord yields a sound of small delight
The song is: of life that lasts so long
To see desire thus crossed with despite
No faith on earth: alas I know no friend!
So with a sigh she makes a solemn end.

Unpleasant is the harmony God knows
When out of tune is almost every string
The sound unsweet, yet all of sorrow grows
And sad the muse, that so is forced to sing
Yet some do sing that else for woe would cry
So dothe my Muse: and so, I swear, do I.[67]

Closely related are poems which speak of the purpose of music being to draw the listener into a state of mourning. This is specifically mentioned in 'A Pastoral Elegy' by Spenser on the death of Sir Philip Sidney.

Thou that with skill canst tune a doleful song,
  Help him to mourn. My heart with grief doth freeze,
Hoarse is my voice with crying, else a part
  Sure I would [sing], though rude: but, as I may,
With sobs and sighs I second will thy song,
  And so express the sorrows of my heart.[68]

---

67 Lyly, in *The Complete Works*, III, 499ff.

68 Edmund Spenser, 'A Pastoral Aeglogue,' lines 9ff.

Humphrey Gifford, in his 'In the praise of music,' begins with reference to the Orpheus story and refers to the power of music to achieve this purpose.

> He played on harp, and sang so sweet,
> As moved them all to moan.
> At sound of his melodious tunes
> The very souls did mourn …[69]

An anonymous poem also pays tribute to the ability of music not to soothe, but to draw the listener into a state of lament.

> Oft thou has with greedy ear
> Drunk my notes and words of pleasure;
> In affection's equal measure
> Now my songs of sorrow hear,
> Since from thee my griefs do grow,
> Whom alive I prized so dear.
> The more my joy, the more my woe.
>
> Music, though it sweetens pain,
> Yet no whit impairs lamenting,
> But in passions like consenting
> Makes them constant that complain,
> And enchants their fancies so
> That all comforts they disdain,
> And fly from joy to dwell with woe.[70]

Curiously, some of these English poets speak of mourning in relationship with music, but found music to be to some degree ineffective. First, Skelton mentions a mourning lover whom music cannot soothe.

> She made him to sing
> The song of lover's lay;
> Musing night and day,
> Mourning all alone,
> Comfort had he none,
> For she was quite gone.[71]

---

[69] Humphrey Gifford, 'In the praise of music,' in Ibid., 325ff.

[70] Anonymous, in Williams, *English Renaissance Poetry*, 281. This poem was set as a madrigal by John Cooper.

[71] John Skelton, 'Philip Sparrow,' in *The Complete Poems of John Skelton*, 80. An elegy to a dead bird, this poem also has some interesting descriptions of singing birds.

A despondent lover in a poem by Wyatt is also not soothed by music, but at least his lute joins him in his mood.

> For of relief
> Since I have none,
> My lute and I
> Continually
> Shall us apply
> To sigh and moan.[72]

How can it be any other way, he asks in another poem?

> How may a mourning heart
> Set forth a pleasant voice?[73]

Sir Walter Ralegh, writing on the death of prince Henry in 1612, doubts that any music is capable of expressing the most profound emotions.

> How can music's saddest tones express
> With sighs or tears a public heaviness?[74]

Sir John Davies, in his 'Orchestra, or A Poem of Dancing,' refers to a number of purposes for music, including one rarely found in this repertoire, for music therapy ('the sick mind's leech').

> But sing a plain and easy melody,
> For the soft mean that warbleth but the ground
> To my rude ear doth yield the sweetest sound …

> And thou, sweet music, dancing's only life,
> The ear's sole happiness, the air's best speech,
> Lodestone of fellowship, charming rod of strife,
> The soft mind's paradise, the sick mind's leech,
> With thine own tongue thou trees and stones canst teach,
> That when the air doth dance her finest measure,
> Then art thou born, the gods' and men's sweet pleasure.[75]

---

72 Wyatt, *Collected Poems*, LI.
73 Ibid., LII.
74 Sir Walter Ralegh, 'What tears, dear prince,' in Bender, *Five Courtier Poets*, 626.
75 Sir John Davies (1569–1626), 'Orchestra or A Poem of Dancing,' in Ibid., 652ff.

In Spenser's *The Faerie Queene* a form of music therapy is used for the benefit of a wounded warrior.

> And all the while most heavenly melody
> About the bed sweet music did divide,
> Him to beguile of grief and agony ...[76]

In a literature that abounds in poetry of love, an important purpose of music is to help woo the ladies. In one unusual case a shepherd breaks his pipe and throws it on the ground when it fails him in this purpose.[77] In this regard, Spenser points to the use of the Lydian mode to help inspire the ladies for love making.

> So was that chamber clad in goodly wise;
> And round about it many beds were dight,
> As whylome was the antique world's guise,
> Some for untimely ease, some for delight,
> As pleased them to use that use it might;
> And all was full of Damsels and of Squires,
> Dancing and reveling both day and night,
> And swimming deep in sensual desires:
> And Cupid still among them kindled lustful fires.
>
> And all the while sweet Music did divide
> Her looser notes with Lydian harmony ...[78]

On Performance Practice

We also find some interesting commentary on musicians and their practice in this repertoire of sixteenth century English poetry. Some musicians were obviously well known, as we can see in the anonymous poem, 'Of the death of Phillips,' honoring the Dutch lutanist and composer, Philip van Wilder, who served as 'Keeper of the King's Instruments' under Henry VIII.

> Bewaile with me all ye that have profest,
> Of musicke tharte by touche of coarde or winde:
> Lay down your lutes and let your gitterns rest,
> Phillips is dead whose like you can not find.
> Of musicke much exceadyng all the rest,
> Muses therefore of force now must you wrest.

---

76 Edmund Spenser, *The Faerie Queene*, Book I, Canto V, xvii.

77 Edmund Spenser, 'The Shepheards Calender,' January, line 72.

78 Edmund Spenser, *The Faerie Queene*, Book III, Canto I, xxxix, xl.

> Your pleasant notes into an other sounde,
> The string is broke, the lute is dispossest,
> The hand is cold, the body in the ground.
> The lowring lute lamenteth now therefore,
> Phillips her friend that can her touch no more.[79]

Another musician is memorialized in Sir Thomas More's 'Epitaph of Abyngdon, the Singer.'

> Let the famed singer, Henry Abyngdon, draw your eyes hither;
> There was a time when he drew your ears with his music.
> Not long ago he sang in a voice marvelous beyond compare
> And played the organ with incomparable skill.
> At first he was the pride of the church at Wells;
> Then the king decided that he should
> Lend his fame to the Chapel Royal.
> Now God has taken him away from the king
> And installed him among the stars
> To add glory to the very inhabitants of heaven.[80]

In the poetry of John Skelton we have a contemporary glimpse of the true wandering minstrel, who was become a rather rare sight in England. His descriptions reveal that Skelton himself was sophisticated in his knowledge of music. First, of particular interest is the suggestion that his melodic improvisation is busy, but makes no sense.

> He solfas too haute, his treble is too high;
> He braggeth of his birth, that born was full base;
> His music without measure, too sharp in his *Mi*;
> He trimmeth in his tenor to counter pardee;
> His descant is busy, it is without mean;
> Too fat is his fancy, his wit is too lean.

Skelton continues by remarking that when he sang to a lute it sounded like 'the sobbing of an old sow!' But this minstrel is no fool, for he has noble students (even though they neither learn to sing from the page or by ear).

> For lords and ladies learn at his school,
> He teacheth them so wisely to solf and to fayne
> That neither they sing well prick-song nor plain:
> This Doctor Devias commenced in a cart,
> A master, a minstrel, a fiddler, a fart.[81]

---

79 Anonymous, 'Of the death of Phillips,' in Rollins, *Tottel's Miscellany*, 162.

80 More, *The Complete Works*, III, Pt. 2, 201ff. Henry Abyngdon (1418–1486) was the court Master of the Children and the first to graduate in music from Cambridge. In Spenser's *The Faerie Queene*, Book II, Canto VI, xxv, a lady singer with 'her skillful art' challenges the birds in singing.

81 John Skelton, 'Against a Comely Coistrown,' in *The Complete Poems*, 35.

Similarly, in his 'The Bouge of Court,' a satire on the dangers of court life, Skelton introduces a visiting minstrel singer, who sings only from rote but wishes he could read music.

> *Princes of Youth* can ye sing by rote?
> Or *Shall I sail with you* a fellowship assay?
> For on the book I cannot sing a note.
> Would to God, it would please you some day
> A ballad book before me for to lay,
> And learn me to sing *re me fa sol!*[82]

He was an older minstrel who had suffered from his years of travel.

> He bit the lip, he looked passing coy;
> His face was belimmed, as bees had him stung:
> It was no time with him to jape nor toy.
> Envy had wasted his liver and his lung,
> Hatred by the heart so had him wrung
> That he looked pale as ashes to my sight.[83]

The minstrel fiddle player, known in Germany as the 'beer fiddler,' is also mentioned by Skelton.

> And what blunderer is yonder that played fiddle diddle?
> He findeth false measures out of his fond fiddle.[84]

Finally, we find a lovely reference to the 'Music of the Spheres' in Greville's Romance, 'Caelica.'

> Atlas upon his shoulders bare the sky,
> The load was heavy, but the load was fair;
> His sense was ravished with the melody,
> Made from the motion of the highest sphere.[85]

---

[82] John Skelton, 'The Bouge of Court,' in Ibid., 45.

[83] Ibid., 46.

[84] John Skelton, 'The Garland of Laurel,' in Ibid., 371.

[85] Fulke Greville, 'Caelica,' XLVII, in Bender, *Five Courtier Poets*, 511.

ART MUSIC

One of the hallmarks of Art Music is the presence of the contemplative listener. A beautiful poem by Thomas Campion describes the reactions of a listener of love songs.

> When to her lute Corinna sings,
> Her voice revives the leaden strings,
> And doth in highest notes appear,
> As any challenged echo clear;
> But when she doth of mourning speak,
> Even with her sighs the strings do break.
>
> And as her lute doth live or die,
> Led by her passion, so must I.
> For when of pleasure she doth sing,
> My thoughts enjoy a sudden spring;
> But if she doth of sorrow speak,
> Even from my heart the strings do break.[86]

George Chapman also provides a remarkable portrait of a listener of a love song.

> Never was any sense so set on fire
> With an immortal ardor, as mine ears;
> Her singing to the strings doth speech inspire
> And numbered laughter, that the descant bears
> To her sweet voice; whose species through my sense
> My spirits; to their highest function rears;
> To which, impressed with ceaseless confluence,
> It useth them as proper to her power,
> Marries my soul, and makes itself her dower.
>
> Methinks her tunes fly gilt like Attic bees
> To my ears' hives, with honey tried to air:
> My brain is but the comb, the wax, the lees,
> My soul the drone, that lives by their affair.
> O, so it sweets, refines, and ravisheth,
> And with what sport they sting in their repair!
> Rise then in swarms, and sting me thus to death,
> Or turn me into swound; possess me whole,
> Soul to my life and essence to my soul![87]

---

86 Thomas Campion, 'When to her Lute,' in Ibid., 316.

87 George Chapman (1559-1634), 'Ovid's Banquet of Sense,' in Jones, *The New Oxford Book of Sixteenth Century Verse*, 682.

In the poetry of Edmund Spenser we find a number of vivid descriptions of the contemplative listener. In his 'Colin Clouts Come Home Again,' one listener is like the 'deer in the headlights,' as we would say today.

> Who all the while, with greedy listfull ears,
> Did stand astonished at his curious skill,
> Like heartless deer, dismayed with thunder's sound.[88]

And later in this work listeners are said to have 'hungry ears.'

> 'Hark then, ye jolly shepherds, to my song,'
> With that they all began to throng about him near,
> With hungry ears to hear his harmony ...[89]

In *The Faerie Queene*, the mythical musician, Arion, performs music which draws not only the ears, but the hearts of the listeners as well.

> Then there was heard a most celestial sound
> Of dainty music, which did next ensue
> Before the spouse: that was Arion crowned;
> Who, playing on his harp, unto him drew
> The ears and hearts of all that goodly crew ...[90]

In this same work, there is a lovely description of music in a pastoral scene where the listeners are enchanted by the combination of music and natural sounds.

> Soon they heard a most melodious sound,
> Of all that might delight a dainty ear,
> Such as attonce might not on living ground,
> Save in this Paradise, be heard elsewhere:
> Right hard it was for wight which it did hear,
> To read what manner music that might be;
> For all that pleasing is to living ear
> Was there consorted in one harmony;
> Birds, voices, instruments, winds, waters, all agree:
>
> The joyous birds, shrouded in cheerful shade
> Their notes unto the voice tempered sweet;
> The Angelical soft trembling voices made
> To the instruments divine respondence meet;
> The silver sounding instruments did meet
> With the base murmur of the water's fall....[91]

---

88 Edmund Spenser, 'Colin Clouts Come Home Again,' lines 7ff.
89 Ibid., lines 51ff.
90 Edmund Spenser, *The Faerie Queene*, Book IV, Canto XI, xxiii.
91 Ibid., Book II, Canto XII, lxxff.

Another poem which reveals the careful listener is quite interesting. A poem by John Lyly, composed ca. 1575–1580, speaks of music not sounding well unless the bass line can be heard. It was this growing awareness of the upper and lower line, something not evident in polyphony, which was to lead to the functional harmony of the Baroque Period.

> The lofty trees whose branches make sweet shades
> Whose arms in Spring are richly dighte with flowers
> Without the root their glory quickly fades
> And all in vain comes pleasant April showers.
> No love can be at all without the heart
> Nor Music made except the Bass takes part.
>
> The princely towers whose pride exceeds in show
> If their foundations be not strong and sound
> Are subject to the smallest winds that blow
> And highest tops are brought to lowest ground.
> No field is sweet where all is scorched with drought
> Nor Music good when so the bass is out.[92]

Finally, Thomas Watson in his collection of sonnets, 'Hekatompathia, Or Passionate Centurie of Love,' begins one sonnet with the famous anecdote about Alexander the Great's having leaped from his dinner table and grasping his sword, all because the musician playing changed to the [ancient] Phrygian mode. But Watson says one should not be surprised that music can change the mind, since it was born in heaven. We notice in particular that this listener was so taken by the music that it remained with him long after the performance.

> Some that reporte great Alexanders life,
> They say, that harmonie so mov'd his mind,
> That oft he roase from meat to warlike strife
> At sounde of Trumpe, or noyse of battle kind,
> And then, that musickes force of softer vaine
> Caus'd him returne from strokes to meat againe.
>
> And as for me, I thinke it nothing strange,
> That musick having birth from heav'ns above,
> By divers tunes can make the minde to change:
> For I my selfe in hearing my sweete Love,
> By vertue of her song both tasted griefe,
> And such delight, as yeelded some reliefe.
>
> When first I gan to give attentive eare,
> Thinking Apolloes voice did haunte the place,
> I little thought my Lady had beene there:
> But whilest mine eares lay open in this case,

---

92 Lyly, *The Complete Works*, III, 452ff.

> Transform'd to ayre Love entred with my will,
> And nowe perforce doth keepe possession still.[93]

FUNCTIONAL MUSIC

Edmund Spenser, in his 'Epithalamion,' depicts the entire day of a wedding celebration. First, we hear the music before the ceremony.

> Hark how the minstrels 'gin to shrill aloud
> Their merry music that resounds from far,
> The pipe, the tabor, and the trembling crowd,
> That well agree withouten breach or jar.
> But most of all the damsels do delight
> When they their timbrels smite,
> And thereunto do dance and carol sweet,
> That all the senses they do ravish quite …

And then inside the Church,

> And let the roaring organs loudly play
> The praises of the Lord in lively notes,
> The whiles with hollow throats
> The choristers the joyous anthems sing,
> That all the woods may answer, and their echo ring.[94]

A frequent form of functional music heard in sixteenth-century England must have been that which welcomed the arrival of nobles. Spenser, in his *The Faerie Queene* pictures a returning Conqueror met by virgins, who have in their hands 'sweet Timbrels all upheld on high.'[95] Soon these instruments are used together with a song, sung by children.

> And to the Maidens' sounding timbrels song
> In well tuned notes a joyous lay,
> And made delightful music all the way …

---

93 Thomas Watson (1557–1592), 'Hekatompathia' (1582), in Sylvester, *The Anchor Anthology*, 554.
94 Edmund Spenser, 'Epithalamion,' in Williams, *English Renaissance Poetry*, 163.
95 Edmund Spenser, *The Faerie Queene*, Book I, Canto XII, viff.

Then a procession takes the Conqueror to the palace.

> And after to his Palace he then brings,
> With shawms and trumpets, and with Clarions sweet:
> And all the way the joyous people sing,
> And with their garments strewn the paved street ...

These trumpets are the ceremonial trumpets which always accompanied the highest aristocrats. A popular song of 1588, 'The Queenes visiting of the campe at Tilsburie' recounts her day there. To the tune of 'Wilsons Wilde,' it contains poetry which describes the music which accompanied a visit by Queen Elizabeth. First we see her in her barge as she traveled,

> She did go with trumpets sounding,
> And with dubbing drums apace:
> Along the Thames that famous river,
> For to view the campe a space.

Next, the troops gathered to meet her.

> How they came marching all together,
> Like a wood in winters weather.
> With the strokes of drummers sounding,
> And with trampling horses than:
> The earth and air did sound like thunder,
> To the ears of every man.

As she reviewed the troops,

> With trumpets sound most loyally,
> Along the Court of guarde she went ...

And again, as she departed.

> And when that she was safely set,
> within her Barge, and past away:
> Her farewell then the trumpets sounded,
> and the cannons fast did play.[96]

Another frequent form of functional music was military music and a poem by Michael Drayton describes the music of battle.

---

[96] Anonymous, 'Queen Elizabeth at Tilbury,' in McClure, *Sixteenth-Century English Poetry*, 174ff.

> They now to fight are gone,
> Armor on armor shone,
> Drum now to drum did groan;
> To hear was wonder,
> That with cries they make
> The very earth did shake,
> Trumpet to trumpet spake,
> Thunder to thunder.[97]

In most early literature references to hearing military trumpets were always associated with fear and a sense of dread, for obvious reasons.[98] One English poet of this period, Humphrey Gifford, was an exception and seemed to be exhilarated by this sound. He wrote, in about 1580,

> Methinks I hear the drum
> Strike doleful marches to the field.
> Tantaria, tantara! Ye trumpets sound,
> Which makes our hearts with joy abound![99]

One important form of aristocratic practice for the military was the tournament, and trumpets are always mentioned in accounts of these. We find especially interesting an allegorical tournament in George Peele's *The Order of the Garter*.

> Therewith I heard the clarions and the shawms,
> The sackbuts, and a thousand instruments
> Of several kinds; and, loudest of them all,
> A trumpet more shrill than Triton's is at sea;
> The same Renown, precursor of the train,
> Did sound,—for who rings louder than Renown?[100]

---

97 Michael Drayton, 'The Ballad of Agincourt,' in Williams, *English Renaissance Poetry*, 262ff. Drayton (1563–1631), born as a son to a tanner, he was brought up as a page in the household of Sir Henry Goodere.

98 Thus Spenser, in *The Faerie Queene*, refers to the sound of the trumpet as 'stern,' in Book I, Canto I, i and as 'shrill' in Book I, Canto V, vi. George Peele, in his *A Farewell to the Generals*, [in A. H. Bullen, ed., *The Works of George Peele* (1888) (Port Washington: Kennikat Press, 1966), II, 238] has a line which speaks of,

> The angry-sounding drum, the whistling fife,
> The Shrieks of men, the princely courser's neigh.

99 Humphrey Gifford, 'For Soldiers,' in Jones, *The New Oxford Book of Sixteenth Century Verse*, 324.

100 George Peele, 'The Order of the Garter,' in Ibid., II, 323. Another poem by Peele, 'Polyhymnia,' [Ibid., 287] also mentions the trumpet in this context.

> Make to the tilt amain; and trumpets sound …

Spenser also writes of the trumpet being used to signal the beginning of a tournament.

> The trumpets sound, then all together run.[101]

Spenser, in his *The Faerie Queene*, uses in his poetry a number of examples of trumpet signals, including to celebrate a victory,[102] to announce the time for departure,

> The trumpets sounded, and they all arose,
> Thence to depart with glee and gladsome cheer.[103]

to signal the time to rest while traveling,[104] the time to rest from work,

> Then shrilling trumpets loudly began to bray,
> And had them leave their labors and long toil
> To joyous feast and other gentle play.[105]

and as a warning signal.

> In readiness, forth to the Town-gate went;
> Where, sounding loud a Trumpet from the wall,
> Unto those warlike Knights she warning sent.[106]

ENTERTAINMENT MUSIC

Sir John Davies describes the lowest of popular music, but even in this case, he observes, such is the power of music that everyone forgets where he is and listens.

> As doth the ballad-singer's auditory,
> Which hat at Temple Bar his standing chose,
> And to the vulgar sings an ale-house story.
> First stands a porter, then an oyster-wife
> Doth stint her cry and stays her steps to hear him,
> Then comes a cutpurse ready with his knife,
> And then a country client presseth near him.
> There stands the constable, there stands the whore,

---

101 Edmund Spenser, *The Faerie Queene*, Book V, Canto III, vi.

102 Ibid., Book I, Canto V, xv.

103 Ibid., Book IV, Canto III, li.

104 Ibid., Book IV, Canto IV, xxxvi.

105 Ibid., Book IV, Canto IV, xlviii.

106 Ibid., Book V, Canto IV, l.

And hearkening to the song mark not each other.
There by the sergeant stands the debtor poor,
And doth no more mistrust him than his brother.
Thus Orpheus to such hearers giveth music …[107]

Finally, an anonymous poet describes a Morris dance in the town square and with a hint of the traditional tempi of these dances a character complains that the bagpipe player plays so fast that the dancers are perspiring.

Hoe who comes here along with bagpiping and drumming?
O the Morris, tis I see, the Morris daunce a comming.
Come Ladies come come quickly,
Come away come I say, O come come quickly,
And see about how trim the daunce and trickly.
Hey ther again! how the bells they shake it!
Hey ho, now for our town, and take it!
Soft awhile, piper, not away so fast! They melt them.
Be hanged, knave, see'st thou not the dauncers swelt them.[108]

---

107 Sir John Davies, in Jones, *The New Oxford Book of Sixteenth Century Verse*, 666.
108 Quoted in McClure, *Sixteenth-Century English Poetry*, 476.

12 SIXTEENTH-CENTURY ENGLISH FICTION

IN A PASSAGE we take to be a description of contemporary England, a character in Robert Greene's *Never Too Late* comments on the decay in letters.

> He called to mind that he was a scholar, and that although in these days Art lacked honor, and learning lacked its due, yet good letters were not brought to so low an ebb, but that there might some profit arise by them to procure his maintenance.[1]

In this case, the character turns to writing for the dramatic stage, which as we know from the extant repertoire had reached a high level of development.

It was for this reason, of course, that some young men wanted to go abroad to 'finish' their education. Greene was apparently one of those who had been criticized by some for traveling to Italy for this reason. In return, he took some satisfaction in pointing out some of the failures of Englishmen as well.

> I am English born, and I have English thoughts, not a devil incarnate because I am Italianate,[2] but hating the pride of Italy, because I know their peevishness: yet in all the countries where I have traveled, I have not seen more excess of vanity than we English men practice through vain glory: for as our wits be as ripe as any, so our wills are more ready than they all, to put in effect any of their licentious abuses …[3]

---

1 Robert Greene, *Never too Late* (1590), in *The Life and Complete Works of Robert Greene*, Alexander Grosart, ed. (New York: Russell & Russell, 1964), VIII, 128ff. Greene (1560–1592) graduated from Cambridge and traveled in Italy and Spain. Although his personal life was perhaps the most sordid of all these writers, little influence of it can be found in his writing. In 1591 he published *Farewell to Folly*, which was inspired, as he says in the preface, by 'the misdeeds of my youth,' as well as *The Repentance of Robert Greene* (1592). His romance, *Pandosto* (1588), was the source of Shakespeare's *Winter's Tale*.

2 We have mentioned above the growing prejudice toward English students who traveled to Italy for further education. Thomas Nashe, in his *Pierce Penilesse His Supplication to the Devil* (1592), in *The Works of Thomas Nashe*, ed. Ronald McKerrow (Oxford: Blackwell, 1966), I, 186, calls Italy the 'Academy of man-slaughter, the sporting place of murder, the Apothecary-shop of poison for all Nations.' He makes the claim that pope Sixtus V (1585–1590) was poisoned by the king of Spain, whom he had invited to dinner. The following pope, according to Nashe, after his election sent someone a note reading '*Sol, Re, Me, Fa*,' which meant *Solus Rex me facit*: 'the king of Spain made me pope.' Nashe (1567–1601) is best known as the author of *The Unfortunate Traveller*, which some consider the first English novel.

3 Robert Greene, 'To the Reader,' in *A Notable Discovery of Coosnage* (1591), in *The Life and Complete Works of Robert Greene*, X, 6. In most cases, we have modernized the English.

He wrote an entire book on Pride as reflected in the English scene. In this work, *A Quip for an Upstart Courtier* (1592), he says his purpose was to reflect,

> the abuses that Pride had bred in England, how it had infected the Court with aspiring Ennui, the City with griping covetousness, and the country with contempt and disdain. How since men placed their delights in proud looks and brave attire, Hospitality was left off, Neighborhood was exiled, Conscience was laughed at, and Charity lay frozen in the streets.[4]

In *Mourning Garment*, Greene offers yet another criticism of English character.

> In Crete you must learn to lie, in Paphos to be a lover, in Greece a dissembler, you must bring home pride from Spain, lasciviousness from Italy, gluttony from England and carousing from the Danes.[5]

No doubt in Greene's mind much of such criticism was aimed at the courtier and we find in his *The Royal Exchange* (1590), a list of four things necessary to be a courtier.

1. Abundance of riches.
2. Ambition and desire of honor.
3. Integrity and quickness of wit.
4. The hope of reward by service.[6]

Another who attacked the courtier in his fiction was John Lyly. He begins his *Euphues, or The Anatomy of Wit* (1578) by introducing a young noble of Athens, whom he says 'had more wit than wealth, and yet more wealth than wisdom.' Since he considered himself above any honest work, he spent his time engaging in what 'wits' do,

> fine phrases, smooth quoting, merry taunting, using jest without mean and abusing mirth without measure.[7]

---

4   Robert Greene, *A Quip for an Upstart Courtier* (1592), in Ibid., XI, 209.

5   Robert Greene, *Mourning Garment* (ca. 1590), in Ibid., IX, 136. Additional criticism of England by Englishmen include John Lyly, in *Euphues and his England*, ed. Morris Croll (New York: Russell & Russell, 1964), 226.

> It is the nature of that country to sift strangers. Everyone that shaketh thee by the hand is not joined to thee in heart.

And Phillip Stubbs, in *The Anatomy of the Abuses in England* (1583), ed. Frederick Furnivall (London: The New Shakespeare Society, n.d.), 23.

> There is not a people more corrupt, wicked, or perverse, living upon the face of the earth.

6   Robert Greene, *The Royal Exchange* (1590), in *The Life and Complete Works of Robert Greene*, VII, 253.

7   Lyly, *Euphues, or The Anatomy of Wit*, in *The Complete Works of John Lyly*, ed. Warwick Bond (Oxford: Clarendon Press, 1967), I, 184. Lyly (1553–1606) is best known for this work and its sequel, *Euphues and His England* (1580). These works are half treatise and half novel and as the novel had not really been invented in England, some consider these works the origin of that form.

Later he bemoans the fact that such young men, so gifted by Nature and Fortune, are only interested in 'the passions of his mind and praises of his Lady.'

> From this comes such vain poetry, such idle sonnets, such enticing songs, which are set forth to the gaze of the world and the grief of the godly.[8]

While on the subject of life at court, Lyly also has a character advise another on how to uncover the 'deceits of thy Lady.'

> Search every vain and sinew of their disposition, if she can not sing at sight, ask her to sing, if she has no cunning to dance request her to trip it, if no skill in Music, offer her the Lute …[9]

ON THE PHYSIOLOGY OF AESTHETICS

Since most of the sixteenth-century English fiction tends toward the light-hearted in character, there is little serious discussion to be found on such topics as the nature of Reason. Robert Greene promises the reader that his *Euphues his Censure to Philautus* will present 'the virtuous minds of true nobility and gentility pleasantly discovered.' In the end, he offers little original thought, and indeed seems eager to qualify his own background in this regard.

> And noble Gentlemen, it may be that report, who is often a false herald of humane actions, hath blabbed that she hath seen some Philosophers' works in my hands, and you therefore suppose that I have their principles in my head: but many handled Orpheus' harp that knew not the secrets of Music, and diverse ones may gaze into Philosopher's conclusions that cannot analyze their reasons …
>
> The Philosopher whom Apollo's Oracle long since graced with the title of a wise man, being demanded what wisdom was, made this answer: A divine influence infused into the minds of men, which being metaphysical, keeps them from committing that whereunto they are forced by sensual appetite. Epictetus called it the touchstone of morality, meaning that as reason is the difference that distinguishes man from brute beast, so wisdom is that perfect index, that shows how far one man excels another in the precious constitution of his mind.[10]

That is how it is supposed to work in theory. But Sir Philip Sidney seems quite exacerbated when he considers the failure of Reason, or the male species for that matter, to deal with feminine beauty.

---

8   Ibid., I, 287.
9   Ibid., I, 254.
10 Robert Greene, *Euphues his Censure to Philautus* (1587), in *The Life and Complete Works of Robert Greene*, VI, 204ff.

But that the beauty of human person is beyond all other things, there is great likelihood of reason, since to them only is given the judgment to discern Beauty; and among reasonable wits, as it seems, that our sex hath the preeminence, so that in that preeminence, Nature countervails all other liberalities, wherein she may be thought to have dealt more favorable toward men. How do men crown themselves with glory, for having either by force brought others to yield to their mind, or with long study, and premeditated orations, persuaded what they would have persuaded? And see, a fair woman shall not only command without authority, but persuade without speaking. She shall not need to procure attention, for her own eyes will chain their ears unto it. Men venture lives to conquer; she conquers lives without venturing.[11]

Greene also acknowledges this silent power of women, in *The Royal Exchange*, where he lists four things which 'do greatly dull the senses.'

1. Delight in women.
2. Cruel adversity.
3. Oppression through famine.
4. Too much prosperity.[12]

On Education

Lyly, in *Euphues*, includes a lengthy section in which he presents his philosophy of education. First, he advises that schoolmasters should be 'not only a teacher of learning but an example of good living.'[13] The principal subject, he says, should be philosophy.[14] While it is pleasant to travel, to read history and study the arts, philosophy is the most profitable.

> Those who cannot attain the knowledge of philosophy apply their minds to things most vile and contemptible. Therefore we must prefer philosophy as the only Princess of all Sciences, with the other arts as waiting maids.

In addition, he believed that while medicine [*Phisicke*] and exercise can contribute to a healthy body, only philosophy can 'cure the wounds of the mind.'

With regard to higher education, Lyly, in this quasi-novel, finds it necessary to protect himself by writing about a fictional university in Athens. It seems clear, however, that he is thinking of the universities in England, where he finds,

---

11 Sir Philip Sidney, *The Countesse of Pembrokes Arcadia*, in *The Prose Works of Sir Philip Sidney*, ed. Albert Feuillerat (Cambridge: Cambridge University Press, 1962), I, Book III, x. Sidney (1554–1586), scholar, poet, diplomat, courtier and soldier, was a key member of Elizabeth's court in its early period. This pastoral romance was written for the entertainment of the author's sister, the Countess of Pembroke. It was the source of Shakespeare's *King Lear* and for Beaumont and Fletcher's *Philaster* of the following generation.

12 Robert Greene, *The Royal Exchange* (1590), in *The Life and Complete Works of Robert Greene*, VII, 314.

13 Lyly, *Euphues, or The Anatomy of Wit*, in *The Complete Works of John Lyly*, I, 268.

14 Ibid., I, 273.

more filthiness than in Sodom and Gomora, more pride than in Rome, more poisoning than in Italy, more lying than in Crete, more private spoiling than in Spain and more idolatry than in Egypt.¹⁵

It is no wonder, he says, that common people say they would rather send their children to the farm than to the university, from where they return,

little better learned, but a great deal worse lived than when they went, and not only unthriftiness in their money, but bankrupt of good manners.

The moral climate in the universities mentioned by Lyly, above, is also mentioned by the sharp-tongued Thomas Nashe. He addresses this general topic and includes a curious anecdote about tigers which is occasionally mentioned in early literature.

Youth being ready to undertake more weightier studies, ought in no case be permitted to look aside to lascivious toys, least the pleasure of the one should breed a loathing of the profit of the other. I wish there were not any, as there are many, who in Poets and Historians, read for no other purpose than serves the feeding of their filthy lust, applying those things to the pampering of their private *Venus*, which were purposely published to the suppressing of that common wandering *Cupid*. These be the Spiders which suck poison out of the honey comb, and corruption out of the holist things, herein resembling ... Tigers, which by the sound of melodious Instruments are driven into madness, by which men are wont to expel melancholy.¹⁶

In general, however, Nashe strongly supports education, although he differs with Lyly when he calls 'the knowledge of Arts, the pathway to honor.' He laments, on the other hand, that he finds learning is no longer enough for promotion. This, he says, 'by many mens' lamentable practice, has become a matter of purchase.'¹⁷

Greene, in his *The Royal Exchange*, lists four characteristics of a good teacher:

1. In the day to look over the lecture he has.
2. In the night by meditation to call it to memory.
3. Privately to resolve his students in all doubts.
4. To be affable with them.

This is followed by a list of four things which teachers aspire to.

1. A multitude of students.
2. Great reward for his pains.
3. The getting of greater knowledge.
4. The hope to obtain fame and honor.¹⁸

---

15 Ibid., I, 274ff.
16 Thomas Nashe, *The Anatomie of Absurditie* (1589), in *The Works of Thomas Nashe*, I, 30.
17 Ibid., 37ff.
18 Robert Greene, *The Royal Exchange* (1590), in *The Life and Complete Works of Robert Greene*, VII, 257ff.

Another of his lists, which he calls, 'Four things which impoverish a man,' bears testimony that values are slow to change. These are the Liberal Arts, Grammar, Logic, Arithmetic and Geometry, of which he concludes,

> all liberal Arts decay, that devotion towards learning is cold, and that it is the poorest condition to be a scholar, all Arts failing except Divinity, Law and Medicine.[19]

ON THE PSYCHOLOGY OF AESTHETICS

Among the fiction writers Love is the emotion most discussed and we find many testimonials to its power. Greene, for example, in his *Ciceronis Amor* (1589), concludes,

> Ladies believe me, Love is of more force than wars, and the looks of women pierce deeper than the strokes of lances.[20]

Philip Sidney, in *The Countesse of Pembrokes Arcadia*, uses the analogy of music to represent the power of love.

> This word, Lover, did no less pierce poor Pyrocles, than the right tune of music touches him that is sick of the Tarantula. There was not one part of his body, that did not feel a sudden motion, while his heart with panting, seemed to dance to the sound of the word …[21]

Later in this romance, Sidney calls Love,

> the bewitcher of wit, the rebel to Reason, the betrayer of resolution, the defiler of thoughts, the underminer of magnanimity, the flatterer of vice, the slave to weakness, the infection of youth, the madness of age, the curse of life and reproach of death …[22]

Historically, we know that poets and comedians have always been able to say things, and point to truths, which the orator cannot. An interesting line in Greene's *Menaphon* suggests that perhaps it was possibile to express some emotions through music which would be held inappropriate if spoken. First, Melicertus sings a description of his love, Samela, after which the latter begs him not to speak further of love. Well, says Melicertus, let me at least sing a madrigal, and Samela gives her consent 'for none loves music more than I.' But the madrigal is also about love, which prompts the following:

---

19 Ibid., 302ff.
20 Robert Greene, *Ciceronis Amor* (1589), in Ibid., VII, 127.
21 Sir Philip Sidney, *The Countesse of Pembrokes Arcadia*, I, Book I, ix.
22 Ibid., III, xii.

Scarce had the shepherd ended this madrigal, but Samela began to frown, saying he had broken his promise. Melicertus alleged if he had uttered any passion, it was sung, not said.[23]

On the other hand, these writers were fully aware that Love and Reason are separated within our faculties. In Robert Greene's pastoral romance, *Menaphon*, a poet reads a sonnet which focuses on this very fact.

> Love is a discord, and a strange divorce
> Between our sense and reason, ...
>
> It is a secret hidden and not known,
> Which one may better feel than write upon.[24]

These last two lines are a remarkable deduction of the organization of the twin hemispheres of our brain. The right hemisphere's archive is indeed a 'secret hidden,' for not only is that hemisphere mute, but its understanding and information is unknown to the speaking and writing left hemisphere. And as the last line indicates, what it knows of love we can feel, but we cannot write or speak of. Greene makes another reference to the separation of Love and Reason in his *Arbasto: The Anatomy of Fortune*.

> Beauty is to be obeyed, because it is beauty, and love to be feared of men, because honored of the Gods. Dare Reason abide the brunt, when beauty bids the battle? can wisdom win the field, when Love is Captain?[25]

A character in Thomas Lodge's *Euphues' Golden Legacie* observes, 'Love admits neither counsel, nor reason,'[26] and another in Sidney's *The Countesse of Pembrokes Arcadia* complains 'my Reason (now grown a servant to passion).'[27] In this latter work we find an extraordinary scene devoted to this subject, as a group of shepherds present a masque which they call, 'The Battle between Reason and Passion.'[28]

> Seven shepherds (which were named the Reasonable shepherds) joined themselves, four of them making a square, another two going a little wide of either side, like wings for the main battle; and the seventh man foremost, like the forlorn hope to begin the skirmish. In similar order came out the seven Passionate shepherds; all keeping the pace of their feet by their

---

23 Greene, *Menaphon* (1589), in *The Life and Complete Works of Robert Greene*, VI, 88.
24 Ibid., VI, 140ff.
25 Greene, in *Arbasto: The Anatomy of Fortune* (1584), in Ibid., III, 197.
26 Thomas Lodge, *Euphues' Golden Legacie* (1590), in *The Complete Works of Thomas Lodge* (New York: Russell & Russell, 1963), II, 46. Lodge (1558–1625) was born to a distinguished London merchant, who was in fact Lord Mayor in 1562–1563. Lodge attended Oxford and later became a law student at Lincoln's Inn.
27 Sir Philip Sidney, *The Countesse of Pembrokes Arcadia*, I, Book I, xiv.
28 Ibid., I, Book II, xxix.

voice, and sundry consorted instruments they held in their arms. And first, the foremost of the Reasonable side began to sing.

REASON. *Thou Rebel vile, come, to thy master yield.*

And the other that met with him answered.

PASSION. *No, Tyrant, no: mine, mine shall be the field.*
REASON. *Can Reason then a Tyrant counted be?*
PASSION. *If Reason will, that Passions be not free.*
REASON. *But Reason will, that Reason govern most.*
PASSION. *And Passion will, that Passion rule the roost.*
REASON. *Your will is will; but Reason reason is.*
PASSION. *Will hath his will, when Reasons will doth miss.*
REASON. *Whom Passion leads unto his death is bent.*
PASSION. *And let him die, so that he die content.*
REASON. *By nature you to Reason faith have sworn.*
PASSION. *No so, but fellowlike together borne.*
REASON. *Who Passion doth ensue, lives in annoy.*
PASSION. *Who Passion doth forsake, lives void of joy …*

Then a mock battle ensues, followed by peace which is concluded with these lines,

REASON. *But yet our strife sure peace in end doth breed.*
PASSION. *We now have peace, your peace we do not need.*

Then did the two square battles meet and instead of fighting embrace one another, singing thus …

REASON. *Yet Passion, yield at length to Reason's stroke.*
PASSION. *What shall we win by taking Reason's yoke?*
REASON. *The joys you have shall be made permanent.*
PASSION. *But so we shall with grief learn to repent …*

As with writers of all centuries, there is the inevitable reflection on the pleasure and pain of Love. In Robert Greene's romance, *Morando* (1587), we find two unusually attractive expositions on the nature of Love, one pro and one con. First, in praise of the virtues of Love, Peratio, says,

The philosophers who have sought precisely to set out the perfect Anatomy of pure love, who set down by pen that which before they tried by experience, weighing wisely the strange affects and force of love, and feeling in themselves the puissance of his power, justly canonized that sacred essence for a God, attributing unto it the title of deity, as a thing worthy of such supernatural dignity. For it doth infuse into the minds of men such virtuous and valorous motions, kindling in men's hearts such glowing coals of natural affection (which before the force of love had touched them, lay buried in the dead cinders of hate) that it doth knit the minds of friends together with such perfect and perpetual amity, as we may justly say with Socrates, they be two bodies and one soul, yea, the common people, although their minds be sotted and almost senseless, yet they have held love in such sacred estimation, that they carefully rewarded them with the title of honor and dignity, who have excelled in that holy affection, esteeming this only virtue (if so basely it may be termed) sufficient of a man to make one a God. But to aim more near the mark, if we rightly consider the force of love, we shall find that there is nothing which so pleasureth a man and profiteth the commonwealth as love … Love maketh a man who is naturally addicted to vice to be endued with virtue, to apply himself to all laudable exercises, that thereby he may obtain his Lover's favor. He coveteth to be skillful in good letters, that by his learning he may allure her to excel in Music, that by his melody he may entice her to frame his speech in a perfect phrase, that his eloquence may persuade her, yea, what nature wanteth he seeketh to amend by nurture, and the only cause of this virtuous disposition is Love.[29]

But, says Silvestro, there is another opinion on Love.

Sir, if you weighed well what love were, you would yield another verdict. Is there anything which man esteemeth more than liberty? Nay, doth he not account it dearer than life: and is not love the loss thereof, and the means to lead him into an endless Labyrinth? Doth it not fetter him that is free, and enthrall the quiet mind in perpetual bondage? Is there anything to be found in Love but lowering, care, calamity, sorrow, sighs, woe, wailings, complaints and misery? What breedeth frenzy and bringeth fury, but Love? What maketh the wise foolish and fools more fond, but Love? What besotteth the senses? What bruiseth the brain? What weakenth the wit? What dulleth the memory? What fadeth the strength? Nay, what leadeth a man to ruth and ruin by Love? … For as soon as it once invades the wit and bewitches the senses, it makes straight a Metamorphosis of the poor Lover's mind: he then rages as though he were haunted with some hellish hag, or possessed with some frantic fury, like one enchanted with some Magical charm, or charmed with some bewitching sorcery, yea he is perplexed with a thousand sundry passions: first free, then fettered: now swimming in rest and now sinking in care: in security and then in captivity: yea turned from mirth to mourning: from pleasure to pain …[30]

In Sidney's *The Countesse of Pembrokes Arcadia*, we find another who discovers no joy in Love.

This bastard Love (for indeed the name of Love is most unworthily applied to so hateful a humor) as it is engendered between lust and idleness; as the matter it works upon is nothing but a certain base weakness, which some gentle fools' call a gentle heart; as his adjoined companions be unquietness, longing, fond comforts, faint discomforts, hopes, jealousies, ungrounded rages, causeless yieldings; so is the highest end it aspires to, a little pleasure with much pain before, and great repentance after.[31]

---

29 Greene, in *Morando* (1587), I, in *The Life and Complete Works of Robert Greene*, III, 88ff.
30 Ibid., 92ff.
31 Sir Philip Sidney, *The Countesse of Pembrokes Arcadia*, I, Book I, xii.

ON THE PHILOSOPHY OF AESTHETICS

In Greene's *A Quip for an Upstart Courtier* (1592) there is a dialogue between a courtier ('Velvet breeches') and a common man ('Cloth breeches') by which the author discusses 'the disorders in all estates and trades.' At the end of the book a trial is organized and one member of each profession[32] is selected as a juror, but one more is needed. Since the arts have not been represented, conveniently a poet, actor and musician come walking along and the discussion relative to which of these might serve as the additional juror provides some insight on the general reputation of these professions.

> As they came near, I discerned the first to be a Poet, the second an Actor, the third a Musician, alias the usher of a dancing school. Well met Master Poet, quoth I, and welcome your friends also, though not so particularly known. So it is, thought none of you three be common wealthsmen, yet from urgent necessity we must be forced to employ you. We have a Jury to be empanelled immediately, which one of you three must help to make up, whichever proves himself the honest man. They are all honest men and goodfellow quoth Velvet breeches, therefore it is no great matter which of them we choose.
>
> The [professors] doubt that, quoth Cloth breeches, for I am of a different opinion. The first, whom by his careless slovenly walk, at first sight I imagined to be a Poet, is a waste good and an unthrift, that he is born to make the taverns rich and himself a beggar: if he have forty pounds in his purse together, he puts it not to usury, neither buys land nor merchandise with it, but a month's supply of wenches and Capons ... He is a king of his pleasure, and counts all others boors and peasants, because although they have money at command they know not, like him, how to domineer with it to any purpose as they should. But to speak plainly, I think him an honest man if he would but live within his compass, and generally is no man's foe but his own. Therefore I hold him a man fit to be on my jury.
>
> Nay, quoth Velvet breeches, I am more inclined to the other two, for this Poet is a proud fellow, and because he has a little wit in his budget will condemn and mislike us that are the common sort of Gentlemen, and think we are beholding to him if he but bestow a fair look upon us. The Actor and the usher of the dancing school are plain, honest, humble men, that for a penny or a cast off piece of clothing will do anything. Indeed quoth Cloth breeches, what you say is true, they are but too humble, for they be so lowly, that they are base minded: I mean not in their looks or apparel, for so they be Peacocks and painted asses, but in the court of life, for they care not how they get money, I mean how basely so they have them, and yet of the two I hold the Actor to be the better Christian, although in his own imagination too full of self liking and self love, and is unfit to be on the Jury ... I must say, that such a plain country fellow as myself, they bring in as clowns and fools to laugh at in their play, whereas they get by us, and for our alms the proudest of them all doth live. Well, to be brief, let him trot to the stage, for he shall be none of the Jury.
>
> And as for you master Usher of the dancing school, you are a leader of all misrule, you instruct Gentlemen to order their feet, while you drive them to misorder their manners, you are a bad

---

32 The order in which the professions are given is apparently intended to reflect the order of the social status of these professions (the arts, not being among the 'common wealthsmen,' are missing). They are in this order: knight, esquire, gentleman, priest, printer, grocer, skinner, dyer, pewterer, saddler, joiner, bricklayer, cutler, plasterer, sailor, ropemaker, smith, glover, husbandman, shepherd, waterman, waterbearer and bellowsmender.

fellow that stands on your tricks and capers, till you make young Gentlemen caper without their lands: why sir to be flat with you: you live by your legs, as a juggler by his hands, you are given over to the pomps and vanities of the world, and to be short, you are a keeper of misrule and a lewd fellow, and you shall be none of the quest ... You are both agreed that the Poet is he that must be the twenty-fourth member of the Jury. They answered both, he, and none but he.[33]

The only interesting comment we find in this literature on the general aesthetic definition of Beauty is found in John Lyly's *Euphues and his England*. He makes the case that Beauty is associated only with the eye. 'Love,' he says, 'comes by the eye, not by the ear: by seeing nature's works, not by hearing women's words.' Thus, we get more pleasure by looking at beautiful pictures, than by eating any meat or hearing any music.[34]

The aesthetic question regarding whether Art should imitate Nature is also rarely mentioned in the works of fiction. Robert Greene in his romance, *Morando*, has a character praise a painter for 'his perfect skill that had so cunningly made a counterfeit of Nature by art.'[35]

ON POETRY

Thomas Nashe, in his preface, 'To the Gentlemen Students,' for Robert Greene's pastoral romance, *Menaphon* (1589) reflects on the decline of poetry in England.

> I will persecute those idiots and their heirs unto the third generation, that have made Art bankrupt of her ornaments, and sent Poetry a begging up and down the Country.[36]

In another place, Nashe seems particularly critical of contemporary epic poetry, poetry which praises the deeds of the great, which had been a very high form of poetry in ancient Greece.

> What political counselor or valiant soldier will find joy or glory of this, that some stitcher, weaver, spendthrift, or fiddler, hath shuffled or slobbered up a few ragged rhymes, in the memory of one's prudence or prowess?[37]

For Nashe, poetry should be more like its reputation in ancient Greece, something akin to philosophy.

> But least I should be mistaken as an enemy to Poetry, or at least not taken as a friend to that study, I have thought it good to make them privy to my mind, by expressing my meaning. I

---

33 Robert Greene, *A Quip for an Upstart Courtier* (1592), in *The Life and Complete Works of Robert Greene*, XI, 291ff.
34 Lyly, *Euphues and his England*, III, 10, contends that when a man decides to be married, he should judge by the ear, and not the eye—meaning on the basis of recommendations.
35 Greene, in *Morando* (1587), I, in *The Life and Complete Works of Robert Greene*, III, 57.
36 Thomas Nashe, 'To the Gentlemen Students,' (1589), in *The Life and Complete Works of Robert Greene*, VI, 27.
37 Thomas Nashe, *The Anatomie of Absurditie* (1589), in *The Works of Thomas Nashe*, I, 24.

account Poetry, as of a more hidden and divine kind of Philosophy, enwrapped in blind Fables and dark stories, wherein the principles of more excellent Arts and moral precepts of manners, illustrated with diverse examples of other kingdoms and countries, are contained: for among the Greeks there were Poets before there were Philosophers, who embraced entirely the study of wisdom ... Poets are most ancient, who to the intent they might allure men with a greater longing for learning, have followed two things, sweetness of verse, and variety of invention, knowing that delight pricks men forward to the attaining of knowledge ... Wherefore seeing Poetry is the very same with Philosophy, the fables of Poets must of necessity be fraught with wisdom and knowledge, as framed by those men who have spent all their time and studies in the one and in the other.[38]

In his *Supplication to the Devil*, Nashe argues for a more favorable attitude toward poetry in general.[39]

> Nor is poetry an art whereof there is no use in a man's whole life, but to describe discontented thoughts and youthful desires: for there is no study which it does not illustrate and beautify.

He also attributes to poetry the raising of the English language from 'barbarism.'

The Medieval Church had long considered poets as liars, because they dwelt in fables, as Nashe has mentioned above. Robert Greene, in *Mamillia*, repeats this criticism and adds painters.

> Prattling Poets I call those who having authority with Painters to faine, lie, and dissemble, seek with *Syrens* songs and enchanting charms of devilish invention, to bewitch the minds of young and tender virgins, under the color of love to draw them to lust, painting out in Songs and Sonnets their great affection, and deciphering in fained rhymes their forged fancy ...[40]

On the Theater

Thomas Nashe saw the actor as someone who was never happy. First because he generally played characters who were socially so much higher than himself, and second because usually they are 'painting forth other mens' imperfections.'[41] His chief criticism of the theater itself was that it failed to seek out new ideas for plots.

> Even as Vultures slay nothing themselves, but prey on that which others have slain, so these [playwrights] inveigh against no new vice, which heretofore by the censures of the learned hath

---

38   Ibid., 25ff.
39   Thomas Nashe, in his *Pierce Penilesse His Supplication to the Devil* (1592), in Ibid., I, 192ff.
40   Robert Greene, *Mamillia* (1583–1593), in *The Life and Complete Works of Robert Greene*, II, 258.
41   Thomas Nashe, *The Anatomie of Absurditie* (1589), in *The Works of Thomas Nashe*, I, 20.

not been sharply condemned, but tear that piecemeal which long since by ancient writers was wounded to the death ... Good God, that those that never tasted of anything save the excrements of Arts, whose threadbare knowledge is bought second hand, is spotted, blemished, and defaced through translators rigorous rude dealing, should prefer their fluttered suits before other mens' glittering gorgeous array, should offer them water out of a muddy pit, who have continually recourse to the Fountain, or dregs to drink, who have wine to sell.[42]

Apart from this criticism, in his *Supplication to the Devil*, Nashe points to the positive educational benefits of the theater. We remind the reader that in sixteenth-century London plays were given at three o'clock in the afternoon.

For whereas the afternoon is the idlest time of the day; wherein men that are their own masters (as Gentlemen of the Court, [lawyers], and the number of Captains and Soldiers about London) do wholly devote themselves to pleasure, and that pleasure they divide among gaming, harlots, drinking or seeing a Play: is it not then better (since, of the four extremes, all the world cannot keep them from choosing one) that they should betake themselves to the least [harmful], which is Plays? Nay, what if I prove Plays to be no extreme; but a rare exercise of virtue? First, the subject of them, for the most part, is borrowed out of our English Chronicles, wherein our forefathers valiant acts (that have long been buried in rusty brass and worm-eaten books) are revived ...[43]

Of even more educational value, he suggests, are plays which illuminate contemporary ills.

They show the ill success of treason, the fall of hasty climbers, the wretched end of usurpers, the misery of civil dissension, and how just God is evermore in punishing murders ... They are sour pills of reprehension, wrapped up in sweet words.

Finally, Robert Greene, attributes the public response to poets and painters to unpredictable Fortune.

The Poets and Painters were not untruthful when they called fortune blind, without good cause, and great reason: for as her gifts are uncertain: so the lot is doubtful, and the chance unlooked for, most often happeneth: she imparteth wealth to the fool and poverty to the wise ...[44]

---

42 Ibid., 20ff.
43 Thomas Nashe, in *Pierce Penilesse His Supplication to the Devil* (1592), in *The Works of Thomas Nashe*, I, 212ff.
44 Robert Greene, *Mamillia*, in *The Life and Complete Works of Robert Greene*, II, 78.

ON THE AESTHETICS OF MUSIC

We find a nice testimonial to the importance of music in Robert Greene's *The Debate Between Folly and Love* (1584–1588). Here, Apollo says,

> Shall I say that Music was only invented by love? yea, truly, for either it mitigates the passions by which men are perplexed, or else augments their pleasure, so that daily they invent diverse kinds of instruments, such as lutes, citrons, viols, flutes, cornetts, bandoras, whereon they play madrigals, sonnets, pavanes, measures, galliardes, and all these in remembrance of Love, for whom men do more than for one another.[45]

By 'Music' here, Apollo clearly meant music of a higher aesthetic, for he mentions, and does not appreciate, the lower forms associated with the pursuit of love.

> And I greatly fear that whereas Love has invented so many laudable sciences, and brought forth so many commodities, that now he will bring great idleness, accompanied with ignorance, that he will cause young Gentlemen to leave feats of arms, to forsake the service of their Prince, to reject honorable studies, and to apply themselves to vain songs and Sonnets, to chambering and wantonness, to banqueting and gluttony, bringing infinite diseases to their bodies, and sundry dangers and perils to their persons: for there is no more dangerous company than Folly.

It is also interesting to read, when Mercury speaks next, of the professions which are associated with Folly.

> How many arts and occupations should be driven out of the world if Folly were banished? Truly the most part of men should either beg for want, or die for hunger? How should so many lawyers, procurators, sergeants, scriveners, embroiderers, painters and perfumers live, if Lady Folly were utterly exiled? Hath not Folly invented a thousand devices to draw a man from idleness, such as tragedies, comedies, dancing schools, fencing houses, wrestling places and a thousand other foolish sports?

On the other hand, in Greene's dedication to Robert Dudley of his *Planetomachia* (1585), a treatise on astrology, he provides a rationale for why man sometimes might prefer inferior entertainments.

> Honor oftentimes hath her eye soon delighted with the sight of a crooked table, as with the view of a curious picture: and as well could Timolus laugh at the homely Music of Pan, as wonder at the heavenly melody of Apollo. The mind wearied with weighty affairs, seeketh soon to be recreated with some pithy concepts, as with any deep contemplations: and rather with sleight devises to procure mirth, than with solemn shows to softer melancholy.[46]

---

[45] Robert Greene, 'The Debate Between Folly and Love,' in Ibid., IV, 212ff.

[46] Robert Greene, in *Planetomachia* (1585), in Ibid., V, 5ff. In his description of the constellation, Orpheus, he misinterprets the Greek myth [Ibid., 20]. He attributes to the astrological influence of Saturn, success in the arts and sciences [Ibid., 46].

Thomas Nashe found the general public to be rather undiscerning with regard to musical taste.

> So senseless, so wavering is the light unconstant multitude, that they will dance after every man's pipe; and sooner prefer a blind harpist that can squeak out a new horn-pipe, than *Alcinous* or *Apollo's* variety, that imitates the right strains of the Dorian melody.[47]

A similar remark of condescension toward the lower classes was made by Sir Philip Sidney. In his *The Countesse of Pembrokes Arcadia*, to describe a person not paying attention to someone talking, he writes that she pays no more attention than 'a tedious talkative cobbler when hearing delightful music'[48]

We find it interesting that Nashe believed that artists were poorly paid due, in large part, to the fact that they themselves did not properly value their art.

> All Artists for the most part are base minded and like the *Indians*, that have store of gold and precious stones at command, yet are ignorant of their value and therefore let the Spaniards, the Englishmen and everyone load their ships with them without molestation …
>
> I know him that had thanks for three year's work, and a gentleman that bestowed much cost in refining of music, and had scarce a fiddlers wages for his labor.[49]

In another book, Nashe adds the character fault of vain-glory to musicians.

> Many excellent Musicians, oddly, are fantastically vain-glorious.[50]

Robert Greene, in his romance *Mamillia*, expresses an objection to music often found in earlier literature, namely that it does not exist except for the duration of the performance. Here, in discussing the mixed qualities of fine things, such as 'the finest glass is the most brittle,' he notes,

> Music is most strong in favor, yet endureth but a small time.[51]

It is in the context of this ancient prejudice, that we can understand a comment by Nashe, in the Prologue of his *Have with You to Saffron-Walden* (1596). In a comment intended to be humorous, assuming that everyone knows it is *not* true, he mentions a person whom he says has,

---

47 Nashe, in his *Pierce Penilesse His Supplication to the Devil* (1592), in *The Works of Thomas Nashe*, I, 225.
48 Sir Philip Sidney, *The Countesse of Pembrokes Arcadia*, I, Book III, v.
49 Nashe, in his *Pierce Penilesse His Supplication to the Devil* (1592), in *The Works of Thomas Nashe*, I, 242.
50 Nashe, in his *Christ's Teares over Jerusalem* (1593), in Ibid., II, 109.
51 Robert Greene, *Mamillia*, in *The Life and Complete Works of Robert Greene*, II, 41.

a perfect unchangeable true habit of honesty, imitating the Art of Music, which the Professors thereof affirm to be infinite and without end.[52]

There is relatively little discussion in this literature of the purposes of music. We find the traditional purpose to soothe in a singer who takes up a harp, in Sidney's *The Countesse of Pembrokes Arcadia*, 'to mollify them as the nature of Music is to do.'[53]

The most universally understood purpose of music is to communicate feelings. One character in Green's *Perimedes* is surprised by the emotional power of her own music. She calls for a lute,

> whereupon singing a mere galliard, the thought to beguile such unacquainted passions, but instead finding that music was like trying quench the flame with oil: feeling the assaults to be so sharp as her mind was ready to yield as vanquished: she began with diverse considerations to suppress the frantic affections …[54]

An important purpose of music in this rather light natured literature is to woo the ladies, as we see in Robert Greene's romance, *Morando*.

> Some practice music to inveigle their minds, playing in the night under their windows, with lutes, *cithrens* and bandoras … Some paint out their passions in songs and sonnets, to move them unto mercy.[55]

A similar passage is found in Greene's *Farewell to Folly*, although here he is describing evil designs, which he associates with Florentine men.

> Some by Music to inveigle the mind with melody, not sparing to spend part of the night under his mistress' window, by such pains to procure her dishonor and his own misfortune … They apply their wits and wiles to work their own woe, penning down ditties, songs, sonnets, madrigals, and such like, shadowed over with the pencil of flattery, where from the fictions of poets they fetch the type and figure of their feigned affection.[56]

---

[52] Thomas Nashe, *Have with You to Saffron-Waldenl* (1596), III, 22.
[53] Sir Philip Sidney, *The Countesse of Pembrokes Arcadia*, Book II, iii.
[54] Robert Greene, *Perimedes* (1588), in *The Life and Complete Works of Robert Greene*, VII, 33.
[55] Robert Greene, in *Morando* (1587), I, in Ibid., III, 106ff.
[56] Robert Greene, *Farewell to Folly* (1591), in Ibid., IX, 291ff.

On Performance Practice

In the works of the sixteenth-century English fiction writers one finds many internal songs. Below we will consider how these songs function with respect to purpose, but here we should like to mention some of the reflections found regarding the contemporary performance practice.

In Sidney's *The Countesse of Pembrokes Arcadia* a singer sings an echo song, producing both parts by the following technique.

> Which he in part to satisfy, began an Eclogue between himself and the *Echo*: framing his voice in those deserte places, as what words he would have the *Echo* reply, unto those he would sing higher than the rest, and so kindly framed a disputation between himself and it.[57]

In Robert Greene's pastoral romance, *Menaphon*, where the text of Menaphon's song is given, we are told that he played something on his pipe between every stanza of the poem, since he could not, of course, play and sing at the same time.[58] The performance of another song by Menaphon is preceded by a prelude on his pipe.[59]

In Thomas Lodge's *Euphues' Shadowe* the description of another song within a romance is interesting with respect to performance practice. In this case, musicians first performed an instrumental version of a madrigal. At its conclusion one of the guests extemporized a madrigal poem to the melody which had just been performed.[60]

In another romance by Lodge, his *Forbonius and Priscaria*, there is a description of a singer who apparently employed considerable body motion while singing. The song itself is described as a 'mournful melody' and we are told he made his lute 'tunable to the strains of his voice.' His listener, however, responded to 'his manifold sighs, aspects, and motions, whereunto he applied his actions …'[61]

As the most universally understood characteristic of music is the communication of feelings, we sometimes find in this literature the criticism of a musician who does not appropriately convey feeling in his performance. Such an example is found in Greene's *Metamorphosis*, where Morpheus is deeply depressed by love. He takes his lute to play 'certain melancholy dumps' and some ladies stand quietly behind him 'to hear what humor the man was in' and heard him sing this 'mournful madrigal.'

> *Rest thee desire, gaze not at such a Star,*
> *Sweet fancy sleep, love take a nap awhile …*

---

[57] Sir Philip Sidney, *The Countesse of Pembrokes Arcadia*, I, Book II, xxix.

[58] Robert Greene, *Menaphon* (1589), in *The Life and Complete Works of Robert Greene*, VI, 40.

[59] Ibid., 59.

[60] Thomas Lodge, *Euphues' Shadowe, The Battle of the Senses* (1592), in *The Complete Works of Thomas Lodge*, Op. cit., II, 22.

[61] Thomas Lodge, *The Delectable History of Forbonius and Priscaria* (London: Shakespeare Society, 1853), 85ff.

But Marpesia, of whom he was singing, 'drew him abruptly from his passions,' criticizing him as follows,

> ... for Phidias ... playing on his pipe, and yet tears dropping from his eyes, as mixing his greatest melody with passions: but I see the comparison will not hold in you, for though your instrument is answerable to his, yet you lack his lukewarm drops, which show, though your music be as good, yet your thoughts are not so passionate ...[62]

We find another criticism of a musician in Sidney's *The Countesse of Pembrokes Arcadia*, where a singer accompanies himself on the Gitterne. We are told he 'ill-played' the instrument and sang in a hoarse voice, with the total impression being 'ill-noised song.'[63] In Greene's preface to his *Ciceronis Amor* (1589), to describe his difficulty in finding the right words he uses an analogy of music which suggests he had heard performances by poor readers.

> If my method be worse then it was wont to be, think that skill in music marde all, For the clef was so dissonant to my note, that we could not put a concord together by fine mark.[64]

Finally, we should mention that Thomas Nashe, in his famous *The Unfortunate Traveller*, claims to have visited an estate in Rome where instead of water spouts in the garden, they had 'great wind instruments ... that went duly in consort, only with this water's rumbling descent.'[65] There was also a banquet house with a mechanical illustration of the so-called 'Music of the Spheres.'

> The heaven was a clear overhanging vault of crystal, wherein the Sun and Moon and each visible Star had his true similitude, shine, situation, and motion, and, by what enwrapped art I cannot conceive, these spheres in their proper orbits observed a kind of soft angelical murmuring music in their often windings and going about; which music the philosophers say in the true heaven, by reason of the grossness of our senses, we are not capable of hearing.

A similar water powered device is mentioned in Sidney's *The Countesse of Pembrokes Arcadia*.

> There were birds also made so finely, that they did not only deceive the sight with their figures, but the hearing with their songs; which the water instruments did make their gorge deliver.[66]

We have mentioned in several places that the consort principle was so universally accepted during the sixteenth century that one even finds references to hunting dogs being organized

---

62 Robert Greene, *Metamorphosis* (1588–1591), in *The Life and Complete Works of Robert Greene*, IX, 98ff.
63 Sir Philip Sidney, *The Countesse of Pembrokes Arcadia*, I, Book II, xxviii.
64 Robert Greene, *Ciceronis Amor* (1589), in *The Life and Complete Works of Robert Greene*, VII, 102.
65 Nashe, in *The Unfortunate Traveller* (1594), in *The Works of Thomas Nashe*, II, 282ff.
66 Sir Philip Sidney, *The Countesse of Pembrokes Arcadia*, I, Book I, xiv.

into consorts corresponding to their voices. Indeed one Englishman recommends this as necessary for the best equipped household!

> If you would have your kennels for sweetness of cry then you must compound it of some large dogs that have deep, solemn mouths ... which must as it were bear the bass in consort, then a double number of roaring and loud-ringing mouths which must bear the counter tenor, then some hollow, plain, sweet mouths which must bear the mean or middle part and so with these three parts of music you shall make your cry perfect.[67]

This must be the only explanation of a comment about hunting dogs in Sidney's *The Countesse of Pembrokes Arcadia*.

> Their cry being composed of so well sorted mouths, that any man would perceive therein some kind of proportion, but the skillful woodsmen did find a music.[68]

We will find similar references to these 'tuned' dogs in the stage plays, including one by Shakespeare in *A Midsummer Night's Dream*!

ART MUSIC

The most beautiful and vivid description of the performance of Art Music in sixteenth-century English fiction is found in Sir Philip Sidney's *The Countesse of Pembrokes Arcadia*. Here we have the very essence of Art Music, with a high quality of music ('for the glory of music'), it is expressing the feelings of the player and is heard by a contemplative listener ('to unpossessed minds of attention').

> The music was of cornetts, whereof one answering the other, with a sweet emulation, striving for the glory of music, and striking upon the smooth face of the quiet lake, was then delivered up to the castle walls, which with a proud reverberation, spreading it into the air; it seemed before the harmony came to the ear, that it had enriched itself in its travel, the nature of those places adding melody to that melodious instrument. And when a while that instrument had made a brave proclamation to all unpossessed minds of attention, an excellent consort followed immediately of five viols, and as many voices; which all being but orators of their master's passions, bestowed this song upon her, that thought upon another matter.[69]

As we have mentioned above, there are numerous internal songs, for which the words, but not the music is given, in this literature. They exist in a broad variety of purpose and style.

---

67 Quoted in Elizabeth Burton, *The Pageant of Elisabethan England* (New York: Scribner's), 190.
68 Sir Philip Sidney, *The Countesse of Pembrokes Arcadia*, I, Book I, x.
69 Ibid., I, Book III, xv.

Sometimes they are to allow a character the opportunity to discover his own feelings, as in Sidney's *The Countesse of Pembrokes Arcadia*, where we find,

> Then she remembered this song, which she thought took a right measure of her present mind.[70]

> Often, of course, these are songs of love. In this same romance, an unnamed 'fellow' sings a song praising Mopsa, calling on all the Greek gods. We are told the singer knows this song from memory.

> These verses are these, which I have so often caused to be sung, that I have them without book.[71]

Another singer reflects on his own emotions, in Robert Greene's pastoral romance, *Menaphon*, where a shepherd sings,

> Tune on my pipe the praises of my Love,
> And midst the oaten harmony recount
> How fair she is that makes thy music mount,
> And every string of thy heart's harp to move.[72]

And in Sidney's *The Countesse of Pembrokes Arcadia*, an older person is by love 'renewed both in his invention, and voice.' He sings,

> Let not old age disgrace my high desire,
> O heavenly soul, in human shape contained:
> Old wood inflam'd, doth yield the bravest fire,
> When younger dooth in smoke his virtue spend.[73]

Often, of course, the purpose of the song is to soothe the feelings of the listener or the performer. In Robert Green's *Arbasto: The Anatomy of Fortune*, a lady sings to soothe her own feelings.

> And with that she sat still as one in a trance, building castles in the air, hanging between fear and hope, trust and despair, doubt and assurance: to rid herself therefore from these dumpes, she took her lute, whereupon she played this dittie.

---

70 Ibid., I, Book II, xxv.

71 Ibid., I, Book I, iii. A 'joyful' song in praise of Pan is found in Book I, xix, and an Hymn to Apollo in Book II, xxviii.

72 Robert Greene, *Menaphon* (1589), in *The Life and Complete Works of Robert Greene*, VI, 83. In the romance, Philomela, a lady sits in the garden and with her lute sings 'many pretty Rondelaies, Borginets, Madrigals, and such pleasant lessons … some of which were of her own composing.' [Ibid., XI, 122ff.] Additional love songs are found in *Ciceronis Amor* (1589), Ibid., VII, 133, 136.

In Sir Philip Sidney, *The Countesse of Pembrokes Arcadia*, I, Book I, xii, we read of the listener 'The dittie gave him some suspicion, but the voice gave him almost assurance, who the singer was.'

73 Sir Philip Sidney, *The Countesse of Pembrokes Arcadia*, I, Book II, i. In Ibid., Book II, xvi, a young lady sings a love song with a 'sweet voice.'

> In time we see that silver drops
> The craggy stones make soft:
> The slowest snail in time, we see,
>
> Doth creep and clime aloft
> With feeble puffs the tallest pine
> In tract of time doth fall:
> The hardest heart in time doth yield
> To Venus luring call.[74]

An unusual reference to a singer seeking solace for himself is found in Greene's pastoral romance, *Menaphon*, where a character is described as 'sometimes lying comfortless on his bed, he would complain to the winds of his woes [in song].'[75]

In Sidney's *The Countesse of Pembrokes Arcadia*, a listener approaches a singer, hoping to find solace.

> But (as a lamentable tune is the sweetest music to a woeful mind) she drew near, in hope to find some companion of her misery.[76]

We are not told if the listener indeed found solace, but the singer certainly found none in his own song.

> For the woeful person (as if the lute had evil joined with the voice) threw it to the ground with such like words: Alas, poor Lute, how much art thou deceived to think, that in my miseries thou could ease my woes, as in my careless times thou was wont to please my fancies? The time is changed, my Lute, the time is changed; and no more did my joyful mind then receive everything in a joyful consideration, then my careful mind now makes each thing taste like bitter juice of care. The evil is inward, my Lute, the evil is inward; which all thou doost doth serve but to make me think more freely of, and the more I think, the more cause I find of thinking, but less of hoping. And alas, what is then thy harmony, but the sweet meats of sorrow? The discord of my thoughts, my Lute, doth ill agree to the concord of thy strings …

A character in Greene's *Never Too Late* sings a song, based on poetry of Ariosto, not to soothe herself exactly, but to clear her mind of thoughts, 'to shake off all fancies.'[77]

---

[74] Robert Greene, in *Arbasto: The Anatomy of Fortune* (1584), in *The Life and Complete Works of Robert Greene*, III, 247ff. A madrigal sung to soothe a character is found in Greene's *Penelopes Web* (1587), in Ibid., V, 179ff., 'pleasant lessons' are sung with lute in *Philomela* [Ibid., XI, 177ff.] and instrumental versions of sonnets for the same purpose in his *Menaphon* [Ibid., VI, 68.

[75] Robert Greene, *Menaphon* (1589), in Ibid., VI, 102ff.

[76] Sir Philip Sidney, *The Countesse of Pembrokes Arcadia*, I, Book II, i. In Book III, vi, a serenade is given outside a lady's window with music designed first to cause her to think of sorrow and then to 'think of it with sweetness.'

[77] Greene, *Never too Late* (1590), in *The Life and Complete Works of Robert Greene*, VIII, 96.

There are also in this literature some remarkable examples of songs which deal with more somber emotions. An internal song in Sidney's *The Countesse of Pembrokes Arcadia* is introduced by the description of a character whose eyes are 'thrown down to the ground, as if the earth could not bear the burdens of his sorrows; at length, with a lamentable tune, he sang.'[78] When he finished singing, 'he struck himself on the breast.'

In Robert Greene's *Arbasto: The Anatomy of Fortune* a man looks at a painting and smiles, then casts it aside and 'taking his lute, played a dumpe, whereunto he warbled out these words,'

> She whose delights are signs of Death,
> Who when she smiles begins to lower:
> Constant in this that still she change,
> Her sweetest gifts time proves but sour:
> I live in care, crossed with her guile,
> Through her I weep, at her I smile.

The old Sire having with sighs sobbed out this sorrowful dittie, I was driven into a maze what the contrary contents of these verses should mean …[79]

A somber hymn, with 'solemn harmony of Music,' is found in Thomas Lodge's *The History of Robert, Second Duke of Normandy*.

> When wasteful wars (fruits of afflicting time)
> Have left our soul devoid of all suspense …[80]

A remarkable example of this darker kind of song is found in Sidney's *The Countesse of Pembrokes Arcadia*. Here, while other shepherds have been singing joyfully and dancing, one young shepherd,

> who neither danced nor sung with the others, but laid all this while upon the ground at the foot of a cypress tree, in so deep a melancholy, as though his mind were banished from the place he loved, to be in prison in his body.

The others beg him to sing, but he begs they pardon him, 'the time being far too joyful to suffer the rehearsal of his miseries.' Nevertheless, eventually he sings.

---

78 Sir Philip Sidney, *The Countesse of Pembrokes Arcadia*, I, Book I, xviii.

79 Robert Greene, in *Arbasto: The Anatomy of Fortune* (1584), in *The Life and Complete Works of Robert Greene*, III, 180ff. A similar song, 'full of melancholy dumps' is found in Greene's *Perimedes*, Ibid., VII, 76ff and another in 79ff. The latter begins,

> Obscure and dark is all the gloomy air,
> The curtain of the night is overspread …

80 Thomas Lodge, *The History of Robert, Second Duke of Normandy*, in *The Complete Works of Thomas Lodge*, II, 68. In Lodge's *The Life and Death of William Long Beard*, Ibid., II, 36, there are texts for three funeral hymns and songs.

> The song I sing old Lanquet had me taught,
> Lanquet, the shepherd best swift Ister knew,
> For clerky reed, and hating what is naught,
> For faithful heart, clean hands, and mouth as true:
> With his sweet skill my unskillful youth he drew,
> To have a feeling taste of him that sits
> Beyond the heaven, far more beyond your wits.
> He said, the Music best thilke powers pleased
> Was jump concord between our wit and will:
> When highest notes to godliness are raised,
> And lowest sinks not down to jote of ill ...

The mixed reaction of the listeners is also interesting.

> According to the nature of diverse ears, diverse judgments straight followed: some praising his voice, others his words fit to frame a pastoral style, others the strangeness of the tale, and scanning what he should mean by it ... But little did the melancholy shepherd regard either his dispraises, or the others' praises ...[81]

In another scene in this same pastoral romance Zelmane, 'whose heart better delighted in woeful ditties, as more according to her fortune,' desires a song. The singer, Lamon, 'with great cunning, varying his voice according to the diversity of the person' began a *Dizaine*. The listeners,

> were stricken in silent consideration; indeed everyone marking, that he heard of another the balance of his own troubles.[82]

We should also note, in this same pastoral, the soliloquy of a man about to die.

> Unhappy eyes, you have seen too much, that ever the light should be welcome to you: unhappy ears, you shall never hear the music of Music in her voice ... Thou hast done thy worst, World ... Exiled Beauty, let only now thy beauty be blubbered faces. Widowed Music, let now thy tunes be roarings and lamentations.[83]

Occasionally there is a song performed while dancing. In Thomas Lodge's *Euphues' Shadowe* (1592), at the conclusion of a banquet, 'the dinner done, and table taken up,' there is music and dancing. First the Gentlemen danced their *Courranto*, after which Philamis commands the cornetts to begin playing a *Barginet*, to which he sings while dancing with Eurinome.[84]

---

81 Sir Philip Sidney, *The Countesse of Pembrokes Arcadia*, I, Book I, xix.
82 Ibid., Book II, xxix.
83 Ibid., Book III, xxii. A song of lamentation is given in Book III, xxv.
84 Thomas Lodge, *Euphues' Shadowe, The Battle of the Senses* (1592), in *The Complete Works of Thomas Lodge*, II, 20ff.

Far more rare is the playing of instruments while dancing, as we find described in this passage from Sidney's *The Countesse of Pembrokes Arcadia*.

> The first sports the shepherds showed were full of such leaps and gambols, as being accorded to the pipe (which they held in their mouths, even as they danced) made a right picture of their chief god Pan, and his companions the Satyrs. Then would they cast away their pipes; and holding hand in hand, dance as it were in a brawl, by only the cadence of their voices, which they would use in singing some short couplets, whereto the one half beginning, the other half should answer. As the one half saying,
> *We love, and have our loves rewarded.*
>
> The others would answer.
> *We love, and are no whit regarded.*
>
> The first again.
> *We find most sweet affections snare,*
>
> With like tune it should be as in choir sent back again.
> *That sweet, but sour despairful care.*
>
> A third time likewise thus:
> *Who can despair, whom hope doth bear?*
>
> The answer.
> *And who can hope, that feels despair?*
>
> Then all joining their voices, and dancing to a faster beat, they would conclude with some such words:
>
> *As without breath, no pipe doth move,*
> *No music kindly without love.*[85]

Sometimes ensembles of instruments join in. In Philip Sidney's *The Lady of May*, as two singers begin to sing they are joined by two groups of instrumentalists.

> But Espilus as if he had been inspired by the Muses, began to sing, whereto his fellow shepherds set in with their recorders, which they bore in bags like pipes, and so of Therions side did the foresters, with the cornetts they wore about their necks like hunting horns.
>
>   *Espilus.*
> Tune up my voice, a higher note I yield,
> Too high concepts the song must needs be high …

---

[85] Sir Philip Sidney, *The Countesse of Pembrokes Arcadia*, I, Book I, xix, first Eclogue.

> *Therion.*
> The highest note comes often from the basest mind,
> As shallow brooks do yield the greatest sound …[86]

At the conclusion of this performance the shepherds and foresters fall into 'great contention' regarding the relative merits of the singers. At the end of the story, however, 'the shepherds and foresters made a full consort of their cornetts and recorders.'

A similar scene is found in *The Countesse of Pembrokes Arcadia*.

> The shepherds attending Philisides went among them and sang an eclogue; one of them answering another, while the other shepherds pulling out recorders (which possessed the place of pipes) accorded their music to the others' voice.[87]

Occasionally a rare and interesting form is mentioned with respect to these internal songs. In Sidney's *The Countesse of Pembrokes Arcadia*, one of the internal songs is described as a 'double Sestina' and includes the following lines,

> *Shamed I have myself in sight of mountains,*
> *And stop my ears, lest I grow mad with Music.*[88]

Sometimes the author is equally careful to emphasize the specific mood of the singer. One singer in Greene's *Never Too Late* is described as singing a Roundley in 'deep consideration of his former fortunes and present follies.'[89]

In Thomas Lodge's *Euphues' Golden Legacie*, a character sings a sonnet of love 'scornfully,'[90] and another sonnet is sung by a character which he made 'when he hath been deeply passionate.'[91]

In Sidney's *The Countesse of Pembrokes Arcadia* a shepherd indicates the purpose of his song is for a 'more large expressing of his passions.' He first plays the melody on his pipe, and then sings.[92] Later in this pastoral romance another singer is even more animated with emotion.

> Taking up the Lute, her wit began to be with a divine fury inspired; her voice would in so beloved an occasion second her wit; her hands accorded the Lute's music to the voice; her panting heart

---

86 Sir Philip Sidney, *The Lady of May*, in Ibid., II, 212.

87 Sir Philip Sidney, *The Countesse of Pembrokes Arcadia*, Ibid., I, Book II, xxi.

88 Ibid., I, Book I, xix.

89 Robert Greene, *Never too Late* (1590), in *The Life and Complete Works of Robert Greene*, VIII, 91. Another singer, in Part II, 'did meditate with himself' as he sang. [Ibid., 122.]

90 Thomas Lodge, *Euphues' Golden Legacie* (1590), in *The Complete Works of Thomas Lodge*, II, 102.

91 Ibid., 48. Another love song in this romance may be found in Ibid., 29 (a madrigal).

92 Sir Philip Sidney, *The Countesse of Pembrokes Arcadia*, I, Book I, xix, Eclogue of Lalus and Dorus. Another singer [Ibid., Book II, ii] sings to a harp and in each verse 'I had broken in the midst with grievous sighs.'

danced to the music; while I think her feet did beat the time; while her body was the room where it should be celebrated; her soul the queen which should be delighted.[93]

In these volumes we have stressed that one of the important hallmarks of art music is the presence of the contemplative listener. In the case of some of these internal songs in sixteenth-century English fiction, the author is careful to call attention to the state of the listener. In Greene's *Never Too Late*, Francesco sings an Ode, accompanying himself on a Citterne, and those listening are described as 'silent auditors to his passions.'[94] Later, Francesco is the listener, while Infida takes her lute and with 'angelic harmony' sings a song. Here is Greene's description of the listener, Francesco.

> While thus Infida sang her song, Francesco sat, as if with Orpheus' melody he had been enchanted, having his eyes fixed on her face, and his ears attendant on her Music.[95]

Lodge, in his *The Life and Death of William Long Beard*, has the character Mirrha sing a 'woefull Lullabie,' but then emphasizes that 'the music of her voice forced them to listen to her.'[96] Another instance where we are told the music itself compelled people to listen is a curious scene in Sidney's *The Countesse of Pembrokes Arcadia*. Two noble ladies are in a lodge, which six female instrumentalists, in peasant attire, appear outside the door.

> Upon their hair they wore garlands of roses and gilliflowers ... Their breasts liberal to the eye ... Their countenances full of a graceful gravity; so as the gesture matched with the apparel, it might seem a wanton modesty, and an enticing soberness. Each of them had an instrument of music in their hands, which consorting their well-pleasing tunes, did charge each ear with insensibility, that did not lend itself unto them. The music entering alone into the lodge, the [noble] ladies were all desirous to see from whence so pleasant a guest was come.[97]

There are also some instances in this literature of an author pointing to a listener who is *not* in a contemplative frame of mind. Lodge, in his *Euphues' Shadowe*, describes the listeners at the conclusion of a song.

> Every one in the company was delighted with this dittie, only Harpaste counted all strings out of tune, since her heart strings were out of temper.[98]

---

93   Ibid., Book II, xi.

94   Greene, *Never too Late* (1590), in *The Life and Complete Works of Robert Greene*, VIII, 62.

95   Ibid., 77.

96   Thomas Lodge, *The Life and Death of William Long Beard* (1593), in *The Complete Works of Thomas Lodge*, II, 11.

97   Sir Philip Sidney, *The Countesse of Pembrokes Arcadia*, I, Book III, ii.

98   Thomas Lodge, *Euphues' Shadowe, The Battle of the Senses* (1592), in *The Complete Works of Thomas Lodge*, II, 23.

Another example is found in Sir Philip Sidney's *The Countesse of Pembrokes Arcadia*, when a man hires 'a fine boy' to sing a song with 'pretty dolefulness to it.' The listening lady, we are told, was polite, but 'otherwise unmoved.'[99]

FUNCTIONAL MUSIC

We find an example of genuine dinner music, as opposed to Art Music *after* the dinner, in Lodge's *Euphues Golden Legacie*. Here there is a scene in which we read, 'About mid dinner, to make them merry Coridon came in … and played them a fit of mirth, to which he sung this pleasant song.'

> *A blithe and bonnie country lass,*
>   *heigh ho the bonnie lass:*
> *Sat sighing on the tender grass,*
>   *and weeping said, will none come woo me?*[100]

A curious form of dinner music is mentioned in Greene's *Mourning Garment*, when shepherds,

> came in with their Timbrels and Cymbals, and played such melody, as the Country then required.[101]

Robert Greene warns young ladies against the dangers in dancing and of the accompanying music.

> Neither do I allow this wanton dancing in young virgins: tis more commendation for them to moderate their manners, than to measure their feet, and better to hear nothing than to listen unto unreverent Music.[102]

Music for a tournament is found in Sidney's pastoral *The Countesse of Pembrokes Arcadia*, where the trumpets announce the decision of the judges.[103]

In this same work we find an example of occupational music, where a shepherdess is knitting 'and singing, and it seemed that her voice comforted her hands to work and her hands kept time to her voice's music.'[104]

---

99 Sir Philip Sidney, *The Countesse of Pembrokes Arcadia*, I, Book III, ix.

100 Thomas Lodge, *Euphues' Golden Legacie* (1590), in *The Complete Works of Thomas Lodge*, II, 135ff. Another example of dinner music can be found in *Euphues, or The Anatomy of Wit*, Ibid., I, 199.

101 Robert Greene, *Mourning Garment* (ca. 1590), in *The Life and Complete Works of Robert Greene*, IX, 213.

102 Robert Greene, *A Disputation Between a He Conny-catcher and a Shee Conny-catcher* (1591), in *The Life and Complete Works of Robert Greene*, Ibid., X, 244.

103 Sir Philip Sidney, *The Countesse of Pembrokes Arcadia*, I, Book I, xvii. In Book III, xiii, a horse, trained to respond to the sound of the trumpet, upon hearing the instrument played leaped forward, causing the surprised rider to almost fall from the saddle.

104 Ibid., I, Book I, ii.

13 ELIZABETHAN PLAYWRIGHTS

AFTER THE GREAT REPERTOIRE of the ancient Greek and Roman playwrights more than one thousand years would pass before anything nearly comparable appears on the dramatic stage. No doubt some form of small civic dramas were acted out during the Dark Ages, but we know nothing of them and can only assume they lead to the late medieval plays sponsored by the Church and by the trade guilds. Real modern theater begins again in England with plays written for the university environment during the middle of the sixteenth century and with the erection of the first professional theater in London in 1576.

The great value in these late sixteenth-century plays for us lies in the fact that with the generation of Thomas Lodge, and particularly with Shakespeare in the following generation, it became an aesthetic principle in playwriting to attempt to make them lifelike—this as opposed to those plays which concerned themselves with Greek gods or allegorical figures. Therefore one finds a broad range of commentary in the dialog which reflects contemporary life. For example, we have cited above evidence to suggest that a change was taking place and it was becoming no longer appropriate for a noble to actually perform music. Thus, one notices in Christopher Marlowe's *Tamburlaine The Great*, Part II, when Tamburlaine returns to find his three sons have not been reared in the aristocratic pursuits of riding, fighting, etc., but rather in dance and lute playing, he says, 'Would make me think them bastards, not my sons.'[1]

There are many references to courtiers, of course, and one that caught our eye is found in Lyly's *Sapho and Phao*, where the question of the value of higher education is raised at the same time. Trachinus observes that in the university, the virtues are 'but shadowed in colors,' while in the court they are seen for what they are: good or bad.

What hath a scholar found out by study, that a courtier hath not found out by practice?[2]

And we have mentioned elsewhere, with respect to the prevailing preference for the consort principle, some indication that some nobles may have even organized their dogs in consorts,

---

1 Christopher Marlowe, *Tamburlaine the Great*, Part II, I, iii. Marlowe (1564–1593) was born into a prosperous family and was well acquainted with many important personages, including Sir Walter Raleigh. The most brilliant talent before Shakespeare, he was killed in a tavern in a fight over a mistress.

2 John Lyly, *Sapho and Phao* (1584), I, i. Lyly (1554-1606) graduated from Oxford in 1569 and aspired to reach a high position in court, although beyond serving in parliament he never reached his goal.

according to the range of their bark. Surely this can be the only explanation for the line in Lyly's *The Maydes Metamorphosis*, where a character says 'I can tune her with my hounds.'[3]

Finally, and most important with respect to the reflection of contemporary practices, where music is used in these plays, either as internal songs or descriptions of performance or as indicated by stage directions, we may be seeing a more accurate description of actual performance practice than might be reflected, for example, in poetry or in court documents, which are mostly concerned with pay notices. Most scholars would agree with Reese, when he observes of these musical references that 'it is quite evident that these were taken from contemporary real-life practices in Elizabethan England.'[4]

Before we look at the plays themselves, we should remind the reader that one attending one of these performances heard a great deal more music than that actually employed in the play. To begin with, performances in the sixteenth century began at three o'clock, with the sounding of a fanfare played three times by trumpets.[5] It was this tradition, of course, which explains the extended brass ensemble written by Monteverdi for the beginning of his *Orfeo*, and his accompanying note that it is to be played three times. In addition, there were brief musical performances between the acts to allow for scene changes. Unlike the better known Intermezzi of Italian comedies, these performances seem to have been unrelated to the play and probably had no underlying dramataic logic. According to one scholar of the Elizabethan stage,

> There was always music between the acts, and sometimes singing and dancing ... At the end the actors would entertain the audience by improvising to any melody the spectators might supply, or by performing what was called a jig, a farcical doggrel improvisation, accompanied by dancing and singing.[6]

As this author indicates, there appear to have been independent concerts performed for the audience after the play itself was completed. One illustration of the evidence for this is a travel diary of 1598 by a visiting German jurist, Paul Hentzner.

> Without the city are some Theaters where English actors represent almost every day tragedies and comedies to very numerous audiences; these are concluded with Music, variety of Dances and the excessive applause of those that are present.[7]

---

3   John Lyly, *The Maydes Metamorphosis*, I, i.

4   Gustave Reese, *Music in the Renaissance* (New York: Norton, 1959), 879.

5   George Peele, 'The Jest of George Peele at Bristow,' in 'The Jests of George Peele,' in A. H. Bullen, ed., *The Works of George Peele* (1888) (Port Washington: Kennikat Press, 1966), II, 390.

> By this time the audience were come, and some forty shillings gathered; which money George put in his purse, and putting on one of the players' silk robes, after the trumpet had sounded thrice, out he comes ...

6   Howard Staunton, *The Plays of Shakespeare* (London, 1858), quoted in Stephen Gosson, *The Schoole of Abuse* (1579), ed. Edward Arber (London, 1868), 80.

7   Quoted in Reese, *Music in the Renaissance*, 881.

On some occasions these affiliated concerts were held before the play, as we know from the diary of Philip, duke of Stettin-Pomerania, relative to his visit to London in 1602.

> For a whole hour before a delightful performance is given on organs, lutes, pandores, mandolines, viols and flutes; and a boy's singing *cum voce tremula* to a double bass so tunefully, that we have not heard the like of it on the whole journey, except perhaps the nuns of Milan did it better.[8]

Given the presence of all these musicians, it is no surprise that from the beginning the theaters had a separate room, below, above or behind the stage called the 'Music Room.' This room, of course, could also be used dramatically to represent heaven or hell, etc., but it was clearly used for the frequent references to off-stage music. Actors also used it when required to speak off-stage, as we see in a stage direction in Rowley's *Thracian Wonder* (1600).

> Pythia speaks in the Musick-room behinde the Curtains ...[9]

But who were these musicians? Simple fanfares may conceivably been played by the actors themselves, as well as the singing of the numerous songs found internally in the plays, but the more difficult instruments such as the shawm, not to mention the ensemble performances called for, would require professional musicians. The most accessible professional musicians would have been the members of the various civic bands (of which each district of London had one), known locally as 'Wait bands.' There is some extant documentation to suggest this was the case. A payment made by Trinity College, Cambridge, for 1552 reads, 'Item, given unto ye Wayttes upon our feast day when ye show was played called Anglia deformata.'[10] On one occasion in 1562, a Chelmsford dramatic production included not only the Bristol Waits, but forty other minstrels.[11] A civic document from 1567 in Newcastle, regarding the performance of a miracle play, lists payment 'to the waites for playeinge before the players.'[12] The Norwich Waits, in 1570, went to court to obtain the privilege of playing regularly in the theaters.

> The whole company of waytes of this Citie did come into this Court and craved that they might have leave to play comedies and Interludes and other such pieces and Tragedies which shall seem to them meete; which petition is granted, they not playing in the Tyme of Divine Service and Sermons.[13]

---

8 Craig Monson, 'Elizabethan London,' in *The Renaissance,* ed. Iain Fenlon (Englewood Cliffs: Prentice Hall, 1989), 326.
9 Quoted in Phyllis Hartnoll, *Shakespeare in Music* (London, 1964), 27.
10 Quoted in Reese, *Music in the Renaissance*, 878ff.
11 E. K. Chambers, *The Elizabethan Stage* (Oxford, 1923), II, 140.
12 Lyndesay Langwill, *The Waits* (Hindrichsen, 1952), 173.
13 J. Bridge, 'Town Waits and their Tunes,' in *Proceedings of the Musical Association* (London, 1927), 81.

And in London in 1601 we find the city magistrates complaining that prior commitments in the public theaters rendered the waits unavailable to perform their civic duties.[14]

The use of these 'extra' musicians, which is to say musicians who do not have dramatic roles in the actual play, can be seen already in the earliest English tragedy, *Gorboduc* (1570), by Thomas Sackville and Thomas Norton. Here, a brief 'Dumb Show' which sets the stage for each act. The stage direction before Act One reads,

> First the Music of Violenze begin to play, during which comes in upon the stage six wilde men clothed in feathers.

This choice of instrument reminds us that until mid-century the strings were amateur instruments at best and were often referred to as 'beer fiddlers' or pictured as peasants playing in the woods, etc. In contrast, the professional musicians played wind instruments and thus Act Two begins,

> First the Music of Cornetts begins to play, during which comes in upon the stage a king accompanied with a number of his nobility and gentlemen.

Act Three begins with 'Music of flutes' which accompanies the entrance of persons in mourning clothes. Act Four begins with the 'Music of oboes' [*Howboies*][15] which accompanies some allegorical 'furies.' And, finally, Act Five begins with soldiers coming on stage, introduced by this phrase,

> First the drums & flutes begin to sound …

They are the instruments we might expect, but we notice they are not called 'Music.'

Music in the Stage Directions

Before we consider the actual dialog of these plays, we must pay at least passing attention to the stage directions. While the dialog must be considered the playwright's main 'message,' the comments he sets in brackets, the stage directions, offer not only information on how music functioned in the theater but, as we have said, to some degree reflects musical practice in real life.

Certainly the stage direction calling for the sounding of a trumpet as a king enters the stage must have been a familiar occurance to members of the audience. Even though the *Gorboduc* example given above suggests that a broad range of associations were already part of common perception, in the generation of playwrights before Shakespeare only this one

---

14 Monson, 'Elizabethan London,' 327.

15 Sixteenth-century England used both the terms oboe and shawm, but so far as anyone knows the instrument in either case was a shawm.

musical metaphor, the association of the trumpet with the king, is consistently used.[16] Thus, in Robert Greene's *Alphonsus, King of Arragon*, when the king enters, the stage direction reads 'Sound Trumpets and Drums within.'[17] Similarly, in Lyly's *Campaspe*, Alexander the Great says, 'let the trumpet sound, strike up the drum, and I will presently leave for Persia.'[18]

The trumpet is also used for persons who function on a level as high as kings, but are not actually kings, as in Greene's *The History of Orlando Furioso* where a stage direction reads 'Enter the twelve Peers of France, with drum and trumpets.'[19] Lesser nobles, however, sometimes enter only to drums, as in Peele's *David and Bethsabe*, 'Enter Joab ... with drum.'[20]

Sometimes the stage directions offer information as to the type of music played. Perhaps the most frequently mentioned form is that of a popular song, the roundelay, as we see in Lyly's *The Woman in the Moone*,

[Exit Shepherds, singing a roundelay in praise of Nature][21]

Sometimes we see a familiar form mentioned, although in unexpected usage, as in George Peele's *The Arraignment of Paris*, where a stage direction requires 'Hereupon enter Nine Knights, in armor, treading a warlike *almain*, by drum and fife.'[22]

We read in the stage directions of forms whose precise musical nature is no longer known, although the general nature is clear from the circumstances in which we find it used, as in the case of a stage direction in Thomas Kyd's *Jeronimo* that calls for 'a dead march within.'[23] More frequent are stage directions referring to various signals of alarm, as in Greene's *The*

---

16 For example, 'Trumpets sound' for a king in Thomas Lodge and Robert Greene, *A Looking Glasse for London and England*, ed. George Glugston (New York: Garland Publishing, 1980), 150.

In the plays of Christopher Marlowe, stage directions call for trumpets to introduce a king in *The Massacre at Paris*, scenes xiv, xvi and xxv; in *Tamburlaine the Great*, Part I, I, i; in *Tamburlaine the Great*, Part II, I, i, iii; but in *The Troublesome Reign and Lamentable Death of Edward the Second*, the king enters with drums and fifes.

In Thomas Kyd's *Jeronimo*, Part I, a trumpet signal, preceding the entrance of the king of Spain, begins the play. At the end of the play trumpets announce the ghost of a courtier!

In George Peele's *Edward I*, 'the trumpets sound' as Edward appears for the first time. In his *The Battle of Alcazar*, V, i, the leader of the Moors, Muly Mahamet Seth enters 'with drums and trumpets.'

17 Robert Greene, *Alphonsus, King of Arragon*, in *The Life and Complete Works of Robert Greene*, ed. Alexander Grosart, (New York: Russell & Russell, 1964), XIII, 351. Trumpets and drums sound again for the duke of Milan. [line 801]. Greene (1560–1592) graduated from Cambridge and traveled in Italy and Spain. Although his personal life was perhaps the most sordid of all these writers, little influence of it can be found in his writing.

18 John Lyly, *Campaspe* (1584), V, iv.

19 Robert Greene, *The History of Orlando Furioso*, line 1081.

20 George Peele, *David and Bethsabe*, ii. In the next generation, in the plays of Marston, sometimes a cornett is used to introduce dukes; the cornett being a kind of lesser trumpet as the duke is a lesser king. Peele (b. ca. 1558) was an actor as well as playwright, graduated from Oxford and lived a rather dissipated life.

21 John Lyly, *The Woman in the Moone*, I, i.

22 George Peele, *The Arraignment of Paris*, I,i, i.s

23 Thomas Kyd, *Jeronimo*, Part I, II, v. Kyd (1558–1594) was a classmate of Edmund Spenser at the Merchant Taylors' School and was imprisoned in 1593 for atheism.

History of Orlando Furioso where several times a drum is instructed in the stage directions to 'Sound a *parle*'[24] and in his *Alphonsus, King of Arragon* where trumpets and drums 'Strike up an alarm awhile.'[25]

A type of fanfare used frequently by Shakespeare in his stage directions is called a 'Flourish.' In Thomas Kyd's *Jeronimo* this is associated with an alarm.[26]

> JERONIMO. We will be as shrill as you: strike an alarm, drum.
> *[They sound a flourish on both sides.]*

This cannot offer us much insight into the stylistic nature of a Flourish, for at the end of the same play a stage direction again calls for a Flourish, but now followed by a funeral march.

Another type of fanfare mentioned in stage directions in the Shakespeare plays is the 'Tucket.' In Thomas Kyd's *The Spanish Tragedy*, a Tucket (far off!) is mentioned in a stage direction and then followed by some dialog which refers to its meaning in this case.

> KING. What means this warning of this trumpet's sound?
> GENERAL. This tells me that your grace's men of war,
>   Such as war's fortune hath reserved from death,
>   Come marching on towards your royal seat,
>   To show themselves before your majesty …[27]

Many times, however, the stage direction calls for music without any hint as to what the music might have been like. Such an example is Lyly's *Endimion* where there is a play within a play, a 'Dumb Show,' which is introduced by, 'Musique sounds.'[28] We wish we were given more information in Greene's *James the Fourth*, which begins with a kind of musical overture, the initial stage note reading only 'Music playing within.'

We are curious what kind of music was played in Christopher Marlowe's *Faustus*, when the stage direction indicates 'Music sounds, and [the ghost of] Helen [of Troy] passeth over the stage'[29] or in his *Tamburlaine the Great*, Part II, when the dying Zenocrate asks for music to ease her passing. A stage direction reads, 'The music sounds and she dies.'[30]

Often the music referred to in the stage directions plays an important role in the structure of the play. Because the music itself has not survived, we often feel, as we do in the

---

24 Robert Greene, *The History of Orlando Furioso*, in *The Life and Complete Works of Robert Greene*, line 395.
25 Robert Greene, *Alphonsus, King of Arragon*, in Ibid., lines 1363ff. In Thomas Kyd, *Jeronimo*, Part I, III, ii, is a stage direction reading, 'Sound Alarum.'
26 Thomas Kyd, *Jeronimo*, Part I, III, i.
27 Thomas Kyd, *The Spanish Tragedy*, I, ii.
28 John Lyly, *Endimion*, II, iii.
29 Christopher Marlowe, *The Tragical History of Dr. Faustus*, scene xii.
30 Christopher Marlowe, *Tamburlaine the Great*, Part II, II, iv.

case of the ancient Greek tragedies, that we are missing a great deal when these works are performed today.

Frequently music is used to introduce a scene and to establish its general character. A rather unusual example is Thomas Nashe's *Summers Last Will and Testament*, in which several scenes open with stage directions calling for ensembles of musicians. If they are not the same people, appearing in different costumes, then this play calls for an extraordinary number of musicians. We see them first at the beginning of the play when they appear as 'Satyrs and Wood-Nymphs, singing.'[31] These singers return to sing a song in line 212, now as three clowns and three maids. Beginning with line 360, the stage directions call for 'a number of shepherds, playing on Recorders.' After line 443, a new scene begins with the arrival of Sol, accompanied by a wind band [*A noyse of Musicians*]. After line 634 the musicians return as hunters, 'blowing their horns.' After Orion says, 'Tosse up your bugle horns unto the stars,' the stage note reads 'Here they go out, blowing their horns, and hallowing, as they came in.' Then almost immediately, after line 803, a group of reapers with sickles enter singing. Finally, after line 967 the singers return, dressed as companions of Bacchus.

Music also is mentioned in stage directions at the ends of scenes, and sometimes we are given some specific information. In the earliest English comedy, *Ralph Roister Doister*, a scene closes with the stage direction 'Here they sing, and go out singing.'[32] In George's Peele's *Edward I* a scene closes with one of the most ancient duties of the trumpeter, the stage direction reading,

Then make the proclamation upon the walls. Sound trumpets.[33]

Often we are simply left wishing for more information in the stage direction, as in Lodge and Greene's *A Looking Glasse for London and England* where a scene ends with 'They draw the curtains and Music plays.'[34]

Frequently the music mentioned in the stage direction is tied directly to stage action. This can be simple and evident, as in Lyly's *The Woman in the Moone*, where a stage direction says 'they dance and sing.'[35] But in some cases the music is more directly involved with dialog as well as with action. In Christopher Marlowe's *Tamburlaine the Great*, Part I, Meander signals his troops to leave by calling out, 'Strike up the drum and march courageously!' The stage direction reads 'Exeunt (drums sounding),' but not before another character has to

---

31 Thomas Nashe, *Summers Last Will and Testament* (1600), in *The Works of Thomas Nashe*, ed. Ronald McKerrow (Oxford: Blackwell, 1966), III, 236. Nashe (1567–1601) is best known as the author of *The Unfortunate Traveller*, which some consider the first English novel.

32 Nicholas Udall, *Ralph Roister Doister*, I, v.

33 George Peele, *Edward I*, xv.

34 Thomas Lodge and Robert Greene, *A Looking Glasse for London and England*, ed. George Glugston (New York: Garland Publishing, 1980), 149. Lodge (1558–1625) was born to a distinguished London merchant, who was in fact Lord Mayor in 1562–1563. Lodge attended Oxford and later became a law student at Lincoln's Inn.

35 John Lyly, *The Woman in the Moone*, III, ii.

ask, 'Drums, why sound ye not, when Meander speaks?'[36] Later in this play, the drums are employed for field signal purposes.

> Then rear your standards; let your sounding drums
> Direct our soldiers to Damascus' walls.[37]

In *Tamburlaine*, Part II, a stage direction reads 'Sound to the battle,' which we presume to be a recognized military trumpet signal.[38] In the same play, for the funeral march for Zenocrate, the stage directions indicate, 'the drums sounding a doleful march.'[39]

In sixteenth-century plays, most stage directions which call for music simply indicate a brief performance, after which the dramatic action resumes. It is rather rare, especially apart from Shakespeare, when this music continues and actually interfaces with the dramatic action. A play which particularly comes to mind is Robert Greene's *Alphonsus, King of Arragon*, which contains three unusual instances of such a use of music.

The play begins with a scene in which the nine Muses appear, with eight of them playing instruments. If nothing else, an ensemble of eight musicians must have been a fairly rare occurrence on stage at this time. The stage direction and initial dialog appear as follows:

> *Enter* Melpomine, Clio, Errato, *with their sisters, playing all upon sundry Instruments,* Calliope *only excepted, who coming last, hangs her head down and plays not her instrument.*
>
> But see whereas the stately Muses come,
> Whose harmony doth very far surpass
> The heavenly music of Apollo's pipe!
> But what means this? Melpomine herself
> With all her sisters sound their Instruments,
> Only excepted fair Calliope,
> Who, coming last and hanging down her head,
> Doth plainly show by outward actions
> What secret sorrow doth torment her heart.[40]

Calliope was the Goddess of Epic Poetry, poetry in praise of great men, and her concern is that this form is dying out. The fact that this is to be a play in praise of the King of Arragon, explains her concern, as well as this opening scene. The scene closes with the appearance of the god of Love, Venus, who offers the solution that if Calliope will just include Love in her school, she will attract many scholars!

---

36 Christopher Marlowe, *Tamburlaine the Great*, Part I, II, ii.

37 Ibid., IV, iii.

38 Christopher Marlowe, *Tamburlaine the Great*, Part II, II, iii, and III, iii. Also, *Tamburlaine the Great*, Part I, II, iv, and III, iii.

39 Christopher Marlowe, *Tamburlaine the Great*, Part II, III, ii.

40 Robert Greene, *Alphonsus, King of Arragon*, in *The Life and Complete Works of Robert Greene*, lines 45ff.

VENUS. Yes Muses, yes, if that she will vouchsafe
    To entertain Dame Venus in her school,
    And further me with her instructions,
    She shall have scholars which will dain to be
    In any other Muses company.
CALLIOPE. Most sacred Venus, do you doubt of that?
    Calliope would think her three times blessed
    For to receive a Goddess in her school,
    Especially so high an one as you,
    Which rules the earth, and guides the heavens too.
VENUS. Then sound your pipes, and let us bend our steps …

In the play proper, another curious instance of the coordination of stage instruction and plot occurs.[41] Here, as Amurack is left alone on stage, the direction reads 'Sound music within.' Amurack responds to the music by saying 'What heavenly Music sounds in my ear,?' and immediately falls asleep! Then Amurack is instructed to speak 'as it were in a dream,' and this dream is interrupted three times by the stage direction 'Sound Instruments a while within.' A very unusual dream with music for the sixteenth century.

Somewhat later in this same play there appears a cult religious, brazen Head on stage, 'which casts flames of fire.' The speech of the priest who attends to this idol is also accompanied by off-stage music, in this case the rumble of drums.[42]

In some cases the playwright appears to depend on the music referred to in the stage direction to justify the following dialog. In Greene's *James the Fourth*, in order to introduce a brief discussion of hunting, hunting music is required by the following stage direction:

After a noise of horns and shoutings enter certain Huntsmen (if you please, singing).[43]

In Thomas Kyd's *Soliman and Perseda*, stage directions call for six separate announcements ('they sound within to the first course') to begin courses in tilting, followed by dialog which comments on the action.[44] Later in this play the stage directions call for a drummer to go to Lucinaes door to announce a game of chance (with 'false Dice').[45]

In George Peele's *Edward I*, a harpist sings, and the stage note indicates the song is sung 'to the tune of *Who list to lead a soldier's life*.'

That you must march, both all and some,
Against your foes with trumpet and drum:
I speak to you from God, that you shall overcome.

---

41 Ibid., lines 932ff.
42 Ibid., lines 1255ff.
43 Robert Greene, *James the Fourth*, IV, i.
44 Thomas Kyd, *Soliman and Perseda*, I, iii.
45 Ibid., II, i.

A character suggests that perhaps the harpist is a prophet, but Jack replies,

> My lords, 'tis an odd fellow, I can tell you, as any is in all Wales. He can sing, rhyme with reason, and rhyme without reason, and without reason or rhyme.[46]

Later in this same play, the wife of the Mayor of London appears, having come from church. The stage direction, 'music before her,' refers to a tradition dating from the Middle Ages by which nobles and civic officials were preceded by musicians. The purpose was to effect an aural 'coat-of-arms,' by which they would be recognized in the distance. Thus, in this case, Queen Elinor asks,

> Glocester, who may this be? A bride or what?
> I pray ye, Joan, go see,
> And know the reason of the harmony.[47]

ON THE PHYSIOLOGY OF AESTHETICS

In the playwrights in the generation before Shakespeare the emphasis was on the action of the court, and one finds little inclination to sit back and contemplate—other than on Love. Philosophers generally are objects of humor, as for instance in Lyly's *Endimion*, which ends with a comment aimed at the soothsayer, Gyptes, and Pythagoras.

> You, Gyptes and Pythagoras, if you can content yourselves in our court, to fall from the vain follies of philosophers to such virtues as are here practiced, you shall be entertained according to your deserts.[48]

Higher education receives little notice as well. Christopher Marlowe makes fun of two famous foreign universities. In his *The Massacre at Paris*, he comments on the secularization of the universities.

> And this for Aristotle will I say,
> That he that despiseth him can never
> Be good in logic or philosophy;
> And that's because the blockish Sorbonnists
> Attribute as much unto their works
> As to the service of the eternal God.[49]

---

46 George Peele, *Edward I*, ii.
47 Ibid., iii.
48 John, Lyly, *Endimion*, in *The Chief Elizabethan Dramatists*, ed. William Neilson (Boston: Houghton Mifflin, 1911), 23.
49 Christopher Marlowe, *The Massacre at Paris*, Scene ix.

In his *Faustus*, the chorus introduces the play by commenting on Dr. Faustus's university education at Luther's university in Wittenberg.

> So soon he profits in divinity,
> The fruitful plot of scholarism graced,
> That shortly he was graced with doctor's name,
> Excelling all whose sweet delight disputes
> In heavenly matters of theology;
> Till swollen with cunning, and self-conceit,
> His waxen wings did mount above his reach,
> And, melting, Heavens conspired his overthrow …[50]

This is followed by the first scene, in which Faustus is in his study wondering what purpose there is to 'live and die in Aristotle's works.' Better, he thinks, to 'Be a physician and heap up gold.'

ON THE PSYCHOLOGY OF AESTHETICS

In Lyly's *Loves Metamorphosis* we find this interesting metaphor using music to express a lady's emotional state.

> SILVESTRIS. My lute, though it has many strings, makes a sweet consent; and a Lady's heart, though it harbor many fancies, should embrace but one love.
> NIOBE. The strings of my heart are tuned in a contrary key to your Lute, and make as sweet an harmony in discords, as your's in concord.
> SILVESTRIS. Why, what strings are in Lady's hearts? Not the base.
> NIOBE. There is no base string in a woman's heart.
> SILVESTRIS. The mean?
> NIOBE. There was never mean in woman's heart.
> SILVESTRIS. The treble?
> NIOBE. Yea, the treble double and treble; and so are all my heartstrings.[51]

We also notice in another of Lyly's plays, *The Maydes Metamorphosis*, the ancient observation that the mental processes associated with Love and Reason do not seem to mix. Aramanthus observes,

> I cannot tell what reason it should be,
> But love and reason here do disagree.[52]

---

50 Christopher Marlowe, *The Tragical History of Dr. Faustus*, I, initial Chorus.
51 John Lyly, *Loves Metamorphosis*, III, i.
52 John Lyly, *The Maydes Metamorphosis*, IV, i.

Regarding Pleasure and Pain, it is the pain of Love that these courtier-playwrights expressed most vividly. We will allow a few lines from Lyly's *Endimion* to be representative of many more. Here, Endimion cries,

> O fair Cynthia! ... Behold my sad tears, my deep sighs, my hollow eyes, my broken sleep, my heavy countenance ...[53]

Tamburlaine, in Marlowe's *Tamburlaine the Great*, Part I, experiences a different kind of pain over love. He is disturbed that a macho figure such as himself could be so affected by love, to be made effeminate, as he calls it. In this soliloquy he is thinking of Zenocrate and reflecting that words cannot express the feelings he has.

> What is beauty, saith my sufferings, then?
> If all the pens that ever poets held
> Had fed the feeling of their masters' thoughts,
> And every sweetness that inspired their hearts,
> Their minds, and muses on admired themes;
> If all the heavenly quintessence they still
> From their immortal flowers of poetry,
> Wherein, as in a mirror, we perceive
> The highest reaches of a human wit;
> If these had made one poem's period,
> And all combined in beauty's worthiness,
> Yet should there hover in their restless heads
> One thought, one grace, one wonder, at the least,
> Which into words no virtue can digest.
> But how unseemly is it for my sex,
> My discipline of arms and chivalry,
> My nature, and the terror of my name,
> To harbor thoughts effeminate and faint!
> Save only that in beauty's just applause,
> With whose instinct the soul of man is touched ...[54]

Nearly all early philosophers point out that Pleasure and Pain seem invariably joined, as in the case that the joy of eating follows the pain of hunger, etc. It often follows that Love is given as a primary example in which Pleasure and Pain are so mixed. Such a passage is found in Kyd's *The Spanish Tragedy*, where Bel-imperia reflects,

> That pleasure follows pain, and bliss annoy.
> Possession of thy love is the only port,
> Wherein my heart, with fears and hopes long tossed,

---

53 John, Lyly, *Endimion*, II, i.
54 Christopher Marlowe, *Tamburlaine the Great*, Part I, V, ii.

Each hour doth wish and long to make resort,
There to repair the joys that it hath lost,
And, sitting safe, to sing in Cupid's choir
That sweetest bliss is crown of love's desire.

We find particularly interesting Horatio's comment which follows.

HORATIO. The less I speak, the more I meditate.
BEL-IMPERIA. But whereon dost thou chiefly meditate?
HORATIO. On dangers past, and pleasures to ensue.[55]

This we take to be one of a number of unconscious references in early literature to the nature of our split-brains, for Horatio clearly associates thinking of love (right hemisphere) with when he is not speaking (left hemisphere).

ON THE PHILOSOPHY OF AESTHETICS

It is surprising that there is so little mention of any of the arts, apart from music, in these plays and we can only assume that it reflects the decline in the appreciation of the arts of which the poets and philosophers complain. There is an occasional allusion to the old debate over the relationship of Art and Nature. For us, the most interesting of these is found in Lyly's *Campaspe* where a character observes that 'art must yield to nature, reason to the appetites, wisdom to affection.'[56] A painter, however, finds more appreciation in his art work than in his model.

Your Majesty knows that painters in their last works are said to excel themselves, and in this [painting] I have so much pleased myself, that the shadow as much delights me, being an artist, as the substance does others that are amorous.[57]

There is even surprisingly little reference to the aesthetics of dramatic literature in these plays. A rare example is found in Kyd's *The Spanish Tragedy*.

HIERONIMO. A comedy?
    Fie! comedies are fit for common wits;
    But to present a kingly troop withal,
    Give me a stately written tragedy …[58]

---

55 Thomas Kyd, *The Spanish Tragedy*, II, ii. Since both love and music are essentially right hemisphere, Horatio is more correct than he can know when he says 'If Cupid sing, Venus is not far.' [Ibid., II, iv.]

56 John Lyly, *Campaspe*, III, v.

57 Ibid., V, iv.

58 Thomas Kyd, *The Spanish Tragedy*, IV, i.

We should mention here a complaint in Sir Thomas More's *Utopia* (1515), which we shall see repeated by Shakespeare in the following chapter, that in the sixteenth century improvisation on stage was a not uncommon event.

> For you spoil and corrupt the play that is in hand when you mix with it things of an opposite nature, even though they are much better. Therefore go through with the play that is acting, the best you can, and do not confound it because another that is pleasanter comes into your thoughts.[59]

Painting is rarely mentioned, although we note that in Lyly's *Campaspe*, a painter says to a student, 'Your hand is not following your mind,'[60] echoing Leonardo's famous comment that art is in the mind, not in the hand. Later this same painter, Apelles, before singing a song about Cupid, makes the interesting observation that he finds it impossible to paint,

> deep and hollow sighs, sad and melancholy thoughts, sounds and slaughters of conceits, a life posting to death, a death galloping from life, a wavering consistency, or an unsettled resolution.[61]

ON THE AESTHETICS OF MUSIC

There are frequent pastoral scenes in these plays in which music plays an important role. Even though we are now in the realm of the mythical gods, perhaps there is some contemporary purpose here as well. At a time when other important writers were complaining about the decline in the appreciation of the arts in England, perhaps this was a means of reminding their audiences that music, since earliest times, had always had some association with the divine.

In Lyly's *Midas* there is a 'music contest' reminiscent to those found so frequently in the works of the ancient Greek lyric poets.[62] This example is particularly remarkable because it is a contest between two of the musical gods, Apollo and Pan. Apollo begins, singing to his lute.

> APOLLO. *My Daphne's Hair is twisted Gold,*
> *Bright stars a-piece her Eyes do hold …*
> NYMPH ERATO. O divine Apollo, o sweet consent!
> THA. If the God of Music should not be above our reach, who should?
> MIDAS. I like it not.

---

59 Quoted in Henry Morley, *Ideal Commonwealths* (Port Washington: Kennikat Press, 1968), 28.

60 John Lyly, *Campaspe*, III, iv.

61 Ibid., III, v.

62 John Lyly, *Midas*, IV, i. One scholar (Halpin, in *Oberon's Vision* [Shakespeare Society, 1843]) makes the outrageous suggestion that this musical contest is a metaphor for the battle between Catholicism and Luther!

PAN. Now let me tune my pipes. I cannot pipe and sing, that's the odds in the instrument, not the art: but I will pipe and then sing; and then judge both of the art and the instrument. [He pipes and then sings]

> Pan's Syrinx was a Girl indeed,
> Though now she's turned into a Reed
> From that dear Reed Pan's Pipe does come,
> A Pipe that strikes Apollo dumb ...

APOLLO. Hast thou finished Pan?
PAN. I, and done well, I think.
APOLLO. Now Nymphs, what say you?
ERATO. We all say that Apollo has shown himself both a God, and of music the god; Pan himself a rude Satyr, neither keeping measure, nor time; his piping as far out of tune, as his body out of form. To thee divine Apollo, we give the prize and reverence.
APOLLO. But what says Midas?
MIDAS. I think there's more sweetness in the pipe of Pan, than in Apollo's lute; I brook not that nice tickling of strings, that contents me that makes one start. What a shrillness came into my ears out of that pipe, and what a goodly noise it made! Apollo, I must needs judge that Pan deserveth most praise.
PAN. Blessed be Midas, worthy to be a God: these girls, whose ears do but itch with daintiness, give the verdict without weighing the virtue; they have been brought up in chambers with soft music, not where I make the woods ring with my pipe, Midas ...
MIDAS. Apollo is angry: blame not Apollo, whom being God of music thou did both dislike and dishonor; preferring the barbarous noise of Pan's pipe, before the sweet melody of Apollo's lute ...

For this misjudgment, another god, Phoebus, casts a spell and gives Midas the ears of an ass, as we learn in a solo song by Apollo.

> When Pan Apollo in music shall excel,
> Midas of Phrygia shall lose his Ass's ears;
> Pan did Apollo in music far excel,
> Therefore king Midas weareth Ass's ears ...

And Midas is in despair.

> I (whom the loss of gold made discontent, and the possessing desperate) either dulled with the humors of my weak brain, or deceived by the thickness of my deaf ears, preferred the harsh noise of Pan's pipe, before the sweet stroke of Apollo's lute, which caused Phoebus in justice (as I now confess, and then as I saw in anger) to set these ears on my head, that have wrung so many tears from my eyes.

In George Peele's *The Arraignment of Paris* the cast includes a large number of Greek gods and the nine Muses. Near the beginning of the play there occurs an extraordinary performance for double choir, a choir of gods on stage and the Muses off-stage. The stage direction describes their music as an echo to the song of birds heard shortly before and indicated by another stage direction, 'An artificial charm of birds being heard within.' The text for the double choir includes the following,

> MUSES. *[within]* The Muses give you melody to gratulate this chance,
>   And Phoebe, chief of sylvan chace, commands you all to dance.
> GODS. Then round in a circle our sportance must be;
>   Hold hands in a hornpipe, all gallant in glee …

This is followed by a solo song by Pan and then another song by the artificial birds. At the conclusion, Juno says 'This welcome and this melody exceed these wits of mine.'[63]

Apollo appears again in Lyly's *The Maydes Metamorphosis*, where he makes the interesting statement,

> By me are learned the rules of harmony.[64]

In Greek mythology, Phoebus was an alternate name for Apollo, but they are separate characters in this play which ends with the characters singing and dancing to Phoebus' harp.

> Since painful sorrows date hath end,
> And time hath coupled friend with friend:
> Rejoice we all, rejoice and sing,
> Let all these groves of Phoebus ring.
> Hope having won, despair is vanished:
> Pleasure revives, and care is banished.
> Then trip we all this Roundelay,
> And still be mindful of the Bay.[65]

To return to our search for reflections of contemporary perspective on aesthetics in music, our attention is first captured by a scene in Lodge and Greene's *A Looking Glasse for London and England*. Here a common citizen has been cheated in a trial. He had been promised a payment of forty pounds and is objecting to the fact that he was paid ten pounds in cash and thirty pounds in Lute strings. We wonder if this suggests that lutes were sufficiently common that their strings were used in barter?[66]

---

63 George Peele, *The Arraignment of Paris*, I, i.

64 John Lyly, *The Maydes Metamorphosis*, III, i.

65 Ibid., V, ii.

66 Thomas Lodge and Robert Greene, *A Looking Glasse for London and England*, ed. George Glugston, ed. (New York: Garland Publishing, 1980), 157. This is one of the earliest English plays in which lower class characters act and speak appropriate to their class.

We find a few interesting comments reflecting what might be considered good qualities in music. First, variety in tonal color seems to have been valued. In Lyly's *Campaspe*, a painter is explaining that a variety of colors makes a good painting, just 'as in music diverse strings cause a more delicate consent.'[67] In this same play there is a suggestion that style means more than technique. After a dance, Syluius thought the music was good, but Diogenes says no,

> The musicians were very bad; they only study to have their strings in tune, never framing their manners to order.[68]

There is a great deal more information regarding contemporary reflections on the purpose of music. First, simple delight was obviously an important purpose of music in sixteenth-century England. In Nashe's *Summers Last Will and Testament*, Summer departs, after long and weary labors, saying,

> Music and poetry, my two last crimes,
> Are those two exercises of delight …[69]

In Peele's *David and Bathsabe*, Adonia says,

> Amnon, thy life was pleasing to thy lord,
> As to mine ears the music of my lute,
> Or songs that David tuneth to his harp …[70]

In this same playwright's *Sir Clyomon and Sir Clamydes*, Clyomon asks,

> Can music more the pensive heart or daunted mind delight …[71]

One also finds many references to the traditional purpose of music in soothing the disturbed listener. In Christopher Marlowe's *Tamburlaine the Great*, Part II, this takes the form of the ancient Greek concept of the use of music to tune the soul.

> The cherubins and holy seraphins
> That sing and play before the King of Kings
> Use all their voices and their instruments
> To entertain divine Zenocrate.
> And in this sweet and curious harmony,
> The god that tunes this music to our souls

---

67 John Lyly, *Campaspe*, III, iv.

68 Ibid., V, i.

69 Thomas Nashe, *Summers Last Will and Testament* (1600), in *The Works of Thomas Nashe*, ed. Ronald McKerrow (Oxford: Blackwell, 1966), III, line 524.

70 George Peele, *David and Bethsabe*, vii.

71 George Peele, *Sir Clyomon and Sir Clamydes*, ii.

Holds out his hand in highest majesty
To entertain divine Zenocrate.[72]

In *Tamburlaine The Great*, Part I, a more traditional form of using music to soothe is found. Here, at a banquet, after Bajazeth is offered water, and flings it to the ground,

> TAMBURLAINE. Fast, and welcome, sir until hunger make you eat. How now, Zenocrate, doth not the Turk and his wife make a goodly show at a banquet?
> ZENOCRATE. Yes, my lord.
> THERIDAMUS. Methnks it is a great deal better than a consort of music.
> TAMBURLAINE. Yet music would do well to cheer up Zenocrate.[73]

A similar purpose is found in Lyly's *Campaspe*, when the king requests a minstrel 'to make him merry.'[74]

With regard to soothing the listener, music in this repertoire is most often called upon with respect to melancholy. An example is found in Lyly's *The Woman in the Moone*, where we find,

> O then to sift that humor from her heart,
> Let us with Rondelays delight her ear:
> For I have heard that Music is a means,
> To calm the rage of melancholy mood.[75]

There are also some instances where music is used to facilitate mourning. In Kyd's *The Spanish Tragedy*, three characters decided to sing a song of mourning, so despondent that it will consist entirely of discords.

> HIERONIMO. Lean on my arm: I thee, thou me, shalt stay,
>   And thou, and I, and she will sing a song,
>   Three parts in one, but all of discords framed—
>   Talk not of chords, but let us now be gone,
>   For with a cord Horatio was slain.[76]

On the other hand, there are several instances where the characters are so sad that the playwright specifies that no music can suffice. In Lodge and Greene's *A Looking Glasse for London and England*, for example, Aluida observes, 'Let the voice of music cease, where

---

72 Christopher Marlowe, *Tamburlaine the Great*, Part II, II, iv.

73 Ibid., Part I, IV, iv.

74 John Lyly, *Campaspe*, V, iv.

75 John Lyly, *The Woman in the Moone*, I, i.

76 Thomas Kyd, *The Spanish Tragedy*, III, xiii.

sorrow dwells.'[77] A similar thought is found in Kyd's *The Spanish Tragedy*, when Hieronimo says 'I'll say his dirge; singing fits not this case.'[78] And the most famous musician of antiquity, David, in Peele's *David and Bathsabe*, mourns his own conduct.

> David, hang up thy harp; hang down thy head;
> And dash thy ivory lute against the stones.[79]

Another important purpose of music for these sixteenth-century courtiers was it helped in wooing the ladies. In the oldest English comedy, Nicholas Udall's *Ralph Roister Doister* (1550), Roister's friend, Merrygreek, recommends music for this purpose.

> In the meantime, sir, if you please, I will go home,
> And call your musicians; for in this your case
> It would set you forth, and all your wooing grace,
> Ye may not lack your instruments to play and sing.

We are not sure what is meant by Roister's following observation,

> Yea, for I love singing out of measure,
> It comforteth my spirits, and doth me great pleasure.[80]

Later in this same play, there is a comic scene in which one of Doister's servants complains about one of her own suitors who uses music to woo but never follows through with marriage.

> So fervent hot wooing, and so far from wiving,
> I trow, never was any creature living;
> With every woman is he in some love's pang;
> Then up to our lute at midnight, *Twangledom twang!*
> Then twang with our sonnets, and twang with our dumps;
> And *Heigho!* from our heart, as heavy as lead-lumps.
> Then to our recorder with *Toodleloodle poop!*
> As the howlet out of an ivy bush should hoop.
> Anon to our gittern, *Thrumpledum thrumpledum thrum,*
> *Thrumpledum, thrumpledum, thrumpledum, thrumpledum, thrum!*
> Of songs and ballads also he is a maker …[81]

---

77 Thomas Lodge and Robert Greene, *A Looking Glasse for London and England*, ed. George Glugston (New York: Garland Publishing, 1980), 218.
78 Thomas Kyd, *The Spanish Tragedy*, II, iv.
79 George Peele, *David and Bethsabe*, v. The prologue begins,
> Of Israel's sweetest signer now I sing …
80 Nicholas Udall, *Ralph Roister Doister*, I, ii.
81 Ibid., II, i.

In Lyly's *Sapho and Phao*, Sybilla gives Phao a lengthy lesson on how to woo a lady. Included are necessary skills in music.

> Can you sing, show your cunning; can you dance, use your legs; can you play any instrument, practice your fingers to please her fancy; seek out qualities.[82]

In one rare case, instead of the purpose of music being to thus influence the ladies, its purpose is to influence the king. In Marlowe's *Edward the Second*, three poor entertainers enter, following which Gaveston observes,

> These are not men for me;
> I must have wanton poets, pleasant wits,
> Musicians, that with touching of a string
> May draw the pliant king which way I please.
> Music and poetry is his delight …[83]

Finally, we should mention that sometimes the purpose of music, in so far as the play is concerned, is for humor. In Christopher Marlowe's *The Jew of Malta*, the title character, Barabas, enters with a lute, disguised as a French musician.

> BELLAMIRA. A French musician! Come, let's hear your skill.
> BARABAS. Must tuna my lute for sound, twang, twang, first …

Then, after Barabas plays,

> PILLA-BORSA. Methinks he fingers very well.
> BARABAS. *[Aside]* So did you when you stole my gold.[84]

There are a few scenes in these plays which contribute insights to performance practice in sixteenth-century England. No topic is so much debated today, relative to early performance practice, as to whether vibrato was used. In Lyly's *Gallathea*, an Alchemist, in discussing the precision necessary to his art, makes a statement which we believe can only be a reference to vibrato. His workers, he says, when they blow on the fire, 'must beat time with their breath, as musicians do with their breasts.'[85]

Another interesting observation seems to reflect musician's attitudes toward keeping up with the increasing technical demands of late Renaissance music. In Lyly's *Midas*, we find in the Prologue,

---

82 John Lyly, *Sapho and Phao*, II, iv.

83 Christopher Marlowe, *The Troublesome Reign and Lamentable Death of Edward the Second*, I, i.

84 Christopher Marlowe, *The Jew of Malta*, IV, vi.

85 John Lyly, *Gallathea* (1592), III, ii.

Gentlemen, so nice is the world, that for apparel there is no fashion, for Music no instrument, for diet no delicate, for plays no invention, but breedeth satiety before noon, and contempt before night … Ask the Musicians, they will say their heads ache with devising notes above *E la*.[86]

In this repertoire there is an occasional use of echo as a dramatic technique. It appears in a song in Peele's *The Arraignment of Paris*, when Thestylis sings 'The strange affects of my tormented heart.' Each line of her song is followed by an echo sung by the shepherds. Most interesting to us is the stage direction, which explains 'The grace of this song is in the Shepherds' echo to her verse.'[87]

ART MUSIC

Most of the Elizabethan plays include the performance of art songs[88] and our purpose here will be to simply give an idea of the breadth of their character and purpose. In the plays of John Lyly these songs are often in three or more parts and concluded by a chorus. In his *Sapho and Phao*, just before a song of this type, we find this curious request by the character Molus:

> I must go by two, or else my master will not go by me: but meet me full with his fist. Therefore, if we shall sing, give me my part quickly: for if I tarry long, I shall cry my part woefully.[89]

Many songs in these plays, of course, are love songs, but we will mention only a rather unusual one. In Lodge and Greene's *A looking Glass for London and England* the king of Cilicia is an unwilling listener of a love song by Aluida, wife of another character.

> ALUIDA. Hear me but sing of love, then by my sighs,
>   My tears, my glancing looks, my changed cheer,
>   Thou shalt perceive how I do hold thee dear.
> KING OF CILICIA. Sing Madam if you please, but love in jest.
> ALUIDA. Nay, I will love, and sigh at every rest.
>   Beauty alas where wast thou borne,
>   Thus to hold thyself in scorn?
>   When as Beauty kist to woo thee,
>   Thou by Beauty doest undo me.
>   Heigho, despise me not.[90]

---

86 John Lyly, *Midas*, in *The Complete Works of John Lyly*, ed. Warwick Bond (Oxford: Clarendone Press, 1967), III, 115.

87 George Peele, *The Arraignment of Paris*, III, ii.s

88 By this we mean that the lyrics of the song are given, but never the music.

89 John Lyly, *Sapho and Phao*, III, ii.

90 Thomas Lodge and Robert Greene, *A Looking Glasse for London and England*, 194.

  In George Peele's *The Arraignment of Paris*, I, ii, Oenone sings a roundelay of love, accompanied by Paris playing a pipe. Act III begins with the stage direction 'Enter Colin, who sings his passion of love.'

There are a surprisingly large number of truly sad songs. In Lyly's *Endimion*, Geron enters singing, and although we are not given the song, we know its character by the opening lines of his son, Eumenides.

> EUMENIDES. Father, your sad music, being tuned to the same key that my hard fortunes is, has so melted my mind, that I wish to hang at your mouth's end till my life's end.
> GERON. These tunes, Gentleman, have I been accustomed with these fifty Winters.[91]

In George Peele's *The Arraignment of Paris*, Mercury requests the company be quiet, while Oenone sings a song of woe.

> MERCURY. She singeth; sirs, be hushed a while.
> Oenone *singeth as she sits*.
>
> Oenone's *Complaint*.
>
> > Melpomene, the Muse of tragic songs,
> > With mournful tines, in stole of dismal hue,
> > Assist a silly nymph to wail her woe,
> > And leave thy lusty company behind.[92]

In Nashe's *Summers Last Will and Testament*, Summer calls for an elegy on death.

> SUMMER. To weary out the time until they come,
> > Sing me some doleful ditty to the Lute,
> That may complain my near approaching death.
> > Adieu, farewell earth's bliss,
> > This world uncertain is,
> > Fond are life's lustful joys,
> > Death proves them all but toys …[93]

There are relatively few references in these plays to instrumental performances and as they generally are concerned with lowly minstrels the dramatic purpose tends to be one of humor. In Lyly's *Mother Bombie* three minstrel fiddlers enter and play. When not appreciated, one of them observes,

> Boy, say no more words! there's a time for all things. Though I should not say it, I have been a minstrel these thirty years, and tickled more strings than thou hast hairs, but yet was never so misused.[94]

---

[91] John Lyly, *Endimion*, III, iv.

[92] George Peele, *The Arraignment of Paris*, III, i.

[93] Thomas Nashe, *Summers Last Will and Testament* (1600), lines 1574ff. George Peele's *The Arraignment of Paris* contains a funeral song in III, ii.

[94] John Lyly, *Mother Bombie*, V, iii.

Later, the character Memphio says of these minstrels,

> Now all are content but the poor fiddlers: they shall be sent for for the marriage and have double fees.[95]

In Lyly's *The Maydes Metamorphosis*, three fairy-musicians make possible a typically blatant example of Elizabethan stage humor.

> 1. FAIRY. Will you have any music Sir?
> 2. FAIRY. Will you have any fine music?
> 3. FAIRY. Most dainty music?
> MOPSO. We must set a face on it now, there's no fleeing. No sir: we are very merry [already] I thank you.
> 1. FAIRY. O but you shall Sir.
> FRISCO. No, I pray you save your labor.
> 2. FAIRY. O Sir, it shall not cost you a penny.
> IOCULO. Where are your fiddles?
> 3. FAIRY. You shall have most dainty instruments Sir.
> MOPSO. I pray you, what might I call you?
> 1. FAIRY. My name is Penny.
> MOPSO. I am sorry I cannot purse you.
> FRISCO. I pray you sir, what might I call you?
> 2. FAIRY. My name is Cricket.
> FRISCO. I would I were a chimney for your sake.
> IOCULO. I pray you, you pretty fellow, what's your name?
> 3. FAIRY. My name is little, little Prick.
> IOCULO. Little, little Prick? O you are a dangerous Fairy, and frighten all the little wenches in the county out of their beds. I care not whose hand I were in, so I were out of yours.[96]

In Lodge and Greene's *A Looking Glasse for London and England*, there is a song by a character disguised as a devil.

> DEVIL. Oh, oh, oh, oh faine would I be,
> If that my kingdom fulfilled I might see.
> Oh, oh, oh, oh.
> CLOWN. Surely this is a merry devil, and I believe he is one of Lucifer's minstrels, hath a sweet voice, now surely, surely, he may sing to a pair of tongs and a bagpipe.[97]

---

95 Ibid., 227.

96 John Lyly, *The Maydes Metamorphosis*, II, ii.

97 Thomas Lodge and Robert Greene, *A Looking Glasse for London and England*, 201.

FUNCTIONAL MUSIC

A rare reference to Church music is found in George Peele's *David and Bathsabe*,

> Sound trumpets, shawms, and instruments of praise,
> To Jacob's God for David's victory.[98]

This is followed by a stage direction which reads, 'Trumpets, etc.'

A stage direction in Greene's *James the Fourth* calls for the director of the play to produce music to celebrate a wedding scene. Of interest here is the range of options the author leaves to the director.

> *[After a solemn service, enter, from the widow's house, a service, musical songs of marriage, or a masque, or whatever pretty triumph you will.]*[99]

References to military music are frequently found in circumstances such as that found in Marlowe's *Edward the Second*, when Sir John calls out 'Sound the trumpets, my lord, and forward let us march.'[100] In most early literature this sound is accompanied with descriptions of feelings of fear and dread on the part of those hearing it, for obvious reasons. We find such a comment in Thomas Kyd's *The Spanish Tragedy*.

> Both the cheerly sounding trumpets, drums and fifes,
> Both raising dreadful clamors to the sky,
> That valleys, hills, and rivers made rebound,
> And heaven itself was frighted with the sound.[101]

In Robert Greene's *Frier Bacon and Frier Bongay*, we have a rare reference to the peace following war.

> But when the stormy threats of wars shall cease:
> The horse shall stamp as careless of the pike,
> Drums shall be turned into timbrels of delight …[102]

An example of the role of music most discussed with respect to the ancient armies, to inspire courage in the soldier, is found in Peele's *Sir Clyomon and Sir Clamydes*.

---

98 George Peele, *David and Bethsabe*, vii.
99 Robert Greene, *James the Fourth*, V, ii.
100 Christopher Marlowe, *The Troublesome Reign and Lamentable Death of Edward the Second*, IV, iv.
101 Thomas Kyd, *The Spanish Tragedy*, I, ii.
102 Robert Greene, *Frier Bacon and Frier Bongay*, lines 2240ff.

Rejoice, then sound of trumpet doth each warlike wight allure,
And drum and fife unto the fight do noble hearts procure …[103]

Aside from the military, the only other occupational music mentioned in any of the plays in this repertoire is found in the early comedy, *Ralph Roister Doister*. First, three household female servants are working when one suggests they sing to ease their work.

Let all these matters pass, and we three sing a song;
So shall we pleasantly both the time beguile now,
And eke despath all our works …[104]

Later these three sing again and the text of the song is given, including,

After drudgery,
When they be weary,
Then to be merry,
To laugh and sing they be free;
With chip and cherry,
Heigh derry derry,
Trill on the bery,
And lovingly to agree.[105]

ENTERTAINMENT MUSIC

Robert Greene, in his *The History of Orlando Furioso* introduces a fiddler to wake up and offer entertainment to Orlando, in a short scene which itself is intended as comic relief.

ORGALIO. Then play a fit of mirth to my Lord.
FIDDLER. Why, he is still mad, is he not?
ORGALIO. No, no: come, play.
FIDDLER. At which side doeth he use to give his reward?
ORGALIO. Why, of any side.
FIDDLER. Doeth he not use to throw the chamber-pot sometimes? It would grieve me should he wet my fiddle-strings.

---

103 George Peele, *Sir Clyomon and Sir Clamydes*, ii.
104 Nicholas Udall, *Ralph Roister Doister*, I, iii.
105 Ibid., II, iii.

This is followed by a stage direction reading, 'He plays and sings any old toy, and Orlando wakes.' Orlando is not pleased and what happens next is made clear by the subsequent stage directions:

[He takes away his fiddle.]
[He strikes and beats him with the fiddle.]
[He breaks it about his head. Exit Fiddler.][106]

---

106 Robert Greene, *The History of Orlando Furioso*, lines 1199ff.

14 SHAKESPEARE

BEFORE CONSIDERING THE TOPIC OF AESTHETICS, as expressed in the works of Shakespeare, we should first like to mention a few of his comments on aspects of the contemporary scene which have been mentioned by other sixteenth-century English writers. First of all, he seemed aware of the exaggerated sense of pride, of which other writers complained. In *Othello*, Iago sings a song about England, which includes the line, 'Tis pride that pulls the country down.'[1] And in *Cymbeline*, Imogen asks,

> Hath Britain all the sun that shines? Day, night,
> Are they not but in Britain? I' the world's volume
> Our Britain seems as of it, but not in it …[2]

More important, for our purpose, Shakespeare also occasionally refers to the decay of the arts, which again was a frequent contemporary complaint among sixteenth-century English writers. In *A Midsummer Night's Dream*, for example, Theseus, duke of Athens, asks what the evening's entertainment shall be.[3]

> Say, what abridgment have you for this evening?
> What masque? what music? How shall we beguile
> The lazy time, if not with some delight?

He is then given a piece of paper listing possible entertainments, the first being quite ridiculous.

> 'The battle with the Centaurs, to be sung
> By an Athenian eunuch to the harp.'

Another, which is judged unsuitable for the occasion, refers to the decline of arts and learning.

> 'The thrice three Muses mourning for the death
> Of Learning, late deceased in beggary.'
> That is some satire keen and critical,
> Nor sorting with a nuptial ceremony.

---

1 *Othello*, II, iii, 88.
2 *Cymberline*, III, iv, 152ff.
3 *A Midsummer Night's Dream*, V, i, 41ff.

In one place, we cannot help wondering if Shakespeare held the male English macho attitudes responsible. We find this in *Timon of Athens*, when Apemantus acuses Timon of having 'a poor unmanly melancholy.'[4] Later Timon observes of Flavius,

> What, dost thou weep? come nearer; then I love thee,
> Because thou art a woman, and disclaim'st
> Flinty mankind, whose eyes do never give
> But through lust and laughter. Pity's sleeping:
> Strange times, that weep with laughing, not with weeping![5]

Shakespeare also comments on the courtier, which was the subject of so much sixteenth-century literature in England and Italy. One courtier, in *Twelfth Night*, seems rather sophisticated.

> He plays the viol-de-gamba and speaks three or four languages word for word without the book.[6]

We get another picture of the courtier, given as Grecian but obviously contemporary, in *The Tragedy of Troilus and Cressida*, when Troilus says,

> I cannot sing,
> Nor heel the high lavolt, nor sweeten talk,
> Nor play at subtle games—fair virtues all,
> To which the Grecians are most prompt and pregnant.
> But I can tell that in each grace of these
> There lurks a still and dumb-discursive devil
> That tempts most cunningly.[7]

In other places, however, Shakespeare is more critical of the institution of the courtier. In *As You Like It* there is a brief dialog which centers on the obsession of manners by the courtiers. Touchstone tells a rural character that he will be damned for never having been to court and the reason quickly shifts to the kind of cause and effect speech often used by the Puritans.

> Why, if thou never wast at court, thou never saw'st good manners. If thou never saw'st good manners, then thy manners must be wicked; and wickedness is sin, and sin is damnation. Thou are in a perilous state, shepherd.[8]

---

4   *Timon of Athens*, IV, ii, 218.
5   *Timon of Athens*, IV, iii, 512ff.
6   *Twelfth Night or What You Will*, I, iii, 23ff.
7   *The Tragedy of Troilus and Cressida*, IV, iv, 93ff.
8   *As You Like It*, III, ii, 37ff.

In the comedy, *The Winter's Tale*, the wandering musician, Autolycus, has disguised himself as a courtier and when asked if he is indeed a courtier, he responds,

> Whether it like me or no, I am a courtier. Seest thou not the air of the court in these enfoldings? hath not my gait in it the measure of the court? receives not thy nose court-odor from me? reflect I not on thy baseness court-contempt? Think'st thou, for that I insinuate, or toaze from thee thy business, I am therefore no courtier?[9]

Hamlet uses the playing of a recorder as metaphor for the courtier's manipulation of others. He says, 'O, the recorders! Let me see one,' and proceeds to give the courtier, Guildenstern, a lesson.

> HAMLET. It is as easy as lying. Govern these ventages with your fingers and thumb, give it breath with your mouth, and it will discourse most eloquent music. Look you, these are the stops.
> GUILDENSTERN. But these cannot I command to any utterance of harmony. I have not the skill.
> HAMLET. Why, look you now, how unworthy a thing you make of me. You would play upon me; you would seem to know my stops; you would pluck out the heart of my mystery; you would sound me from my lowest note to the top of my compass. And there is much music, excellent voice, in this little organ, yet cannot you make it speak. 'Sblood, do you think I am easier to be played on than a pipe? Call me what instrument you will, though you can fret me, yet you cannot play upon me.[10]

Finally, we should point out that in *Timon of Athens* Shakespeare creates a shallow, cynical courtier, the 'opposite to humanity,' to whom he gives the name *Apemantus*.

There are two passages which refer to the contemporary custom of young men going abroad, especially to Italy, to finish their education. This, as we have seen, was particularly attacked by the religious right in England. In one play, Shakespeare seems sympathetic to this custom. At the very beginning of *The Two Gentlemen of Verona*, Valentine desires to travel, observing, 'Home-keeping youth have ever homely wits.' On the other hand, in *Richard II*, Shakespeare seems to take the other side of the question, as he has the duke of York observe,

> The open ear of youth doth always listen—
> Report of fashions in proud Italy,
> Whose manners still our tardy apish nation
> Limps after in base imitation.[11]

In this regard, perhaps we should also mention that Hamlet's parents beg him not to pursue his desire to go to school in Wittenberg, but to stay and remain as their chief courtier.[12]

---

9   *The Winter's Tale*, IV, iv, 797ff.
10 *Hamlet*, III, ii, 345ff.
11 *Richard II*, II, i, 20ff.
12 *Hamlet*, I, ii, 117ff.

We have mentioned the prevalence of the consort principle in sixteenth-century music and several references which suggest that this principle was even extended to the organization of hunting dogs! Shakespeare also mentions this, in *A Midsummer Night's Dream*, when Theseus says,

> Slow in pursuit, but matched in mouth like bells,
> Each under each. A cry more tunable
> Was never holla'd to, nor cheered with horn.[13]

Finally, it will be evident to anyone reading the works of Shakespeare that one of his private joys as a writer was to make plays on words. Frequently these involve associations with music and we will let two examples, from *Troilus and Cressida* and *Romeo and Juliet*, represent many.

> ULYSSES. She will sing any man at first sight.
> THERSITES. And any man may sing her, if he can take her clef; she's noted.[14]
>
> ......
>
> TYBALT. Mercutio, thou consort'st with Romeo.
> MERCUTIO. Consort? What! dost thou make us minstrels? And thou make minstrels of us, look to hear nothing but discords.[15]

ON THE PHYSIOLOGY OF AESTHETICS

Shakespeare does not engage in extended comment on the nature or working of the mind and the senses. One passage, however, attracted our attention as an example of the unconscious prejudice which we have seen throughout history in favoring the right hand over the left. We understand today that this is the left hemisphere of the brain, which thinks and writes, expressing prejudice toward the left hand—which is controlled by a right hemisphere of which the left is completely unaware and whose existence it denies. In *King Henry VI: Part III*, Shakespeare associates weeping with the left and a smile with the right, as the king says,

> She on his left side, craving aid for Henry;
> He on his right, asking a wife for Edward.
> She weeps, and says her Henry is deposed;
> He smiles, and says his Edward is installed.[16]

---

13 *A Midsummer Night's Dream*, IV, i, 123.
14 *The Tragedy of Troilus and Cressida*, V, ii, 10ff.
15 *Romeo and Juliet*, III, i, 40ff.
16 *King Henry VI: Part III*, III, i, 43ff.

Another passage which we find interesting with regard to the organization of the mind is found in *Richard II*, when the imprisoned king reflects on thought.

> My brain I'll prove the female of my soul,
> My soul the father, and these two beget
> A generation of still-breeding thoughts …[17]

On Education

Curiously enough, for so literate a man, Shakespeare never makes a point of praising formal education, not to mention higher education. In *King Henry VI: Part II*, he even seems to take the position of the religious right in questioning general education. Cade, leader of a rabble of citizens, says to one of the king's lords,

> Thou hast most traitorously corrupted the youth of the realm in erecting a grammar-school; and whereas, before, our forefathers had no other books but the score and the tally …[18]

We suspect that Shakespeare, who must have regarded himself as largely self-taught and a student of experience, provides his most personal reflection on education in *The Taming of the Shrew*. Here, the young gentleman, Lucentio, idealistically observes that he shall devote himself to that part of philosophy which teaches that happiness is achieved through virtue. His servant, Tranio, arguing for a much more practical approach to education, advises his master, on the contrary, not to let philosophy (and the Liberal Arts) get in the way of happiness.

> *Me pardonato*, gentle master mine:
> I am in all affected as yourself,
> Glad that you thus continue your resolve
> To suck the sweets of sweet philosophy.
> Only, good master, while we do admire
> This virtue and this moral discipline,
> Let's be no stoics nor no stocks, I pray;
> Or so devote to Aristotle's checks
> As Ovid be an outcast quite abjured.
> Balk Logic with acquaintance that you have
> And practice Rhetoric in your common talk.
> Music and Poetry use to quicken you;
> The Mathematics and the Metaphysics,

---

17 *Richard II*, V, v, 6ff.
18 *King Henry VI: Part II*, IV, vii, 27ff.

> Fall to them as you find your stomach serves you.
> No profit grows where is no pleasure tane ...[19]

And of course we must not fail to mention the famous reference on the importance of learning from Nature, found in *As You Like It*. Here, Duke Senior observes,

> And this is our life, exempt from public haunt,
> Finds tongues in trees, books in the running brooks,
> Sermons in stones, and good in everything.[20]

ON THE PSYCHOLOGY OF AESTHETICS

The one emotion which many sixteenth-century English writers seem to dwell on is melancholy, an association which we regard as worthy of further study. Shakespeare has created a character, Jaques, in his *As You Like It*, who has a propensity for melancholy, which he says he loves more than laughing. He offers a little dissertation on this emotion.

> I have neither the scholar's melancholy, which is emulation; nor the musician's, which is fantastical; nor the courtier's, which is proud; nor the soldier's, which is ambitious; nor the lawyer's, which is politic; nor the lady's, which is nice; nor the lover's, which is all these. But it is a melancholy of mine own, compounded of many simples, extracted from many objects, and indeed the sundry contemplation of my travels, in which my often rumination wraps me in a most humorous sadness.[21]

In *All's Well That Ends Well*, Shakespeare associates the melancholy noble with one who is always singing.

> Why, he will look upon his boot and sing; mend the ruff and sing; ask questions and sing; pick his teeth and sing.[22]

In two passages, Shakespeare mentions the importance of the face for the expression of emotions. In *Macbeth*, Duncan says,

> There's no art,
> To find the mind's construction in the face ...[23]

---

19 *The Taming of the Shrew*, I, iii, 25ff.
20 *As You Like It*, II, i, 15ff.
21 *As You Like It*, IV, i, 10ff.
22 *All's Well that Ends Well*, III, ii, 6ff.
23 *Macbeth*, I, iv, 13ff.

And in *Romeo and Juliet*, Juliet complains to her nurse,

> Now good sweet Nurse—O Lord, why look'st thou sad?
> Though news be sad, yet tell them merrily;
> If good, thou sham'st the music of sweet news
> By playing it to me with so sour a face.[24]

Of particular interest to us is Shakespeare's use of the metaphor of out of tune music for a character's emotional unbalance, a device many earlier writers also employed. In *The Comedy of Errors*, a character speaks of 'my feeble key of untuned cares'[25] and in *Much Ado About Nothing*, Hero asks Beatrice,

> Do you speak in the sick tune?[26]

In *Hamlet*, Ophelia uses the same metaphor.

> O what a noble mind is here overthrown!
> The courtier's, soldier's, scholar's eye, tongue, sword;
>
> ......
>
> And I, of ladies most deject and wretched,
> That sucked the honey of his music vows,
> Now see that noble and most sovereign reason,
> Like sweet bells jangled, out of tune and harsh ...[27]

We also find reference in Shakespeare to the fact that Reason and the Emotions exist separately, again reflecting the twin hemispheres of our brain. In *The Two Gentlemen of Verona*, Julia complains that because Proteus does not speak (left hemisphere) of Love, there must be little Love (right hemisphere). She says, 'His little speaking shows his love but small.' Her waiting-woman, Lucetta, says, No, 'Fire that's closest kept burns most of all.'[28] Another reference to the separation of Love and Reason is found in *The Merry Wives of Windsor*. Falstaff begins a letter which reads,

> Ask me no reason why I love you; for though Love use Reason for his physician, he admits him not for his counselor.[29]

---

24 *Romeo and Juliet*, II, iv, 20ff.
25 *The Comedy of Errors*, V, i. 315.
26 *Much Ado About Nothing*, II, iv, 35.
27 *Hamlet*, III, i, 155ff.
28 *The Two Gentlemen of Verona*, I, ii, 29ff.
29 *The Merry Wives of Windsor*, II, i, 4.

And in Shakespeare's poem, 'The Rape of Lucrece,' we find,

> All orators are dumb when beauty pleadeth …[30]

Shakespeare's only specific reference to the philosophical topic of Pleasure and Pain is found in a comment on Love in his poem, 'Venus and Adonis.' Here he makes the comment shared by many earlier writers, that Pleasure and Pain are always connected.

> For I have heard it is a life in death,
> That laughs and weeps, and all but with a breath.[31]

ON THE PHILOSOPHY OF AESTHETICS

On Poetry

In the comedy, *The Two Gentlemen of Verona*, there is a humorous dialog, full of double meanings, which reflects the fact that some poetry was still sung.

> JULIA. Some love of yours hath writ to you in rime.
> LUCETTA. That I might sing it, madam, to a tune.
>   Give me a note; your ladyship can set.
> JULIA. As little by such toys as may be possible;
>   Best sing it to the tune of 'Light o' Love.'[32]
> LUCETTA. It is too heavy for so light a tune.
> JULIA. Heavy! belike it hath some burden, then?
> LUCETTA. Ay; and melodious were it, would you sing it.
> JULIA. And why not you?
> LUCETTA. I cannot reach so high.
> JULIA. Let's see your song. *[Taking the letter.]* How now, minion!
> LUCETTA. Keep tune there still, so you will sing it out.
>   And yet, methinks, I do not like this tune.
> JULIA. You do not?
> LUCETTA. No, madam; it is too sharp.
> JULIA. You, minion, are too saucy.
> LUCETTA. Nay, now you are too flat.
>   And mar the concord with too harsh a descant.
>   There wanteth but a mean to fill your song.
> JULIA. The mean is drowned with your unruly bass.[33]

---

30 'The Rape of Lucrece,' 268.
31 'Venus and Adonis,' 413ff.
32 This song is mentioned again in *Much Ado About Nothing*, II, iv, 37.
33 *The Two Gentlemen of Verona*, I, ii, 83ff.

In Shakespeare's comedy, *As You Like It*, he makes fun of the Roman Church's (and contemporary Puritan) frequent accusation that the poets are liars, that they feign and deal in fables.

> AUDREY. I do not know what poetical is. Is it honest in deed and word? Is it a true thing?
> TOUCHSTONE. No, truly, for the truest poetry is the most feigning, and lovers are given to poetry. And what they swear in poetry may be said, as lovers, they do feign.
> AUDREY. Do you wish then that the gods had made me poetical?
> TOUCHSTONE. I do truly, for thou swear'st to me thou are honest. Now if thou were a poet, I might have some hope thou didst feign.
> AUDREY. Would you not have me honest?
> TOUCHSTONE. No, truly, unless thou were hard favored. For honesty coupled to beauty is to have honey a sauce to sugar.[34]

We find this issue mentioned again in *Twelfth Night*,

> OLIVIA. I forgive you the praise.
> VIOLA. Alas, I took great pains to study it, and 'tis poetical.
> OLIVIA. It is the more like to be feigned …[35]

and in *Timon of Athens*,

> APEMANTUS. Art not a poet?
> POET. Yes.
> APEMANTUS. Then thou liest: look in thy last work, where thou hast feigned him a worthy fellow.
> POET. That's not feigned; he is so.
> APEMANTUS. Yes, he is worthy of thee, and to pay thee for thy labour; he that loves to be flattered is worthy of the flatterer.[36]

Shakespeare mentions epic poetry in his poem 'The Rape of Lucrece.'

> Feast-finding minstrels, tuning my defame,
> Will tie the hearers to attend each line …[37]

We should point out that one play, *Pericles, Prince of Tyre*, is itself presented as a work of epic poetry. Gower, a medieval poet who presents this story to Shakespeare, begins,

> To sing a song that old was sung,
> From ashes ancient Gower is come,

---

34 *As You Like It*, II, iii, 13ff.
35 *Twelfth Night or What You Will*, I, v, 177ff.
36 *Timon of Athens*, I, i, 247ff.
37 'The Rape of Lucrece,' 817ff.

> Assuming man's infirmities,
> To glad your ear, and please your eyes.
> It hath been sung at festivals,
> On ember-eves, and holy-ales;
> And lords and ladies in their lives
> Have read it for restoratives …

On the Theater

An important play within a play affords Shakespeare the opportunity to make several reflections on the writing of plays. First, he makes fun of the growing specialization of the form, which now he enumerates as,

> tragedy, comedy, history, pastoral, pastoral-comical, historical-pastoral, tragical-historical, tragical-comical-historical-pastoral …[38]

In this same scene he indicates that an excellent play is one 'well digested in the scenes, set down with as much modesty as cunning.'

Shakespeare also gives a definition of the purpose of historical plays at a time before history books were commonly available to the general public. In the words of Hamlet he says of plays,

> they are abstract and brief chronicles of the time. After your death you were better have a bad epitaph than their ill report while you live.[39]

In *The Taming of the Shrew*, which is itself in entirety a play within a play, a Messenger provides a purpose of comedy.

> Seeing too much sadness hath congealed your blood,
> And melancholy is the nurse of frenzy:
> Therefore [the doctors] thought it good you hear a play
> And frame your mind to mirth and merriment,
> Which bars a thousand harms and lengthens life.[40]

The religious right in England had, by the end of the sixteenth century, begun attacking plays and actors in published treatises and in sermons. The actors were held to be, like the poets, participants in untruths. Shakespeare saw this from a somewhat different perspective, having been an actor himself. He looked with resignation on the fact that the actor expends

---

38 *Hamlet*, II, ii, 391ff.
39 *Hamlet*, II, ii, 513ff.
40 *The Taming of the Shrew*, I, ii, 140ff.

so much emotion for something which is after all not real. Shakespeare, through Hamlet, observes of the actor,

> Is it not monstrous that this player here,
> But in a fiction, in a dream of passion,
> Could force his soul so to his own conceit
> That from her working all the visage wann'd,
> Tears in his eyes, distraction in 's aspect,
> A broken voice, and his whole function suiting
> With forms to his conceit? and all for nothing![41]

And of course, Macbeth, in one of Shakespeare's most familiar passages, speaks of life, but the analogy also speaks of his perspective of acting.

> Life's but a walking shadow, a poor player
> That struts and frets his hour upon the stage,
> And then is heard no more. It is a tale
> Told by an idiot, full of sound and fury,
> Signifying nothing.[42]

In *Hamlet*, Shakespeare gives some very specific advice on acting, which we may imagine was the product of his own experience.[43] First, he does not like actors who gesture too much, 'saw the air too much with your hand.' He also questions great displays of emotion, especially for a general public whose experience has not prepared them to view such emotional expression.

> O it offends me to the soul to hear a robustious periwig-pated fellow tear a passion to tatters, to very rags, to split the ears of the groundlings, who for the most part are capable of nothing but inexplicable dumb-shows and noise.

Then he directly addresses the actor.

> Be not too tame neither, but let your own discretion be your tutor. Suit the action to the word, the word to the action, with this special observance, that you overstep not the modesty of nature; for anything so overdone is from the purpose of playing, whose end, both at the first and now, was and is to hold, as 'twere, the mirror up to nature, to show virtue her own feature, scorn her own image, and the very age and body of the time his form and pressure. Now this overdone, or come tardy off, though it makes the unskillful laugh, cannot but make the judicious grieve …

---

41   *Hamlet*, II, ii, 537ff.
42   *Macbeth*, V, v, 25ff
43   *Hamlet*, III, ii.

Also from his experience, as a playwright, he adds, no improvisation, please!

> And let those that play your clowns speak no more than is set down for them …

Another reference to actors is found in *Coriolanus*, when Coriolanus comments in passing,

> Like a dull actor now,
> I have forgot my part …⁴⁴

On Painting

While Shakespeare mentions painting a number of times in his plays, he does not reveal much regarding his own understanding of aesthetics in painting. The few insights we can deduce in this regard come from the single, but ancient, question regarding whether Art should imitate Nature. He mentions this question in *Timon of Athens*, where the suggestion is made that the artist has surpassed nature.

> PAINTER. It is a pretty mocking of the life.
>   Here is a touch; is 't good?
> POET. I'll say of it,
>   It tutors nature: artificial strife
>   Lives in these touches, livelier than life.⁴⁵

Shakespeare brings up this question again in the comedy, *The Winter's Tale*, where Polixenes, in disguise at a shepherd's cottage, offers a rather philosophic view of the question.

> Yet nature is made better by no mean
> But nature makes that mean: so, over that art,
> Which you say adds to nature, is an art
> That nature makes.⁴⁶

Shakespeare touches on this once more in his poem, 'Venus and Adonis,'

> Look, when a painter would surpass the life,
> In limning out a well-proportioned steed,
> His art with nature's workmanship at strife,
> As if the dead the living should exceed …⁴⁷

---

44 *Coriolanus*, V, iii, 44ff.
45 *Timon of Athens*, I, i, 43ff.
46 *The Winter's Tale*, IV, iv, 103ff.
47 'Venus and Adonis,' 289ff.

A brief reference to technique is found in *King Lear* where the Earl of Kent observes, 'A stone-cutter or a painter could not have made him so ill, though they had been but two hours o' th' trade.'[48]

ON THE AESTHETICS OF MUSIC

What can we deduce from his writings about Shakespeare's general aesthetic views on music? To begin with it seems clear that he was aware of the old Scholastic misunderstanding, by which music was taught as a branch of mathematics. He leaves this clue in *The Taming of the Shrew*, when Hortensio presents himself in the disguise of a music teacher, Shakespeare has him introduced as a man 'Cunning in music and the mathematics.'[49]

Shakespeare also seems to have been well read with respect to earlier theories on music, as we can see in his several references to the ancient Greek notion of the 'Music of the Spheres.' The most extended of these is found in *The Merchant of Venice*, where Lorenzo reflects,

> How sweet the moonlight sleeps upon this bank!
> Here will we sit, and let the sounds of music
> Creep in our ears; soft stillness and the night
> Become the touches of sweet harmony.
> Sir, Jessica: look, how the floor of heaven
> is thick inlaid with [patterns] of bright gold:
> There's not the smallest orb which thou behold'st
> But in his motion like an angel sings,
> Still choiring to the young-eyed cherubins;
> Such harmony is in immortal souls;
> But, whilst this muddy vesture of decay
> Doth grossly close it in, we cannot hear it.[50]

But, to use the expression of Shakespeare's contemporary, Morley, there is a 'science and mystery' to music and Shakespeare was also aware of the 'mystery,' as we can see in *Much Ado About Nothing*, where Benedick hears music and observes,

> Now, divine air! now is his soul ravished! Is it not strange that sheeps' guts should hale souls out of men's bodies?[51]

---

48 *King Lear*, II, ii, 51.

49 *The Taming of the Shrew*, II, ii, 57.

50 *The Merchant of Venice*, V, i, 61ff. Additional references to the 'Music of the Spheres,' can be found in *As You Like It*, II, vii, 6; *Henry VIII*, IV, ii, 85ff and *Twelfth Night or What You Will*, III, i, 109.

51 *Much Ado About Nothing*, II, iii, 55ff.

We believe that as Shakespeare looked around at the cast of real characters he came in contact with in sixteenth-century England, he must have concluded that the more refined also had an interest in, and perhaps even performed, music of a higher aesthetic level. There are hints of this throughout his plays, but it is voiced most clearly by Lorenzo, in *The Merchant of Venice*.

> The man that hath no music in himself,
> Nor is not moved with concord of sweet sounds,
> Is fit for treasons, stratagems, and spoils;
> The motions of his spirit are dull as night,
> And his affections dark as Erebus:
> Let no such man be trusted.[52]

Shakespeare obviously felt the same applied to women. In *Much Ado About Nothing*, there is a young noble of Padua, Benedick,[53] who is a confirmed bachelor, determined never to marry. But, on one occasion he does list the qualities a woman must have, should he decide to marry. She must be rich, good-looking, noble and an excellent musician.[54] Also, Othello includes music among the virtues of his wife.

> To say my wife is fair, feeds well, loves company,
> Is free of speech, sings, plays, and dances well.
> Where virtue is, these are more virtuous.[55]

We suspect Shakespeare's own taste in music tended to be more conservative and that Juliet was expressing his preference, and not the lark's, in *Romeo and Juliet*.

> It is the lark that sings so out of tune,
> Straining harsh discords and unpleasing sharps.[56]

The same preference, stated in a more positive way, is clear in his praise of harmony in his 'Sonnet VIII.'

> Music to hear, why hear'st thou music sadly?
> Sweets with sweets war not, joy delights in joy:
> Why lov'st thou that which thou receiv'st not gladly,
> Or else receiv'st with pleasure thine annoy?
> If the true concord of well-tuned sounds,

---

52 *The Merchant of Venice*, V, i, 91ff.
53 The spelling of the name is a typical example of Shakespeare's humor, like the preacher 'Martext' in *As You Like It*.
54 *Much Ado About Nothing*, II, iii, 26ff.
55 *Othello*, III, iii, 209.
56 *Romeo and Juliet*, III, v, 27ff.

By unions married, do offend thine ear,
They do but sweetly chide thee, who confounds
In singleness the parts that thou shouldst bear.
Mark how one string, sweet husband to another,
Strikes each in each by mutual ordering;
Resembling sire and child and happy mother,
Who, all in one, one pleasing note do sing:
Whose speechless song, being many, seeming one,
Sings this to thee: 'Thou single wilt prove none.'

It also seems clear that Shakespeare was observant of changes in contemporary taste, in particular the emergence of the preference for string instruments in England, which we believe forms part of the background for a passage in *Othello*. We remind the reader that 'noise' was an English synonym for wind music, hence his play on this word. Cassio meets a group of musicians and tells them he will pay them to play something brief. They play and then a clown enters and initiates the following exchange.

CLOWN. Why, masters, have your instruments been at Naples, that they speak i' th' nose thus?
MUSICIAN. How, sir? how?
CLOWN. Are these, I pray, called wind instruments?
MUSICIAN. Ay, marry, are they, sir.
CLOWN. O! thereby hangs a tail.
MUSICIAN. Whereby hangs a tale, sir?
CLOWN. Marry, sir, by many a wind instrument that I know. But, masters, here's money for you; and the general so likes your music that he desires you, of all loves, to make no more noise with it.
MUSICIAN. Well, sir, we will not.
CLOWN. If you have any music that may not be heard, to't again; but (as they say) to hear music the general does not greatly care.
MUSICIAN. We ha' none such, sir.
CLOWN. Then put up your pipes in your bag, for I'll away. go; vanish into air; away!
       Exeunt Musicians.[57]

On the Purposes and Use of Music

The purpose of music most frequently mentioned by earlier writers was its ability to soothe the listener or player, as we see in *Henry VIII*, when the rejected queen Katherine calls for music to soothe her feelings.

---

57 *Othello*, the beginning of Act III.

QUEEN. Take thy lute, wench; my soul grows sad with troubles;
Sing and disperse 'em, if thou canst. Leave working.

Song

Orpheus with his lute made trees,
And the mountain tops that freeze,
Bow themselves, when he did sing:
To his music plants and flowers
Ever sprung, as sun and showers
There had made a lasting spring.

Every thing that heard him play,
Even the billows of the sea,
Hung their heads, and then lay by.
In sweet music is such art,
Killing care and grief of heart
Fall asleep or, hearing, die.[58]

In *Romeo and Juliet*, after Juliet has taken a sleeping potion and appears to have died, three musicians who had been called for entertainment are about to leave, realizing that it is an inappropriate time for their kind of music.[59] Peter, the servant to Juliet's nurse, asks them to stay and play music to soothe his feelings.

PETER. O Musicians, because my heart itself plays 'My Heart is Full'—O play me some merry dump to comfort me.
1. MUSICIAN. Not a dump, we, 'tis no time to play now.

Shakespeare now turns this into a comic scene as the musicians and Peter argue over possible tunes they might play. Peter begins to quote one,

When Griping griefs the heart doth wound,
(And doleful dumps the mind oppress,)
Then music with her silver sound—

Peter breaks off, asking what the last line means. A musician answers that it means musicians make their sound for silver (coins).

Shakespeare in his fairy tale, *The Tempest*, has Ariel, a musician of the spirit world, sing to soothe the survivors of a shipwreck. One of these, Ferdinand, reflects,

This music crept by me upon the waters,
Allaying both their fury and my passion
With its sweet air …[60]

---

58   *Henry VIII*, III, i.
59   *Romeo and Juliet*, IV, iv, 131ff.
60   *The Tempest*, I, ii, 459ff

In the same play, Prospero, the duke of Milan, turned magician, after hearing the 'solemn music' requested in the stage direction, observes,

> A solemn air and the best comforter
> To an unsettled fancy, cure thy brains,
> Now useless, boil'd within thy skull …[61]

There are two rather unusual references to the purpose of music being to soothe. The first comes in *Macbeth* where the witches offer music and dance.

> 1 WITCH. Ay, sir, all this is so. But why
>   Stands Macbeth thus amazedly?
>   Come, sisters, cheer we up his sprites,
>   And show the best of our delights.
>   I'll charm the air to give a sound,
>   While you perform your antic round …
>   *Music. The Witches dance, and vanish.*[62]

Shakespeare, in his comedy, *As You Like It*, creates a character, the cynical malcontent, Jaques, who is soothed by melancholy emotions. Amiens, a professional singer, sings a song which ends,

> Come hither, come hither, come hither!
> Here shall he see
> No enemy
> But winter and rough weather.

> JAQUES. More, more, I prithee, more.
> AMIENS. It will make you melancholy, Monsieur Jaques.
> JAQUES. I thank it. More, I prithee, more. I can suck melancholy out of a song as a weasel sucks
>   eggs. More, I prithee, more.
> AMIENS. My voice is ragged; I know I cannot please you.
> JAQUES. I do not desire you to please me; I do desire you to sing. Come, more: another stanzo.
>   Call you 'em stanzos?
> AMIENS. What you will, Monsieur Jaques.
> JAQUES. Nay, I care not for their names; they owe me nothing. Will you sing?
> AMIENS. More at your request than to please myself.[63]

There are two instances in the plays where music is not effective in its capacity to soothe. In *Richard II* the queen is depressed and her ladies-in-waiting suggest, as means of cheering

---

[61] *The Tempest*, V, i, 63ff.
[62] *Macbeth*, IV, i, 136ff.
[63] *As You Like It*, II, v.

her up, bowling, dancing and telling tales, all of which the queen rejects. Finally a lady suggests music, but the queen rejects that as well.

> LADY. Madam, I'll sing.
> QUEEN. 'Tis well that thou hast cause.
>   But thou shouldst please me better, wouldst thou weep.
> LADY. I could weep, madam, would it do you good.
> QUEEN. And I could sing, would weeping do me good,
>   And never borrow any tear of thee.[64]

In the second instance, Shakespeare provides the reason why music does not soothe. Jessica in *The Merchant of Venice* says, 'I am never merry when I hear sweet music.' Lorenzo answers, 'The reason is, your spirits are [in]attentive.'[65]

A closely related purpose of music is to refresh the mind, as we find in *The Taming of the Shrew*, when Lucentio, in criticizing a pretended music teacher, observes,

> Preposterous ass, that never read so far
> To know the cause why music was ordained!
> Was it not to refresh the mind of man
> After his studies or his usual pain?[66]

Perhaps the most universally understood purpose of music is to express feelings. Before we consider some of Shakespeare's illustration of this purpose, we might point out that the more basic purpose of music simply to communicate is referred to by analogy in *Richard II*, after the king has exiled the duke of Norfolk for life. The latter responds,

> My native English, now I must forgo;
> And now my tongue's use is to me no more
> Than an unstringed viol or a harp,
> Or like a cunning instrument cased up …[67]

So direct is music in expressing emotions, that in *The Merry Wives of Windsor*, a singer almost begins to cry in the middle of her own song.[68] In *Twelfth Night*, Viola speaks of the variety of possible emotional expression,

> I can sing,
> And speak to him in many sorts of music.[69]

---

64 *Richard II*, III, iv, 3ff.
65 *The Merchant of Venice*, V, I, 77.
66 *The Taming of the Shrew*, III, i, 9ff.
67 *Richard II*, I, iii, 160ff.
68 *The Merry Wives of Windsor*, III, i, 18.
69 *Twelfth Night or What You Will*, I, ii, 59ff.

In *The Merchant of Venice*, Portia calls for music while Bassanio makes his choice of three caskets, one of which wins Portia as his wife. Portia instructs the musicians, that if he picks the wrong one, they are to play something sad,

> Let music sound while he doth make his choice;
> Then, if he lose, he makes a swan-like end,
> Fading in music …

But if he selects the correct one,

> He may win;
> And what is music then? then music is
> Even as the flourish when true subjects bow
> To a new-crowned monarch …[70]

In the comedy, *Twelfth Night*, Shakespeare makes fun of the universally understood purpose of music to express emotions. Of course, what is usually understood is that music expresses the emotion truthfully and accurately. Shakespeare's joke is in having the singer and listeners all respond with emotions that have nothing to do with the music. First, the duke asks to hear,

> That old and antique song we heard last night,
> Methought it did relieve my passion much,
> More than light airs …

Shortly after, Viola, when asked how she likes this tune, reflects,

> It gives a very echo to the seat
> Where love is throned.

Shakespeare further prepares the audience for his jolt by having the duke observe that this song is often sung by women while working at spinning and weaving. But when this song is finally sung by the court singer, Feste, it turns out to be a dark and morbid song about death!

> Come away, come away, death,
> And in sad cypress let me be laid.
> Fie, away; fie, away, breath;
> I am slain by a fair cruel maid …

---

70 *The Merchant of Venice*, III, ii, 45ff.

Shakespeare completes this absurd scene by having the singer say he takes *pleasure* in singing this particular song.[71]

Finally, in *Henry VIII*, the despondent former queen Katherine requests music expressing her state of feelings.

> KATHERINE. Cause the musicians play me that sad note
>   I named my knell, whilst I set meditating
>   On that celestial harmony I go to.

This is followed by the stage direction, 'Sad and solemn music.' This music continues as Katherine has a Vision. When she wakes up, she says,

> Bid the music leave.
> They are harsh and heavy on me.
>   *Music ceases.*[72]

In one case, Shakespeare points to the effectiveness of music to express melancholy, an emotion much dwelled on in sixteenth-century England. In *The Two Gentlemen of Verona*, Proteus pretends to help his rival, Thurio, court Silvia by encouraging him to organize a serenade, by which he can impress her with the sincerity of his melancholy.

> For Orpheus' lute was strung with poets' sinews,
> Whose golden touch could soften steel and stones,
> Make tigers tame and huge leviathans
> Forsake unsounded deeps to dance on sands.
> After your dire-lamenting elegies,
> Visit by night your lady's chamber-window
> With some sweet consort; to their instruments
> Tune a deploring dump; the night's dead silence
> Will well become such sweet-complaining grievance.[73]

Thurio agrees with the plan and suggests going into the city 'To sort some gentlemen well skilled in music' to sing the serenade for him. When the serenade, for which Shakespeare gives the words, occurs, the focus is on Julia, in disguise as a boy, who unhappily hears this serenade to another woman.

> HOST. How now! are you sadder than you were before?
>   How do you, man? The music likes you not.
> JULIA. You mistake; the musician likes me not.

---

71 *Twelfth Night or What You Will*, II, iv. At the beginning of Act III, Viola asks this musician, 'Do you live by the tabor?' 'No,' he answers, 'I live by the Church.' She asks, 'Art thou a churchman?' No, he says, I live in a house *by* the Church!

72 *Henry VIII*, IV, ii, 85ff.

73 *The Two Gentlemen of Verona*, III, ii, 78ff.

HOST. Why, my pretty youth?
JULIA. He plays false, father.
HOST. How? Out of tune on the strings?
JULIA. Not so; but yet so false that he grieves my very heartstrings.
HOST. You have a quick ear.
JULIA. Ay; I would I were deaf; it makes me have a slow heart.
HOST. I perceive you delight not in music.
JULIA. Not a whit,—when it jars so.
HOST. Hark! what fine change is in the music!
JULIA. Ay, that change is the sprite.
HOST. You would have them always play but one thing?
JULIA. I would always have one play but one thing.[74]

One important purpose of music for the sixteenth-century courtier was as an aid in wooing the ladies, which Shakespeare acknowledges through several serenades in his plays. The *Twelfth Night or What You Will* begins with one of Shakespeare's most familiar lines, an homage to the relationship of love and music.

If music be the food of love, play on!
Give me excess of it, that surfeiting,
The appetite may sicken and so die.
That strain again! It had a dying fall;
O, it came over my ear like the sweet sound
That breathes upon a bank of violets,
Stealing and giving odor.

In *All's Well That Ends Well* there is a reference to a persistent serenader.

Every night he comes
With music of all sorts and songs composed
To her unworthiness: it nothing steads us
To chide him from our eaves, for he persists
As if his life lay on it.[75]

In *Cymbeline*, in a scene intended to be humorous, Cloten arranges a morning serenade by a group of string players in an attempt to woo Imogen.

CLOTEN. It's almost morning, is't not?
1. LORD. Day, my lord.
CLOTEN. I would this music would come. I am advised to give her music o' mornings; they say
  it will penetrate

---

74 *The Two Gentlemen of Verona*, IV, ii, 40ff.
75 *All's Well that Ends Well*, III, vii, 44ff.

> *Enter Musicians.*
>
> Come on; tune. If you can penetrate her with your fingering, so; we'll try with tongue too: if none will do, let her remain; but I'll never give o'er. First, a very excellent good-conceited thing; after, a wonderful sweet air, with admirable rich words to it: and then let her consider.
> *Song*
>> Hark! hark! the lark at heaven's gate sings,
>> And Phoebus 'gins arise,
>> His steeds to water at those springs
>> On chalic'd flowers that lies;
>> And winking Mary-buds begin
>> To ope their golden eyes:
>> With everything that pretty is,
>> My lady sweet, arise:
>> Arise, arise!
>
> So, get you gone. If this penetrate, I will consider your music the better; if it do not, it is a vice in her ears, which horsehairs and calves'-guts, nor the voice of unpaved eunuch to boot, can never amend.
> *Exeunt Musicians.*[76]

The serenade had no effect, for Cloten complains, 'I have assail'd her with musics, but she vouchsafes no notice.'

Another purpose of music is to express love, as testified to by that most famous of lovers, Cleopatra.

> Give me some music: music, moody food
> Of us that trade in love.[77]

A purpose of music frequently mentioned by ancient philosophers was music therapy. Shakespeare makes only two references to this, the first in *Pericles, Prince of Tyre*. Thaisa is thought to have died aboard ship and her body is placed in a box and thrown over the side. She is washed ashore in Ephesus, where she is revived by a skillful physician. Shakespeare does not discuss the physician's medical techniques, but uses the mystery of music, with its long association with music therapy, as a metaphor for the healing process.

> The rough and woeful music that we have,
> Cause it to sound, beseech you.
> The viol once more;—how thou stirr'st, thou block!
> The music there! I pray you, give her air.[78]

---

76 *Cymberline*, II, iii, 7ff.
77 *Antony and Cleopatra*, II, v, 1ff.
78 *Pericles, Prince of Tyre*, III, ii, 99ff.

The second reference to music therapy is found in *Richard II*, when the imprisoned king, having heard some music, says,

> This music mads me. Let it sound no more,
> For though it have helped mad men to their wits,
> In me it seems it will make wise men mad.
> Yet blessing on his heart that gives it me!
> For 'tis a sign of love …[79]

The closely related purpose of music, to affect one's character is mentioned in *The Tempest*, when the duke of Milan, turned magician, calls for,

> Some heavenly music—which even now I do—
> To work mine end upon their senses …[80]

Shakespeare provides a much more vivid illustration of this purpose, including music's effect on animals, in *The Merchant of Venice*. Lorenzio, speaking of the power of music, observes,

> For do but note a wild and wanton herd,
> Or race of youthful and unhandled colts,
> Fetching mad bounds, bellowing and neighing loud,
> Which is the hot condition of their blood;
> If they but hear perchance a trumpet sound,
> Or any air of music touch their ears,
> You shall perceive them make a mutual stand,
> Their savage eyes turned to a modest gaze
> By the sweet power of music: therefore the poet
> Did feign that Orpheus drew trees, stones, and floods;
> Since nought so stockish, hard, and full of rage,
> But music for the time doth change his nature.[81]

Shakespeare makes only one reference to contemporary performance practice. This, a criticism, is found in *Richard II*, following a stage direction reading, 'The music plays,' when the king observes,

> Music do I hear?
> Ha, ha! Keep time. How sour sweet music is
> When time is broke and no proportion kept![82]

---

79 *Richard II*, V, v, 61ff.s
80 *The Tempest*, V, i, 57ff.
81 *The Merchant of Venice*, V, i, 79ff.
82 *Richard II*, V, v, 41ff.

On Music Education

The first of two references to music education in the plays of Shakespeare is an observation on children's performance. In *A Midsummer Night's Dream*, after the prologue of a play within a play, Hippolyta observes,

> Indeed he hath played on his prologue like a child on a recorder; a sound, but not in government.[83]

In the comedy, *The Taming of the Shrew*, the nobleman, Baptista, observing that his daughter, Bianca, loves music and poetry, decides to hire a 'schoolmaster' in those subjects to come to the palace to instruct both his daughters. Hortensio, desiring to woo Bianca, disguises himself as a music teacher and is hired, but he first must give a music lesson to the older sister, the 'shrew' Kate. After this ill-fated lesson, he reports to the father that Kate hit him over the head with his lute and called him a 'fiddler,' an intended derogatory reference to an instrument still associated with peasants.

> BAPTISTA. How now, my friend! why dost thou look so pale?
> HORTENSIO. For fear, I promise you, if I look pale.
> BAPTISTA. What, will my daughter prove a good musician?
> HORTENSIO. I think she'll sooner prove a soldier.
>   Iron may hold with her but never lutes.
> BAPTISTA. Why, then thou canst not break her to the lute?
> HORTENSIO. Why, no; for she hath broke the lute to me.
>   I did but tell her she mistook her frets
>   And bowed her hand to reach her fingering;
>   When, with a most impatient devilish spirit,
>   'Frets, call you these?' quoth she; 'I'll fume with them';
>   And, with that word, she stroke me on the head,
>   And through the instrument my pate made way.
>   And there I stood amazed for a while.
>   As on a pillory, looking through the lute,
>   While she did call me rascal, fiddler.[84]

When Hortensio arrives to give a music lesson to Bianca,[85] he finds her having a Latin lesson with another gentleman, Lucentio, who also wishes to woo her. When he tries to interrupt, Bianca tells him to go tune his instrument while she finishes with Lucentio. Hortensio interrupts again,

---

83 *A Midsummer Night's Dream*, V, i, 123ff.
84 *The Taming of the Shrew*, II, i, 145ff.
85 *The Taming of the Shrew*, III, i.

HORTENSIO. Madam, my instrument's in tune.
BIANCA. Let's hear.—O fie! the treble jars.
LUCENTIO. Spit in the hole, man, and tune again.

When it is finally his turn, Hortensio tells Lucentio to leave. Lucentio, correctly guessing that Hortensio is another suitor, decides to stay and listen.

HORTENSIO. You may go walk and give me leave a while;
   My lessons make no music in three parts.
LUCENTIO. Are you so formal, sir? *[Aside]* Well, I must wait
   And watch withal; for, but I be deceived,
   Our fine musician groweth amorous.
HORTENSIO. Madam, before you touch the instrument
   To learn the order of my fingering,
   I must begin with rudiments of art
   To teach you gamouth [diatonic scale] in a briefer sort,
   More pleasant, pithy, and effectual,
   Than hath been taught by any of my trade;
   And there it is in writing, fairly drawn.
BIANCA. Why, I am past my gamouth long ago.
HORTENSIO. Yet read the gamouth of Hortensio.
BIANCA.
     'Gamouth' I am, the ground of all accord,
     'A re,' to plead Hortensio's passion;
     'B mi,' Bianca, take him for thy lord,
     'C fa ut,' that loves with all affection;
     'D sol re,' one clef, two notes have I;
     'E la me,' show pity or I die.
   Call you this gamouth? tut, I like it not.
   Old fashions please me best; I am not so nice
   To change true rules for odd inventions.

MUSIC IN THE STAGE DIRECTIONS

A great deal of information about performance practice in sixteenth-century England can be gained from Shakespeare's notations in the margins known as stage directions. The music he calls for here is often for the purpose of introducing his characters.

The aristocratic trumpeter, and the music he played, served as an aural coat-of-arms or flag, announcing from the distance the identity of the noble who was approaching. One sees this reflected numerous times in the Shakespeare plays, although by no means every time a noble appears. Why Shakespeare calls for such fanfares in his stage directions when he does is not entirely clear.

That Shakespeare recognized this ancient tradition is documented in the text itself, as in *All's Well That Ends Well*, following a stage direction 'Trumpets sound,' Lafeu says, 'The king's coming; I know by his trumpets.'[86] Similarly, in *Titus Andronicus*, Lucius says, 'The trumpets show the emperor is at hand.' This is followed by the stage direction,

> *Sound trumpets. Enter Emperor and Empress ...*[87]

This link between the noble and his music was so important that we see in *Measure for Measure* the duke, upon his return to Vienna, will not enter through the city gates until his trumpets arrive. He gives the order, 'bid them bring the trumpets to the gate.'[88]

Shakespeare also used this well-known tradition to lend verisimilitude to his plot development on occasion. For example, *The Taming of the Shrew* begins with a drunk derelict, named Sly, whom a noble finds and, for his own amusement, takes him to his palace, dresses him in fine clothes, etc., in order to convince the man, when he awakes, that he is a noble who has been asleep many years. Thus, when the stage direction indicates 'Sound trumpets,'[89] it is part of the necessary atmosphere to make Sly believe what he has been told. Similarly, it is the stage direction, 'Sound the Trumpets,' for the entrance the three gentlemen *disguised* as Russian nobles in *Love's Labour's Lost*, which helps lend them authenticity.[90]

We should also mention that since it was a tradition for these plays themselves to begin with a trumpet fanfare, it is no surprise to find Shakespeare, when presenting a play within a play in *A Midsummer Night's Dream*, requiring before the actor's prologue a 'Flourish of Trumpets.' When the players enter, the stage direction again reads 'with a trumpet before them.'[91]

---

86 *All's Well that Ends Well*, V, ii, 42ff. Similar uses of trumpet fanfares can be found in:
   King Henry IV: Part I, V, i., for the entrance of the Earl of Worcester and for the king's entrance in V, ii and V, iv.
   King Henry IV: Part II, V, v, for the entrance of king Henry V.
   King Henry VI: Part I, IV, ii, for the entrance of a general and in V, iii, duke Reignier, titular king of Naples, enters to a trumpet.
   King Henry VI: Part II, III, iii; III, i and V, v, for the entrance of the king.
   Richard II, I, iii, for the arrival of the king.
   Richard III, III, i, for the entrance of the prince of Wales and others and for the arrival of Richard in IV, iv.
   Henry VIII, I, for the exit of the king and for the entrance of the Lord Mayor, V, v.
   Titus Andronicus, I, i, for the entrance of the sons of Titus (with drums).
   Antony and Cleopatra, III, ii, for the exit of Antony and the entrance of Antony, IV, v.
   Timon of Athens, I, i, for the entrance of Timon and V, iii for the entrance of Alcibiades.

87 *Titus Andronicus*, V, iii.

88 *Measure for Measure*, IV, v.

89 *The Taming of the Shrew*, I, i, 76. As part of the preparations, the Lord says,

   Procure me music ready when he wakes
   To make a dulcet and heavenly sound ...

90 *Love's Labour's Lost*, V, ii, 164.

91 *A Midsummer Night's Dream*, V, i, 111ff.

Sometimes Shakespeare calls for specific musical forms to provide these musical introductions. We cannot know today what was understood in the sixteenth century by *Flourish*, *Sennet*, or *Tucket*, other than the fact that they all seem to fulfill the function of a fanfare. Nevertheless, it might be profitable to consider briefly Shakespeare's use of these forms.

Flourish

The most frequent appearance of a Flourish in the stage directions is for the entrance or exit of important personages. A typical example is found in *King Henry VI: Part III*, II, ii, which begins with stage direction,

> *Flourish. Enter the King, the Queen ... and young Prince, with drum and trumpets.*[92]

Usually, it appears that the Flourish was performed by trumpets, and sometimes with drums indicated, as we see in the final scene of *Henry VI: Part III*, which begins with a Flourish for the entrance of the king and queen and ends with the king's lines,

> Sound drums and trumpets! farewell sour annoy!
> For here, I hope, begins our lasting joy.[93]

A very rare exception is the inclusion of oboes, which we find at the beginning of *King Henry VI: Part II*, where Shakespeare has a stage direction requesting,

> *Flourish of Trumpets: then hautboys. Enter King ...*

There are a few instances in Shakespeare where the stage directions call for a Flourish by cornetts. In the plays of the following generation, the cornett is sometimes used as a kind

---

92 Also IV, i and IV, vi, for the entrance of the king and III, iii, for the entrance of the French king. Additional examples of a Flourish can be found in:
Richard II, II, ii, for the entrance of the king reads 'Drums. Flourish and colors'; II, ii for the entrance of the king; V, vi, for the entrance of several dukes; II, i, for the exit of several dukes and III, iii, for the exit of the king.
Richard III, II, i, for the entrance of king Edward IV and IV, iv, for the exit of Richard.
Troilus and Cressida, III, iii, for the entrance of military commanders.
All's Well That Ends Well, III, i and III, iii, for the entrance of the duke of Florence.
Henry VI: Part I, I, ii, for the entrance of the Dauphin Charles.
Henry VI: Part II, IV, ix, for the exit of the king and queen.
Henry V, several times for the entrance of the Chorus; II, iv, for the entrance of the French king and III, iii, to enter a town.
Titus Andronicus, III, i, for the entrance of Caesar and the beginning of Act II, for the entrance of Aaron.
Hamlet, I, ii and II, ii, for the entrance of the king and II, ii, 365, for the entrance of actors for a play within a play.
King Lear, II, ii, for the exit of nobles.
Macbeth, I, iv, for the exit of king Duncan.
Antony and Cleopatra, I, i, for the entrance of Antony; II, iii, for the exit of Antony; II, vi and IV, v, for the entrance of Agrippa and Caesar.

93 *King Henry VI: Part III*, final two lines.

of lesser trumpet, for announcing lesser nobles such as dukes. This does not seem to be the case in Shakespeare, however, it does appear that he uses other instruments than trumpets to represent non-English kings. Thus, we see the call for a 'Flourish of Cornets' for the arrival of the king of France in *All's Well that Ends Well*[94] and in *The Merchant of Venice*, the prince of Morocco is ushered off, and the prince of Arragon on, by 'Flourish of Cornets.'[95]

In this regard, we know of only one instance where an oboe consort performs the music for the entrance of an important person. In *Henry VIII*, I, iv, the stage direction calls for 'Hautboys' for the entrance of Cardinal Wolsey, which seems appropriate for it was widely known that he maintained a personal consort of this type.

What clues do we have regarding the style of a 'Flourish?' This question is made difficult by the varying circumstances in which we find the stage direction. Sometimes it is associated with festive moments, as in *Henry VI: Part I*, i, ii, where Charles calls for a banquet to celebrate victory[96] or in *Henry VI: Part III*, where a coronation seems to require a Flourish.

> HASTINGS. Sound, trumpet! Edward shall be here proclaimed;
>   Come, fellow soldier, make thou proclamation.
>   *Flourish. Sound.*
> SOLDIER. Edward the Fourth, by the grace of God, King of England and France, and Lord of
>   Ireland, etc.[97]

Similarly, in *Titus Andronicus* 'Flourish' is found several times as the crowd cheers Caesar.[98] In *Coriolanus* there are three Flourishes played by cornetts and all share a certain joyous emotion with the text. The stage direction in II, i, 'A Flourish. Cornets,' is followed by a line reading, 'The town is taken!' perhaps suggests a sense of celebration. 'Flourish, Cornetts. Exeunt in state,' is found in II, i, 200, and in II, iii, 175, a Senator says, 'To Coriolanus come all joy and honor!' which is followed by a stage direction 'Flourish cornets.'

In a similar mood, there are entrances which seem like festive processions, as in *Henry VI: Part III*, where, after a battle, the stage direction reads,

> *Flourish. Enter King Edward, in triumph* ...[99]

Perhaps, such a procession implies a strong metric beat, for in the following scene (V, iv) the queen, and later Edward, each enter to 'Flourish. March.' Similarly, in *Titus Andronicus*, at the end of V, i, Lucius says, 'And we will come. March away.' This is followed by the stage

---

94 *All's Well that Ends Well*, I, ii. Again when he enters and exits in Act II.
95 *The Merchant of Venice*, II, vii, viii.
96 *King Henry VI: Part I*, the end of Act I.
97 *King Henry VI: Part III*, IV, vii, 69ff.
98 *Julius Caesar*, I, ii.
99 *King Henry VI: Part III*, V, iii.

direction, 'Flourish.' For the entrance of the king of Denmark, in *Hamlet*, the stage direction is more specific.

Danish March. Sound a Flourish.[100]

In some cases, however, there is a more militant or somber moment associated with the Flourish, as in *Richard III*, when Richard threatens to kill Queen Elizabeth and the Duchess of York,

    KING RICHARD. A flourish, trumpets! strike alarum, drums!
      Let not the heavens hear these tell-tale women
      Rail on the Lord's annointed. Strike, I say!
          Flourish, Alarums.[101]

In *Titus Andronicus*, I, i, a 'Flourish' is called for as part of a funeral scene.

On less frequent occasions, a 'long Flourish' is called for and it seems reasonable to suppose that time was needed for a brief procession on stage, which seems clear in *Titus Andronicus*, I, i, 234.

A long flourish till they come down.

A similar stage requirement may have been necessary, although it is not evident in the text, in *Richard II*. First, the king decides to have a trial by combat between his cousin Bolingbroke and Mowbray, Duke of Norfolk. The Lord Marshal calls out 'Sound trumpets and set forward combatants.' This is followed by the stage direction 'A charge sounded.' But then the king abruptly changes his mind and stops the fight. This is followed the stage direction 'A long flourish.'[102]

SENNET

Several times in his plays Shakespeare calls for a 'Sennet' in the stage directions. As we have said, the *Sennet*, *Flourish* and *Tucket* are all assumed to be specific kinds of fanfares, although their distinction is unknown today. The distinction must have been clear to the sixteenth-century English audience, however, for in *Coriolanus*, II, i, 140, following the line 'Hark! The trumpets.' is a stage direction 'Flourish' and only four lines later a stage direction reads 'Sennet. Trumpets sound.' In other words, since it was in both cases performed by trumpets, it must represent a stylistic distinction. Similarly, in *King Henry VI: Part I*, the fact that a stage

---

100 *Hamlet*, III, ii, 89.
101 *Richard III*, Iv, iv, 152ff.
102 *Richard II*, I, iii, 118ff. Also, *Coriolanus*, I, ix.

direction calls for two of them in a row, 'Sennet. Flourish.,'[103] also suggests the distinction had some meaning for the contemporary audience. In this case, since the reference in the line before is to a coronation, perhaps a common style is indicated for them both in this case.

> We here create you Earl of Shrewsbury;
> And in our coronation take your place.

We also note that in the above case, as well as later (V, i), this music he heard in a palace room, rather than outdoors.

A Sennet is called for in the stage directions often to introduce a noble character to a scene, as in *King Henry VI: Part II*, (within a palace) for the entrance of the king 'Sound a Sennet'[104] and again (III, i) for the king's entrance into the Abbey of Bury St. Edmunds.[105]

Otherwise a variety of emotional moods are associated with the Sennet. A Sennet is called for in the stage directions after Warwick says, 'Long live King Henry! Plantagenet, embrace him' in *King Henry VI: Part III*.[106] More somber circumstances in which a Sennet is heard are found in *Richard III*, (III, i) when the Prince of Wales is taken to be imprisoned in the Tower and in *Henry VIII* (II, iv), before the divorce trial of Queen Katherine before Cardinal Wolsey.

Tucket

The Tucket is used only rarely in the Shakespeare plays and the only consistent feature is that it is always identified with a trumpet. For example, in *King Lear* where a stage direction reads 'Tucket within,' it is followed by the question 'What trumpet's that?'[107] and in *The Merchant of Venice*, V, i, 134, for the arrival of Bassanio, 'A tucket sounds,'[108] followed by the line, 'I hear his trumpet.'[109]

In *Timon of Athens*, I, ii, a trumpet plays a Tucket to introduce the players of a masque, held during a banquet.

---

103 *King Henry VI: Part I*, III, iii, following line 27.

104 *King Henry VI: Part II*, I, iii.

105 See also *King Lear*, I, i, for the entrance of the king.
Macbeth, III, i, for the entrance of Macbeth as king.
Antony and Cleopatra, II, vii, for the entrance of Caesar, Antony and others.
Coriolanus, II, ii, for the entrance of 'Patricians, Tribunes of the People, etc.'
Richard III, IV, ii:

> [A Room of State in the Palace]
> Sound a Sennet. Enter Richard in pomp ...

106 *King Henry VI: Part III*, I, i, 205ff.

107 *King Lear*, II, iv, 196.

108 *The Merchant of Venice*, V, i, 134

109 See also *Troilus and Cressida*, I, iii, 215.

Alarum

The most frequent specific form of music called for in the stage directions is the Alarum, usually associated with battle. A fitting example is found in *Troilus and Cressida*, where, following the stage direction, 'Sound Alarum,' Troilus describes the sound for us.

> Peace, you ungracious clamors! Peace, rude sounds![110]

The same adjective to describe the sound is uttered by Macbeth,

> Make all our trumpets speak; give them all breath.
> Those clamorous harbingers of blood and death.
> *Exeunt. Alarums continued.*[111]

The association which Macbeth makes here with the Alarum, as opposed to other signals, is made quite clear in *Henry VI: Part II*, IV, viii. This scene begins with the stage direction,

> *Alarum and Retreat. Enter again Cade, and all his rabblement.*

Cade then speaks.

> Up Fish Street! down St. Magnus' corner! kill and knock down! throw them into Thames!
> *Sound a parley.*
> What noise is this I hear? Dare any be so bold to sound retreat or parley, when I command them kill?[112]

In three instances, *King Henry VI: Part II*, IV and *Antony and Cleopatra*, III, viii, 13 and IV, viii, such battle 'Alarums' are called for relative to sea battles. It seems unusual, but in three cases an Alarum is used to introduce a character to a scene.[113]

---

[110] *The Tragedy of Troilus and Cressida*, I, i, 86. Numerous battle 'Alarums' are found in *King John*, *King Henry V* and *Coriolanus*. Alarums to signal the beginning of battle are also found in *King Henry VI: Part III*, II, iii; *King Henry VI: Part II*, IV, iii and *King Henry VI: Part I*, where the Dauphin Charles cries,

> Sound, sound Alarum! we will rush on them.

In *Richard III* an alarm before a battle precedes one of Shakespeare's most familiar lines,

> A horse! a horse! my kingdom for a horse!

[111] *Macbeth*, V, vi.

[112] That the distinction between these signals must have been obvious is suggested in *Henry VI: Part I*, I, v, where the stage direction calls for three signals in sequence, 'Alarum, Retreat, Flourish.'

[113] For the entrance of Richard Plantagenet, duke of York at the beginning of *King Henry VI: Part III*, and again in I, iv; and in *King Henry VI: Part III*, II, vi, for the entrance of Clifford.

It may perhaps be assumed that there were a variety of kinds of Alarms, for Shakespeare specifies in his stage directions 'A short Alarum,'[114] a 'Low alarum'[115] and a 'Loud alarum.'[116]

In most cases we assume this signal was performed by trumpets, as we see in *King Lear*, V, iii, 176, where the stage direction is preceded by 'Trumpets, speak!' In one case, however, a preceding line of dialog indicates the alarm was performed by a drum.[117]

Retreat

'Alarum and Retreat,' is given in a stage direction in *King Henry VI: Part III*, after which Edward speaks,

> Now breathe we, lords: good fortune bids us pause,
> And smooth the frowns of war with peaceful looks.[118]

This must have been a familiar military signal, as military signals go, and a happy one if it implied an enemy retreat. This is the sense in *King Henry IV: Part I* when the Prince of Wales says, 'The trumpet sounds retreat, the day is ours.'[119]

Parley

In *King Kenry VI: Part I*, Joan of Arc says, 'Summon a parley; we will talk with him,' followed by the stage direction, 'Trumpets sound a parley.'[120] This was apparently the signal intended later, when Talbot orders,

> Go to the gates of Bordeaux, trumpeter;
> Summon their general unto the wall.[121]

A somewhat more insistent example is found at the end of *Timon of Athens*, when Alcibiades announces,

---

114 *King Henry VI: Part I*, I, v; *King Henry VI: Part III*, I, iv and *All's Well That Ends Well*, IV, i.

115 *Julius Caesar*, V, v.

116 *Julius Caesar*, V, ii.

117 *All's Well That Ends Well*, IV, i. In *Antony and Cleopatra*, IV, v, the stage direction calls for 'Alarum. Drums and trumpets.'

118 *King Henry VI: Part III*, II, vi, 31ff.

119 *King Henry IV: Part I*, V, iii, 161. Additional examples of retreat can be found in *Troilus and Cressida*, III, i, 137 and IV, v, 73ff; *Henry VI: Part I*, II, ii; *Macbeth*, V, vii; *Antony and Cleopatra*, IV, v, 75 and *Coriolanus*, I, ix.

120 *King Henry VI: Part I*, III, iii, 36.

121 *King Henry VI: Part I*, IV, ii, 1.

Sound to this coward and lascivious town
Our terrible approach.
> *Sounds a parley.*[122]

In *Richard II* we have a signal for a parley with an answer, the stage direction reading 'Parle without, and answer within; then a flourish.'[123]

A wide variety of additional trumpet signals are used by Shakespeare in his plays, including a signal to mount the horses[124] and to announce a messenger, such as the stage direction 'Enter one blowing' in *King Henry VI: Part III*, II, i.[125] In *King John*, II, i, stage directions call for both an English and French Herald, each with his trumpet. In *King Lear* a herald with trumpets forms a momentarily important role in the plot.

> ALBANY. Come hither, herald. Let the trumpet sound,
>   And read out this.
>   *A trumpet sounds.*
>   *Herald reads.*
>
> *If any man of quality or degree within the lists of the army will maintain upon Edmund, supposed Earl of Gloucester, that he is a manifold traitor, let him appear by the third sound of the trumpet. He is bold in his defense.*
>
> | 'Edm. Sound!' | 1. Trumpet |
> | HERALD. Again! | 2. Trumpet |
> | HERALD. Again! | 3. Trumpet |
>
> *Enter Edgar, armed, at the third sound, a trumpet before him.*
>
> ALBANY. Ask him his purposes, why he appears
>   Upon this call o' th' trumpet.[126]

In *The Tragedy of Troilus and Cressida*, we find an example of the use of military signals so valued by the ancient Greeks, which was to inspire the soldier. Here, the Trojan commander, Aeneas, commands,

> Trumpet, blow loud.
> Send thy brass voice through all these lazy tents,
> And every Greek of mettle, let him know
> What Troy means fairly shall be spoke aloud.
>   *The trumpets sound.*[127]

---

122 *Timon of Athens*, V, iv.

123 *Richard II*, III, iii, 62. Additional examples of the 'parley' can be found in *King Henry VI: Part III*, V, i, 16; *King John*, II, i, 207; *King Henry IV: Part I*, III, iii; *Henry V*, III, iii, 123 and *Coriolanus*, I, iv.

124 *Antony and Cleopatra*, III, ii, 24.

125 See also *Timon of Athens*, I, i, 267.

126 *King Lear*, V, iii, 128ff.

127 *The Tragedy of Troilus and Cressida*, I, iii, 261ff.

Shakespeare sometimes uses a military signal to establish some form of identification essential to the plot. In *King Henry VI: Part I*, Talbot has placed his troops outside when visiting the countess of Auvergne, suspecting treachery. When she accuses him of being but a 'shadow,' he responds 'I will show you.' A stage direction follows,

Winds his horn. Drums strike up; a peal of ordnance. Enter Soldiers.

After which, Talbot, says, 'How say you, madam?'[128]

Later in this same play a drum signal, given in the stage direction as 'Drum sounds afar off,' identifies the progress of the enemy troops.

Hark! by the sound of drum you may perceive
Their powers are marching unto Paris-ward.[129]

Still later, an identical stage direction produces a more somber reaction.

Hark! Hark! the Dauphin's drum, a warning bell,
Sings heavy music to thy timorous soul.[130]

A similar drum signal alerts Richard to the enemy in *Richard III*. During his speech to his troops the audience hears,

Drum afar off.

Hark! I hear their drum.
Fight, gentlemen of England! fight, bold yeomen![131]

Stage directions for drums often accompany soldiers onto the stage, as in *Henry VI: Part II*, IV, ii and the beginning of Act V.[132] The most common form also includes the troops' flag. For example, the armies of Oxford, Montague, Somerset and Clarence enter separately with 'drum and colors' in *King Henry VI: Part III*, V, i.[133] And, they are used to signal an exit, as we see later in this same play, when Montgomery says, 'Drummer, strike up, and let us march away,' which is followed by the stage direction,

The drum begins to march.[134]

---

128 *King Henry VI: Part I*, II, iii, 38ff.

129 *King Henry VI: Part I*, III, iii.

130 *King Henry VI: Part I*, IV, ii, 40ff. In *King John*, II, i, 76, upon hearing the 'churlish drums,' the French ambassador, Chatillion, says, 'To parley or to fight; therefore prepare.'

131 *Richard III*, V, iii, 360. For additional examples of 'Drum afar off,' see *Coriolanus*, I, iv, 20ff and *Henry VI: Part III*, I, ii, 70.

132 See also *Timon of Athens*, IV, iii and *Henry VI: Part III*, IV, iii.

133 *Richard III*, V, ii, troops enter with drum and colors. In *Richard II*, III, iii, several dukes enter with 'drum and colors.' See also *Hamlet*, V, ii; *King Lear*, IV, iv; V, iii and *Macbeth*, V, ii.

134 *King Henry VI: Part III*, IV, vii, 50.

We find such a call for an individual exit in *Timon of Athens*, when Timon says, 'beat thy drum, and get thee gone.'[135]

In *All's Well That Ends Well*, there is a discussion of the loss of a drum in battle, which in the sixteenth century was a trophy collected when one defeated an enemy regiment. Before a discussion of how the drum might be recovered, this dialog reminds us how important this symbol was.

> 2. LORD. A pox on it! let it go: 'tis but a drum.
> PAROLLES. 'But a drum!' Is it 'but a drum?' A drum so lost! ...
> BERTRAM. Well, we cannot greatly condemn our success: some dishonor we had in the loss of that drum; but it is not to be recovered.[136]

The stage direction notes also call for military music other than simple signals and fanfares. We wish Shakespeare had given us more description in *King Henry VI: Part I*, where his stage directions call for both a 'French March' and an 'English March.'[137] And perhaps an Italian March was expected when Shakespeare calls for 'A march afar,' in *All's Well That Ends Well*, as the troops approach the walls of Florence.[138]

'A march' for the entrance of Edward, Prince of Wales begins Act II of *King Henry VI: Part III* and again in II, ii, as well as for the entrance of Warwick and his army (II, i).

King Henry VI: Part I begins with the stage direction 'Dead March,' played for the funeral of King Henry V. While there is no indication of instrumentation here, at the beginning of Act II a stage direction includes 'their drums beating a dead march.' *Coriolanus* ends with stage direction, 'A dead march sounded.'

One also finds in the stage directions the call for music which is not military in nature. We wish we could hear the music Shakespeare envisioned in *Cymbeline*, when he requests 'Solemn music' for a procession during a dream by Posthumus. This unusually lengthy stage direction suggests a number of musicians.

> *Solemn music. Enter, as in an apparition, Siclus Leonatus, father to Posthumus, an old man, attired like a warrior; leading in his hand an ancient matron, his wife, and mother to Posthumus, with music before them. Then, after other music, follow ...*[139]

---

135 *Timon of Athens*, IV, iii, 101.

136 *All's Well that Ends Well*, III, vi, 38ff. A similar tradition existed for the capture of the banner which hung from trumpets, which is mentioned in *King Henry V*, IV, ii, 61ff.

137 *King Henry VI: Part I*, III, iii.

138 *All's Well that Ends Well*, III, v. 'A march afar off' is also found in *Hamlet*, V, ii, 358. In *Julius Caesar*, IV, ii, there is a stage instruction for 'Low march within.'

139 *Cymberline*, V, iv.

The evidence is that when a larger number of musicians were required, it was made possible through the participation of the civic musicians known as 'Waits.' They certainly must have been present in this play when later, for a scene of celebration in Rome, the stage direction reads 'Trumpets, hautboys, drums beat, all together.' The following line, by a messenger, lists even more instruments,

> The trumpets, sackbuts, psalteries, and fifes,
> Tabors, and cymbals …[140]

In *The Tempest*, the spirit-musician, Ariel, plays 'solemn music' (II, i), as opposed to a tune she plays later on the tabor and pipe (III, ii). The expression 'Solemn music' was used in sixteenth-century England to represent what we would call beautiful music today, as seems to be suggested later in this play (III, iii). The stage direction 'Solemn and strange music' is followed by the lines,

> ALONSO. What harmony is this? My good friends, hark!
> GONZALO. Marvelous sweet music.

In *The Tempest* we also find stage directions for 'Soft music,' in III, iii and IV, i, as opposed to 'a noise of hunters' V, i.

Some music referred to in the stage directions is intended for dancing, including 'Music plays' in *Love's Labour's Lost*[141] and 'Sing and dance' in *A Midsummer Night's Dream*.[142] In only one instance, in *Much Ado About Nothing*, are we given the instrumentation for dance music, 'Strike up, pipers!'[143]

Finally, in *A Midsummer Night's Dream* there is special music to put characters asleep[144] and later to wake them up.[145]

> [Horns and they awake.]

The oboe consort was an indoor ensemble, found when guests are being entertained. In *Hamlet* we find 'Hautboys play' in reference to a kind of prelude for 'The dumb-show,' a play within a play.[146] In *Macbeth*, I, vi, we find 'Hoboyes and torches' and in the following scene dinner is served with,

---

140 *Coriolanus*, V, iv, 46ff.

141 *Love's Labour's Lost*, V, ii, 222.

142 *A Midsummer Night's Dream*, V, i, 390.

143 *Much Ado About Nothing*, the final line. In *The Winter's Tale*, IV, iv, a stage direction calls for a dance by shepherds and shepherdesses.

144 *A Midsummer Night's Dream*, IV, i, 84.

145 *A Midsummer Night's Dream*, IV, i, 138.

146 *Hamlet*, III, ii, 131.

Hoboyes. Torches. Enter a Sewer, and divers Servants with dishes ...

In *Timon of Athens*, I, ii, there is also a banquet scene, where the stage direction calls for 'Hautboys playing loud music.' During this banquet there is a masque featuring 'Cupid and Ladies of the Amazons,' who play lutes and dance. After the masque, the guests dance with the Amazons to music which the stage directions identify as 'a lofty strain or two of the hautboys.'

In *Antony and Cleopatra* the stage direction reads only 'Music plays' while servants bring in a banquet.[147] It is likely Shakespeare used oboes here as well, for later in this play (IV, iii) a stage direction reads 'Music of the hautboys is under the stage,' referring to music of the underworld performed from the 'music room.' In *Coriolanus*, IV, v, as well, we suspect that the banquet scene carrying the stage direction, 'Music plays,' refers to the oboe consort.

While the oboes performed the banquet music, it was still a trumpet signal which called the guests to the table. Thus, in *Othello*, a stage direction reads 'Trumpets within' and Iago remarks, 'Hark how these instruments summon you to supper.'[148]

Horns usually appear associated with hunting and a typical stage direction reads,

Wind horns. Enter a Lord from hunting, with his train.[149]

In *Titus Andronicus*, Titus and his sons are hunting in a forest near Rome. The stage directions call several times for 'Wind horns,' one of which calls for a specific hunting signal, the playing of 'a peal.'[150]

ART MUSIC

In *The Tragedy of Troilus and Cressida*, we find a description of an instrumental ensemble concert of pure Art Music.

PANDARUS. What music is this?
SERVANT. I do but partly know, sir; it is music in parts.
PANDARUS. Know you the musicians?
SERVANT. Wholly, sir.
PANDARUS. Who play they to?
SERVANT. To the hearers, sir.
PANDARUS. At whose pleasure, friend?
SERVANT. At mine, sir, and theirs that love music.[151]

---

147 *Antony and Cleopatra*, II, vii.

148 *Othello*, IV, ii, 194.

149 *The Taming of the Shrew*, I, i.

150 *Titus Andronicus*, II, ii.

151 *The Tragedy of Troilus and Cressida*, II, iii, 16ff. In line 44 the ensemble is referred to as a broken consort.

Internal Art Songs are frequently found in these plays, usually unaccompanied. An exception may have been intended by the stage direction 'Here Music,' in *The Merchant of Venice* (III, ii). For the most part these are love songs and one of the most beautiful is that sung by Desdemona in *Othello*.

> The poor soul sat sighing by a sycamore tree,—
>   Sing all a green willow.
> Her hand on her bosom, her head on her knee,—
>   Sing willow, willow, willow.
> The Fresh streams ran by her, and murmur'd her moons.
>   Sing willow, willow, willow.
> Her salt tears fell from her, and softened the stones.
>   Sing willow, willow, willow.[152]

Measure for Measure, Act IV begins with Mariana, the pathetic and jilted fiancée of the duke's deputy, on stage with what the stage direction only calls a 'Boy singing,' for whom Shakespeare provides the text of a love song. When Mariana sees the duke coming, she tells the boy, 'Break off thy song, and haste thee quick away.' When the boy leaves and the duke arrives, she attempts to explain this was not a romantic encounter, but merely music to soothe her feelings. The duke seems to remind her that such music can get her into trouble.

> MARIANA. I cry you mercy, sir, and well could wish
>   You had not found me here so musical.
>   Let me excuse me, and believe me so,
>   My mirth it much displeased, but pleased my woe.
> DUKE. 'Tis good; though music oft hath such a charm
>   To make bad good, and good provoke to harm.

Among the more unusual songs is an off-stage song from the spirit world, heard by the witches in *Macbeth*, III, v, for which Shakespeare provides only the first line, 'Come away, come away.'

In these books we have contended that the presence of the contemplative listener is a primary hallmark of art music. We find such a case in *Pericles, Prince of Tyre*, where Pericles, who identifies himself as,

> A gentleman of Tyre, my name, Pericles;
> My education been in arts and arms ...[153]

has apparently performed before King Antiochus during a banquet. Shakespeare provides the king's reaction the following day to what must have been art music.

---

152 *Othello*, IV, iii, 43ff. She repeats the last line of this song just before she dies. [V, ii, 295]

153 *Pericles, Prince of Tyre*, II, iii, 87ff.

> Sir, I am beholding to you
> For your sweet music last night: I do
> Protest my ears were never better fed
> With such delightful pleasing harmony.[154]

Another example is found in *Timon of Athens*, where there is a banquet, the music for which is identified in the stage direction only as 'Music.' Soon after the banquet begins, Timon says to his guests, 'feast your ears with the music awhile.'[155] We might also mention the analogy in *Richard II*, when the ill John of Gaunt observes,

> Oh, but they say the tongues of dying men enforce attention like deep harmony.[156]

Shakespeare, in *The Merchant of Venice*, also makes reference to the fact that there must be a proper environment for a contemplative listener.

> PORTIA. Music! hark!
> NERISSA. It is your music, madam, of the house.
> PORTIA. Nothing is good, I see, without respect;
>   Me thinks it sounds much sweeter than by day.
> NERISSA. Silence bestows that virtue on it, madam.
> PORTIA. The crow doth sing as sweetly as the lark
>   When neither is attended, and I think
>   The nightingale, if she should sing by day,
>   When every goose is cackling, would be thought
>   No better a musician than the wren,
>   How many things by season seasoned are
>   To their right praise and true perfection![157]

In this same play, Shylock speaks of the varying pleasures of different persons, one of which is music,

> And others, when the bagpipe sings i' the nose,
> Cannot contain their urine …[158]

---

[154] *Pericles, Prince of Tyre*, II, v, 25ff.
[155] *Timon of Athens*, III, vi, 30.
[156] *Richard II*, II, i, 5ff.
[157] *The Merchant of Venice*, V, i, 105ff.
[158] *The Merchant of Venice*, IV, i, 50.

FUNCTIONAL MUSIC

Shakespeare almost never mentions church music in his plays. In the comedy, *The Winter's Tale*, a brief mention in passing is made by a clown who is discussing the plans for a rural feast. Among the things organized, he mentions a,

> three-man song-men all, and very good ones; but they are most of them means and basses: but one Puritan amongst them, and he sings psalms to hornpipes.[159]

In *Henry VIII*, Shakespeare supplies a rather detailed account of the coronation procession through Westminster of Anne Boleyn. Before the queen the stage directions calls separately for trumpets and 'Hautboys.' The following elements of the procession include 'A lively flourish of trumpets,' 'Choristers, singing' and concluding with 'a great flourish of trumpets.' In the dialog which follows a gentleman describes the coronation itself, including,

> The rod, and bird of peace, and all such emblems
> Laid nobly on her: which performed the choir,
> With all the choicest music of the kingdom,
> Together sung *Te Deum*.[160]

Another procession is mentioned in *Julius Caesar*. When Caesar first enters, the stage direction mentions only 'in solemn procession, with music.' No instruments are referred to, but Shakespeare may have intended something resembling a Roman trumpet, for Caesar hears a voice over the music and asks,

> Who is it in the press that calls on me?
> I hear a tongue, shriller than all the music …[161]

A wedding hymn in *As You Like It* is accompanied by what the stage direction note calls 'Still Music.'[162]

A genuine hunting song is found in *As You Like It*, sung by foresters on having killed a deer. The character requesting the song commands, 'Sing it. 'Tis no matter how it be in tune, so it make noise enough.'[163]

Functional Music for the trumpet is found in *King Henry V*, where the king commands,

> Take a trumpet, herald.
> Ride thou unto the horsemen on yon hill.[164]

---

159 *The Winter's Tale*, IV, iii, 39ff.
160 *Henry VIII*, IV, i, 40ff.
161 *Julius Caesar*, I, ii, 18ff.
162 *As You Like It*, V, iv, 99.
163 *As You Like It*, IV, ii.
164 *King Henry V*, IV, vii, 47ff.

References to military music are found frequently in the dialog, as before a battle in *Richard III*, when Richmond concludes a speech to his soldiers,

> Sound drums and trumpets, boldly and cheerfully;
> God and Saint George! Richmond and victory![165]

And Hotspur, in *King Henry IV: Part I*, cries,

> Sound all the lofty instruments of war,
> And by that music let us all embrace,
> For, heaven to earth, some of us never shall
> A second time do such a courtesy.[166]

The sound of the military trumpet is described several times. In *The Taming of the Shrew*, it is called a 'clang'[167] and in *Richard II*, Bullingbrooke speaks of the 'brazen trumpet.'[168] In *King John*, the Dauphin of France says, 'What lusty trumpet thus doth summon us?'[169] Perhaps another reflection of the sound of the sixteenth-century trumpet is found in the Epilogue of *Henry VIII*, which apologizes to the audience for fear 'We've frightened with our trumpets.'

In *The Tragedy of Troilus and Cressida*, Ajax gives a vivid and extraordinary portrait of the military trumpet player.

> AGAMEMNON. Give with they trumpet a loud note to Troy,
>   Thou dreadful Ajax, that the appalled air
>   May pierce the head of the great combatant
>   And hale him hither.
> AJAX. Thou trumpet, there's my purse;
>   Now crack thy lungs, and split thy brazen pipe!
>   Blow, villain, till thy sphered bias cheek
>   Outswell the colic of puffed Aquilon.
>   Come, stretch thy chest and let thy eyes spout blood;
>   Thou blowest for Hector.[170]

---

165 *Richard III*, V, iii, 288ff.

166 *King Henry IV: Part I*, V, ii, 98ff.

167 *The Taming of the Shrew*, I, iv, 210.

168 *Richard II*, III, iii, 35.

169 *King John*, V, iii, 118.

170 *The Tragedy of Troilus and Cressida*, IV, v, 3ff. This description reminds us of a similar passage in the medieval 'Song of Roland,' which Shakespeare must have known.

> Roland, racked with agony and pain
> and great chagrin, now sounds his ivory horn;
> bright blood leaps in a torrent from his mouth;
> the temple has been ruptured in his brain.

There is one reference in the dialog to military music aboard ships, when the Chorus, in *Henry V*, says,

> Hear the shrill whistle which doth order give
> To sounds confused.[171]

In *All's Well That Ends Well*, when Parolles wishes to say that he has had enough of military service, he tells the audience,

> [Aside.] I'll no more drumming; a plague on all drums![172]

A similar farewell to war is expressed by Othello.

> Farewell the neighing steed, and the shrill trumpet,
> The spirit-stirring drum, the ear-piercing fife …[173]

Finally there is a reference to music to drink a toast. In *Hamlet*, the king offers a toast to Hamlet, with the stage direction indicating that the trumpets play throughout.

> And let the kettle to the trumpet speak,
> The trumpet to the cannoneer without,
> The cannons to the heavens, the heaven to earth:
> Now the king drinks to Hamlet![174]

ENTERTAINMENT MUSIC

The most refined indoor entertainment music was the masque, which is mentioned several times in the plays. In *Henry VIII*, the king and others enter as maskers, while the stage direction calls for 'Hautboys.' No actual masque is given in the text, only the stage direction 'Music. Dance.'[175] Capulet and his guests participate in a masque in *Romeo and Juliet* which also consists primarily of music and dancing, judging by the stage direction 'Music plays and they dance.'[176]

The possibility of an outdoor masque is mentioned in *The Merchant of Venice*. Shylock wants no serenades by his house.

---

171 *King Kenry V*, III, Chorus, 9ff.
172 *All's Well that Ends Well*, IV, iii, 264.
173 *Othello*, III, iii, 396ff.
174 *Hamlet*, V, ii, 269ff.
175 *Henry VIII*, I, iv, 82ff.
176 *Romeo and Juliet*, I, iv, 134ff.

> What! are there masques? Hear you me, Jessica:
> Lock up my doors; and when you hear the drum,
> And the vile squealing of the wry-necked fife,
> Clamber not you up to the casements then,
> Nor thrust your head into the public street
> To gaze on Christian fools with varnished faces,
> But stop my house's ears, I mean my casements;
> Let not the sound of shallow foppery enter
> My sober house.[177]

Regarding genuine popular music, we should mention first a passage in which Shakespeare comments on the value of popular music in general. In *As You Like It* a rather light love song is performed ('With a hey, and a ho …'). Upon being criticized by Touchstone, the singer says 'You are deceived, sir. We kept time; we lost not our time.' Touchstone answers,

> By my troth, yes. I count it but time lost to hear such a foolish song.[178]

The stage direction 'Enter Music' refers to tavern music, with no further indication as to its nature, in *Henry IV: Part II*, II, iv. In several cases, however, Shakespeare supplies the actual text for songs sung in taverns. These include *Romeo and Juliet*, where the text of a bawdy song is given,[179] in *Othello*, a drinking song sung by Iago[180] and a sailor's drinking song is found in *The Tempest*, II, ii.

For a drinking song in *Antony and Cleopatra*, Enobarbus says,

> All take hands.
> Make battery to our ears with the loud music;
> The while I'll place you; then the boy shall sing.
>   *Music plays*

A few lines later we get an indication of the wind instruments meant by 'loud music' referred to above. Menas says,

> These drums! these trumpets, flutes! what!
> Let Neptune hear we bid a loud farewell
> To these great fellows …
>   *Sound a flourish with drums.*[181]

---

177 *The Merchant of Venice*, II, v, 28f.

178 *As You Like It*, V, iii, 34ff.

179 *Romeo and Juliet*, II, iii, 120ff.

180 *Othello*, II, iii, 65.

181 *Antony and Cleopatra*, II, vii, 123ff.

Finally, in the comedy, *The Winter's Tale*, Shakespeare provides a detailed description of the wandering minstrel. This musician appears with a repertoire of songs which must represent a broad sampling of sixteenth-century popular music in England.

> SERVANT. O master! if you did but hear the peddler at the door, you would never dance again after a tabor and pipe; no, the bagpipe could not move you. He sings several tunes faster than you'll tell money; he utters them as he had eaten ballads and all men's ears grew to his tunes.
> CLOWN. He could never come better: he shall come in: I love a ballad but even too well, if it be doleful matter merrily set down, or a very pleasant thing indeed and sung lamentably.
> SERVANT. He hath songs for man or woman, of all sizes; no milliner can so fit his customers with gloves: he has the prettiest love songs for maids, so without bawdry, which is strange; with such delicate burdens of dildos and fadings, 'jump her and thump her'; and where some stretch-mouthed rascal would, as it were, mean mischief and break a foul gap into the matter, he makes the maid to answer, 'Whoop, do me no harm, good man'; puts him off, slights him with 'Whoop, do me no harm, good man.'
> POLIXENES. This is a brave fellow.
> CLOWN. Believe me, thou talkest of an admirable conceited fellow. Has he any unbraided wares?
> SERVANT. He hath ribands of all the colors i' the rainbow; points more than all the lawyers in Bohemia can learnedly handle; though they come to him by the gross … why, he sings 'em over, as they were gods or goddesses …
> CLOWN. Prithee, bring him in, and let him approach singing.
> PERDITA. Forewarn him that he use no scurrilous words in 's tunes.[182]

Later this minstrel, named Autolycus, offers more detail regarding his repertoire as he offers some published ballads for sale.

> CLOWN. What hast here? ballads?
> MOPSA. Pray now, buy some: I love a ballad in print, a-life, for then we are sure they are true.
> AUTOLYCUS. Here's one to a very doleful tune, how a usurer's wife was brought to bed of twenty money-bags at a burden; and how she longed to eat adders' heads and toads carbonadoed.
> MOPSA. Is it true, think you?
> AUTOLYCUS. Very true, and but a month old.
> DORCAS. Bless me from marrying a usurer!
> AUTOLYCUS. Here's the midwife's name to 't, one Mistress Taleporter, and five or six honest wives' that were present. Why should I carry lies abroad?
> MOPSA. Pray you now, buy it.
> CLOWN. Come on, lay it by: and let's first see more ballads; we'll buy the other things anon.
> AUTOLYCUS. Here's another ballad of a fish that appeared upon the coast on Wednesday the fourscore of April, forty thousand fathom above water, and sung this ballad against the hard hearts of maids; it was thought she was a woman and was turned into a cold fish, for she would not exchange flesh with one that loved her. The ballad is very pitiful and as true.
> DORCAS. Is it true too, think you?

---

182 *The Winter's Tale*, IV, iv, 207ff.

AUTOLYCUS. Five justices' hands at it, and witnesses more than my pack will hold.
CLOWN. Lay it by too: another.
AUTOLYCUS. This is a merry ballad, but a very pretty one.
MOPSA. Let's have some merry ones.
AUTOLYCUS. Why, this is a passing merry one, and goes to the tune of 'Two maids wooing a man'; there's a scarce a maid westward but she sing it: 'tis in request, I can tell you.
MOPSA. We can both sing it: if thou 'lt bear a part thou shalt hear; 'tis in three parts.[183]

Later, Autolycus, in a soliloquy, tells us that while they were looking at his ballads he stole their purses.[184]

---

[183] *The Winter's Tale*, IV, iv, 276ff.
[184] *The Winter's Tale*, IV, iv, 665ff.

BIBLIOGRAPHY

Aber, Adolf. *Die Pflege der Musik unter den Wettinern und Wettinischen Ernestinern Von den Anfängen bis zur Auflösung der Weimarer Hofkapelle 1662*. Bückeburg, 1921.
Acta des Printzen tzu Uranieun und Frawlein Annen tzu Saxen Beylager, 1561. Dresden: Royal Archives.
Agrippa, Henry Cornelius. *De occulta Philosophia*. Translated by Donald Tyson, in *Three Books of Occult Philosophy*. St. Paul: Llewellyn Publications, 1993.
———. *Of the Vanitie and Uncertaintie of Arts and Sciences* [1569, in English]. Edited by Catherine Dunn. Northridge, CA: California State University, Northridge Press, 1974.
Allen, P. S. *Erasmus*. Oxford, 1934.
Altenburg, Detlef. *Untersuchungen zur Geschichte der Trumpete im Zeitalter der Clarinblaskunst*. Regensburg: G. Bosse, 1973.
Anglo, Sydney. *The Great Tournament Roll of Westminster*. Oxford: Clarendon Press, 1968.
Anonymous pencil drawing, *NürnbergerSchembarthandschrift*, Nürnberg, Germanisches Nationalmuseum, Hs. 5664, D2, Fol.66.
Anonymous. 'Tom Tel-Troths Messaage,' in *Miscellaneous*, VI. Edited by Frederick Furnivall. Valduz: Kraus Reprint, 1965.
———. *A second and third blast of retreat from plays and theatres* [1580]. New York: Johnson Reprint Corporation, 1972.
Ascham, Roger. *The Schoolmaster* [1579]. Edited by Lawrence Ryan. Ithaca: Cornell University Press, 1967.
———. *The Whole Works of Roger Ascham*. Edited by Rev. A. Giles. London: John Russell Smith, 1864.
Baines, Anthony, 'Two Cassel Inventories.' *The Galpin Society Journal* 4 (June 1951): 30–38, http://www.jstor.org/stable/841260
———. *Woodwind Instruments and Their History*. New York: Norton, 1962.
Bell, Clair, 'A Glance into the Workshop of Meistergesang.' *Publications of The Modern Language Association of America* (June, 1953).
Bender, Robert. *Five Courtier Poets of the English Renaissance*. New York: Washington Square Press, 1967.
Bianco, Franz Joseph von. *Die alte Universität Köln und die spätern Gelehrten-Schulen dieser Stadt*. Köln: C. Gehly , 1856.
Boos, Heinrich. *Thomas und Felix Platter*. Leipzig: Hirzel, 1878.
Bossert, G. 'Die Hofhantorei undter Herzog Christof.' *Württembergische Vierteljahrescheftes für Landesgeschichte* (1898).
Brenet, M. 'Notes sur l'introduction des instruments dans les églises de France.' *Riemann-Festschrift*. Leipzig: Hesse, 1909.
Bridenbaugh, Carl. *Vexed and Troubled Englishmen*. New York: Oxford University Press, 1968.
Bridge, J. 'Town Waits and their Tunes.' *Proceedings of the Musical Association*. (London, 1927)
Brooke, Arthur. *Romeus and Juliet*. Vaduz: Kraus Reprint, 1965.
Bryskett, Lodowick. *A Discourse of Civill Life*. Edited by Thomas Wright. Northridge: San Fernando Valley State College, 1970.
Bullen, A. H. *The Works of George Peele*. Port Washington: Kennikat Press, 1966.
Burton, Elizabeth. *The Pageant of Elizabethan England*. New York: Scribner, 1958.

Buszin, Walter. 'Luther on Music.' *The Musical Quarterly* 32, no. 1 (January, 1946): 80–97, http://www.jstor.org/stable/739566

Carpenter, Nan Cooke. *Music in the Medieval and Renaissance Universities*. Norman: University of Oklahoma Press, 1954.

Cavendish, George. *The Life and Death of Cardinal Wolsey*. London: Published for the Early English Text Society by the Oxford University Press, 1959.

Chambers, Frank. *The History of Taste*. New York: Columbia University Press, 1932.

Cherbuliez, Johann Steiner. *Neujahrsblatter der Allgemeinen Musikgesellschaft Zürich*. Zürich, 1964, CXLVIII.

Christensen, Carl. *Art and the Reformation in Germany*. Athens: Ohio University Press, 1979.

———. 'Dürer's 'Four Apostles' and the Dedication as a Form of Renaissance Art Patronage.' *Renaissance Quarterly* (1967), XX.

Chybinsky, A. 'Polnische Musik und Musikkultur der 16. Jahrhunderts in ihren Beziehungen zu Deutschland.' *Sammelbände der Internationalen Musikgesellschaft* (1911–1912).

Cochlaeus, Johannes. *Tetrachordum Musices* [1511]. Translated by Clement Miller. Rome: American Institute of Musicology, 1970.

Coclico, Adrian. *Compendium Musices* [1552]. Translated by Albert Seay. Colorado Springs: Colorado College Music Press, 1973.

Crewdson, H. A. F. *The Worshipful Company of Musicians*. London: C. Knight, 1971.

Cross, Wilbur L. and Brooke, Tucker, ed. *The Yale Shakespeare Complete Works*. New York: Barnes & Noble, 1993.

Daalder, Joost. *Sir Thomas Wyatt Collected Poems*. London: Oxford University Press, 1975.

Devillers, Leopold. *Essai sur l'harmonie de la musique à Mons*. Mons: Dequesne-Masquillier, 1868.

Dugdale, William. *The History of Saint Paul's Cathedral*. London, 1818.

Duncan, Edmondstoune. *The Story of Minstrelsy*. London: Walter Scott Publishing Co., 1968.

Dunlop, Ian. *Palaces and Progresses of Elizabeth I*. London, 1962.

Dürer, Albrecht. *Albrecht Dürer, Diary of his Journey to the Netherlands*. Grennwish, CT: New York Graphic Society, 1971.

———. *The Writings of Albrecht Dürer*. Translated by William Conway. New York: Philosophical Library, 1958.

Eby, Frederick. *Early Protestant Educators*. New York: McGraw-Hill, 1931.

Ehmann, Wilhelm. *Tibilustrium*. Kassel: Bärenreiter, 1950.

Erasmus, Desiderius. *Epistles*. London: Longmans, Green, 1901.

———. *The Collected Works of Erasmus*. Toronto: University of Toronto Press, 1992.

———. *The Colloquies of Erasmus*. Translated by Craig Thompson. Chicago: University of Chicago Press, 1965.

Erler, Georg. *Leipziger Magisterschmäuse*. Leipzig: Giesecke & Devrient, 1905.

Federhofer, Helmutt. *Musikpflege und Musiker am Grazer Habsburgerhof*. Mainz: Schott, 1967.

Federman, Maria. *Musik und Musikpflege zur Zeit Herzog Albrechts*. Kassel: Bärenreiter Verlag, 1932.

Fox, Lilla M. *Instruments of Processional Music*. London: Lutterworth Press, 1967.

Fronsperger, Lienhart. *Fünff Bücher von Kriegsregiment*. Frankfurt, 1555.

Garside, Charles. *Zwingli and the Arts*. New Haven: Yale University Press, 1966.

Garzoni, Tomaso. *Allgemeiner Schauplatz aller Kunst, Professionen und Handwerker.* Franckfurt am Mäyn: In Verlag Matthaei Merians Sel. Erben, 1659.
Gattuso, Susan. '16th Century Nuremberg.' In *The Renaissance.* Edited by Iain Fenlon. Englewood Cliffs: Prentice Hall, 1989.
Giustinian, Sebastian. *Four Years at the Court of Henry VIII.* London: Smith, Elder, & Co., 1854.
Glarean, Heinrich. *Dodecachordon.* Translated by Clement Miller. American Institute of Musicology, 1965.
Gosson, Stephen. *The Schoole of Abuse* [1579]. Edited by Edward Arber. London: A. Murray & Son, 1868.
Green, Robert. *Carde of Fancie* [1587], in *The Life and Complete Works of Robert Greene.* Edited by Alexander Grosart. New York: Russell & Russell, 1964.
Grosart, Alexander. *The Complete Poems of Sir Phillip Sidney.* Freeport: Books for Libraries Press, 1970.
Grove, George. *The New Grove Dictionary of Music and Musicians.* Edited by Stanley Sadie. London: Macmillan, 1980.
Hall, Edward. *Chronicle, containing the history of England.* London: J. Johnson, 1809.
Hallett, P. E. *The Life and Illustrious Martyrdom of Sir Thomas More.* London: Burns, Oates & Washbourne, 1928.
Harrison, Frank and Joan Rimmer. *European Musical Instruments.* London: Studio Vista, 1964.
Harrison, George, ed. *The Elizabethan Journals.* New York: MacMillan, 1939.
Hayes, Gerald. *King's Music.* Oxford: Oxford University Press, 1937.
Henderson, Daniel. *The Crimson Queen.* New York: Duffield and Green, 1933.
Hooker, Richard. *The Works of Mr. Richard Hooker.* Oxford: Clarendon Press, 1888.
Jackson, Samuel. *Huldreich Zwingli.* New York: Putham, 1901.
Janssen, Johannes. *History of the German People After the Close of the Middle Ages.* Translated by A. Christie. New York: AMS Press, 1966.
Jones, Emrys, ed. *The New Oxford Book of Sixteenth Century Verse.* Oxford: Oxford University Press, 1991.
Kade, R. 'Antonius Scandellus (1517–1680). Ein Beitrag zur Geschichte der Dresdener Hofkapelle.' *Sammelbande der Internationalen Musikgesellschaft* (1913/1914), XV.
Kastner, Georges. *Manuel Général de Musique Militaire.* Paris: Didot, 1848.
Kellner, Altmann. *Musikgeschichte des Stiftes Kremsmünster.* Kassel: Bärenreiter, 1956.
Kessler, Johannes. *Johannes Kesslers Sabbata mit kleineren Schriften und Briefen.* St. Gall: Fehr'sche Buchhandlung, 1902.
Keussen, Hermann. 'Die alte Universität,' in *Universität Köln.* Köln: Verlag des Kölnischen geschichtsvereins e. v., 1929.
Kindeldey, Otto. *Orgel und Klavier in der Musik des 16. Jahrhundert.* [Sl], 1910.
Köchel, Ludwig Ritter von. *Kaiserliche Hof-Musikkapelle in Wien von 1543–1867.* New York: G. Olms, 1976
LaFontaine, Henry Cart de. *The King's Musik.* London, 1909.
Langwill, Lyndesay. *The Waits.* London: Hindrichsen, 1952.
Listenius, Nicolaus. *Musica* [1537]. Translated by Albert Seay. Colorado Springs: Colorado College Music Press, 1975.
Lodge, Thomas and Robert Greene. *A Looking Glasse for London and England.* Edited by George Glugston. New York: Garland Publishing, 1980.
Lodge, Thomas. *A Defence of Poetry, Music and Stage-plays.* London: Shakespeare Society, 1853.
———. *The Complete Works of Thomas Lodge.* New York: Russell & Russell, 1963.
———. *The Delectable History of Forbonius and Prisceria.* London: Shakespeare Society, 1853.

Luther, Martin. *Luther's Works*. St. Louis: Concordia, 1961.
Lyly, John. *Euphues and his England*. Edited by Morris Croll. New York: Russell & Russell, 1964.
———. *The Complete Works of John Lyly*. Edited by Warwick Bond. Oxford: Clarendon Press, 1967.
Magnus, Olaus. *Historia de gentibus septentrionalibus*. Rome: I.M. de Viottis, 1555.
McClure, Norman, ed. *Sixteenth-Century English Poetry*. New York: Harper & Brothers, 1954.
McFarlane, I. D. 'Clément Marot and the World of Neo-Latin Poetry.' *Literature and the Arts in the Reign of Françis I*. Lexington: French Forum, 1985.
McGuigan, Dorothy. *The Habsburgs*. Garden City, NY: Doubleday, 1966.
McKerrow, Ronald. *The Works of Thomas Nashe*. Oxford: Blackwell, 1966.
Melanchthon, Philip. *Loci Communes* [1555]. Translated by Clyde Manschreck, in *Melanchthon on Christian Doctrine*. New York: Oxford University Press, 1965.
———. *Melanchthon, Selected Writings*. Translated by Charles Hill. Minneapolis: Augsburg Publishing House, 1962.
Memmingen, Germany. *Stadtarchiv*. MS. 1/1.
Memmingen, *Stadtarchiv*. Ratsprotokollbuch, 1517–1519.
Miller, Clement A., ed. *The Dodecachordon of Heinrich Glarean*. Rome: American Institute of Musicology, 1965.
Miller, Clement A. 'Erasmus on Music.' *The Musical Quarterly* 52, no. 3 (July 1966): 332–349, http://www.jstor.org/stable/3085961
———. 'The Dodecachordon: Its Origins and Influence on Renaissance Musical thought.' *Musica Disciplina* (1961).
Monson, Craig. 'Elizabethan London,' in *The Renaissance*. Edited by Iain Fenlon. Englewood Cliffs: Prentice Hall, 1989.
More, Thomas. *The Complete Works of St. Thomas More*. New Haven: Yale University Press, 1981.
Morley, Henry. *Ideal Commonwealths*. Port Washington: Kennikat Press, 1968.
Morley, Thomas. *A Plain and Easy Introduction to Practical Music*. Edited by R. Alec Harriman. New York: Norton, n.d.
Moser, H., 'Zur Mittelalterichen Musikgeschichte der Stadt Köln.' *Archiv für Musikwissenschaft* (1918).
Motley, John. *History of the United Netherlands*. New York: Harper, 1860.
Müller, Johann, *Regiomontanus on Triangles*. Translated by Barnabas Hughes. Madison: The University of Wisconsin Press, 1967.
Murray, John. *Antwerp in the Age of Platin and Brueghel*. Norman: University of Oklahoma Press, 1970.
Nashe, Thomas. *The Anatomie of Absurditie* [1589], in *The Works of Thomas Nashe*. Edited by Ronald McKerrow. Oxford: Blackwell, 1966.
Neilson, William. *The Chief Elizabethan Dramatists*. Boston: Houghton Mifflin, 1911.
Nichols, John G. *Literary Remains of King Edward the Sixth*. London, 1857.
Nichols, John. *The Progresses and Public Processions of Queen Elizabeth*. London: Printer to the Society of Antiquaries of London, 1788.
Northbrooke, John. *A Treatise Against Dicing, Dancing, Plays and Interludes* [1577]. London: The Shakespeare Society, 1843.
Nürnberg, *Germanisches Nationalmuseum*. (Sign. HB 235).
Ornithoparchus, Andreas. *Musicae active mirologus* [1517]. Edited by Gustave Reese and Steven Ledbetter. New York: Dover, 1973.

Panoff, Peter. *Militärmusik in Geschichte und Gegenwart*. Berlin: K. Siegismund, 1944.
Paule, G. *The Life of the most reverend and religious prelate John Whitgift Lord Archbishop of Canterbury*. London, 1612.
Peacham, Henry. *The Complete Gentleman*. Edited by Virgil Heltzel. Ithaca: Cornell University Press, 1962.
Pietzsch, G. 'Beschreibungen deutscher Fürstenhochzeiten von der Mitte des 15. bis zum Beginn des 17. Jahrhunderts als musikgeschichtliche Quellen.' *Anuario Musical* (1960), XV.
Polk, Keith, 'Instrumental music in the Urban Centres of Renaissance Germany.' *Early Music History*, VII.
Praetorius, Michael. *Syntagma Musicum*. Wolfenbütel, 1619.
Prescott, Hilda F. M. *A Spanish Tudor*. New York, 1940.
Puttenham, George. *The Arte of English Poesie* [1589]. Edited by Edward Arber. London, 1869.
Rastall, Richard. 'Some English Consort-Groupings of the Late Middle Ages.' *Music & Letters* 55, no. 2 (April 1974): 179–202, http://www.jstor.org/stable/733853
Rathgeb, Jacob. *A True and Faithful Narrative ...* [1602] in *England as seen by Foreigners*. Edited by William Rye. New York: Blom, 1967.
Reese, Gustave. *Music in the Renaissance*. New York: Norton, 1959.
Reichert, Georg. *Erasmus Widmann (1572–1634)*. Stuttgart: W. Kohlhammer, 1951.
Ruhnke, Martin. *Beiträge zu einer Geschichte der deutschen Hofmusikkollegien im 16. Jahrhundert*. Berlin: Merseburger, 1963.
Russell, Joycelyne. *The Field of Cloth of Gold*. New York: Barnes & Noble, 1969.
Sachs, Curt. *Musik und Oper am kurbrandenburgischen Hof*. Berlin: J. Bard, 1910.
Salmen, Walter. *Musikleben im 16. Jahrhudert*. Leipzig: Deutscher Verlag für Musik, 1976.
Sandberger, Adolf. *Beiträge zur Geschichte der bayr. Hofkapelle unter Orlando di Lasso*. Leipzig: Breitkopf & Härtel, 1894.
Saxl, J. 'Dürer and the Reformation.' *Lectures*. London: Warburg Institute, 1957.
Schaal, R. 'Die Musikinstrumenten-Sammlung von Raimund Fugger.' *Archiv für Musikwissenschaft* (1964), XXI.
Schünemann, Georg. 'Sonaten und Feldstücke der Hoftrompeter.' *Zeitschrift für Musikwissenschaft* (1935).
Senn, Walter. *Musik und Theater am Hof zu Innsbruck*. Innsbruck: Österreichische Verlagsanstalt , 1954.
Severen, Louis Gilliodts-Van. 'Les ménesstrels de Bruges,' in *Essais d'Archéologie Brugeoise*. Bruges: L. de Plancke, 1912.
Sidney, Philip. *The Prose Works of Sir Philip Sidney*. Edited by Albert Feuillerat. Cambridge: Cambridge University Press, 1962.
Sittard, Josef. *Geschichte der Musik und des Theaters am Württembergischen hofe*. Stuttgart: Kohlhammer, 1890.
Skelton, John. *The Complete Poems of John Skelton*. Edited by Philip Henderson. London: Dent, 1959.
Smithers, Don. *The Music and History of the Baroque Trumpet*. London: J. M. Dent, 1973.
Stads Rekeningen. Ghent: Meyer-van Loo, 1540–1541, vol. 246v.
Stahl, Wilhelm. *Musikgeschichte Lübecks*. Kassel: Bärenreiter, 1952.
Stechow, Wolfgang. *Northern Renaissance Art 1400–1600*. Englewood Cliffs, NJ: Prentice-Hall, 1966.
Sternfeld, Frederick. 'Music in the Schools of the Reformation.' *Musica Disciplina* (1948).
Stevens, John. *Music & Poetry in the Early Tudor Court*. London: Methuen, 1961.
Stokes, Francis. *On the Eve of the Reformation*. New York: Harper & Row, 1909.

Stoltzer, Thomas. 'Exultabo te,' in *Das Chorwerk*, Nr. 6. Edited by Otto Johannes Gombosi. Wolfenbüttel: Kallmeyer, 1930.
Strunk, Oliver. *Source Readings in Music History*. New York: Norton, 1950.
Stubbs, Philip. *The Anatomy of the Abuses in England* [1583]. Edited by Frederick Furnivall. London: The New Shakespeare Society, n.d.
Stuhlfauth, Georg. 'Künstlerstimmen und Künsternot aus der Reformationsbewegung. *Zeitschrift für Kirchengeschichte* (1937), LVI.
Suppan, Wolfgang. *Lexikon des Blasmusikwesens*. Freiburg: Blasmusikverlag Schulz, 1976.
Sylvester, Richard, ed. *The Anchor Anthology of Sixteenth-Century Verse*. Garden City: Anchor Books, 1974.
Thornbury, G. W. *Shakespeare's England*. London: Longmans, Brown, Green and Longmans, 1856.
Thornley, I. D. *The Great Chronicle of London*. London: G.W. Jones at the sign of the Dolphin, 1938.
Rollins, Hyder, ed. *Tottel's Miscellany 1557–1587*. Cambridge: Harvard University Press, 1965.
Trojano, Massimo. *Discorsi Delli Triomfi. Giostre, Apparat. E delle cose piu notable ...* Monico, 1568.
Van Aerde, Raymond. *Ménestrels Communaux ... à Malines, de 1312 a 1790*. Mechelen, 1911.
Vander Straeten, Edmond. *La Musique aux Pays-Bas*. New York: Dover, 1969.
Wallner, B. 'Ein Instrumentenverzeichnis aus dem 16. Jahrhundert,' in Festschrift zum 50. Geburtstag Adolf Sandberger. München, 1918.
Wallner, Bertha Antonia. *Musikalische Denkmaler der Steinätzkunst*. München: J.J. Lentnersche Hofbuchhandlung, 1912.
Walter, Johann. *Wittenberg Gesangbuch* [1537], quoted in Oliver Strunk, *Source Readings in Music History*. New York: Norton, 1950.
Wangermeé, Robert. *Flemish Music and Society in the Fifteenth and Sixteenth Centuries*. New York: F. A. Praeger, 1968.
Werner, Arno. *Städtische und fürstliche Musikpflege in Weissenfels*. Leipzig: Breitkopf & Härtel, 1911.
Werner, Arno. *Vier Jahrhunderte im Dienste der Kirchenmusik*. Leipzig: Merseburger, 1933.
Williams, John, ed. *English Renaissance Poetry*. Fayetteville: The University of Arkansas Press, 1990.
Woodfill, Walter. *Musicians in English Society from Elizabeth to Charles I*. Princeton, NJ: Princeton University Press, 1953.
Wyatt, Thomas. *Sir Thomas Wyatt, Collected Poems*. Edited by Joost Daalder. London: Oxford University Press, 1975.
Zwingli, Ulrich. *Ulrich Zwingli, Selected Works*. Edited by Samuel Jackson. Philadelphia: University of Pennsylvania Press, 1901.

INDEX

A

Adam von Fulda, 16th century German composer, 143
Adrian VI, 16th century pope, 8, 11, 38
Aesculalpius, mythical son of Apollo, 16
Agazzari, Agostino, 16th century Italian writer, 168
Agricola, Martin, 1486–1556, *Musica Instrumentalis Deutsch* [1528], 75, 104
Agrippa, Henry, 1486–1536, German philosopher, 60ff, 67, 69ff
Albert V of Munich, 16th century , 74, 133, 147
Albert, 16th century Duke of Prussia, 9, 136
Albertus Alasco, 16th century Palatine of Siradia [Poland], 230
Alexander the Great, 40, 194
Amsdorf, bishop in Naumberg, 142
Anacharsis, 6th century BC philosopher, 207
Anna van Borssele, Princess of Veere, 16th century Dutch noble, 14
Arion, mythical Greek musician, 40
Aristonicus, ancient Greek musician, 194
Aristotle, 384–322 BC, 17, 26, 117 fn. 44, 80ff, 120, 186, 209, 324
Arnobius, d. 330, celebrated teacher of rhetoric, 38
Arthur, mythical king of England, 21
Ascham, Roger, 1616–1568, tutor to Elizabeth I, 76, 185ff, 202, 207, 212, 229
Athenaeus, Greek historian, 44
August, 16th century Elector of Saxony, 136
Augustanus, Jacobus, d. 1577, merchant in Krakow, personal consort, 140

B

Babst, publisher of the *Hymnal* of 1545, 95
Brooke, Arthur, 16th century English poet, 270
Brumel, 16th century composer, 138
Bryskett, Lodowick, 1546–1612, English writer, 200, 203, 214ff, 218
Bucholczer, Noe, 16th century German poet, 131
Bugenhagen, Johann, 1485–1558, German education critic, 63ff
Byrd, William, 1540–1623, English composer, 218, 245, 271

C

Calvin, John, preacher, 75
Campion, Thomas, 1567–1620, English poet, musician, 272, 279
Case, John, 16th century English music critic, 218
Casimir, Margrave of Brandenburg, d. 1527, 143
Castiglione, Baldassare, 1478–1529, Italian writer, 184ff, 188
Charles V, emperor elected in 1519, 68, 226
Christian I of Saxony, 1560–1591, 134ff, 146
Christopher, 16th century Bishop of Basel, 58
Christopher, 16th century Duke of Württemberg, 134
Cicero, 106–43 BC, Roman orator, 19, 30, 86
Clément, Jacques (Clemens non Papa), Flemish composer, 144
Cochlaeus, Johannes, 1479–1552, professor at Köln, *Tetrachordum Musices*, 104, 106, 114
Coclico, Adrian, 1499–1562, professor at Wittenberg, *Compendium Musices*, 103, 125
Colet, John, friend of Erasmus, 16
Coninc, Pieter, 16th century Dutch goldsmith, instrument maker, 3
Constable, Henry, 1562–1613, English poet, 257ff
Coperario, 218
Copernicus, Nicholas, 1473–1543, astronomer, 82
Cordatus, Conrad, friend of Luther, 83
Cyrus, ancient general, 186

D

Daniel, Samuel, English poet, 268
David, Old Testament king, 38, 48, 112, 195, 269, 333
Davies, Sir John, 1569–1626, English poet, 256ff, 275, 285
De la Rue, Pierre, 119

Deering, 247
Dorilaus, early philosopher, 107
Drake, Sir Francis, 1540–1596, 241
Drayton, Michael, 1563–1631, English poet, 257, 283ff
Dürer, Albrecht, 1471–1528, 4, 68ff

E

Earl of Hertford, 16th century English noble, 235
Earl of Leicester, 16th century English Lord, 5, 231
Edward VI, 1547–1553, King of England, 227ff
Elizabeth I, 1558–1603, Queen of England, 183, 221ff, 229ff, 283
Empedocles, ancient philosopher, 40
Emser, Jerome, 1477–1527, lecturer at Erfurt, 82ff
Eobanus, 16th century German poet, 30
Epictetus, ancient philosopher, 289
Erasmus, Desiderius, 1469–1536, humanist, philosopher, 2ff, 7ff, 57, 84, 114, 201, 223
Eyselin, Jörg, civic musician in Memmingen, 140

F

Ferdinand I, 1503–1564, Emperor, Holy Roman Empire, 139, 144, 147
Ferdinand II, 1529–1595, archduke at Innsbruck (1572), 137, 142
Ferrabosco, the father, 218
Field, John, 16th century English Puritan writer, 220
Fletcher, Giles, 1546–1611, English poet, 265
Francis, Duke of Brabant, 16th century, 5
Frederick the Wise of Wittenberg, 16th century German noble, 76, 110
Friedrich, Count Palatine, 1486–1525, 140
Fronsperger, Lienhard, military manual of 1555, 148
Fugger, Hans Jakob, 138
Fugger, Raimund, merchant at Augsburg [instrument collection], 141

G

Gabrieli, Giovanni, 1554–1612, 157, 159, 162, 170, 175
Gaffurio, Franchinus, 1451–1522, music theorist, *de Harmonia musicorum*, 116, 122
Galen, 2nd century AD, medical writer, 120, 185ff, 212
Gallus, Jakob, *Opus Musicum* [1587], 145
Gibbons, 247
Gifford, Humphrey, 16th century English poet, 271ff, 274, 284
Glarean, Heinrich, 1488–1563, *Dodecachordon* [1547], 35, 104, 114
Gosson, Stephen, 1555–1624, English writer, 192ff, 199, 206ff, 210ff, 239
Green, Robert, 1560–1592, English writer, 188, 287ff, 294ff, 297ff, 306ff, 319ff, 322ff, 330ff, 339
Greville, Fulke, 1554–1628, English poet, 254, 265ff, 278
Griselius, 16th century scholar and poet at Wittenberg, 130
Gwin, Matthew, 16th century professor at Oxford, 230

H

Hendrich Lübeck, 16th century court trumpeter, 148
Henry VIII, 1491–1547, 17, 183, 200, 220ff, 220ff, 223ff, 238, 247, 276
Hentzner, Paul, 16th century German jurist, 316
Heydenreich, Caspar, publisher of conversation with Luther in 1542, 95
Hieronymus of Udine, 16th century Italian cornett player in Munich, 138
Hippocrates, early medical writer, 120
Holbein, Hans, 1497–1543, German artist, 69
Homer, ancient Greek poet, 119
Hooker, Richard, 1553–1600, important English philosopher, 212, 221ff
Howard, Henry, 262
Howell, Thomas, 1566–1581, English poet, 261
Hueber, Wolf, 16th century civic musician at Freistadt, Austria, 140
Hut, Abraham, Stadtpfeifer in Swickau, 148
Hutten, Ulrich von, German author, 58

I

Isaac, 138
Ismenias of Themes, early music therapist, 40

J

Joachim II of Brandenburg, 1505–1571, 134, 146
Johann Georg, North German Elector, 1571–1598, 112, 133
Johann von Sachsen, 16th century duke, 139

Johann, Duke of Saxony, 16th century, 143
Josquin des Prez, 1450–1521, Franco-Flemish composer, 98, 119, 125, [study with] 127ff, 138
Julius II, 1443–1519, pope, 52

K

Karl II, (Charles II), 1540–1590, Archduke of Graz [funeral, 1590], 147
Kessler, Johannes, priest at St. Gall, 67
Kirchmaier, Thomas, 16th century Luthern lawyer, 144
Knox, John, 1505–1572, Protestant leader, 201
Köchel, Ludwig, early musicologist, 133
Kugelmann, Johann, 16th century German composer, 136
Kugelmann, Paul, 16th century German composer, 136
Kyd, Thomas, 1558–1594, English playwright, 319ff, 322, 326ff, 332ff, 338
Kytson, Thomas, 16th century English merchant, 245

L

Laneham, Robert, 16th century English noble, 231ff
Lassus, Orlando, 1532–1594, Franco-Flemish composer, 62, 74, 77, 138, 144, 147, 218
Latomus, music theorist quoted by Erasmus, 36
Lauterbach, Anthony, publisher of conversation with Luther in 1538, 88, 91
Lee, Edward, 16th century English scholar, 13
Leo X, 16th century pope, 13, 79
Leone of Nola, Ambrogio, quoted by Erasmus, 36
Listenius, Nicolaus, 1500–1550, *Musica* [1537], 112

Lodge, Thomas, 1558–1625, English playwright, 196ff, 260, 293, 303ff, 308ff, 315, 321, 330ff, 335ff
Ludwig III, Duke of Württemburg, 1568–1593, 137, 143
Ludwig, Duke of Württemberg (1575), 149
Luther, Hans, a son to Luther, 86ff
Luther, Martin, 1483–1546, 1, 8ff, 63ff, 67, 75, 79ff , 112, 253, 325
Lyly, John, 1554–1606, English poet, playwright, 272, 281, 297, 288ff, 315, 319ff, 324, 325ff, 330ff, 332, 334ff,
Lynche, Richard, fl. 1596–1601, 263

M

Marenzio, 218
Margaret of Austria, 1480–1530, regent of the Netherlands, 3, 139
Marlowe, Christopher, 1564–1593, English playwright, 315, 320ff, 324, 326, 331, 334, 338
Martial, Latin poet, 19
Mary Tudor, 1553–1558, Queen of England, 228
Maximilian II, 1564–1576, emperor, 103, 114, 139, 140, 142
Maximus Tyrius, 193
Melanchthon, Philipp, 1497–1560, a leader in the Reformation, 9, 62ff, 69, 76, 90, 112, 125
Melville, James, [hears Elizabeth perform], 229
Michael de Verona, 16th century composer, 124
Monteverdi, Claudio, composer, 180, 316
More, Sir Thomas, 1478–1535, Archbishop of Canterbury, 7, 18, 201, 205ff, 213, 253ff, 262, 265, 277, 328

Moritz, Landgraf of Hesse-Cassel, 134ff, 142
Morley, Thomas, 1557–1602, English writer on music, 184, 215ff, 245, 260
Mouton, 16th century composer, 138
Müchelon, Sebastianus, professor, University of Leipzig in 1505, 103

N

Nagel, Hans, 16th century member of the Antwerp civic band, 3
Nashe, Thomas, 1567–1601, English writer, 184, 291ff, 297ff, 321, 331
Nero, 37–68 AD, Roman Emperor, 107
Neuschel, 16th century instrument maker in Nürnberg, 136
Northbrooke, John, 16th century English Puritan preacher, 189ff, 209ff
Norton, Thomas, 16th century English playwright, 318

O

Obrecht, Jacob, 1457–1505, Dutch composer, 35
Ockeghem, Johannes, 1410–1497, composer, 38, 119
Ornithoparchus, Andreas, prof. at Leipzig. *Musice active micrologus* [1517], 106ff
Ottheinrich, Elector at Heidelberg, 16th century, 142
Ovid, 43 BC – 17 AD, Roman poet, 30, 84, 86

P

Padovano, Annibale, 138, composer
Palestrina, 168
Pan, Greek mythical figure [reflecting 16th c. English manners], 188

Peacham, Henry, 1576–1643, English writer on manners, 134, 185, 187ff, 202ff, 208, 217ff, 223
Pedoamis, Ascpmois, 1st century writer quoted by Erasmus, 45
Peele, George, b. 1558, English playwright, 284, 319ff, 323, 329ff, 335ff, 338ff
Pfefferkorn, Johannes, German humanist writer, 57
Phalereus, Demetrius, 4th century BC, 21
Phalèse, Perre, 16th century publisher, 3, fn. 11
Philip de Monte, 1521–1603, composer, 156
Philip, 16th century Duke of Stettin-Pomerania, 317
Philip, Archduke, 24
Philipps von Hessen, 16th century, 133
Plaser, Ulrich, civic musician in Memmingen, 140
Plato, 424–347 BC, Greek philosopher, 38, 186
Pliny, Roman writer, 27
Plutarch, 46–120 AD, 46, 194
Ponte, Petrus, 16th century Dutch poet, 1
Praetorius, Michael, 1571–1621, German composer, author, 77, 139, 153ff
Puttenham, George, 16th century English literary critic, 208
Pythagoras, 570–490 BC, Greek philosopher, 17, 40ff, 193, 197, 324

Q

Quickelberg, Samuel, 16th century German humanist, physician, 74

R

Ralegh, Sir Walter, 1552–1618, English politician, poet, 268, 275
Ratgeb, Jörg, 16th century German painter, 68
Reuchlin, Johannes, 16th century lawyer in Württemberg, 57
Rhau, Georg, German publisher [*Symphoniae lucundae*, 1538], 88, 93
Riemenschneider, Tilmann, 16th century German wood carver, 68
Rowley, William, 16th century playwright, 317
Rubeanus, Crotus, 16th century German fiction writer, 58, 114
Rudolf II [welcome in Breslau, 1577], 150

S

Sackville, Thomas, 16th century English playwright, 318
Sappho, ancient lyric poet, 207
Saxo the Grammarian, Danish historian, 71
Scandello, Antonio, 1517–1580, German composer, 142
Schöner, John, 1477–1547, German writer, 57, 133
Schütz, Heinrich, 1585–1672, composer, 177
Seneca, Roman philosopher, 22
Senfl, Ludwig, 1486–1543, composer in Munich, 91, 138
Shakespeare, William, 1564–1616, 305, 315, 320, 322, 341ff
Sidney, Philip Sir, 1554–1586, English poet, 198ff, 204ff, 208ff, 211, 258ff, 264ff, 273, 289ff, 295, 301ff, 304ff
Sigismund, Emperor (1533), 146

Skelton, John, 1460–1529, English poet, 253ff, 264, 274, 274, 277ff
Socrates, 295
Spanberg, Johann, poet, 113
Spenser, Edmund, 1552–1599, English poet, 249, 266, 270ff, 273, 276ff, 280, 282, 285ff
St. Augustine, 354–430, 190
St. Paul, 48ff
Sternfeld, Frederick, 16th century German educational philosopher, 65
Stoltzer, Thomas, 1480–1526, court composer in Hungary, 136
Striggio, Allesandro, 1573–1630, composer, 147
Strozzi, Bernardo, 16th century German composer, 167
Stubbs, Philip, 16th century English writer, 195, 203, 211, 239
Susato, Tielman, d. 1561, trombonist, leader of the Antwerp civic band, 2ff

T

Terpander, Greek musician, 40
Thomsen, Magnus, 16th century court trumpeter, 148
Timotheus, ancient musician, 40
Troiano, Massimo, 16th century singer, diarist in Munich, 147
Tubal, inventor of music [Old Testament], 111
Turberville, George, 1540–1595, English poet, 258
Twenger, Johann, 16th century German artist, 150
Tye, 220

U

Udall, Nicholas, 333
Ulrich von Hutten, 16th century German fiction writer, 114

V

Valckenborck, Lucas, 16th century Dutch painter, 4
Van Dorp, Maarten, 16th century Humanist, 12
Van Winckle, Corneilis, 16th century trombonist in Ghent, 3
Vaux, Thomas, 1510–1556, 261
Verdonck, Corneille, 1563–1625, Franco-Flemish composer, 1
Viadana, Lodovico, 1560–1627, 16th century Italian composer, 162, 172, 175
Virdung, Sebastian, b. 1465, *Musica getutscht* [1511], 104
Virgil, 70–19 BC, Roman poet, 40, 86, 115, 119
Vogtherr, Heinrich, 16th century German writer, 68

W

Walter, Johann, 1496–1570, poet, music adviser, friend to Luther, 57, 86, 89, 94, 146
Warham, William, Archbishop of Canterbury, 16th century, 28, 33
Watson, Thomas, 1557–1592, English poet, 281
Weelkes, 247
Whythorne, Thomas, 16th century English writer, 184
Wilder, Philip van, 1500–1553, English court lutenist, 226, 276
William of Munich, son to Duke Albert V, 138
Wolsey, 1473–1530, English cardinal, 2, 220, [his wind band] 225, 253
Wotton, Sir Henry, 16th century English poet, 257
Wyatt, Thomas, 1503–1542, English poet, 261ff, 269ff

Z

Zeno, Greek philosopher, 36
Zwingali, Ulrich, 1484–1531, Swiss Reformation leader, 63ff, 67, 75

ABOUT THE AUTHOR

Dr. David Whitwell is a graduate ('with distinction') of the University of Michigan and the Catholic University of America, Washington DC (PhD, Musicology, Distinguished Alumni Award, 2000) and has studied conducting with Eugene Ormandy and at the Akademie für Musik, Vienna. Prior to coming to Northridge, Dr. Whitwell participated in concerts throughout the United States and Asia as Associate First Horn in the USAF Band and Orchestra in Washington DC, and in recitals throughout South America in cooperation with the United States State Department.

At the California State University, Northridge, which is in Los Angeles, Dr. Whitwell developed the CSUN Wind Ensemble into an ensemble of international reputation, with international tours to Europe in 1981 and 1989 and to Japan in 1984. The CSUN Wind Ensemble has made professional studio recordings for BBC (London), the Köln Westdeutscher Rundfunk (Germany), NOS National Radio (The Netherlands), Zürich Radio (Switzerland), the Television Broadcasting System (Japan) as well as for the United States State Department for broadcast on its 'Voice of America' program. The CSUN Wind Ensemble's recording with the Mirecourt Trio in 1982 was named the 'Record of the Year' by The Village Voice. Composers who have guest conducted Whitwell's ensembles include Aaron Copland, Ernest Krenek, Alan Hovhaness, Morton Gould, Karel Husa, Frank Erickson and Vaclav Nelhybel.

Dr. Whitwell has been a guest professor in 100 different universities and conservatories throughout the United States and in 23 foreign countries (most recently in China, in an elite school housed in the Forbidden City). Guest conducting experiences have included the Philadelphia Orchestra, Seattle Symphony Orchestra, the Czech Radio Orchestras of Brno and Bratislava, The National Youth Orchestra of Israel, as well as resident wind ensembles in Russia, Israel, Austria, Switzerland, Germany, England, Wales, The Netherlands, Portugal, Peru, Korea, Japan, Taiwan, Canada and the United States.

He is a past president of the College Band Directors National Association, a member of the Prasidium of the International Society for the Promotion of Band Music, and was a member of the found-

ing board of directors of the World Association for Symphonic Bands and Ensembles (WASBE). In 1964 he was made an honorary life member of Kappa Kappa Psi, a national professional music fraternity. In September, 2001, he was a delegate to the UNESCO Conference on Global Music in Tokyo. He has been knighted by sovereign organizations in France, Portugal and Scotland and has been awarded the gold medal of Kerkrade, The Netherlands, and the silver medal of Wangen, Germany, the highest honor given wind conductors in the United States, the medal of the Academy of Wind and Percussion Arts (National Band Association) and the highest honor given wind conductors in Austria, the gold medal of the Austrian Band Association. He is a member of the Hall of Fame of the California Music Educators Association.

Dr. Whitwell's publications include more than 127 articles on wind literature including publications in Music and Letters (London), the London Musical Times, the Mozart-Jahrbuch (Salzburg), and 39 books, among which is his 13-volume *History and Literature of the Wind Band and Wind Ensemble* and an 8-volume series on *Aesthetics in Music*. In addition to numerous modern editions of early wind band music his original compositions include 5 symphonies.

David Whitwell was named as one of six men who have determined the course of American bands during the second half of the 20th century, in the definitive history, *The Twentieth Century American Wind Band* (Meredith Music).

A doctoral dissertation by German Gonzales (2007, Arizona State University) is dedicated to the life and conducting career of David Whitwell through the year 1977. David Whitwell is one of nine men described by Paula A. Crider in *The Conductor's Legacy* (Chicago: GIA, 2010) as 'the legendary conductors' of the 20th century.

> 'I can't imagine the 2nd half of the 20th century—without David Whitwell and what he has given to all of the rest of us.' Frederick Fennell (1993)

www.ingramcontent.com/pod-product-compliance
Lightning Source LLC
Chambersburg PA
CBHW080723300426

44114CB00019B/2470